PETERSBURG: THE PHYSIOLOGY OF A CITY

PETERSBURG

The Physiology of a City

Edited by

NIKOLAI NEKRASOV

Translated from the Russian with an introduction and notes by

Thomas Gaiton Marullo

NORTHWESTERN UNIVERSITY PRESS

EVANSTON, ILLINOIS

Northwestern University Press
www.nupress.northwestern.edu

Printed in the United States of America

10 9 8 7 6 5 4 3 2 1

Library of Congress Cataloging-in-Publication Data

Fiziologiia Peterburga. English
Petersburg : the physiology of a city / edited by Nikolai Nekrasov ; translated from the Russian and annotated by Thomas Gaiton Marullo.
p. cm.
ISBN 978-0-8101-2573-5 (pbk. : alk. paper)
1. Saint Petersburg (Russia)—Social life and customs. 2. Saint Petersburg (Russia)—Intellectual life. I. Nekrasov, Nikolai Alekseevich, 1821–1877. II. Marullo, Thomas Gaiton. III. Title. IV. Title: Physiology of a city.
DK557.N413 2009
947.21073—dc22

2009019634

∞ The paper used in this publication meets the minimum requirements of the American National Standard for Information Sciences—Permanence of Paper for Printed Library Materials, ANSI Z39.48-1992.

For George Gibian,

May he rest in peace

CONTENTS

PREFACE

In a review of *Petersburg: The Physiology of a City* (*Fiziologiia Peterburga*) in April 1845, a twenty-four-year-old Nikolai Nekrasov wrote: "Before us is a book which is exceedingly noble-looking, exceedingly dear, exceedingly entertaining, and exceedingly edifying (*preblagoobraznaia, premilaia, prezabavnaia, prenazidatel'naia*) . . . a book which dances in a Russian choral dance and which features the most variegated mix: humor and truth, joy and sadness, intelligence and mischief, witty observation and bitter taunt." The goal of such a work, Nekrasov continued, was equally laudatory if daunting. Collectively, the writers who fashioned *Petersburg*—a two-volume anthology of poetry and prose, criticism and drama—sought nothing less than an encyclopedia of life in Russia's imperial capital. The concerted effort was to "disclose all the mysteries of our social life; all the wellsprings . . . of our domestic existence; all the sources of our street happenings; the pace and direction of our civic and moral formation; the character and method of our pleasures and delights; the typical characteristics of all ranks of our population; and finally, all the features of Petersburg as a city, a port, a capital, as the extreme border of Rus', and as the 'window on Europe'!"

Addressing *Petersburg* as a living entity, Nekrasov focused further on the work's intent. Like no previous work in Russian literature, it sought to expose Peter's city and to show that all that glittered was not gold. "Oh, most intelligent work!" Nekrasov continued, "You have assumed a task that is difficult, delicate, and even dangerous. You must uncover mysteries . . . seized from corners and spied from keyholes. But you are a physiology . . . a history of our internal life . . . profound and dark; covered with tinsel and lights; and masked in resplendent facades, tasty dinners, and surface cleanliness and light . . . and into which you must reflect a bold ray of truth!"

Even the tone and tenor of the work had to be empirical and precise: physiological. "Your probings," Nekrasov concluded, "must be subtle and precise; your views, observant and farsighted; your emotions, genuine and enduring; and your humor, accurate and affable. . . . Your writers must act unanimously to fulfill your enduring goal!"[1]

With *Petersburg,* Nekrasov had good reason for his enthusiasm—and demands. He was, after all, both the editor and the publisher of the work. Indeed, little did Nekrasov know that his first serious venture[2] into the world of Russian literary commercialism would, over the next thirty years (he died in 1878), catapult him from his already lofty status as one of Russia's greatest nineteenth-century poets to even greater acclaim as the first publisher-advocate of both Fyodor Dostoevsky and Leo Tolstoy,[3] as well as the editor of both *The Contemporary* (*Sovremennik*) and *The Fatherland Notes* (*Otechestvennye Zapiski*), the most respected journals of their time.

Nekrasov, though, took even deeper (and more legitimate) satisfaction in *Petersburg* for what he and others then (and later) discerned as its importance in the national written expression. Specifically, the work was hailed as a "programmatic manifesto"[4] of the much-vaunted Natural school in Russian literature, a movement that embraced the youthful writings of such authors as Nekrasov, Dostoevsky, and Ivan Turgenev; which, beginning around 1840, sought to root in native soil the content and form of European urban realism; and which, as did Western writers of the city, made everyday people the new heroes and heroines of literature.

In content, Nekrasov and the other contributors to *Petersburg* sought socioscientific investigation of urban denizens. In form, they appealed to a broad spectrum of low or noncanonical literary and nonliterary genres, shapes, and tonalities. In journalism, Nekrasov and company looked to essay, sketch, feuilleton, pamphlet, chronicle, and exposé; in theater, they

1. N. Nekrasov, "Fiziologiia Peterburga," in *Polnoe sobranie sochinenii i pisem v piatnadtsati tomakh,* vol. 11, bk. 1 (Leningrad: Nauka, 1989), 186.

2. Two years earlier, Nekrasov had published an almanac, entitled *Articles in Poetry Without Pictures* (*Stateiki v stikhakh bez kartinok,* 1843).

3. Specifically, Dostoevsky's 1845 work *Poor Folk* (*Bednye liudi*) and Tolstoy's 1852 piece *Childhood* (*Detstvo*), both of which were the first fictional piece of each writer.

4. E. Ol'khovskii, *Peterburgskie istorii: Gorod i intelligentsiia v minuvshem stoletii (1810–1910-e gody)* (St. Petersburg: Kul'tInform Press, 1998), 18; M. Peppard, *Nikolai Nekrasov* (New York: Twayne, 1967), 39. It is also of interest to note that *Petersburg: The Physiology of a City* (with the original illustrations) was reprinted in Russia in 1984 and 1991. See V. Nedzvetskii, *Manifest sotsial'noi belletristiki: Fiziologiia Peterburga* (Moscow: Sovetskaia Rossiia, 1984); V. Kuleshov, *Znamenityi al'manakh Nekrasova. Fiziologiia Peterburga* (Moscow: Nauka, 1991).

appealed to pageant, musical, vaudeville, melodrama, burlesque, slapstick, and farce; in fiction, they opted for romance, memoir, diary, travelogue, confession, pastoral, and pulp fiction;[5] in street entertainment, they singled out the puppet show, *gulian'ia,*[6] and *balagan;*[7] in oral tradition, they elected anecdote, legend, and *skaz;*[8] and in folk art, they moved to print, woodcut, and engraving.

5. Pulp fiction, or *lubochnaia literatura,* has its origins in the so-called *lubki,* or prints and cuts made from copper and wood and sold at fairs by wandering peddlers. In both the nineteenth and twentieth centuries, varied assortments and collections of *lubki* came to designate anything in print, including mass-produced lithographs, chapbooks, and editions.

Like the humble English chapbooks they resembled, native pulp fiction advanced Russian workers and peasants from illustrated readings (translations, reworkings, and originals) ranging from folklore, fairy tales, hagiography, epic folk poems (*byliny*), religious and moral tales, and philosophical commentaries (all often updated and/or adapted) to more modern and imaginative works. Genres included poetry, prose, songs, romance, travelogues, adventure tales, war stories, chivalrous pieces, and popular historical fiction.

Noteworthy in Russian pulp fiction was the growing individualism of its heroes and heroines, particularly their willingness to take control of their lives. Indeed, the personalities and plots were seductive if revolutionary. Knights and bandits, merchants and rogues moved beyond superstition, resignation, and xenophobia to freedom, mobility, and success. Most important, perhaps, the heroes and heroines of *lubochnaia literatura* helped redefine what it meant to be Russian both at home and abroad.

Concerning pulp fiction, Nekrasov and other progressive Russian writers and reviewers were of two minds. On the one hand, they disliked the fact that Russian readers were reading at low levels; on the other hand, they rejoiced that the domestic public was interested in literacy and literature and that, however implicitly, it was absorbing new and positive images and ideals. With pulp fiction, progressive Russian authors and critics also learned the aesthetic likes and dislikes of the public; and, whatever their misgivings about *lubochnaia literatura,* they were not above or adverse to adapting much of the content and form of such writing to their own works. Indeed, in this time of literary commercialism, the line between canonical and pulp fiction was not always clear. For instance, the publishing ventures of Alexander Smirdin and the artistic creations of Nikolai Gogol were often seen as straddling the fence between the two modes of writing.

It is also revealing to note that Nekrasov, as if to establish a tie between *Petersburg* and pulp fiction, preceded a review of his work with comments on Ivan Snegirev's study, *O lubochnykh kartinkakh,* published in Moscow in 1844. See *Sovremennik* 38, no. 5 (1845): 251–52.

For the classic study of *lubochnaia literatura* in the second half of the nineteenth century, see J. Brooks, *When Russia Learned to Read, 1861–1917* (Princeton, N.J.: Princeton University Press, 1985).

6. *Gulian'ia* was the generic name for a wide assortment of fairs, carnivals, and celebrations in Russia in both the nineteenth and twentieth centuries.

7. *Balagany* were temporary wooden theaters which were erected specifically for the Russian carnivals of Shrovetide and Easter week. Accommodating as many as fifteen hundred spectators, *balagany* typically featured lavish productions constructed on three or four raised platforms with scores of participants, punctuated by interludes of single scenes with several characters. For more on *balagany,* see A. Leifert, *Balagany* (Petrograd: Izdanie ezhenedel'nika petrogradskikh gosudarstvennykh akademicheskikh teatrov, 1922).

8. *Skaz* is a narrative technique that mirrors oral discourse with its hesitations, corrections, and grammatical mistakes.

In so doing, Nekrasov and the other writers of *Petersburg* accomplished several key goals. They expertly bound a colorful documentary on life in Russia's imperial and cultural capital into an artistic treatise that commented insightfully on the sociopolitical, cultural, literary, and economic dimensions of the city. In *Petersburg,* Nekrasov and his confreres also continued the momentum of the so-called civic or progressive trend in Russian literature. That is, they steered the national written tradition away from the tsarist demands for autocracy, orthodoxy, and nationality in art; and, with their own sense of literary realism, they closed what was to them the worrisome gap between Nikolai Gogol's 1842 epic *Dead Souls* (*Mertvye dushi*) and two 1847 novels, Ivan Goncharov's *A Common Story* (*Neobyknovennaia istoriia*) and Alexander Herzen's *Who Is to Blame?* (*Kto vinovat?*).

The writers of *Petersburg* also followed through on what was a new and popular trend in Russia—they strove to advance the people and themes of the national written expression from the well-worn tropes of lords and peasants, masters and men, to what may be seen as the middling layers of the population. Their spotlight focused on officials and merchants, organ-grinders and yardkeepers, all of whom, in real life, had the clout (and rubles) to demand that Russian literature represent their cares and concerns. Indeed, it is plausible to say that in *Petersburg,* Nekrasov and company bowed—willingly—to "consumer sovereignty."[9]

To this first-time English edition of *Petersburg* I was tempted to add the subtitle "on with the show"; and for a key reason. Its writers, for all their diverse themes and styles, shared a fascination with stage and *spektakl'* through which they followed Gogol in moving Russian literature from the salons to the street but without the great writer's penchant for the gothic, bizarre, and grotesque. Rather, in *Petersburg,* Nekrasov and company celebrated Russia's northern Venice in a joyful exultation of its daily life, citizens, and culture. In fact, it can be argued that no other work of the so-called Petersburg tradition of Russian literature looked to the city of its inspiration with such joy and hope for what St. Petersburg represented to Russia since its founding, that is, a place of civilization and enlightenment

9. Brooks, *When Russia Learned to Read,* xvi.

for a country caught, tragically if chronically, between West and East and, equally sad to say, between the divine impulses of creativity and the satanic urges for destruction. In this regard also, *Petersburg* provides an insightful slice-of-life view of a people without whom the story of Russia's imperial city cannot be told. It gives poignant witness to a "folk . . . who filled marshes, drained swamps, built palaces and cathedrals, ran machines, and defended [their home] against enemies."[10] It also places this group at the "center of a centuries-long conversation that Russians have carried on among themselves about what their nation is and what it needs to become."[11]

It is my hope that this edition of *Petersburg* will serve as a literary, social, and economic reference not only to classical studies of Russia's imperial and cultural capital but also to recent (and magisterial) investigations into St. Petersburg, for example, W. Bruce Lincoln's *Sunlight at Midnight: St. Petersburg and the Rise of Modern Russia* (Boulder, Col.: Basic Books, 2000), and Julie Buckler's *Mapping St. Petersburg: Imperial Text and Cityshape* (Princeton, N.J.: Princeton University Press, 2005). In particular, I extend Buckler's claim that a fuller accounting of writing about St. Petersburg is essential, particularly the sociocultural middle of the city (the least studied aspect of Russian urban culture).[12] In this edition of *Petersburg,* I also advance three of Butler's key assertions: (1) the geographical material entity that is St. Petersburg finds expression in an equally complex structure of diverse literary forms rooted in specific sites of urban life; (2) although myriad fictional works about St. Petersburg failed to achieve the status of Alexander Pushkin's "The Bronze Horseman" ("Mednyi Vsadnik") or Fyodor Dostoevsky's *Crime and Punishment* (*Prestuplenie i Nakazanie*), they played an active part in the myth of Russia's imperial city; and (3) Russian literature and culture of the nineteenth century drew not only from the negotiation between the privileged

10. W. Bruce Lincoln, *Sunlight at Midnight: St. Petersburg and the Rise of Modern Russia* (Boulder, Col.: Basic Books, 2000), 13.

11. Ibid.

12. Buckler is correct to see the reasons for such neglect as twofold: (1) critics and scholars have dismissed the sociocultural middle of St. Petersburg as unlike the established bourgeoisie of England and France; and (2) they have reviled this group as the refuge of vulgar epigones who corrupted aristocratic and folk cultures with economic (read: capitalist) concerns. See J. Buckler, *Mapping St. Petersburg: Imperial Text and Cityshape* (Princeton, N.J.: Princeton University Press, 2005), 5.

elite and the illiterate peasantry but also from the intervention of middle and diverse urban groups only now coming under historical research and reassessment.[13] It is with additional reference to Buckler's work that I define my own thinking both on *Petersburg* and on Russian urban realism as a whole.

I also intend that this edition of *Petersburg* extend, in a seminal way, the dynamics of urban writing, culture, and carnival as defined not only by such critics as Victor Shklovsky, Mikhail Bakhtin, Vladimir Toporov, and Yuri Lotman but also by such cartographers as Denis Wood, J. B. Harley, James Duncan, and David Ley who, since the late 1970s, have considered maps and mappings in new and fruitful ways.[14] With reference to Shklovsky, I explore how the poetry and prose of *Petersburg* affirmed the images and ideas of the Formalists on literary adaptation and innovation, particularly of urban texts.[15] Considering Bakhtin's seminal work, *Rabelais and His World,* I show that as did the author of *Gargantua and Pantegruel,* the contributors to *Petersburg* rooted their humor in the "city square, the town fair, and the carnival"[16] as well as in a folk who, in its culture, opposed the ruling classes with "its own conception of the world, its own forms and imagery."[17] Pointing to Toporov and Lotman, I contend that the structure of *Petersburg* drew in part from the city as a "complex semiotic mechanism,"[18] from the coalescence and collision of urban signs, symbols,

13. Buckler writes: "Only since the 1990s has attention begun to rest seriously upon the unwritten middle round of the imperial period, with Russians taking an interest in the historical bases for market democracy, and with academic fashion in the West . . . treating aesthetic categories such as 'middlebrow,' 'mainstream,' and 'everyday' more generously." Ibid., 4, 15–16.

Initial investigations into this area have been unsatisfactory, though. As E. Ol'khovsky observes, scholars have written a great deal about *Petersburg,* but they have not explored the "urban studies" (*gorodovedenie*) implicit in the work, particularly its treatment of everyday life. Ol'khovskii, *Peterburgskie istorii,* 18.

14. See D. Wood et al., *The Power of Maps* (New York: Guilford, 1992); J. Duncan and D. Ley, eds., *Place/Culture/Representation* (London: Routledge, 1993); J. Harley, "Deconstructing the Map," *Cartographica* 26 (1989): 2–20; J. Harley, "Maps, Knowledge, and Power," in *The Iconography of Landscape: Essays on the Symbolic Representation, Design, and Use of Past Environments,* ed. Dennis Cosgrove et al., 277–312 (Cambridge: Cambridge University Press, 1988).

15. See, for instance, V. Shklovskii, "Ob ocherke i romane: O tipakh romana," in *Literaturnyi kritik,* no. 8 (1835): 166–76, as well as his many articles on the feuilleton.

16. M. Bakhtin, *Rabelais and His World,* trans. H. Iswolsky (Bloomington: Indiana University Press, 1984), 146.

17. Ibid., 473.

18. See I. Lotman, "Simvolika Peterburga i problemy semiotiki goroda," in *Izbrannye stat'i v trekh tomakh,* vol. 2 (Tallinn: Alekandra, 1992), 13, 14.

and codes with woodcut,[19] icon, folklore, and the oral triad of rumor, anecdote, and gossip.

Finally, reflecting upon Wood, Harley, and their fellow cartographers, I distinguish how *Petersburg* was not so much a "transparent opening to the world" as it was a "particular human way . . . of looking at it."[20] It can be argued that the writers of *Petersburg* disputed the ideas of maps as mirrors and windows: "accurate, transparent, and neutral."[21] Rather, they saw cartography as aesthetics and discourse with its own subjects and themes.[22] In a conscious and purposeful way, the writers of *Petersburg* breathed life into types and daguerreotypes that were rectangular, black-and-white, and static—the stuff of science—making them into metaphors of urban landscape that were colorful, figurative, and rhetorical—the stuff of art. In so doing, they transformed the streets, stores, buildings, bridges, canals, inscriptions, signs, and other municipal accoutrements of their environs into a *poema* of national identity and pride for Russia's imperial capital and its citizens. What Nekrasov and company did in *Petersburg,* therefore, was not neutral or value-free; rather, they structured their mappings of urban life as "dialogical assertions," " 'thick' texts," and "mythical geographies"[23] to move not only St. Petersburg but also Russia to new progress, civilization, and enlightenment and, as is always the case in the homeland, to have Russian literature point the way.[24]

Like mapmakers in the age of exploration, the contributors to *Petersburg* sought "to construct, not reproduce" their world.[25] They drew

19. For instance, much of what Lotman values in the Russian woodcut, that is, its ties to folk carnival and theater, bears directly upon the "Petersburg" tradition in Russian literature in general and Nekrasov's *Petersburg* in particular. See I. Lotman, "Khudozhestvennaia priroda russkikh narodnykh kartinok," in *Narodnaia graviura i fol'klor v Rossii XVII-XIX vv (k 150–letiiu so dnia rozhdeniia D. A. Rovinskogo): materialy nauchnoi konferentsii,* ed. I. Danilova, 247–67 (Moscow: Sovetskii khudozhnik, 1976).

20. Harley, "Deconstucting the Map," 3.

21. Wood, *Power of Maps,* 22, 141.

22. Ibid., 22, 60; and Harley, "Deconstructing the Map," 12. Interestingly, such cartographers also adopt the same ideas on signs and codes as the semioticians. See, for instance, Wood, *Power of Maps,* 137.

23. Harley, "Maps, Knowledge, and Power," 277; Harley, "Deconstructing the Map," 7–12.

24. "Maps are never value-free images," Harley writes, "except in the narrowest Euclidean sense they are not in themselves either true or false. Both in the selectivity of their content and in their signs and styles of representation, maps are a way of conceiving, articulating, and structuring the human world which is biased towards, promoted by, and exerts influence upon particular sets of social relations." Harley, "Maps, Knowledge, and Power," 278.

25. Wood, *Power of Maps,* 17.

their plan of Peter's city with an eye to the size of images, the thickness of lines, the intensity of light, and the nuance of colors and tones.[26] Like any text—visual or otherwise—they selected, omitted, simplified, and classed information from "a cornucopia of images, bewildering in their variety."[27] Consciously and unconsciously, the writers of *Petersburg* appealed to fictional mappings to "show this . . . but not that."[28] They established formulas and rules, created hierarchies and symbols, and chose rhetorical styles and means of expression. The ostensible goal was to look for data that were concrete, recurring, and uniform to shape mental structures, as well as to define a sense of self and place in the world. The more seductive task, though, was to invert the status quo, to challenge imperial authority and power, and to vaunt new modes, geometries, and geographies (political, social, and cultural). In fashioning *Petersburg,* Nekrasov and company intuited that maps are "moments in the process of decision-making";[29] that they are "value-laden images . . . [that] contribute to dialogue in a socially constructed world";[30] and that "make connectives effective in the ongoingness of daily living."[31] Indeed, in the conjoining of mapping and mind-set, metaphor and myth, Nekrasov and company also understood that they assumed "heavy responsibilities"[32] in fashioning topologies that empowered their readers and worked toward their understanding and betterment as citizens of Russia and the world.

I note here that in my edition of *Petersburg,* I have relied on the original text of the work published in 1845. I also have used familiar spellings

26. "The map has a discursive tone," Wood writes, "soft/loud, even/dynamic, complacent/agitated, polite/aggressive, soothing/abrasive." Ibid., 131.

27. "Inevitably, unavoidably, necessarily," Wood writes, "all maps embody their authors' prejudices, biases, and partialities (not to mention the less frequently observed art, curiosity, elegance, focus, care, imagination, attention, intelligence, and scholarship their makers bring to their labor)." Ibid., 4, 24.

Similarly, Edward Imhof writes: "Due to scale restrictions, the cartographer makes a selection, classifies, standardizes; he undertakes intellectual and graphical simplifications and combinations; he emphasizes, enlarges, subdues, or suppresses visual phenomena according to their significance to the map. In short, he *generalizes, standardizes,* and *makes selections;* and, he recognizes the many elements which interfere with one another, lie in opposition and overlap, thus *coordinating* the content to clarify the geographical patterns of the region." E. Imhof, *Cartographic Relief Representation* (Berlin: Walter de Gruyter, 1982), 357 (italics in the original).

28. Wood, *Power of Maps,* 48.

29. Ibid., 185.

30. Harley, "Maps, Knowledge, and Power," 278; Harley, "Deconstructing the Map," 7, 11, 13, 14.

31. Wood, *Power of Maps,* 12.

32. Ibid., 188, 192.

of proper names in the text and the body of the notes and more precise, scholarly transliterations in the source citations. For this reason, many names appear with two spellings, for example, "Belinsky" in the text but "Belinskii" in source citations. Several of the contributors to *Petersburg* wrote under pen names, a frequent convention in Russia. The signatures under which the authors were originally published, whether nom de plume or initials, appear at the end of each article.

Dates for letters, memoirs, and critical essays and reviews have been rendered according to the New Style calendar whenever this could be ascertained. Also, except where noted otherwise, all translations of quotations from Russian sources in the footnotes are mine.

For their invaluable assistance at various stages in the preparation of this work, I wish to acknowledge—for what has to be the millionth time in my thirty-three years as a professor of Russian and Russian literature—the members of the Slavic Reference Service of the Slavic Department of the Library of the University of Illinois. Like my other studies, this work never would have come to be without the assistance of Helen Sullivan, Christopher Condill, Jan Adamczyk, Mary Aquila, Suleyman Sarihan, and Katya Dunatov, all of whom unearthed sources, researched footnotes, and answered myriad questions about Nekrasov and company. By now, readers of my works should recognize a pattern: invariably, I choose topics which are of interest to me and (I hope) scholars and aficionados of Russian literature and culture but which soon are beyond my knowledge and ken to pursue in a sustained and meaningful way. Hence the numerous e-mails, telephone calls, and requests for prayers and emotional support which "Reverend Mother" Helen and the devoted members of her (pre-Vatican II) order field often on a daily basis, and for which they will wear triumphal crowns in heaven.

I also owe a profound debt of gratitude to professors Gary Saul Morson of Northwestern University and Kathleen Parthé of the University of Rochester, both of whom offered excellent recommendations and advice; to freelance editor Lori Meek Schuldt, and to Anne Gendler and Mike Levine at Northwestern University Press, who produced this manuscript; to Professor Gregory Sterling, associate dean of the College of Arts and Letters here at Notre Dame, who provided funds for research; to Professor David Gasperetti, chair of the Department of German and

Russian Languages, who cleared my academic runway; to Professor Alain Toumayan of the Department of Romance Languages and Literatures, who assisted me with *physiologie;* to Kenneth Kinslow and the staff of the Department of Interlibrary Loan of the Theodore M. Hesburgh Library here at Notre Dame for obtaining many of the materials for this work; to Cheryl Reed, who prepared the manuscript; and to Steven Atwood and Kaitlin Spillane, who served as my research assistants for this project and who, like the members of the Slavic Reference Service, handled my endless requests with grace, energy, and aplomb.

Again, I also wish to cite my wife, Gloria Gibbs Marullo, who, delighted that I chose a topic other than Ivan Bunin, was even more supportive in this venture on Russian realism; and also my cats, Bernadette Marie, Monica Anne, Benedict Joseph, Gonzaga Gaiton, and Francis Xavier, all of whom took turns in keeping me sane and whole after I had exhausted the patience and good cheer of everyone else.

Finally, it is with special fondness that I salute the memory of Professor George Gibian, professor of Russian literature at Cornell University, who for more than thirty years was a loyal teacher, mentor, and colleague, and who deserves the credit along with Gloria, Sister Mary Colleen Dillon of the Sisters of Notre Dame, Covington, Kentucky, and Helen Sullivan and the members of the Slavic Reference Service, for whatever success and achievement I have attained.

From the bottom of my heart, thank you all.

T.G.M.
August 15, 2007
Feast of the Assumption of the Blessed Virgin Mary

EDITOR'S INTRODUCTION

Thomas Gaiton Marullo

As is often the case in their cultural history, Russian writers and readers drew their interest in physiology from Western Europe, in part from England[1] but more directly from France. They had many choices. Indeed, the Gallic urge to study a nation and its people as a living organism—healthy in some respects, ailing in others—often bordered on obsession. Already in 1782, French writers and readers were poring over Louis-Sébastien Mercier's four-volume *Table of Paris,* which featured "investigations among all classes of citizens . . . the moral physiognomy of a huge capital."[2] In France, also, the popularity of Johann Lavater's ten-volume *The Art of Knowing People by Their Physiognomies* (1806–9)[3] and of Jean Anthelme Brillat-Savarin's eight-volume *The Physiology of Taste* (1825) gave rise to similar multitomed self-portraits of various nationalities and groups,[4] as well as to studies,

1. See, for instance, K. Meadows, ed., *Heads of the People; or, Portraits of the English* (London: R. Tyas, 1840–41). Also consider the widespread Russian acclaim for the works of Charles Dickens in Russia in the mid-nineteenth century. For instance, excerpts from his 1836–37 work *Sketches by Boz, Illustrative of Everyday Life and Everyday People,* were published in *Literary Additions to the Russian Invalid* (*Literaturnye pribavlenniia k Russkomu Invalidu*) in November 1839.

2. L. Mercier, *Tableau de Paris,* vol. 1 (Amsterdam: n.p., 1782), iii–iv.

3. J. Lavater, *L'art de connaître les hommes par la physionomie,* 10 vols. (Paris: L. Prudhomme, 1806–9). Johann Lavater was a Swiss writer, Protestant pastor, and founder of "physiognomics," an antirational religious and literary movement that posited the interaction between mind and body and that sought a demonstrable presence of the divine in life.

Although Lavater's 1775–78 four-volume *Physiognomishche Fragmente zur Beförderung der Menschenkenntnis und Menschenliebe* established his reputation throughout Europe, it was his *L'art de connaître* that insured his fame. In fact, so popular was *L'art de connaître* with writers and readers that it was republished in 1825 and, as evidence of the wide interest in physiognomies in Western Europe at the near midcentury, also in 1841 and 1845.

In 1841, Lavater's *L'art de connaître* appeared in Russia under the longer title *Physiognomics; or, The Art of Recognizing People by the Features of Their Face, Their Likeness to Various Animals, and So Forth* (*Fizionomistika, ili iskusstvo raspoznavat' liudei po chertam ikh litsa, ikh skhodstvu s razlichnymi zhivotnymi i t.d.*).

Lavater's work was warmly received in Russia. See, for instance, S. Kutorga, "Lafater i Gall'," *Biblioteka dlia chteniia* 72, no. 3 (1845): 1–33.

4. See, for instance, *Les Français peints par eux-mêmes; encyclopédie morale du dix-neuvième siècle,* 9 vols. (Paris, L. Curmer, 1840–42); A. Saillet, *Les enfants peints par eux-mêmes* (Paris: Dessesserts, 1841); J. K. Meadows and E. de La Bedolliere, *Les anglais peints par eux-mêmes* (Paris: L. Curmer, 1842); and G. Grandville, *Les animaux peints par eux-mêmes* (Paris: Hetzel, 1841–42).

directories, and catalogs of Paris and other cities.[5] In fact, scholars estimate that in the first half of the 1840s, there existed somewhere between 130 and 160 pocket physiologies that French citizens carried with them at all times.[6]

Particularly intriguing to the Gallic public were the self-styled travelogues of pilgrims, hermits,[7] and even the devil[8] through the French capital. Also welcome were works that dissected Paris and other urban centers vertically and horizontally. Investigations into neighborhoods, suburbs, and other localities took their place among inquiries into many-tiered buildings and their occupants from attics to cellars.[9] In all these works, the focus

5. See, for instance, C. Ladvocat, *Paris, ou le livre de cent-et-un* (Paris: Chez Ladvocat, 1831–34); and H. Martin, *Nouveau Tableau de Paris au XIX-e siècle* (Paris: M-me Charles Bechet, 1834).

For instance, *Paris ou le livre de cent-et-un* came out in fifteen volumes. It featured works by Jules Janin, Paul de Kock, Alexandre Dumas-père, Francois-René de Chateaubriand, the Marquis de Custine, and Victor Hugo, and it contained sketches and essays ranging from the public library to the morgue. (A two-volume translation of selections from the work was published in Boston in 1833.)

In the introduction to *Paris ou le livre de cent-et-un,* the editor wrote: "The plan of this book is very simple. One must survey contemporary Paris . . . and show it as it is: indefinite, capricious, irascible, impatient, poor, bored, always yearning eagerly for art and excitement, even though it is not easy to agitate it, often absurd, sometimes sublime." See *Paris ou le livre de cent-et-un,* vol. 1 (1831), vi.

6. T. Iakimovich, *Frantsuzskii realisticheskii ocherk* (Moscow: Akademiia nauk SSSR, 1963), 158.

7. The concept of the literary "hermit"—a recluse-observer of life, removed from the "things of this world"—had been quite well known throughout European literature from the end of the eighteenth century on. The figure, though, became extremely popular with a work by the French writer Étienne de Jouy entitled *The Hermit from Chaussée d'Antin; or, Observations on French Customs and Mores at the Beginning of the Nineteenth Century* (*L'Hermite de la Chaussée d'Antin, ou Observations sur les Moeurs and les Usages Français au Commencement du XIXe siècle*), which was published in five volumes in Paris between the years 1815 and 1817. The work was translated into English in London in 1815, in Philadelphia in 1816, and in St. Petersburg, between 1825 and 1828.

In this work, Jouy sought to catalog the "differences of mores and habits which cast each section of Paris as a sort of nation apart"; to seize "the general character of Parisians and the particular physiognomy of this great city"; and to identify "the vices, the faults, and the foolishnesses, as well as the very virtues" that distinguish one group from another. See Jouy, *The Hermit from Chaussée d'Antin,* vol. 3 (1817), 292–93.

In later years, Jouy wrote *Hermits* from Provence, Italy, Switzerland, and other locations; many of these works were also translated into Russian.

Such fictional anchorites also engaged the scholarly attention of Shklovsky. See Shklovskii, "Ob ocherke i romane," 169–76.

8. See, for instance, *Le Diable à Paris: Paris et les Parisiens; Mouers et Cotumes, Caractères, et Portraits des Habitants de Paris, Tableau Complete de Leur Vie Priveé, Publique, Politique, Artistique, Litteraire, Industrielle, Etc., Etc.,* 20 vols. (Paris, J. Hetzel, 1845–46).

9. Consider, for instance, Jules Janin's picture of such a building in his 1830 work *La Confession.* "Here there is something more curious than the Egyptian pyramids, the Kremlin, and the Swiss icehouses, something more wondrous than miracles, to behold with one's eyes those who come and go with such outlays of energy and means. Here is a large Parisian apartment building on a crowded block, filled with

was the lives of urban denizens from all classes of society. The diversity was as striking as it was democratic. Aristocrats and beggars, writers and hacks, bosses and clerks, entrepreneurs and idlers, socialites and prostitutes: all were subjects for French physiologists, ranging from well-respected writers to petty journalists and hacks.

There was also in France a plethora of literary physiologies on a wide range of subjects. For instance, from 1825 to 1844, Honoré de Balzac wrote a series of such works, including, in 1829, *The Physiology of Marriage;* in 1830, *The Physiology of Dressing* and *The Gastronomic Physiology;* in 1841, *The Physiology of the Civil Servant;* and in 1844, *The History and Physiology of French Boulevards.* To these can be added physiologies by other writers on husbands, musicians, voters, clerks, usurers, tailors, cuckolds, and the bourgeoisie.[10] Women were also claimed in French physiologies, with maidens and nuns at one end of the spectrum and viragoes and prostitutes at the other. Even King Louis-Philippe was not immune from physiology.[11]

As different and engaging as such works were at the time, they shared several flaws. European collections or anthologies of physiologies tended to be both monographic and encyclopedic. Indeed, they often drowned their readers in chaotic waves of description and detail. From multitome works[12] to pocket editions, no one thing claimed the exclusive focus; anything and

---

people from its foundation to its very roof. [In it are] the extreme luxury on the first floor, the extreme poverty under the roof, and the enterprise and activity of its middle." J. Janin, *La Confession* (Paris: M. Levy, 1861), 217–19.

It should be noted that in fictional physiologies of St. Petersburg, the horizontal dissection of apartment buildings was a favorite technique of Yakov Butkov in his two-part 1845–46 work *The Petersburg Heights* (*Peterburgskie vershiny*) and of Dostoevsky in his 1861 novel *The Insulted and the Injured* (*Unizhennye i oskorblennye*). It also appears in *Petersburg,* in Evgeny Grebenka's "The Petersburg Quarter" ("Peterburgskaia Storona").

10. For instance, Paul de Kock, in his 1841 piece *Physiologie de l'homme marié* (*Physiology of the Married Man*), distinguished among husbands "who are anxious to please their wives"; husbands "who are affectionate with their wives in public"; the "jealous husband"; and, the pièce de resistance, "the husband . . . you yourselves know well." See "Physiologie," in *La grande Encyclopedie universelle du XIX siècle,* ed. P. Larousse, vol. 12 (Paris: Administration du grand dictionnaire universel, 1865), 918.

11. See J. Janin, "Le Roi," in *Les Francais peints par eux-mêmes,* vol. 5 (1842), 81–107.

12. For instance, the 1845–46, twenty-volume French physiological compilation *The Devil in Paris: Paris and the Parisians* was subtitled *The Mores and Customs, Characters and Portraits of the Inhabitants of Their Personal, Social, Political, Artistic, Literary, Working Lives and So Forth.* Translated into Russian almost immediately, the work featured Satan and damned souls (former Parisians, of course) who are bored with hell, miss the bodily delights and comforts of the French capital, and who, as if to herald Mikhail Bulgakov's *The Master and Margarita* more than a hundred years later, commission a devil to visit the city as a dandy-reporter on the goings-on there.

everything (big and small) were fair and random game. Essays on peoples and professions; portraits of mores and movements; articles on geography, history, and economics; and works of poetry and prose were all grist for writers' mills. Topics for physiological discussion began with descriptions of wedding nights and of new year's celebrations and ended with discussions of silk hats, blue stockings, and cigars.[13] Leave it to the French: there were even physiologies on corsets and the cancan![14]

European assemblies of physiologies—their characters, plots, language, even illustrations—also tended to be scientific: serious, static, and stiff. Their writers took their empiricism too literally. Whether they analyzed or synthesized reality, whether they looked at life through "a microscope or a telescope,"[15] they did so with eyes that were cold, ears that were deaf, a nose that was blocked, and a heart that was dead. First they dissected a character from head to toe; then they set the object of their scrutiny against an equally lifeless background, that is, a rote if numbing roster of streets, buildings, and vicinities.

Further, writers of European physiologies tended to draw their heroes and heroines with the well-worn images and ideas of classical and sentimental fiction. Billing their works as "moral encyclopedias of the nineteenth century,"[16] they praised virtue and censured vice as entities that were formal, philosophical, and abstract. In no way did they see morality as informing real life. In truth, European writer-physiologists sought to remedy these flaws. With varying success, they chose narrative and exposition over facts;

Compare also Janin's remarks in his introduction to *The French as Painted by Themselves.* "We wish to find a method," he wrote, "by which after we die, we can leave traces of the so-called personal life of people.... We want to think about the fact that sometime our grandchildren will want to know what we did in our time; how we were clothed, what kind of dresses our wives wore, what were our homes like, what were our customs and entertainments . . . what did we understand by . . . Beauty. About us they will want to know everything: how we went horseback riding, how our tables were set, what wines we preferred." See J. Janin, introduction to *Les Francais peints par eux-mêmes,* vol. 1 (1840), iv–v.

13. See, for instance, Balzac's 1830 piece *The Physiology of a Cigar;* and Frédéric Soulié's 1841 work *The Physiology of the Silk Stocking,* a catalog-description of such apparel for various ages and ranks, for example, aristocratic, married, and unmarried women.

14. See Iakimovich, *Frantsuzskii realisticheskii ocherk,* 293; "Physiologie," 918.

15. See V. Belinskii, *Polnoe sobranie sochinenii v trinadtsati tomakh,* 13 vols. (Moscow: Akademiia nauk, 1953–59), vol. 6 (1955), 268. Also consider the assertion by Ley and Duncan that "by adopting the discourse of science, thus claiming to grasp the whole, to assume a commanding position, the survey 'captures' the world in miniature. The world is mimetically reduced to the text." Duncan and Ley, *Place/Culture/Representation,* 2.

16. Iakimovich, *Frantsuzskii realisticheskii ocherk,* 158.

dialogues and scenes over figures. By and large, though, they were unable to overcome the academic aspects of physiology.[17] In fact, it was only when European physiologies moved from collections or anthologies to the novels and short stories of the period—Honoré de Balzac's *Father Goriot, Lost Illusions,* and *The Human Comedy* are pertinent examples—that the writers were able to surmount the shortcomings of such writing.

Russian writers and readers were well acquainted with European physiologies—in theory and practice, in originals, translations, and reworkings.[18] Pyotr Chaadaev, in the first of his 1836 *Philosophical Letters* (*Filosofskie pis'ma*), noted the phenomenon by asserting that what makes up the "atmosphere of the West is not history and psychology, but the physiology of the European individual."[19] Indeed, so familiar were Russians with French fictional physiologies that Osip Senkovsky, as "Baron Brambeus," noted in an 1842 review for the *Library for Reading* (*Biblioteka dlia chteniia*), "Russians know Paris better than Parisians themselves."[20]

Initially, the response of native writers and readers to European physiologies vacillated between feigned interest and outright hostility. At times, Russian critics and reviewers regarded fictional physiologies as harmless and transient fads in literature. "A special type of fashionable writing

17. Indeed, Russian reviews of such moralizing could be harsh. "There has appeared a Frenchman named Jouy who has brought into fashion systematic articles on mores," Nikolai Polevoi wrote in 1832. "He has written several volumes—but he has gotten tired. From what? It seems . . . precisely because he wanted to philosophize, to pursue vice and stupidity in a methodical manner. . . . Would it not have been better for Jouy . . . to describe whatever comes his way?" N. Polevoi, "Vmesto predisloviia," *Novyi zhivopisets,* part 1 (Moscow: I. Stepanov, 1832), 13.

18. See, for instance, an 1842 piece entitled *The Physiology of Someone in Love: Reworked from the French* (*Fiziologiia vliublennogo: Peredelana s frantsuzskogo*), in which the author classed love with such parameters as weight, age, sex, location, vocation, season of the year, and temperament, that is, "full-blooded, passionate, melancholic, diffident, indifferent, nervous and of strong constitution."

Also consider a work, again made mostly of translations from the French, entitled *The Translator; or, One Hundred and One Stories and Many More Anecdotes, Old, New, and Contemporary, Regarding Thoughts, Rules, Judgments, Opinions, and So Forth; On Exploits, Bravery, Virtue, Intelligence, Stupidity, and Simple-Heartedness; and Including Witticism, Expression, Epigrams, Puns, and the Like, Along with Characteristic Essays, Portraits, and Similar Sundry Items.* See *Perevodchik ili sto odna povest' i sorok sorokov anekdotov, drevnikh, novykh i sovremennykh; myslei, pravil, suzhdenii, mnenii i pr.; podvigov khrabrosti, dobrodeteli, uma, gluposti, prostodushiia, i prostykh slov, vyrazhenii, epigramm, kalamburov, i pr.; kharakteristicheskikh ocherkov, portretov i pr. i pr.* (St. Petersburg: I. P. Bocharova, 1843).

19. P. Chaadaev, "Pervoe pis'mo. Filosofskie pis'ma," in *Stat'i i pis'ma* (Moscow: Sovremennik, 1987), 39.

20. See O. Senkovskii, review of *Parizh v 1838 i 1839 godakh: Putevye zapisi i zametki,* by Vladimir Stroev, in "Literaturnaia letopis': Novye knigi; Fevral' 1842," *Biblioteka dlia chteniia* 50 (1842): 55.

has appeared recently [in the form] of physiologies," a reviewer for the *Fatherland Notes* wrote in 1841. "[There is] . . . 'The Physiology of the Priest' . . . 'The Physiology of a Married Man' . . . 'The Physiology of Lovers' . . . 'The Physiology of a Wanderer' . . . 'The Physiology of a Prankster' . . . and 'The Physiology of a Governmental Official.' Undoubtedly, readers will allow us to pass over in silence similar insignificant works. Indeed, many of them will drop out of sight before we can even note their titles."[21]

Similarly, Pavel Annenkov wrote in his *Letters from Abroad* (*Pis'ma iz-za granitsy*) on November 29, 1841: "I also must mention so-called physiologies, but with the light hand of a jester. . . . Thousands of these works, complete with pictures and engravings, have appeared, literally flooding our libraries. What is not a physiology these days! There are physiologies of workers, deputies, soldiers, idlers, and the like. There are physiologies of gloves . . . and even of cabbies' horses. Soon I will see a physiology of an idle Slav who wanders several countries with my picture in it."[22]

Other times, though, Russian reviewers and critics saw European physiologies as annoying, even noxious incursions into the national written expression. "As is our laudatory custom not only to seize upon everything that arrives here from Paris," a reviewer wrote in the *Northern Bee* (*Severnaia pchela*) in 1843, "but also never to figure out for whom one or another item is intended, our journals have begun to translate bits and pieces of Parisian physiologies. . . . What a gain for Russian literature! . . . Such people will learn the great 'Parisian mysteries,'[23] they will . . . flaunt their knowledge of Parisian 'loose women,' 'lorgnettes,' 'bons vivants,' 'boulevards,' and 'eating-houses' to such an extent that they will astound the most desperate Parisian idler. Do you think we are joking? . . . What some people will not do to indulge the tastes of their readers! . . . These physiologies are filthy things."[24]

21. "Frantsuzskaia literatura," *Otechestvennye zapiski* 18, no. 6 (1841): 19.

22. P. Annenkov, "Pis'ma iz-za granitsy: Pis'mo VIII," *Otechestvennye zapiski* 20, no. 1 (1842): 23.

23. The reference is to Eugene Sue's 1842–43 work *Les Mystères de Paris.*

24. Others were outraged at the Gallic ridicule of entire social classes. A Russian translation of Paul de Kock's 1841 work *Physiology of a Married Man,* published in 1842, provoked Senkovsky to write a defensive—and physiological—review of the work.

Physiology of a Married Man was for Senkovsky the "most dull slander of a witty Parisian Homer on . . . a most oppressed class: husbands. Husbands are the outcasts of Europe. Everyone insults them—wives, mothers-in-law, fathers-in-law, aunts, gossips, novelists, poets, comedians, artists, wood engravers on wood, steel engravers, lovers . . . and even booksellers who sell their honor openly in various types

The perceived filth of French and English physiological fiction set many Russian writers and critics on edge. Portraits of everyday people were already in questionable taste, they asserted; but pictures of torsos in decline and decay were for them outrageous and inadmissible. "Can the waxen image of a rotting corpse or the picture of a drunkard vomiting and convulsing from a hangover be a subject for art?" Nikolai Polevoi complained in 1842. "The mistake of earlier writing, you say, was that it painted nature in rouge and portrayed life on stilts. Perhaps so, but to depict only the dark sides of nature and life, to choose only dirt and manure, debauchery and vice, do you not fall into the other extreme?"[25]

Very quickly, though, Russians warmed to physiological writing; and for several reasons. The first was literary, the primary champion of the phenomenon in France being the liberal critic Vissarion Belinsky. "One cannot but agree," Belinsky wrote in 1843, "that the French are remarkable masters . . . especially when they write about the most routine subjects—their everyday conversations and discussions—in a way that is lively, skillful, playful, light, and witty. In such writing [our Russian writers] would do well to compete with them."[26]

---

of prose, poetry, and caricatures. . . . These men and women call themselves 'the party of the weak,' but they are powerful, cruel, and enduring. They are in a grand conspiracy against the black servile people known under the humorous name of 'husbands.'" See O. Senkovskii, review of *Fiziologiia zhenatogo cheloveka Pol'-de-Koka,* by Paul de Kock, in "Literaturnaia letopis': Novye knigi; Mart 1833," *Biblioteka dlia chteniia* 57 (1843): 68. Also see Z. Z., "Russkaia literatura," *Severnaia pchela,* no. 81 (1843): 523.

25. See N. Polovoi, "Pokhozdeniia Chichikova, ili 'mertvye dushi': Poema N. Gogolia," *Russkii vestnik,* no. 6 (1842): 41–42.

26. Belinsky offered little initial hope, though, that, in physiological writing, Russian writers could vie with their French counterparts. In his review of 1843 Russian translations of Louis Couailhac's *The Physiology of the Theater in Paris and the Provinces* (1842) and James Rousseau's *The Physiology of a Hedonist* (1842), Belinsky wrote: "One cannot be surprised at the lightness, playfulness, and wit which the French reproduce their national life . . . in their [fictional] 'manners.' They are not like our hundred-pound . . . labored, and disquieting articles in which financial speculators ogle Russian existence . . . but show it only inside out, not like life at all. . . . Such works people buy only for the pictures."

In a similar vein, Belinsky was also unhappy with Russian translations of French physiologies. "In no way can we rejoice over [the rendering] of physiologies into Russian," he continued. "What appears in France as triflings, as jokes and games, as a break from work, and as a witty word, uttered at a merry table over a glass of champagne—is in this country regarded with such reverence . . . with such laughable and pitiful worship that our translators, not understanding irony, take as serious affairs the very jokes of contributors to French physiologies. . . . Meanwhile, the pedants cry out: 'Look at French literature! What nonsense fills it these days!' That is it exactly—[the view of] *a sick man of a healthy one.* The French are guilty that they can joke but also get down to business; but we are proud . . . because we do not do anything important right and render gracious follies in plump and corpulent language." See Belinskii, *Polnoe sobranie sochinenii,* vol. 7 (1955), 80–81.

Belinsky was not alone in such a view. French physiologies on select concepts and themes also received widespread Russian approval. Regarding an 1844 physiology entitled *The Streets of Paris,*[27] a reviewer wrote in the *Fatherland Notes* in August 1844: "How many interesting things the writers [in this work] tell about Parisians and foreigners who come to admire Paris and to make merry in its environs."[28] Similarly about the 1840–42 nine-volume physiology entitled *The French as Painted by Themselves,*[29] Faddei Bulgarin wrote, "There is no possibility even to enumerate all the good [things in this work] and so we can only limit ourselves with the advice to read and acquire this splendid edition."[30]

A second reason for the Russian interest in French physiologies was financial. Like it or not, native writers and editors, publishers, and booksellers sensed that the reading audiences in their country were no longer aristocrats and intellectuals exclusively; rather, they were becoming as widespread and democratic as their counterparts in the West. Despite their disparagement of what they regarded as low literature—"a repulsive insect in human form,"[31] one critic wrote in 1843—members of the Russian literary caste could not ignore the allure of the almighty ruble.[32]

"The fact of the matter is," a previously quoted reviewer for the *Northern Bee* continued in 1843, "that in France, England, and Germany . . . the janitor reads, the servant reads, the cabbie reads, the housekeeper reads. Just as educated people need their own books, encyclopedias, theater, and newspapers, so do janitors, servants, cabbies, and housekeepers need their own literature, their own writers. . . . [Hence] the [growth of]

27. L. Lurine, ed., *Les rues de Paris: Paris ancient et moderne; origines, histoire, monuments, costumes, moeurs, chroniques et traditions* (Paris: G. Kugelmann, 1844).

28. "Inostrannaia literatura: Frantsuzskaia literatura," *Otechestvennye zapiski,* 32, no. 1, otdel. vii (1844), 11–12. (The word "otdel" means "section" or "part." Russian journals of the time were divided into *otdely* labeled "history," "literature," "science," and so forth. The *otdel* for literature could and did appear everywhere in a particular issue without any consistency in numbering.)

29. See previous footnote 4 to Editor's Introduction.

30. F. Bulgarin, "Frantsuzy, spisannye s natury frantsuzami," *Severnaia pchela,* no. 130 (1840): 520.

31. See Z. Z., "Fiziologiia vivera," *Severnaia pchela,* no. 137 (1843): 546–47.

32. Such a statement should be taken quite literally. "One ruble silver for a miniature picture gallery," Bulgarin wrote in his physiological work *Pictures of Russian Mores,* "Nothing could be cheaper!" F. Bulgarin, *Kartinki russkikh nravov,* bk. 1 (St. Petersburg: I. A. Iungmeister, 1842), iii.

'physiologies.' . . . Indeed, the entire rear courtyard of readers is in ecstasy over physiologies."[33]

Such individuals also had money to spend. Throughout the 1830s and into much of the 1840s, Russians enjoyed marked peace and prosperity.[34] Particularly in St. Petersburg, law and order reigned supreme. Aristocrats were comfortable; merchants, prosperous. With apologies to Gogol and Dostoevsky, even the petty clerk could participate, albeit vicariously, in the glittering life of Russia's imperial capital. True, there was frustration and anger at the old order, particularly the censorship; but for individuals with small stakes in national life, their desire was for the status quo (political, social, and economic). Even the majority of aristocrats and educated citizens, having reconciled themselves to the limits imposed by Tsar Nicholas, worked creatively and successfully within his system.[35] "No dissonances marred the general harmony," a Russian observer noted in the 1840s, "for there was a conservative monarchial element in all strata [of society] and there seemed to be no possibility of any other."[36]

No doubt about it, money could be made with physiologies. "There exists an entire *Gostinyi Dvor*[37] of Russian mores," a critic from the *Library for Reading* wrote in 1843. "People who sell such wares . . . rake in the dough. . . . The trade in Russian mores has reached feverish heights: There are even speculators and stock exchanges of such things. . . . People who buy ten Russian mores get the eleventh one free! . . . Who needs such things?"[38]

33. Z. Z, "Fiziologiia vivera," 523.

34. The statistics are impressive. By 1843, the currency was stable and industry expansive. Raw cotton imports for Russian thread rose from 5,400,000 pounds in 1831 to 40,400,000 pounds in 1848; the production of beet sugar from 540,000 pounds in 1825 to 38,286,000 pounds in 1850. Similarly, the number of factories increased from 5,261 in 1835 to 8,020 in 1848; and, in the same period, the number of industrial workers more than doubled, from 210,568 to 483,542. Finally, the export of grain, one of Russia's most important foreign trade commodities, moved from 7,100,000 silver rubles in 1820 to 11,074,000 in 1840, and, with the 1846 repeal of the Corn Laws in England would by the 1860s rise to 37,508,000 silver rubles. W. Bruce Lincoln, *Nicholas I: Emperor and Autocrat of All the Russias* (Bloomington: Indiana University Press, 1978), 270–71.

35. Ibid., 239. Also consider Lincoln's caution on focusing too exclusively on Russian dissidents alone in this period. Ibid., 152.

36. Ibid., 152.

37. *Gostinyi Dvor,* or Guest Market, built in the late eighteenth century, is not only the oldest and largest shopping center in St. Petersburg but one of the first department stores in the world.

38. "Literaturnaia letopis'," *Biblioteka dlia chteniia* 57 (March–April 1843), otdel. VI, 16.

With such a question, of course, the reviewer was kidding no one. Russians on both sides of the literary market did!

Most crucially, perhaps, the Russian interest in physiologies was seen by many writers, editors, and publishers as fostering national aspirations for political and philosophical progress. Initially, such a belief drew from the Russian fascination with France as the birthplace of liberty, equality, and fraternity, as well as from a Gallic fixation not only over what the eye could see but also, more important, what it could not, that is, the hidden or secret qualities of national life. "France had the categorical solutions for all questions of a social, political, or moral character," Annenkov recalled in his memoirs, "[but] in our country it was the hidden France, and not the France in plain view, which was the object of interest."[39] The consensus was also that physiological writing was what every cultured country applauded and did and that Russians had everything to gain from socioscientific studies of their people and land. "In our time [the urge for] analysis has developed so forcefully throughout all of Europe," a reviewer for the *Finnish Herald* (*Finskii Vestnik*) wrote in 1845, "that manners writing has almost overtaken refined literature. In our country this direction draws not from fashion but as a consequence of our historical development. . . . We are beginning to turn to a critical investigation of our very selves. To be sure, such a transition must be the first step toward . . . genuine civilization."[40]

It was only a matter of time, then, before Russian writers and publishers tried their hand at physiology. Already in 1825, writer-critics such as Polevoi were demanding that, regarding fictional physiologies, native writers should take up "Russian paints . . . and brushes. We have our own customs and peculiarities that still await artists."[41] Indigenous literati accepted the physiological challenge wholeheartedly, even as quantity outdid quality. In 1835, for instance, Vladimir Stroev published *Scenes from Petersburg Life* (*Stseny iz Peterburgskoi zhizni*), which focused on the love and long-winded dialogues between a dreamy-eyed heroine and an

39. P. Annenkov, "*Zamechatel'noe desiatiletie, 1838–1848,*" in *Literaturnye vospominaniia* (Moscow: Gosudarstevennoe izdatel'stvo khudozhestvennoi literatury, 1960), 207.

40. F. Dershau, "Ot redaktsii 'Finskogo vestnika'," *Finskii vestnik,* no. 1 (1845): 3–4.

41. Also see N. Polevoi, "Obozrenie russkoi literatury v 1824 godu," *Moskovskii telegraf,* no. 2 (1824), 143.

equally flighty poet more than on any genuine interest or concern for the imperial.

In 1842, Russian readers leafed through an edition, entitled *Additions* (*Nastavki*), which portrayed the trade, gardens, churches, history, festivities, and even the Jewish citizens of the Haymarket Square, while ignoring the notoriously seamy side of life there. Beginning in 1842, also, there appeared in St. Petersburg the first of what was to be a twelve-part series of notebooks, entitled *Daguerreotype* (*Dagerrotip*), which—despite its claims to light reading, an encyclopedic embrace of St. Petersburg, and a fictional recourse to the latest advances in photography—featured enough of the likes of Polevoi, Nestor Kukol'nik, and Vladimir Benediktov to be dismissed by readers and reviewers alike.

Early Russian forays into fictional physiologies also wavered between the silly and the salacious. In 1841, for instance, there appeared two sketches, entitled "The Physiology of a Nose" ("Fiziologiia nosa")[42] and "The Physiology of Womanly Beauty" ("Fiziologiia zhenskoi krasoty"). In fact, when it came to physiologies, the Russians could be as frivolous as the French. In 1843 and 1844, Polevoi, writing under the name of Ivan Balakirev, published a physiological edition with the heading *True and Untrue Tales: Small Articles Torn from a Large Book Called "The World and People: Philosophical-Philanthropic-Humorous-Old Fashioned-and-Artistic Essays."* (*Byli i nebylitsy: Stateiki, vyrvannye iz bol'shoi knigi, nazyvaemoi "Svet i liudi. Filosofsko-filantropichesko-gumorichesko-starichesko-zhivopisnye ocherki"*). In *True and Untrue Tales,* Balakirev cared little about science and sobriety. The work, he claimed, was "neither a blank page nor a book"; rather, it was something "akin to a letter of recommendation and a hothouse watermelon; to Crimean wines, widow's tears, and first loves; to maidenly drawings and a concert of amateurs; to the essentials that the Japanese, flies, ravens, and fools have in the world." To Balakirev, such subjects were as "inexhaustible as the pride of an actor, the keys of an official, the compromises of conscience, the rhythms of a poor poet, the

42. "If the nose were not situated in the middle of the face," the Russian physiologist wrote, "it would have no reason for its existence. If the olfactory organ were the center of our being, the window of our soul, then it would be in some other place [on the human body]." See "Kaleidoscop: Fiziologiia nosa," *Literaturnaia gazeta,* no. 55 (1841), 217.

ambition of a collegiate registrar, the songs of an Italian composer, and the proofs of a German philosopher."[43]

Two early examples of serious and sustained physiological activity were Alexander Bashchutsky's 1834 two-volume work *Panorama of St. Petersburg* (*Panorama Sanktpeterburga*) and his 1841–42 edition *Ours, Copied from Nature by the Russians* (*Nashi, spisannye s natury russkimi*).[44] In such undertakings, Bashchutsky's heart was in the right place. "We do not have a history of Petersburg," he wrote in the introduction to *Panorama*, "We do not even have a description, a travel guide, or a simple directory which . . . could put forth even an essay of its huge scope."[45] Bashchutsky's head was also not far from the mark. To remedy this "terrible failing"[46] of literature in the imperial capital, he sought in *Panorama* to "draw . . . a broad and diverse picture of the capital . . . to show both its beauty and faults . . . to examine the successes of the arts, sciences, and professions . . . to capture the key features of mores, habits, folk life, and the communal

43. I. Balikrev, ed., *Byli i nebylitsy: Stateiki, vyrvannye iz bol'shoi knigi, nazyvaemoi, "Svet i liudi: Filosofsko-filantropichesko-gumorichesko-starichesko-zhivopisnye ocherki"* (St. Petersburg: V. S. Semeneko-Kramarevskii i A. E. Maslov, 1843), i.

44. It should be noted here that fictional anthologies and almanacs were not new in Russian literature. Such editions as *Polar Star* (*Poliarnaia Zvezda,* 1823–35), *Mnemosyne* (*Mnemozina,* 1824–25), *Uranius* (*Uraniia,* 1826), *Northern Flowers* (*Severnye tsvety,* 1825–32), and *Nevsky Almanac* (*Nevskii al'manakh*) (1825–33) were followed by *Daybreak* (*Dennitsa,* 1830–34), *The New Painter of Society and Literature* (*Novyi zhivopisets obshchestva i literatury,* 1832), *Housewarming* (*Novosel'e,* 1833–34), *One Hundred Russian Writers* (*Sto russkikh literaturov,* 1839), *Morning Sunrise* (*Utrennaia zaria,* 1839–43), *Russian Discourse* (*Russkaia beseda,* 1841–43), and, as has already been noted, Nekrasov's own *Articles in Poetry Without Pictures* (*Stateiki v stikhakh bez kartinok,* 1843).

Although such earlier (and later) collections sometimes featured genuine literature—*Housewarming,* for instance, published Pushkin's *The Little House in Kolomna* (*Domik v Kolmne*) and Gogol's *How the Two Ivans Quarreled* (*Povesti o tom, kak Ivan Ivanovich posorilsia s Ivanom Nikiforivichem*); the fables of Ivan Krylov; the poetry of Vasily Zhukovsky, Pyotr Vyazemsky, and Ivan Kozlov; and translations of Shakespeare, Dante, and Goethe—they were often seen as too frivolous and eclectic to feature the programs (political, social, and artistic) that both literary and conservative groups were demanding for Russian literature in the mid-1840s. Since almanacs catered typically to small circles of patrons and readers, they were also ill suited for the new financial concerns of publishers and writers.

"The fashion for almanacs has passed," a reviewer for *Literary Gazette* (*Literaturnaia gazeta*) wrote in 1843. "At a time when every line of poetry is weighed for its gold and every line of prose is measured in *arshins,* when all of literature is now a firm or, more accurately, a market, when anyone comes with a work of his own manufacture in the hope of catching maidens, almanacs of the good old days cannot live or succeed." See "Kritika i biografiia: Utreniaia zaria. Al'manakh na 1843, izdannyi I. Vladislavlevym," *Literaturnaia gazeta,* no. 1 (1843): 13.

45. A. Bashchutskii, *Panorama Sanktpeterburga,* bk. 1 (St. Petersburg: Tipogragiia vdovy Pliushara s synom, 1834), iv–v.

46. Ibid., v.

living of various classes, and finally to acquire . . . all the facts for a most rapid and precise knowledge of Petersburg."[47]

Bashchutsky's venture was not successful, though, and for a simple reason. From *Panorama* everyone knew what to expect with a dedication that read: "To His Imperial Majesty, Lord Emperor Nikolai Pavlovich, Autocrat of All Russia, with Gratitude, from Your Faithful Subject, Alexander Bashchutsky." Even a slow-witted audience could read between the lines with claims by the writer that the "appearance of the folk deceives the inexperienced eye"; that "under its coarse and heavy surface, one finds individuals who are strong, active, alive, adroit, noisy, thoughtful, articulate, precise, humorous, and good-hearted"; and, the pièce de résistance, that "the folk preserve patriarchal virtue and hospitality in full force." Lest anyone doubt the virtues of the common people in the northern Palmyra, Bashchutsky elaborated: "To help the poor, to comfort the orphan, to respect the old, to honor the dead, and to defend what is just, this is the universal inclination [of the folk in St. Petersburg]."[48]

Complementing the virtue-sans-vice in Bashchutsky's *Panorama* was the fact that his heroes and heroines lived in what later would be called a "snow-globe world" in which peace was endemic and the silence deafening. "On the streets [of Petersburg]," he wrote unabashedly, "there is no fighting or unruly behavior. . . . There are also no shouters . . . troublemakers . . . or coarse cabbies. At night there is quiet and calm. Even on the most deserted and far-flung streets safety is absolute."[49]

Bashchutsky's well-meaning if fanciful "moral physiology of a city and its people"[50] was seen as so sentimental and idealized[51] that the *Panorama of Petersburg* was dismissed by *both* liberal and conservative critics as

47. Ibid., vii–viii.

48. Ibid., bk. 3, 14, 31–32.

49. Ibid., 182.

50. Ibid., 9.

51. Compare Bashchutsky's waxing too eloquently on the death of a water-carrier: "In the eyes of the suffering man were two huge tears which were like two pearls, brilliant with the tints of the sun. . . . Neither I nor anyone else could convey all the ineffably sad, all the bitter and mysteriously imploring feelings that pressed down on my soul! This silent drama of the death of a poor man, this trait of faith and of sincere memory on the threshold of another life, affected me and illumined my mind in an instructive way. It seemed to me that at this very minute I became better in my soul and that I was a thousand times happier than I thought I could ever be; that I, who complained of life, was not worthy of a similar end!" See A. Bashchutskii, "Vodovoz," *Nashi, spisannye s natury russkimi,* no. 1 (1834): 14.

"caricatures" and "mirages."[52] The numbers speak for themselves. Whereas a work like the 1840–42 nine-volume *The French as Painted by Themselves*[53] had almost twenty-three thousand readers in France, Bashchutsky's *Ours, as Copied from Nature by the Russians* claimed only eight hundred in Russia.[54]

Such lack of success in physiological fiction did not discourage Russian readers, though. Just the opposite: it only whetted their appetite for more. By 1843, national excitement over the genre, particularly its pictures of everyday life, rivaled that of the French. "Russian mores are the most remarkable in the world," a critic from the *Library for Reading* wrote in 1843. "Everyone is writing about them. Everyone is outlining, drawing, and painting them. Each morning there appears a new picture, a new essay, outline, rough sketch, story, fairy tale, *poema,* and novel—all on Russian mores."[55]

Literary conservatives—Bulgarin, Senkovsky, Polevoi, and others—were particularly unhappy with Russian ventures into fictional physiology; but for reasons other than those noted earlier. They were often less than thrilled with the scientific approach that native physiologists were taking

52. See "Zhurnal'naia vsiakina vsiachina," *Severnaia pchela* (January 2, 1842), 2; and, "Smes'," *Severnaia pchela,* no. 81 (1842): 322. Also see Belinskii, *Polnoe sobranie sochinenii,* vol. 6 (1955), 560.

53. Iakimovich, *Frantsuzskii realisticheskii ocherk,* 158.

54. See V. Vereshagin, *Russkie illiustrirovannye izdaniia XVIII i XIX stoletiia (1720–1870)* (St. Petersburg: Tipografiia V. Kirshbauma, 1898), 152.

Russian attempts at physiology also extended into the countryside and abroad. See, for instance, I. Miatlev's *The Sensations and Observations of Mrs. Kudryukova Abroad* (*Sensatsii i zamechaniia gospozhi Kudriukovoi za granitseiu,* 1840); V. Burnashev's *Sunday Gatherings for Young People: A Book for the Good Russian People* (*Voskresnye posidelki: Knizhka dlia dobrogo russkogo naroda,* 1844); D. Begichev's *Provincial Scenes* (*Provintsial'nye stseny,* 1845); and N. Kirilov's *Types of Contemporary Mores* (*Tipy sovremennykh nravov,* 1845).

Not surprisingly, Russian physiologies for the folk were even more conservative than those for the urban masses. As typified by *Sunday Gatherings,* the watchword was "Christian virtue," that is, "obey superiors; keep arguments inside the hut; and observe courtesy . . . calm, heartfelt service, honesty and truth . . . patience for the boss's failings . . . gratitude to the master . . . [and] resignation to the will of God." There was even advice for refuge from thunderstorms and for recipes for "strongest and cheapest house vinegar."

The titles of the moral tales in *Sunday Gatherings,* though, say it all, for example, "About How the Small Boy Weaned His Father Away from Drink," "About What Happened to the Incident with the Curious Girl," "About the Harm of Being in Sweat and Swimming in Cold Water," "About How to Recognize Lazy Masters at First Glance," "About the Tragedy That Occurs When Simple Girls Surrender to the Flattering Promises of Frivolous City People," and "How It Is Harmful and Dangerous to Surrender to Sorcery, Magic, the Evil Eye, Flying Snakes, Falling Stars, and So Forth."

55. "Literaturnaia letopis'," *Biblioteka dlia chteniia* 57 (1843): 16.

in their works, that is, like naughty children, they were telling the secrets (good and bad) of family life in the imperial capital. Nothing, it seemed, was sacred to Russian writers of physiology. A reviewer from the *Library for Reading* was particularly nonplussed. Fictional physiologists, he complained in 1834, had to "be out at night... on the streets and under the gates . . . first to listen in on the conversations of yardkeepers . . . and then to record whom they addressed and where they went off to." The approach had to be encyclopedic, however intimate or intrusive. Lest anyone miss the point, an inclusive if unnerving "you" and "yours" entered into the job description. Anyone in Russia who thought to pick up a physiological pen "should know by heart all the alleyways of the city, all the staircases of the homes, and all the secrets and gatherings of its masters. He should describe to you all your innermost mores and customs . . . to specify the first name, last name, rank, and residence not only of your friends and family . . . but also of every passerby walking or riding down the street."

That done (!), the reviewer continued, the Russian physiologist now had to get serious about his task. "Armed with the knife of an anatomist," he was to "open up the body of Petersburg society, cut and push back its folds, and without mercy, show to you the boils and abscesses in the innards of all your friends and acquaintances." On the physiological list were specific issues and concerns. The writer of such a genre should "tell the entire world . . . who has a dirty entranceway, who has elegant furniture, who has on his table a bottle of Lafitte standing next to a bottle of *kvas,* who eats and drinks what and even how much, what these people ride around in . . . [and] how they feed their horses and servants."

No holds were barred in the physiological quest, the reviewer from the *Library for Reading* bemoaned. Doors should be opened, curtains parted, candles lit. Everything was fair game for discussion and review. "Without permission," the Russian physiologist was to enter "the servant quarters and see how your valets and maids are dressed . . . to step into your kitchen and praise your cook . . . to peek into your cabinet and exclaim about your poor china . . . even to look into your bedrooms and see what your wives and daughters are doing there!"

With friends like Russian physiologists, the reviewer concluded, who needed enemies? Half in earnest, half in jest, he added that if such physiological fashion continued in the national literature, Peter's city would lose its magisterial if mystical allure. It would even become a ghost town. Citizens would be too embarrassed to stay; provincials would be too loath to come. Having read physiologies of the imperial mecca, the reviewer lamented, "I cannot imagine how to go on living in St. Petersburg. In the public panorama, without any frills, we have been so exposed to provincials that they now know our most significant secrets and have the keys to our mores."[56]

Bulgarin and company were also annoyed that early native physiologies were for them not sufficiently Russian. "Look around you," a critic from the *Library for Reading* wrote in 1843. "Russian mores are nowhere to be seen! One wipes his eyes, dons his glasses, and looks around. . . . But just the same, Russian mores are nowhere to be found!" Rather, in homeland physiologies, the reviewer continued, Russian readers and reviewers meet "only a fermentation of inclinations, concepts, and customs . . . [that are] fickle, colorless, and vague . . . a meld of mores that are French, German, English, Italian, Tatar, and Turkish . . . but nothing that [is] enduringly, particularly, and exclusively Russian!"[57]

Paradoxically, though, Bulgarin and his colleagues also became upset when domestic physiologists were too Russian, when they advanced from scientific to social, in sketches that showed the dark and seamy side of life in Peter's city. Just as indigenous conservative writers and critics had attacked the appeal of such writing among the lower classes in France, so now did they assail the popularity of such prose with similar groups in Russia. "Repel from our country this incursion by the enemy, you guardians of the Russian land and mind!" a critic from the *Northern Bee* exhorted Russian citizens in 1841. "Our literature can do without Paul-de-Kock-like physiologies just as our novels can dispense with those stinking Petrushkas and those eating-house fleas that . . . jump into our literature from abroad."[58] When it came to domestic physiologies, therefore, there was no winning with Bulgarin and his group. Russian physiologists were damned when they did not portray the homeland and damned when they did.

56. "Literaturnaia letopis'," *Biblioteka dlia chteniia* 8, no. 4 (1835): otdel. VI, 45–46, 48.

57. "Literaturnaia letopis'," *Biblioteka dlia chteniia* 57 (1843): 16.

58. See "Russkaia literatura: Ocherki, ili litsevaia storona i iznanka roda chelovechestva," *Severnaia pchela,* no. 84 (1843): 554.

Conservative Russian editors and writers did not reject fictional physiology entirely, though. Despite their uneasiness with such writing, they could not close their eyes to the fact that the genre, beyond literary and financial boons, also bestowed social and political blessings. Armed with their own version of physiologies, Bulgarin and others believed that they could fill what they correctly saw as the growing vacuum in Russian literature with writing that countered the so-called Gogolian direction (*gogolevskoe napravlenie*) in the national written expression. They were also confident that they could address their concerns for Russianness in domestic physiologies: the images and ideals of autocracy, nationality, and Orthodoxy that Nicholas I had imposed on the homeland since the Decembrist Revolt of 1825.

The time was right for such a coup: Alexander Pushkin had died in 1837, Mikhail Lermontov in 1841, and Ivan Krylov in 1844. Nikolai Gogol, after writing *Dead Souls* in 1842, had left literature. Ivan Turgenev was only coming to public notice; Nekrasov was seen as a *podenshchik,* or "day laborer"; Alexander Herzen had not yet published in its entirety his novel *Who Is to Blame?* and Ivan Goncharov, Alexander Ostrovsky, Dmitri Grigorovich, Mikhail Saltykov-Shchedrin, and Fyodor Dostoevsky still had not lent their voices to native fiction.[59] Further, many Russian writers believed that the national written expression had become too depressing and dark to be of value to its readers. As Gogol lamented to Nikolai Yazykov in January 1845, "We have an old generation of writers, masters only at depressing young people, but without the intelligence to set them to labor and effective work. How can up to now so little concern have been shown with investigations into the nature of the individual when such knowledge is the key source of everything?"[60]

59. Even these writers came under the spell of physiology. "Most likely, you know," Goncharov's hero says in his 1848 work "Correspondence Between a Petersburg Citizen and a Provincial" ("Perepiska mezhdu peterburgtsem i provintsialom"), "every part of the human body has its own physiognomy . . . which expresses clearly, as if it were water, the character . . . of the individual. Do you believe such a thing? If not, I ask only one question: Where did craniology, physiology, palmistry, and other sciences come from? What kind of people studied such things: Gall, Lavater, and other great men." See I. Goncharov, "Perepiska mezhdu peterburgtsem i provintsialom," *Sovremennik,* no. 10 (1848): 6.

60. See Gogol's letter to Yazykov, written on January 2, 1845, in N. Gogol, *Polnoe sobranie sochinenii v chetyrnadtsati tomakh,* vol. 12 (Moscow: Akademiia nauk SSSR, 1952), 444–45.

Complicating matters was the fact that the stakes for readers were also high. In St. Petersburg in 1840, of a population of roughly 470,000 citizens, fully 70 percent were from the middle and lower classes, including 30,000 *raznochintsy,* or "nonaristocratic intellectuals"; 54,000 merchants and petit bourgeois; 24,000 tradesmen; 22,000 servants; 120,000 peasants; and 22,000 prisoners.[61]

Bulgarin and company thus informed their physiological works with their own cares and concerns. In 1842, for example, Bulgarin published *Russian Conversation* (*Russkaia beseda*) and *Mosquitoes* (*Komary*); a year later, he published *Essays of Russian Mores; or, The Right and Wrong Side of the Human Race* (*Ocherki, ili litsevaia storona i iznanka roda chelovecheskogo*). In all three works,[62] together with reviews and articles in the *Northern Bee,* Bulgarin made clear his own ideas on physiological realism. In his view, a tidy if simplistic duality governed literature and life. "It is impossible," Bulgarin wrote in *Essays of Russian Mores,* "that everyone in the world be rich, intelligent, healthy, happy, industrious, and irreproachable. . . . There also exists the 'wrong side' of things, that is, poverty, stupidity, sadness, laziness, and vice. All of us . . . are obliged to attend to this wrong side of humanity as if [it were] spots on silk."[63]

Further, Bulgarin insisted that only the right side—and never the wrong—should be the stuff of Russian physiological writing. Wholesome

61. A. Tseitlin, *Stanovlenie realizma v russkoi literature* (*Russkii fiziologicheskii ocherk*) (Moscow: Nauka, 1965), 95.

62. Bulgarin's attempts at physiology aptly illustrate Harley's idea of the often conservative if reactionary nature of mappings. That is, monarchs and popes ordered maps to "reinforce the legal statutes, territorial imperatives, and values stemming from the exercise of political power" (Harley, "Maps, Knowledge, and Power," 282). Power is exerted on *and* with cartography, Harley continues, so that ideas and authority can be maintained over boundaries and population, as well as on such activities as commerce, administration, and defense. "Maps helped create myths which assisted in the maintenance of the territorial status quo. As communicators of an imperial message, they have been used as aggressive complements to the rhetoric of speeches, newspapers, and written texts, or to the histories and popular songs extolling the virtues of the empire" (Harley, "Deconstructing the Map,"12).

To this Wood adds: "Maps are required for us all to keep track of each other and what we are up to. . . . Maps connect us to all the other aspects of the vast system of codes, laws, contracts, treaties, covenants, deals, and so on in which we have immersed ourselves" (Wood, *Power of Maps,* 39).

63. F. Bulgarin, "Izvoshchik-nochnik," *Ocherki* (St. Petersburg: Tipografiia Eduarda Pratsa, 1843), 17.

and edifying, official and Orthodox,[64] pious and patriotic—these were the criteria for indigenous fiction.[65] "Artists who copy from nature," he argued in the *Northern Bee* in 1845, "must choose only that which is graceful and proper. . . . In nature there are a great many things which must never enter into . . . literature and art, and which a person of good breeding must also turn away from."[66] Bulgarin, together with his colleagues, fought tooth and nail any perceived movement in Russian literature from "classical Olympus and romantic Valhalla"[67] to "pulp pictures and heroes with black eyes, wearing torn shapeless sacks, and speaking the language of . . . courtyards."[68]

In this simple and tidy art, also, Bulgarin contended that, in physiologies, native writers portrayed a folk that was faceless and abstract. Let the French have their types, Bulgarin sniffed, Russians needed neither diversity nor prosaic complications. "In France," he wrote in the *Northern Bee* in 1841, "every social class has its own favorite spots, its own places at the theaters, even its own theaters, coffeehouses, and fashions. Every social class bears the mark of originality. . . . But in our country, what distinguishes professionals or tradesmen? Precisely nothing. An undertaker is the same as an artisan, and when he enters the home of a rich deceased person to arrange for a funeral, in no way is he different from a contractor

64. Consider for instance, the story in *Mosquitoes,* entitled "The Beggar; or, The History of Riches" (*Nishchii ili istoriia bogatstva*) in which a wealthy merchant son, after years of carousing, goes bankrupt, is abandoned by all—and finds joy both in the Almighty and in his diminished position in life. "I thank God," the hero affirms, "that He has deprived me of riches, but that He has sent me comfort in faith . . . [and has taught me] to live by the ancient Russian proverb: 'Know thy place!' ('*Znai sverchok svoi shestok*!')." F. Bulgarin, *Komary* (St. Petersburg: n.p., 1842), 68, 78.

The preference for nonsecular literature continued for at least another decade. For instance, at the end of Tsar Nicholas's reign, an official pronouncement from the Ministry of Education affirmed that only religious works should be published for the folk because "books of spiritual content bolster the simple people's faith and hope in holy Providence for new labor and for the benign bearing of all types of privation, whereas secular books only . . . lead them away from their work and try their patience." A. Kotovich, *Dukhovnaia tsenzura v Rossii (1799–1855)* (St. Petersburg: Rodnik, 1909), 309.

65. Consider the claim by Duncan and Ley that "topography is also a science of domination, confirming boundaries, securing norms, and treating questionable social conventions as unquestioned social facts" (*Place/Culture/Representation,* 1).

66. F. Bulgarin, "Smes'," *Severnaia pchela,* no. 106 (1845), 422.

67. F. Bulgarin, "Zhurnal'naia vsiakina vsiachina," *Severnaia pchela,* no. 69 (1847): 275.

68. Ibid.

who delivers wood, bricks, hay, and straw. . . . Russian merchants are also all of similar cut. . . . Writers and scholars . . . are one and the same."[69]

Bulgarin even claimed that for Russian physiologists to cross the borders of class, language, and the like, that is, for individuals from higher castes to write about men, women, and children from lower ones, was on the one hand an exercise in self-futility and deception and on the other hand a preoccupation with the darkness even amid the light. Only a conservative writer-critic like Bulgarin could let a thousand flowers bloom in St. Petersburg in the 1840s.[70] Imagining that he had encountered a writer from the Natural school eager to portray "all the burden and grief"[71] of a peasant, Bulgarin sounded off in the *Northern Bee* in 1843, "What for? Who could like such a thing? There is enough sadness in the world; and, if an individual from his 'heights' looks at the lower levels of society, such grief will seem to him to be a hundred times more oppressive. It means nothing to a peasant to carry a bundle of wood . . . in bad weather or snowstorms; but if you and I were to do such a thing, we would be unhappy. Look at an individual according to his situation and where there are shadows, insert bright colors."[72] Let sleeping dogs lie, Bulgarin argued; the more distant and remote the folk were, the better.[73]

69. F. Bulgarin, "Peterburskie tipy," *Severnaia pchela,* no. 22 (1841): 87.

70. Needless to say, such optimism had its fans. "No one like Bulgarin," an anonymous critic from the *Library for Reading* wrote, "can discover in the dark and dirty earth such brilliant diamonds, which, although black, are diamonds just the same." "Literaturnaia letopis'," *Biblioteka dlia chteniia* 57 (1843): 16.

71. As quoted in Tseitlin, *Stanovlenie realizma,* 135.

72. Ibid.

73. It gets worse. For instance, in *Essays of Russian Mores,* Bulgarin wrote: "I prefer drivers who dedicate themselves to their heavy labor in a willing way." Such virtue, Bulgarin insisted, had its own (mutual) reward. He continued: "'Here, old man, is a ten-ruble note,' I said to him, '. . . for today I have met a good Russian man and have learned that in any calling, an honest man can be happy'" (*Ocherki russkikh nravov,* 18).

Indeed, Bulgarin could be quite the philosopher. Compare such lines from his *Pictures of Russian Mores* as "Who is poor and who is rich? The answer to that question depends on how each [of us] understands his life-view" and "For a long time now I have considered the beggar not only to be the richest and even the happiest individual in the world, since he does not know loss, does not have unrealizable dreams, being limited to a daily existence" (Bulgarin, *Kartinki,* 1, 29).

Bulgarin was fooling no one, though. "How little truth . . . knowledge of Russian life, Russian mores, and finally, the simple facts of Russian contemporary existence of all classes of society," a reviewer from *Literary Gazette* wrote in 1843, "Bulgarin's portrait of a night driver is colorless and not at all like the Russian original, or even any member of the folk. . . . Rather, all we have here is a repetition, for the one-hundred-and-first time, of worn moral sentiment." "Kritika i bibliografiia: Ocherki russkikh

Bulgarin and company were particularly incensed by portraits of ordinary men and women that departed from their conservative norms. A particular litmus test for them was the fictional *chinovnik,* or "civic official," petty and otherwise. "The world of civic officials," Bulgarin wrote in a physiological sketch about this type in *Russian Conversation,* "is completely unto itself. It has absolutely nothing in common with the world of the gentry, or the merchants, or the petit bourgeois. In the world of civic officials, nothing is borrowed; everything is original, its own. The world of civic officials has its own language, literature, intelligence, and wit. It has its own fashions, cooking, and even its own dances."[74] In no way, Bulgarin continued, could this group, the ultimate pillar of official society, do any wrong; and any affirmation to the contrary smelled of slander, revolution, and the Gogolian direction. In fact, it was over the fictional *chinovnik* that the battle lines over Russian physiology were often drawn. "Talking about civic officials," Bulgarin wrote, "do not think that I intend to talk about bribes! No, civic officials do not take bribes! That is the province of scribes and clerks, that group of quill drivers, that afflicted tribe!"[75] The critic Leopold Brant concurred. "It is time to stop typing clerks!" he thundered in 1842. "We have grown accustomed to seeing them in a false mirror . . . as caricatures . . . on the painted sign over the barbershop on Gorkhovaya street."[76]

---

nravov, ili litsevaia storona i iznanka roda chelovecheskaia; Soch. F. Bulgarina," *Literaturnaia gazeta,* no. 7 (1843): 134.

74. F. Bulgarin, "Chinovnik," *Russkaia beseda,* vol. 3 (St. Petersburg: Pechatnia E. Evdokimova, 1842), 5.

75. Bulgarin was sufficiently honest, though, to note that *chinovniki* had their bad days. Such individuals, he insisted, "could not be indifferent at how some people rise above others and become rich suddenly! Their hearts grew hard, and smiles rarely appear on their faces." He was, however, careful to keep his civic officials under wraps. No Dostoevskian rebels were they! "Sometimes civil clerks," Bulgarin continued, "grumble. . . . 'At whom?' you ask. In no way at anyone! Only at fate!" Even more revealing, perhaps, Bulgarin was not above canonizing his *chinovniki,* even as he unwittingly buried them. "Eternal memory and peace to your ashes, kind souls," Bulgarin ended his sketch. "Much paper have you used up in life, many pens have you minced, many rivers of ink have you spilled, and many mountains of sealing wax have you melted. But you have never written lampoons, nor denunciations, nor stupid or vicious criticism. You have not forced anyone to shed tears, or to ruin another's reputation with your tongue, or to burn someone's heart with your slander! You have lived a life of toil, and here is your reward: the kind word of an honest man and a place with God!" Ibid., 7, 18.

76. Like Bulgarin, Brant had very clear if simplistic ideas about national types. "We would do well," he continued, "to become acquainted with a genuine Russian gentry maiden (*baryshnia*), a girl about nineteen years old, with blue eyes, rosy cheeks, and light-brown curls. . . . Tell us how sweet, happy, mournful she is . . . how she loves and suffers . . . remind us of Pushkin's Tat'yana!" L. Brant, *Opyt*

Chinovniki aside, the breadth and depth of the conservatives' search for aberrations in native physiological fiction was impressive. The concern was not only about Russian literature but also about Russian life. Bulgarin and company had very definite ideas on national freedom and order, identity and success, as well on the function of writing to support (or negate) their views of the world. Above all, the folk was not to get any ideas from what it had read, the fear being that the Russian public, if presented with fictional portraits of unhappy citizens, would rock the empire with revolution and repression. Shades of Joseph Stalin a century later, even Nicholas I kept a watchful eye on physiological writing.[77] "There are new worries among the censors," Alexander Nikitenko wrote in his diary on January 22, 1842. "One of the pieces [in Bashchutsky's *Ours, as Copied from Nature by the Russians*], an essay entitled 'The Water Carrier,' has caused an uproar. Truly, the democratic direction of the work is beyond a doubt, that is, the folk endure oppression but, in their virtue, they do not stir. The emperor is very displeased. To everyone's surprise, though, the matter has been handled quietly. . . . Benkendorf summoned the author and gave him a restrained warning."[78]

Despite the risks, political[79] and financial,[80] progressive editors and writers challenged the conservative hegemony over literary physiology.

---

bibliograficheskogo obozreniia ili ocherk poslednego polugodiia nashei literatury s oktiabria 1841 g. po aprel' 1842 g. (St. Petersburg: Tipografiia glavnogo upravleniia putei soobshcheniia i publichnykh zdanii, 1842), 54, 56.

77. Apparently, so did Vladimir Lenin. Bashchutsky's *Ours, as Copied by the Russians* was included in his Kremlin library. See A. Bessonova et al., *Biblioteka V. I. Lenina v Kremle* (Moscow: Izdatel'stvo vsesoiuznoi knizhnoi palaty, 1961), 500.

78. Doubtless, Nicholas had to be upset by such lines as: "[The water carrier] does not complain, he does not hope. He sees clearly what . . . is possible for him to live . . . and work like as animal" (Bashchutskii, "Vodovoz," 24).

79. See Kotovich, 300-302. The tsar's concern for popular fiction was long-standing. Indeed, when it came to popular reading, his ministers trod lightly. For instance, when in 1834 the tsar's minister of education, Sergei Uvarov, was asked to permit the publication of Russian equivalents to the English *Penny Magazine* and the German *Heller Mag,* he asked the censors, "Is it useful to allow the introduction and implantation here of this type of cheap literature that has the aim and immediate consequence of acting upon the lower-class reading public?" They replied that secular literature was incompatible with the existing order. To this reply Nicholas affixed an addendum, saying, "Completely true. By no means allow." See Brooks, 299.

Also see A. Nikitenko, *Moia povest' o samom sebie i o tom, "chemu svidietel' v zhizni byl": zapiski i dnevnik (1804–1877 gg.),* vol. 1 (St. Petersburg: Gerold, 1905), 312–22.

80. In 1842, the famous publisher and bookseller Alexander Smirdin faced bankruptcy, being over 500,000 rubles in debt.

They too believed that as goes art, so goes the nation—its very essence and identity. As early as 1828, forward-looking literati were taking issue with Bulgarin's idea of physiological mores. The simple, abstract and pristine view of Russian physiological life that Bulgarin was selling, many homeland readers and reviewers were not buying. "Mr. Bulgarin seems to have a monopoly on portraying mores," a critic from the *Moscow Herald* (*Moskovskii vestnik*) wrote at this time, "but a writer without his own view, profundity, insightfulness, and irony, but only with outworn rules, can never succeed in this type of writing."

"Mr. Bulgarin," the critic continued, "will never create a picture of contemporary characters and customs that is bright, diverse, and variegated. . . . He does not describe Russian mores but reworks foreign pieces into Russian. In Bulgarin's works, one meets a long-forgotten list of moral allegories, without any warm emotion or poetic thought. In his works one also often runs into humorous anachronisms which no one believes. Finally, not unlike our old comic writers, Bulgarin forces his character to tell others their faults in an innocent way . . . as if they have not been crafty and sly, or have hidden anything foolish inside them."[81]

A decade or so later, Belinsky picked up the charge against conservative physiologists. Even at this stage in his distinguished career (he died in 1848), the feet of the great critic may have walked on Russian soil, but his head still roamed in German clouds. Since 1840, Belinsky had championed French positivism, for example, the Gallic ability to espouse new ideals, to transform ideas into action, to draw from common sense and practicality, to develop a society that was intense and intellectual, and, most important, to posit a close interaction between French literature and national life. On the lighter side, Belinsky also relished (and envied) the ability of Parisians and their neighbors to see wit and humor in everything, to laugh at themselves, and to live life without guilt, pretense, and excess. Even though Belinsky was disenchanted with German idealism—its tenets at variance with Russian existence—he continued to linger around the Rhine. Schiller, Schelling, and Hegel still captured his fancy. Particularly enduring to Belinsky was the idealist-romantic view of a country as an organism that was vital, coherent, and just. He also clung to the idealist-romantic concept

81. "Obozrenie russkoi slovesnosti za 1827 god," *Moskovskii vestnik,* no. 1 (1828): 77.

that just as national ideas or spirits particularize a universal idea-absolute of ongoing freedom, progress, and humanity, so do national literatures contribute written expression to vaunt such ideals to the world. It was to Belinsky's delight that Pushkin, Lermontov, and Gogol were assuming a global presence on the literary stage and enhancing the healthful ontology of native and universal life. New homeland writers needed to be nurtured, though, if Russia were to enter fully into the community of civilized lands.

Nodding again to German philosopher-intellectuals of the 1830s and 1840s, Belinsky cherished the notion that it was ideas that forged art, that so long as writers were inspired by thoughts that were rational, progressive, and humane, they would bear fictional fruit. Mindful of Russian reality, though, Belinsky added this flourish: even artists of only modest talent could do great things if their heads were screwed on tight. Such individuals and their writing, Belinsky insisted, could be as quintessential a manifestation of the national spirit as literary geniuses.[82] After all, Belinsky believed, it was such writers as Mikhail Lomonosov who had set the stage for Pushkin. New talents, he continued, were constantly needed to pave the way for new geniuses. More important, perhaps, middling writers served as mediators between high and low literature, insuring enduring interchange and innovation on both sides of the national literary equation.

Like many critics, Russian and others, Belinsky was at his best when he censured, not sanctioned. Bulgarin and his physiology (theory and

82. Bowing to necessity, Belinsky thought and wrote long and hard on the difference between what he saw as genius and talent. Not surprisingly, he was clearer on the nature of the latter than the former. For Belinsky, talent lacked the universality and independence of genius. It required cultivation and hard work; it depended on social and historical circumstances; it moved along with the masses and the trends of the times. Talent, Belinsky also argued, featured technical skill, expressive ability, even imagination. It created works, enjoyed temporary success, and even forged entire trends in literature. Most important, perhaps, talent gave adequate expression to the ideas and values of an age, a nation, a society. Writers with talent, Belinsky also affirmed, were diligent litterateurs and honest journeymen of their trade. They moved at will between field marshals and plain soldiers to forge new paths for literature.

As a corollary to his views on talent, Belinsky showed a great tolerance for *belletristika,* that is, popular literature which, though not true art, meets a legitimate need in society and has a rightful place in the national written expression. Indeed, with a blessing to the folk, Belinsky saw *belletristika* as a matter not only of social expediency but also of historical necessity. For him, a shift to the masses, their interests, and their values was a key mark of a forward-looking, independent, and original literature.

For a sampling of Belinsky's 1845 pronouncements on talent and *belletristika,* see, for instance, Belinskii, *Polnoe sobranie sochinenii,* vol. 9 (1955), 160–63, 310–11, 454–56.

practice) were prime targets. "Our homegrown suppliers of text to accompany pictures, that is, the editors of so-called *Russian Mores,*" the great critic sniffed in an 1843 review of Paul de Kock's *The Physiology of a Married Man,* "will never achieve one tenth of the art which the French . . . do in their physiologies. . . . Will you find in 'Russian' compositions of this type even one hundredth of the wit and knowledge of life, of the observation and originality which strike us on every page in a small physiology written by Paul de Kock?"[83] Bulgarin's *Pictures of Russian Mores,* Belinsky continued, was not a study of Russian life but merely empty allegory and moralizing rhetoric: an "empty toy . . . a trifle."[84]

Other progressives joined in the assault. They were not happy with Bulgarin in 1828; they were even less so a generation later. "Long gone is the time when Bulgarin passed for a humorist and a writer of mores," a critic from *Literaturnaia Gazeta* wrote in 1845. "Nowadays people demand not only imagination and debate but also real life and characters from the folk captured in an accurate way. For such things, it is not enough merely to write in a smooth manner; one must also have a gift for observation and a good knowledge of Russian existence. . . . Bulgarin's *Essays* features nothing that is Russian and even less that is social; rather, the work is filled with mannerslike thoughts first on one thing, then on another. The Russian public has become very discerning, though. Readers can distinguish gold from tinsel. They are shown goods from both inside and out, but they are not moved to buy."[85]

Sadly, the battle between progressives and conservatives over Russian physiological fiction failed to move the genre forward. In fact, it locked the genre in a stalemate. Complaints, particularly about viable essays and sketches on St. Petersburg, continued unimpeded. "Up until now," a reviewer for the *Russian Invalid* (*Russkii invalid*) wrote in 1844, "we Russians have cared little about pictures of our personal existence in general and still less about portraits of life in St. Petersburg, particularly what makes the city great, instructive, engaging, amusing, and original. Besides address calendars and two or three works, no less dry . . . we have almost nothing on Petersburg."

83. Ibid., vol. 7 (1955), 23–24.

84. Ibid., vol. 6 (1955), 538.

85. *Literaturnaia gazeta,* no. 18 (1845): 312; as quoted in Tseitlin, *Stanovlenie realizma,* 136.

As before, the desire was for incursion into imperial urban life. "All that we have about Petersburg," the reviewer continued, "takes in only the external, surface form of our capital. . . . Physiologies that capture Petersburg in its entirety, we do not have. . . . To any observant physiologist how engaging . . . is our Petersburg population with its diverse images, calibers, stripes, and tongues! . . . [Consider only] the officer, the clerk, the writer, the bookseller, the actor, the organ-grinder, the Russian merchant, the French woman salesclerk, the German woman salesclerk, the Russian shoemaker, the German shoemaker, and so forth. All these people, all the inhabitants are of one and the same Petersburg, but among them there are differences, so many interesting shades and nuances which, without fail, must be captured since they harbor the genuine character of Petersburg."

One wondered what the problem was, the reviewer contended, when the diversity of Russia's northern Palmyra, its abundance of sights, sounds, and smells, provided subjects for endless physiological works. "Looking attentively at the movement on Petersburg streets . . . at the distinctiveness of the buildings," he concluded, "reading unerringly the signs plastered on buildings, the faces looking out from windows, the people walking or riding along . . . listening attentively to the scattered conversations, the specialness of the sounds coming from the homes, and breathing in the very air—one will begin, finally and little by little, to understand all the great diversity of Petersburg streets."[86]

Although Belinsky and company derided the fictional products and opinions of the conservatives at every turn, they were at a loss as to what to offer in their place. Such anxiety was only momentary, though. "Around that time (1843–44)," Grigorovich recalled, "small volumes under the general title 'Physiology' began to show up in quantity in the shops selling foreign books; each volume contained the description of some type taken from Parisian life. . . . Imitators immediately began to appear in Russia. . . . Nekrasov, whose practical mind was always on the lookout, conceived the idea of undertaking to publish something in this line; he imagined a publication in several small volumes: *Petersburg*."[87]

86. "Zhurnal'nye otmetki," *Russkii invalid*, no. 170 (1844): 977–78.

87. D. Grigorovich, *Literaturnye vospominaniia* (Moscow: Khudozhestvennaia literatura, 1987), 77.

The joy and excitement over no less than two volumes of *Petersburg: The Physiology of a City* was beyond measure.[88] Like a long-childless couple hailing, in both giddiness and surprise, the arrival of a blessed event, Belinsky and the other contributors to the work stood proud that they, at long last, had given birth to a physiology of their own to present to the Russian reading world.[89] *Petersburg* featured four pieces by Belinsky, the introduction ("Vyystuplenie") to the work, "Petersburg and Moscow" ("Peterburg i Moskva"), "The Alexander Theater" ("Aleksandrinskii Teatr"), and "The Literature of Petersburg" ("Peterburgskaia Literatura"); two by Nekrasov, "The Petersburg Corners" ("Peterburgskie ugly") and "The Bureaucrat" ("Chinovnik"); two by Grigorovich, "The Petersburg Organ-Grinders" ("Peterburgskie Sharmanshchiki") and "The Lottery Ball" ("Lotereinyi Bal"); one by Vladimir Dal', "The Petersburg Yardkeeper" ("Peterburgskii dvornik"); and one by Mikhail Kul'chitsky, "The Omnibus" ("Omnibus").

From Belinsky and his colleagues, the collective sigh of relief was almost audible. In their idealist-romantic minds, they had yet another example of national literature and spirit to add to universal culture and being. Pushkin, Lermontov, and Gogol were not blips on the national and universal cultural scene. Bulgarin and other conservatives were fighting only delaying, rear-guard actions in the march of Russian literature forward. With *Petersburg,* Belinsky and his colleagues had new proof that Russia and its people were ideal and organic; that their identity, idea, and inner life were alive and well; and that they heralded a bright future, in sync with the laws, ironclad and immutable, of history, progress, and the like.[90]

88. The first volume of *Petersburg* appeared on April 5, 1845; the second volume on August 28 that same year.

89. Expectations from readers and reviewers for *Petersburg* were as high as those of its contributors. They, too, it seemed, were in a carnival mood. "With pleasure we note an advertisement," a critic wrote in the *Literary Gazette,* "that soon there will be published a book entitled *The Physiology of Petersburg,* which promises to acquaint us with the lives of the rich and poor in the city, what they do, how they squander their money, how they make merry, what they like and no not like.

"'Wonderful! Wonderful!' we think. 'It will be a useful thing.' . . . But suddenly it occurred to us . . . Will there not be an article about 'how people eat in Petersburg'? . . . And if not, what will be the good of this work? . . . But, Messrs. Compilers of *The Physiology* . . . if you do not show us how people in Petersburg eat and drink . . . your work will be a mediocre one . . . like a man without his stomach!" "Perepiska doktora Pufa," *Literaturnaia gazeta,* no. 6 (1845): 6.

90. Consider Belinsky's 1840 statement that "the presence of a literature vouches for the historical existence of a nation" (*Polnoe sobranie sochinenii,* vol. 4 [1954], 414).

With *Petersburg,* also, Belinsky and his company believed that they were joining with European confreres to move fictional realism (and all it meant) to new and greater heights. They, too, now had a national literature which represented not only masters and men but all social classes, especially the middling groups: a genuine expression of all the Russian people. They, too, had works which could shine bright ideals amid dark realities; express the "innermost depths and pulsation"[91] of their land; and move Russia to an equal and honored place with England, Germany, and France.

With what Belinsky and company trumpeted as the strengths and innovations of *Petersburg,* the Russian public agreed wholeheartedly. The work was a financial success, the entire run of the work being snatched up immediately by avid readers and reviewers.

Bulgarin and his cohorts attacked *Petersburg* unrelentingly. "This so-called new literary school (already a genuine school!) tortures and torments us," Bulgarin wrote in the *Northern Bee* in 1846 with a specific eye to Nekrasov's work. "It forces us to read boring and flaccid absurdities, to describe in words some drunk, a repulsive woman, a pitiful writer, a dirty room, that is, so-called nature in life under the name of physiologies. . . ."[92]

The locus for their inspiration and settings, Bulgarin continued, was equally fanciful, farcical, and sordid. "These young writers," he wrote, "are creating a new world—one with 'corners'[93] no less—and in these 'corners' are stored all the treasure of their mind[94] . . . and taste as manure for the soil

91. Ibid., vol. 1 (1953), 24.

92. See F. Bulgarin, "Zhurnal'naia vsiakaia vsiachina," *Severnaia pchela,* no. 55 (1846): 219.

93. The reference is to Nekrasov's "The Petersburg Corners," the most controversial section in *Petersburg.*

94. The idea of "corners" as a seedbed for Russian literature became a literary football in Bulgarin's opposition not only to *Petersburg* but also to other products of progressive urban realism. Bulgarin wrote in 1847: "The new literary school has gained for itself the flattering epithet, 'natural,' i.e., it searches for poetry diligently and exclusively only in the dark corners and alleys of life."

Also see Ia. "Vospominaniia Faddeia Bulgarina," *Severnaia pchela,* no. 34 (1847): 155.

Similarly, Pyotr Karatygin wrote this couplet for an 1847 one-act vaudeville entitled "The Natural School" ("Natural'naia shkola"):

> We are staunch champions of nature,
> Geniuses of court backyards!
> The mob of Petersburg corners,
> Wanderers and caretakers are our bards.

of the new Russian literature!"[95]

In his anger over *Petersburg,* Bulgarin was only getting started. "Tell me, please," he thundered in another issue of the *Northern Bee* that same year, "What is the use, what is the delight, what is the entertainment that one finds in a truthful description of the life of a yardkeeper or in the characteristics of a drunken woman and so forth? Truly are such things copied from nature. But what is the point? Talent—you say? Such a talent is like a gift for catching insects."[96]

Belinsky was not to be silenced, though. If Nekrasov had waxed eloquently about *Petersburg* in general, the great critic did the same for individual contributors in particular. Dal' was the first on Belinsky's list. "It seems to us," Belinsky wrote in 1847, "that Mr. Dal', having written Russian fairy tales and stories, has been looking for a genuine road for his talent, and that having written 'The [Petersburg] Yardkeeper' . . . he has found it. . . . The physiological sketches of Mr. Dal', we consider to be pearls of contemporary Russian literature, and we wish and hope that he will turn his rich

---

My, my natury priamye pobomiki,
Genii zadnikh dvorov!
Nashi geroi: brodiagi da dvorniki,
Chern' peterburgskikh uglov.

Also see *Severnaia pchela,* no. 269 (1846), as quoted in Tseitlin, *Stanovlenie realizma,* 93.

Characteristically, Belinsky picked up the gauntlet thrown down by the conservatives. Responding to Bulgarin, he wrote: "*Corners* are refuges of poverty, despair, and debauchery which one reaches only by going through dirty courtyards on one's knees" (*Polnoe sobranie sochinenii,* vol. 10 [1956], 297, italics in original).

The notion of "corners" should be taken literally, since in the 1840s many people in St. Petersburg were living in single rooms, separated from one another by a hanging blanket or bedspread. In fact, in 1844, members of the first government commission to investigate the living conditions of workers in the imperial city found that as many as fifty men, women, and children, including several with tuberculosis and syphilis, lived in a single room which measured no more than twenty feet on one side. Lincoln, *Sunlight at Midnight,* 131, 134.

95. Similarly, about *Petersburg,* an anonymous reviewer from the conservative journal the *Lighthouse* (*Maiak*), wrote in 1845: "Can it be, my Messrs. Physiologists, that Petersburg does not have splendid and gracious things, people, and subjects . . . the lively description of which can engage . . . without revulsion? . . . And can it not be that people with unspoiled and graceful taste can become carried away by the most dirty aspects in the life of a yardkeeper, a lackey, a cook, a clerk, a woman of the evening, or a street doll who flits about the sidewalks of Nevsky Prospekt? . . . This is not a physiology of Petersburg, but of the Petersburg rabble [*chern'*], and as such, it is unacceptable both to society and even to the subjects whom the authors attempt to depict." "Fiziologiia Peterburga, sostavlennaia iz trudov russkikh literaturov," *Maiak* 22 (1845): 7.

96. See F. Bulgarin, "Zhurnal'naia vsiakina vsiakaia," *Severnaia pchela,* no. 110 (1846): 438.

and powerful talent primarily to this kind of writing. . . ."[97] Grigorovich rated a close second. "Mr. Grigorovich's 'The Petersburg Organ-Grinders,'" Belinsky continued, "is a charming and gracious picture, drawn with the pencil of a talented artist. Here one sees observation, the ability to notice and seize upon the characteristic features of a phenomenon and to render them with poetic accuracy. Mr. Grigorovich is a young writer who only just now is beginning to write. Such a beginning augurs great hopes for the future."[98]

The work that impressed Belinsky most favorably, though, was Nekrasov's "The Petersburg Corners," with its sordid (and daring) picture of drunkards, prostitutes, and the like. According to Avdot'ya Panaeva, a private reading of the work by Nekrasov for colleagues and friends prompted an impassioned response from the great critic. "Belinsky had already read 'The Petersburg Corners,'" Panaeva recalled in her memoirs, "but he listened to [Nekrasov's] reading with great attention, as well as watched the impression . . . it was making on the other listeners. I noticed that the realism of 'The Petersburg Corners' affected the audience greatly. After Nekrasov finished his reading amid acclaims to the author, Belinsky walked about the room, saying, 'Yes, ladies and gentlemen! Literature must acquaint readers with all aspects of our social life. Long overdue is the time to consider material questions and the important role they play in the development of society.' And on this theme, Belinsky spoke for a long time."[99]

At first glance, the writers of *Petersburg* seem to follow closely upon European fictional physiologists. They, too, seek not so much realism as hyperrealism. Obsessed with socioscientific approaches to life—"only ignorance can look with indifference on the great successes . . . of physiology,"

97. Belinskii, *Polnoe sobranie sochinenii,* vol. 10 (1956), 82–83.

98. Regarding "The Petersburg Organ-Grinders," even a reviewer from the *Northern Bee* was complimentary in a begrudging way. "Having understood the full importance of his chosen subject," the reviewer wrote, "[Grigorovich] flashes with genuine feeling, brought forth by the pitiful lot of the poor organ-grinder." Quoted in Tseitlin, *Stanlovenie realizma,* 148. Also see Belinskii, *Polnoe sobranie sochinenii,* vol. 9 (1955), 55.

99. A. Panaeva, *Vospominaniia* (Moscow: Khudozhestvennaia literatura, 1972), 97. Even in these enlightened times, though, the realism in Nekrasov's "Petersburg Corners" did not go unchallenged in the Belinsky circle. Vasily Botkin, for instance, complained that "such realism should not be allowed in literature" (98).

Timofei Granovsky wrote in 1847[100]—they style themselves as scientists, surgeons,[101] and sociologists who travel to and through the metropolis to fashion detailed, even documentary, sketches and essays[102] that applaud

100. T. Granovskii, "Istoricheskaia literatura vo Frantsii i Germanii," *Sovremennik* 5, nos. 9–10, otdel. III (1847): 2. Similarly, Apollon Maikov wrote: "In the same way that physiology examines how the laws of mechanics, physics, and chemistry relate to each other in the physical organism, so does philosophy examine the law of political economy, law, and pedagogy in the life of society as an organic body. . . . A fact of sociological life is as complex as a physiological fact." Quoted in V. Maikov, *Kriticheskie opyty (1845–1847)* (St. Petersburg: N.A. Lebedev, 1891), 583.

101. Russian journals of this time were filled with articles and reviews about physiologies on humans and animals. See, for instance, "The Physiology of the Human Brain" ("Fiziologiia chelovecheskogo mozga") in *Otechestvennye zapiski,* no. 11 (1847): 34–94, and no. 12 (1847): 146–210; and "The Physiological Phenomena of Nutrition" ("Fiziologicheskie iavleniia pitaniia") in *Otechestvennye zapiski,* no. 1, otdel. VIII (1846): 53–56; and no. 2, otdel. VIII (1846): 132–37.

102. In Russia, the so-called physiological sketch (*fiziologicheskii ocherk*) draws from several sources. In the eighteenth century, Russian writers and readers thrilled to the satirical essays of the journals of Nikolai Novikov, his model being Joseph Addison and Richard Steele's publications, *The Tatler* (1709–11) and *The Spectator* (1711–12, 1714).

In the first third of the nineteenth century, the sketch was a favorite form of such Russian writers as Konstantin Batyushkov, Nikolai Polevoi, Kondraty Ryleev, Ivan Krylov, Vladimir Odoevsky, and Faddei Bulgarin. With the sketch, these individuals could fashion armchair travelogue-strolls through Russia's capital cities and pursue meditative explorations into "everyday" (*bytovoi*) and "manners-descriptive" (*nravopisatel'nyi*) scenes of Russian people and life. Further, the fact that sketch was idiosyncratic, elastic, and diverse gave Batyushkov and company leeway to capture both Moscow and St. Petersburg from orientations that were sociopolitical, topographic, and stylistic.

Batyushkov's 1811 sketch "Stroll Through Moscow" ("Progulka po Moskve") was a particularly well-received picture of Muscovite urban life. "The splendid April mornings and quiet May nights attract . . . holiday crowds," Batyushkov wrote. "A good tone demands sacrifice: from noon on, the dandy and the coquette, the old newsmonger, and the greasy usurer skip about from all the corners of Moscow to Tverskaya Boulevard. What strange attire, what faces!" K. Batiushkov, *Polnoe sobranie sochinenii* (Moscow: Sovetskii pisatel', 1964), 384–85.

If initial forays into physiological sketch were acclaimed by Russian readers, they were censured by Russian critics. What was to like, a critic from the *Moscow Herald* wondered in 1828, when such writing lacked "thought, irony, and insight" as well as "its own view of the world"? "Obozrenie russkoi slovesnosti za 1827," *Moskovskii vestnik* 7, no. 1 (1828): 77.

Despite such criticism, the sketch became such a popular genre that it entered into the Russian literary canon. Writers such as Alexander Pushkin, Alexander Griboyedov, Mikhail Lermontov, and especially Nikolai Gogol wrote sketch-stories about ordinary urban men and women who loved and lost in battles with nature, fate, and the devil amid settings that were romantic, gothic, and grotesque.

It should be noted, though, that none of the aforementioned writers wrote "physiologies" in the strict sense of the word. They cared little for detailed lessons in geography and history. They also did not pursue socioscientific approaches to reality or seek encyclopedic descriptions of classes, circles, and professions.

The physiological rendition of the sketch enjoyed widespread popularity in the Russian literature throughout the 1840s, and, as a dominant genre of the time, became a key factor in the development of both urban and village prose. (Scholars count no fewer than seven hundred exemplars of the genre between 1839 and 1848.)

societal strengths, expose weaknesses, and prescribe treatments and cures.[103] Their writings present, argue, and conclude; they dig into the essence and roots of things; they show regularities and tendencies in life; they are clinical and clear; they are short, sweet, and to the point. As fictional cartographers, they see mappings as "fundamental to the process of lending order to the world."[104]

The contributors to *Petersburg* also take care that in their works, law and order move in sync with defined beginnings, middles, and ends. Life is ordinary and everyday; an enduring present overrides past and future. Days flow into nights in idyllic fashion, without the surges and bends that mark much of Russian urban fiction. Further, in *Petersburg,* Nekrasov and his colleagues dispense with the Gogolian penchant for fictional instability of chaos. Disembodied voices, illogical discrepancies, outlandish hyperboles, arbitrary assumptions, numbing digressions, sudden improvisations, irritating evasions, and multiplying tones and attitudes do not complicate their empirical portraits of people and events.

Also in keeping with the socioscientific stance of European writer-physiologists, the outlook of the contributors to *Petersburg* is all-inclusive: synchronic and diachronic. On the one hand, Nekrasov and company seek to fashion type[105] and daguerreotype[106] in Euclidean time and space. Self-

103. Bulgarin contested the urge for analysis in fiction. "Nowadays it is the fashion," he wrote in 1846, "to take the most usual and simple situations and forcibly to track down and squeeze some kind of unprecedented, noble, and meaningful side, to analyze, in a precise way, the 'internal world' of the heart and soul, in other words, to make a mountain out of a molehill." F. Bulgarin, "Zhurnal'naia vsiakaia vsiachina," *Severnaia pchela,* January 26, 1846, 36.

104. See R. Rundtstrom, "A Cultural Interpretation of Inuit Map Accuracy," *Geographical Review* 80, no. 2 (April 1990): 155.

105. Consider Ivan Panaev's 1844 remark that "we now all write 'types' and consider ourselves to be 'typical' writers." As quoted in V. Vinogradov, *Evoliustiia russkogo naturalizma: Gogol' i Dostoevskii* (Leningrad: Akademiia, 1929), 304.

106. The daguerreotype, invented in 1839, caused a sensation in both Europe and Russia. The new invention, a writer for the *Northern Bee* wrote in 1839, "captures the ways of the sun more clearly and faithfully than people with brushes and pencils!" ("Smes': Dagerotipy v Petersburge," *Severnaia pchela,* no. 237 [1839]: 1; "Eshche neskol'ko slov o dagerotipe," *Severnaia pchela,* no. 39 [1839]: 1–2). That same year, the editors of the *St. Petersburg News* (*Sanktpeterburgskie vedomosti*) published a story concerning a traveling salesman who, with the aid of a daguerreotype, successfully sued for divorce from his unfaithful wife ("Smes': Usoversenstvovaniia dagerotipa," *Sanktpeterburgskie vedomosti,* no. 271 (1839): 1081.

Not everyone was happy with daguerreotype, though. Women cared little for the new contraption. "Although, as of late, the technical aspects of the daguerreotype have improved greatly," an anonymous reviewer for the *Fatherland Notes* commented in 1842, "it still has not yet managed to force the sun

styled mapmakers, their concern is for "great bundlings of borders,"[107] for innumerable delineations of space, physical and social. Nekrasov and his fellow physiologists class nationalities, professions, and worldviews; they observe torsos, clothes, and routines; they study streets, byways, and alleyways; they peer into corners, apartments, and homes. On the other hand, the writers of *Petersburg* also examine the past of their subjects to construct biographies and family histories so as to underscore their strengths, weaknesses, and the like. Everything is cause for interest and investigation. Even the "modest fellow lodgers" who inhabit the cracks under the wallpaper in Grebenka's "The Petersburg Quarter" are classed as "personal incidentals" worthy of physiology!

Most notably, perhaps, the writers of *Petersburg* keep their selections aloof from disaster, natural and supernatural. Neither they nor their characters accept Gogol's famed dictum that in St. Petersburg "everything is an illusion, everything is a dream, everything is not what it seems."[108] Not a single scene in Nekrasov's work features the sleets and fires, fogs and floods which compared Peter's city to Atlantis and other ruined meccas (mythic and real), and which, to such writers as Pushkin, Gogol, Dostoevsky, and (later) Andrei Bely gave to it an aura of impending apocalypse, cataclysm, and doom. Even perfunctory mentions of poor climate transmute to lavish descriptions of summer gardens and the like.

The urban mapping-topologies in *Petersburg* bypass sinister melancholy, existential indifference, and tomblike claustrophobia; they also eschew yawning abysses, shadowy underworlds, and specters of death and death-in-life. Nowhere does the comic draw from the tragic, the melodramatic from the mundane, or the supernatural from the trivial. Nowhere

to capture viable portraits of women. In the eyes of each and every daguerreotype, one always sees a deathlike pall which ruins the physiognomy of the entire face. That is why among portraits done by Parisian opticians, one finds few feminine pictures. Right away women notice that daguerreotypes not only minimize their natural beauty but also reduce the charm of their subjects."

"If opticians do not correct this serious shortcoming," this same reviewer warned, "our beautiful women will never choose the daguerreotype over painting, even though the daguerreotype captures portraits in several seconds. A woman would rather agree to sit for three hours before an obliging artist than allow her face to be ruined by a daguerreotype in thirty seconds." "Smes'," *Otechestvennye zapiski* 23 (1842): 197.

107. Wood, *Power of Maps,* 11.

108. N. Gogol, "Nevskii Prospekt," *Polnoe sobranie sochinenii v chetyrnadtsati tomakh,* vol. 3 (Moscow: Akademiia nauk SSSR, 1938), 45.

is there a blurred line between the animate and inanimate, the true and false, the vulgar and sublime. Nowhere is Russia's imperial capital seen as a "city of the mind, deprived of grace."[109] With the mappings in *Petersburg,* Nekrasov and company keep both Peter's city and its citizens safe and secure.

Rather, the writers of *Petersburg* see the northern Palmyra as the realest of real places. In contrast to the urban world of Gogol, for instance, in which everything is upside down, out of joint, and rife with physical *ne to* ("not that") and metaphysical *neizvestno pochemu* ("it is unknown why"),[110] the people, places, and things in *Petersburg* are locked securely, tongue and groove. Here the imperial city is hero, not antihero; here it is unity, not atmosphere.[111] Self-conscious rationality and reality are triumphant, the order of the day. Superstition, the supernatural, and the bizarre—the stuff of wild tales, enduring legends, intriguing anecdotes, and colorful gossip[112]—are dismissed as innocuous or silly, the butt of humor and logic, system and science. (Consider, for instance, the stories of the birch log, Aksinya Ivanovna, and the white Negro in Grebenka's "The Petersburg Quarter.) In their works, the writers of *Petersburg* champion "stone over water"[113] as well as an almost epic equipoise and calm. To their taste, the Bronze Horseman stays put; the devil avoids Nevsky Prospekt; and street-lamps light up the surroundings—nothing more. Like Pushkin, the writers of *Petersburg* love the city of Peter's making. Unlike him, though, they do so without reservation.[114] Like Dostoevsky, they see the imperial city as

109. As is the case in Gogol's portraits of the imperial city. See D. Fanger, *Dostoevsky and Romantic Realism: A Study of Dostoevsky in Relation to Balzac, Dickens, and Gogol* (Evanston, Ill.: Northwestern University Press, 1998), 115, 120, 123.

110. Ibid., 123.

111. Rightfully, Fanger states precisely the opposite about Gogol's Petersburg. See ibid., 114.

112. Consider Lotman's remark: "If we look . . . to the life of the mass population, we cannot help being struck immediately by the enormous number of rumors, oral tales about unusual occurrences, a special kind of urban folklore which played so great a part in the life of the 'Palmyra of the North' since its founding. . . . One might have expected the medieval tradition of visions and prophecies would be more a part of the Moscow tradition than of 'rationalist' and 'European' Petersburg. But it was Petersburg where such things flourished." I. Lotman, "The Semiosphere," *Universe of the Mind: A Semiotic Theory of Culture,* trans. Ann Shukman (Bloomington: Indiana University Press, 1990), 195.

113. Ibid., 12.

114. Consider Dostoevsky's paraphrase: "I love thee, city of Peter's making. Sorry, I don't love it. Windows, godforsaken holes—and monuments." See N. Strakhov, *Biografiia, pis'ma i zametki iz zapisnoi knizhki F. M. Dostoevskogo* (St. Petersburg: A. S. Suvorin, 1883), 359.

"the most fantastic city, with the most fantastic history of all the cities of the north."[115] Unlike him, though, they relish its earthly delights, not its mystical horrors.

As a literary work, though, Nekrasov's *Petersburg* exhibits a number of features that distinguish it not only from other anthologies and collections of the period but also from much of Russian realistic writing as a whole.

For one thing, the work's contributors were a diverse, even motley, mix of ages, ranks, and stations. Dal' was forty-four; Grigorovich, forty-six. Grebenka was thirty-three; Belinsky, thirty-four. Youthful were only Nekrasov, who was twenty-four, and the twenty-eight-year-old Kul'chitsky, who, sadly, died in 1845, several months after he published his work.[116] Some of the writers of *Petersburg* were educated formally; others were not. (Only Kul'chitsky had graduated from the university.) Nonetheless, Nekrasov and company shared common ground and perspectives; and for a straightforward reason. They were in the vanguard of what would become an enduring feature of mid- and later nineteenth-century Russian political and cultural life: members of the petty gentry and equally prosaic déclassé who had come to St. Petersburg from the provinces and who, in the imperial city, had spent time with the very middling classes who would be the subjects of their stories. Of the writers of *Petersburg,* only Panaev was born in the imperial city. Dal' and Grebenka hailed from Ukraine; Belinsky was born in Sveaborg (near Helsinki), Grigorovich in Simbirsk, Nekrasov in Yaroslavl', and Kul'chitsky in Kharkov. Further, for several of these individuals, literature was a second career. Dal' had been a physician in the military; Grebenka had taught literature in secondary schools; Grigorovich had studied to be an engineer; Kul'chitsky and Panaev had worked as civil servants. The writers of *Petersburg* championed the downtrodden and demanded change in Russian life; but they also admired people who, like

115. See Dostoevsky's 1862 work *Winter Notes on Summer Impressions* (*Zimnie zametki o letnikh vpechatleniiakh*), chapter 3.

116. How wrong, then, was an 1847 reviewer from the *Northern Bee* who noted the social and educational shortcomings of the writers of *Petersburg* and their ilk: "Onto the literary scene there now have entered scores of young people, without a definite place in life, half gifted and half educated, with pretensions to fame and talent, and with extremely poor means [to accomplish anything in life]." *Severnaia pchela,* no. 8 (1847); as quoted in Tseitlin, *Stanovlenie realizma,* 93.

themselves, negotiated native existence on its own terms and who, despite the adversities and obstacles, led lives of meaning and success.

Also, like the conservatives, the writers of *Petersburg* were well aware of the literary dilemma, that is, with the passing of Russia's aristocratic writers, the national written expression was in desperate need of middling writers. It was also their belief, though, that fate had deemed them, as Westerners, the self-selected progeny of Peter the Great, to fill in the void. With special claim to speak for and to a popular audience, the contributors to *Petersburg* accepted the challenge. What they lacked in education and finesse, they more than made up for in energy and chutzpah and in trial-and-error approaches to literary supply and demand. Unlike the conservatives, the writers of *Petersburg* did not regard their readers with condescension or contempt. Rightfully, they understood literary consumers as equals who, although often unsophisticated, even semiliterate, had fictional expectations and who would buy Russian poetry and prose only if such writing was to their liking.

For this reason, every step (and often misstep) that the authors of *Petersburg* took into Russian literature redounded to their fame. For once in their often tortured lives, they were swimming downstream. Time and taste were on their side. National art was thickening around the middle,[117] the result of indulgent melds of printed and oral modes; of street and folk art; of journalism, drama, and pulp. In their fiction, the contributors to *Petersburg* were like seasoned cooks who used a fistful of this and a handful of that to satisfy the public hunger for literature of every cast, register, and hue. Entrepreneurs in mind and at heart, Nekrasov and his colleagues worked day and night, combing the streets for subjects, taking artistic and financial risks, and stealing shamefully from other texts (high and low, written and oral)—anything for a ruble. Indeed, their works bore witness to values, confidence, and drive as much as they did the writers' penchant for physiology.

As editor of *Petersburg,* Nekrasov is exemplar-hero of the time. He was not only the son of an often drunk and abusive police chief despot but also witness to suffering peasants, prisoners, and Volga boatmen. Having come to Petersburg in 1838, Nekrasov had big if naive hopes for success. "To enter

117. Buckler, *Mapping St. Petersburg,* 13.

the university," he recalled, "was my only goal. . . . I was spurred on by dreams that, at long last, I would escape my poverty, and that I would be given a warm corner and a piece of bread which I would eat . . . in the firm hope . . . that I would repay the noble hand who fed me with the labors of my entire future life, with everything that would advance my head . . . and heart."[118] Nekrasov failed miserably, though, the result being that he nearly died of starvation. At one point, he subsisted on only fifteen kopecks a day.[119]

"Wrapped tightly in my overcoat and shivering from the cold," Nekrasov's autobiographical hero wrote in his 1840 sketch "The Poet Has Disappeared Without a Trace" ("Bez vesti propavshii piita"), "I lay on the blanket in the middle of my bed and began to think about how I could obtain ink for writing. After three hungry days, it was imperative for me to write an article upon which all the hopes of my poor stomach rested. . . . My circumstances were straitened in every possible way. I did not have a penny to my name; I had sold all my things."[120]

Throughout the trials and travails, though, Nekrasov showed an iron will. "I promised myself," he recalled of his early years in Peter's city, "that I would not die in some attic. No, I thought, I would not be like those who perished before me. I would try no matter what."[121] Nekrasov thus had

118. As quoted in V. Evgen'ev-Maksimov, *Nekrasov i Peterburg* (Leningrad: Leningradskoe gazetno-zhurnal'noe i knizhnoe izdatel'stvo, 1947), 14–15.

119. Nekrasov's youthful suffering in St. Petersburg so impressed Belinsky that he saw the fledgling writer not only as a kindred spirit but also as a progressive artist with a great future. "Oh, gentlemen," Belinsky told his colleagues, "you are happy that you are starving but that you will sit down to a tasty dinner and eat with great appetite. Nekrasov, though, has known pain in his stomach from hunger and did not even have a piece of dry bread to still that pain. I give you my word that Nekrasov has talent, and more important, a knowledge of the Russian people, an ignorance of which we are all guilty of. . . . I am convinced that he will make a name for himself in literature." Quoted in Panaeva, *Vospominaniia,* 98.

Panaev concurred. "From the very beginning," he recalled, "Nekrasov made a very pleasant impression on Belinsky. Belinsky loved Nekrasov for his sharp, somewhat embittered mind, for the suffering which he encountered at a very early age . . . for his bold, practical view of life, that is, beliefs that were beyond his years, and which he took from the slums and sufferings of his life and which Belinsky always envied in a tormenting type of way." I. Panaev, *Literaturnye vospominaniia* (Moscow: Gosudarstvennoe izdatel'stvo khudozhestvennoi literatury, 1950), 248.

120. N. Nekrasov, "Bez vesti propavshii piita," in Nekrasov, *Polnoe sobranie sochinenii,* vol. 7 (1983), 42. Real-life personages concurred. "When it was cold," the actor A. Shubert recalled, "Nekrasov looked particularly pitiful. He was pale and dressed poorly. He was always shivering and huddled up. . . . His arms were bare and red. . . . Around his neck was a torn red scarf." V. Evgen'ev-Maksimov, *Nekrasov i teatr* (Moscow: Iskusstvo, 1948), 27.

121. I. Oksman, ed., *N. A. Nekrasov: V vospominaniiakh i dokumentakh* (Leningrad: Akademiia, 1930), 44.

neither the time nor the inclination to be a philosopher, organic or otherwise. Quickly, he became practical. "There existed a chasm between me and idealism. . . . [As a youth] I began to kill it in myself and to develop a practical sense. Idealists angered me. Life had passed them by, and they never thought anything about it. They were always in their dreams and everyone took advantage of them. I rarely spoke in their presence, but when I began getting drunk with them—and they were masters at that!—I began to speak against this idealism with such cynicism that I simply scared them. I vaunted a cruel egoism and an ancient rule: 'an eye for an eye, and a tooth for a tooth.' "[122]

The future editor of *Petersburg* did anything and everything to survive. For a piece of bread, he wrote letters for peasants and primers for children. He drew posters for booths; he translated works from the French; he wrote prose, verse, and drama (comedies, vaudevilles, and skits that were mostly translations and adaptations of French works); and he penned essays and reviews of plays and books, often without knowing anything about them.[123] By hook or by crook, he learned how to satisfy Russian tastes.

However undeveloped his talent at this time, Nekrasov was a master of physiology. His poetry and prose, drama and criticism featured usurers and bureaucrats, actors and landowners, prostitutes and cabbies, editors and writers—including not-so-veiled images of Bulgarin as the "highly respected one" (*pochtenneishii*) and "ass-man" (*Zadarin*).[124]

Like Belinsky, Nekrasov was concerned about the failure of physiology in the national written expression. On the one hand, he fretted over the penchant of the Russian public to look to Paris for sketches of urban life. "With every year," Nekrasov wrote in 1844, "the passion for things foreign surpasses the attachment to what is good and ours here. . . . One must confess that . . . many of us pay more attention to every engraving that comes out of Paris than, for example, the artistic treasures in the Hermitage

122. Ibid., 60–61.

123. It was Nekrasov's early criticism that first attracted the attention of Belinsky. In fact, his anonymous reviews were so much like those of the great critic that the reading public was often confused as to their true authorship.

124. See Nekrasov's 1841 play *Morning in the Editorial Office: Vaudeville Scenes from Journalistic Life* (*Utro v redaktsii: Vodevil'nye stseny iz zhurnal'noi zhizni*); and chapter 5 of his 1843–48 novel *The Life and Adventures of Tikhon Trostnikov* (*Zhizn' i pokhozhdeniia Tikhona Trostnikova*).

Museum."[125] On the other hand, Nekrasov blamed homeland literati for turning Russian eyes westward, since they had failed to imbue their physiologies with a genuinely national cast. "Not without cause," he continued, "are [we writers] reproached for coldness to all that is ours, Russian, and domestic, no matter how remarkable and colossal it might be."[126]

Also as was the case with Belinsky, Nekrasov was particularly outraged by the attempts of Bulgarin and other conservatives to co-opt physiology into official nationality and art. In such matters, Nekrasov could be as "furious" as Vissarion. "Our literature," he wrote in 1844 in a review of Bulgarin's *Essays of Russian Mores* (and by implication, other fictional physiologies of its ilk), "is so wretchedly conscious of its feebleness . . . that it has become a business firm and a market in which, for the amusement of buyers, sellers showcase rotten goods in a premeditated way. Having forgotten sense and shame, [our literature] wallows in triflings . . . puts on a clown's hat . . . dances on its haunches . . . and dashes off to lavish printings, wild titles, and extravagant advertisements . . . all so that the public will be forced to throw it a few pennies which have become its single goal, idol, and destroyer!"[127]

Bulgarin's *Essays,* Nekrasov continued, was typical of the lot. Its humor was "old-fashioned and shallow," its curiosity "puerile," its wit "strained, heavy, garish, and crude," and its pictures "pale, lifeless, and as far removed from reality as the sky from the earth."[128] Caveat emptor, Nekrasov warned; sellers of Bulgarin's *Essays* were guilty of false advertising. To his fans, Bulgarin compared to "Walter Scott and Karmazin"; he was the "linchpin of Russian literature, the founder of the Russian novel, the reformer of the Russian language."[129] Whatever, Nekrasov smiled spitefully, but as evidenced by his *Essays,* Bulgarin was no physiologist.

Partially in response to Bulgarin and other conservatives, Nekrasov sought to stretch his own physiological muscles. Two 1844 feuilleton cycles, entitled "Features from a Characterization of the Petersburg Population" ("Cherty is kharakteristiki peterburgskogo naseleniia") and "Chronicle

125. See Nekrasov, "Literaturnye novosti," *Polnoe sobranie sochinenii,* vol. 12 (1995), 145.

126. Ibid.

127. N. Nekrasov, "'Ocherki russkikh nravov, ili litsevaia storona i iznanka chelovecheskogo roda': Sochinenie Faddeia Bulgarina," in Nekrasov, *Polnoe sobranie sochinenii,* vol. 11 (1989), 81–82.

128. Ibid., 82.

129. Ibid., 90.

of a Petersburg Resident" ("Khronika peterburgskogo khroniltelia"), were particularly popular with the public. In the latter piece, Nekrasov, under the name of I. Pruzhinin or "Spring Man," poses as a *skaz*-type narrator who bounces about the imperial city with comic low-style observations about the people and places there. Particularly noteworthy in "Chronicle" is Nekrasov-Pruzhinin's quarrel with the aristocratic tradition of Russian literature: a playful (but purposeful) swipe at Pushkin's "The Bronze Horseman." At first, Nekrasov-Pruzhinin appropriates Pushkin's work as his own. "What a majestic, beautiful, and illustrious spectacle the Neva presents," he intones, "when, having broken the icy fetters which inhibited its triumphant flow into eternity. . . ." Suddenly, though, Nekrasov-Pruzhinin realizes that, like Gogol's narrator in *Dead Souls* (and Dostoevsky's speakers in his mature novels), he is not up to the task.[130] Epic—Pushkinian or Gogolian—is not for him. "No, I cannot," he laments. "I wanted to begin from the heights, to relate everything as good writers do. But such labor is beyond my strength."[131] Happily for Russian literature, Nekrasov-Pruzhinin has other (read: physiological) talents to lend to the national written expression.

Nekrasov's *Petersburg* also models distinctive features in and of itself, the most obvious being the localized character of the work. Notwithstanding Nekrasov's extravagant claims, *Petersburg* is not an encyclopedia of Russian life. Rather, its contributors focus on the imperial city almost exclusively. Indeed, St. Petersburg is for them the center of the (Russian) world. If the participants of *Petersburg* acknowledge Moscow, the provinces, and other locales, they do so only to note the superiority of St. Petersburg in all respects. Further, unlike their literary confreres before and after them, Nekrasov and company avoid literary monumentalization: the extremes of their city's myth. They do not sing of mansions and slums, of the Winter Palace and Haymarket Square;[132] references to the rich and poor, to grand Nevsky Prospekt and dark narrow streets, are perfunctory and fleeting. (The clavichord-like wooden planks that make up the streets

130. Such reticence, of course, was also common in the sermons and saints' tales of the medieval era as well as in many forms of eighteenth-century writing in both Russia and Europe.

131. Nekrasov, *Polnoe sobranie sochinenii,* vol. 12 (1995), 54–55.

132. Consider Buckler's remark that the "'Petersburg text' sustains a social-moral focus on city slums, a fact proudly cited by cultural chroniclers, who consider this pervasive theme a centerpiece of the literary tradition." See Buckler, *Mapping St. Petersburg,* 159.

in Grebenka's "The Petersburg Quarter" are seen as "very amusing.") Rather, the writers of *Petersburg* focus on everything in between: worlds unto themselves. Indeed, their self-styled interest in middlings and melds—physical, social, and aesthetic—move them to believe that they are doing something new not only for Russian literature but also for writing about the northern Venice. With youthful rashness, Nekrasov and company dismiss all that had been penned about St. Petersburg previously. "Do we not love our Petersburg?" Nekrasov asked in 1844. "Are we so little interested in all that is so original, splendid, engaging, and jovially merry in this city? And why is so little being written about it now?"[133] To their taste, it is *Petersburg* which raises the aesthetic bar in the national written expression about Russian urban life.

With self-righteous zeal, Nekrasov and his comrade-physiologists plumb the urban depths for places, plots, and personalities that heretofore in literature had been undocumented, unrepresented, even invisible. In fact, given their focus, it comes as little surprise that in *Petersburg,* Nekrasov and his fellow writers are as drawn to the middles on the outskirts of the city as they are to those at its center. In either case, they are strikingly precise about routes and streets, neighborhoods and locales, markets and stores. They even choose maps embedded in other mappings! Nowhere in their stories is there the idea of St. Petersburg as terra incognita or worse, of coldly anonymous locales cut and dried into endless squares from which there is no escape or meaning. Indeed, the tone for Russia's northern capital is as instructive as it is comforting. If readers are uncertain or unawares of the people and environs in their midst when they begin *Petersburg,* they come away fully cognizant of them when they finish. For them location moves to a "sense of place."[134]

Another feature of *Petersburg* that separates it from other works of its type is the sheer exuberance with which its writers celebrate all the groups of Peter's city. No matter where the location or what the event (formal or informal)—for example, the puppet show in Grigorovich's "The Petersburg Organ-Grinders" or the freezing of the Neva in Grebenka's "The Petersburg Quarter"—they opt for carnivalesque communities that

133. Nekrasov, *Polnoe sobranie sochinenii,* vol. 12 (1995), 146.

134. J. Agnew, "Representing Space: Space, Scale, and Culture in Social Science," in Duncan and Ley, *Place/Culture/Representation,* 263.

are open and spontaneous, informal and free. Literally and metaphorically, *Petersburg* is rife with the noises of the crowd, the melodies of bands, the colors of booths, and the entreaties of barkers inviting onlookers to join in the fun. As Grebenka notes in "The Petersburg Quarter," "everywhere there is life!" In this carnivalesque atmosphere, also, the contributors to *Petersburg* seek a highly democratic approach, that is, a leveling of classes in which all doors are open, all curtains drawn, so that for the moment at least, everyone enjoys liberty, equality, and fraternity. What church and state have failed to do, Nekrasov and company, as fictional physiologists, have accomplished. Indeed, what Russian critics applauded in the fun-loving feuilleton can also be said about *Petersburg.* It, too, "appears in living rooms, strolls down the streets, travels to theaters, dances at balls, sweeps through the book and music stalls, yawns at literary evenings and at concerts of music lovers. Everywhere and anywhere it looks, listens, and understands. . . . It expresses everything; from it there is no salvation . . . it devours everything in its path."[135]

In *Petersburg,* even Belinsky is in a carnivalesque mood. Absent in his contributions to the work are the humorless tone, the moral earnestness, the grim purpose, the bleak cynicism, and the strident demands that Russia and Russians conform to his ideas and ideals of life. Rather, Belinsky's pieces in *Petersburg* sparkle with energy, humor, and wit. They are also remarkably straightforward and focused, without the pedantry and preaching as well as the sudden changes of thought, manner, and address that mark many of his critical writings. True, the great critic takes issue with what he sees as classical and romantic types or with anyone who does not see Peter and his city as the physical, intellectual, and cultural hope of the world. Also not surprising is that, like everyone else at the time, Belinsky bemoans the lack of works in the national written expression that focus on *both* of Russia's capitals and that are genuinely historical, middling, and/or realistic. He censures romantics and philosophers, Slavophiles and theatergoers; he chides readers and writers, critics and authorities (literary and otherwise) as fickle and fragmented, fractious and false. (The faux formation of all four groups, not to mention their preference for Polevoi and Kukol'nik over Schiller and Shakespeare, were particular bones of contention.) At

135. "Smes': Peterburgskaia khronika," *Literaturnaia gazeta,* no. 5 (1843): 101.

the same time, though, Belinsky rejoices in the vast diversity—physical and social—of his land. Youthful lyricism, tongue-in-cheek resignation, and an "if you can't beat 'em, join 'em" attitude toward literature and life also pervade his attempts at physiology. All three of Belinsky's contributions are cases in point: portraits of people who live the good life. With gusto, the men and women in these works relish dinners, feasts, and balls. (Food is a major entertainment in Nekrasov's work.) They also gad about in costume-clothes; devour newspapers, journals, and books (foreign and Russian); and buy apartments and homes. Their daily agendas are informed by strolling down Nevsky Prospekt; visiting family, friends, and social institutions, particularly theaters; acting in a "good light and tone"; and vaunting their likes and dislikes in wild applause or rabid hisses. In no way does Belinsky condemn such goings-on; even the great critic, it seems, cannot resist the urge to join in the carnivalesque fun!

Another salient and distinguishing characteristic of *Petersburg* is its theatricality. Its writers see all the city as a stage, both explicitly and implicitly.[136] There are in the work formal setups, such as the Alexander Theater, wooden theaters, and living-room tableaux, often with stylized scenes, one embedded inside another. There are also impromptu gatherings: puppeteers perform in spacious yards to pedestrians rushing in from all sides onto the streets below, and to spectators peering out from hundreds of windows of tiered stories above. Explicit or implicit, trained or amateur, self-styled actors and actresses appeal to gesture, mime, even acrobatics, on the one hand, and to music, song, and dance, on the other. Either way, spectacle is the order of the day; either way, the house is always full. In *Petersburg,* also, writers focus on people and things not only onstage but also, and more important, off. In their view, two yardkeepers sweeping the street and conversing about life hold the same dramatic presence as trained thespians in Petersburg's theaters. Pursuant to the investigative nature of the work, writers also deem as stageworthy the hidden, even prosaic aspects of urban

136. Consider the following statement by Denis Cosgrove and Stephen Daniels: "The present cultural turn in human geography has introduced metaphors and analogies more in keeping with an emphasis on meaning than function. . . . System and organism give way to spectacle, theater, and text. . . . Theater itself had the meaning not only of a playhouse, but also a conspectus, a place, region, or text in which phenomena are presented together for public understanding." S. Daniels and D. Cosgrove, "Spectacle and Text: Landscape Metaphors in Cultural Geography," in Cosgrove et al., *Iconography of Landscape,* 57, 58.

life. Individuals and happenings concealed in the Petersburg Quarter are just as interesting as, if not more interesting and vital than, their counterparts on display on Nevsky Prospekt. There is also among the contributors to *Petersburg* the idea that life, especially in Russia, is inherently theatrical, that the line between life and stage, actors and audience is ill defined, if it exists at all. Drama is not only the province of such real-life actors as Pyotr Karatygin and Pavel Mochalov. Rather, almost any character in Nekrasov's work performs instinctively, as if on cue, whether the spotlight shines or him or not. Crowds also exhibit a theatrical flair. Be they in a theater, on the street, or in an omnibus, they often stage a show all their own, as engaging and entertaining as the actors!

Petersburg also exhibits an unabashedly Russian tone. Although the contributors to the work champion Western culture and civilization, they are not above making fun of what they deem the less-desirable elements of Germany and France. As a cook in Grebenka's "The Petersburg Quarter" notes, French bouillon and artichokes are not for him or his diners; *shchi* and *kvas* more than fit the bill. The French may boast their accomplishments, he adds, but the Russians "will beat them every time." (The "war of '12" and ludicrous woodcuts of Napoleon are pertinent examples.) Even cockroaches in the soup are welcomed as "servants" at patrons' beck and call! The writers of Nekrasov's work also cannot resist the temptation to poke fun at Western progress. The newly invented vehicle in Kulchitsky's "The Omnibus," for instance, does not speed passengers to their destination; rather, it is the locus for time-honored human chaos (crowdedness, intoxication, and quarreling) among French, Germans, and Russians of all classes and types.

In a more positive vein, the writers of *Petersburg* seek Russianness by unearthing a governing psychology and principle, a mission and idea that define and distinguish their city (and by extension, their homeland) from the cities and countries on the other side of Europe.[137] The modus operandi is from analysis to synthesis, to assert in the words of Virgil, *ab*

137. As Conley writes, "The cartographic projects . . . coordinates archeological and geographic information that builds a case for national supremacy and identity. The latter is confined to local areas that manufactured both a regional and national consciousness . . . that ultimately established a firm spacial coherence." See T. Conley, *The Self-Made Map: Cartographic Memory in Early Modern France* (Minneapolis: University of Minnesota Press, 1996), 16.

uno disce omnes, that is, "from one to know all."[138] (Or, as Dal' wrote in his 1845 physiological sketch "The Russian Officer's Servant" ("Russkii denshchik"), "Such was Yakov, and such will be all Yakovs, or at the very least, the majority of them."[139] Probing and penetration to universality and wholeness—an organic understanding of national life—are the goals.[140]

As the writers of *Petersburg* see it, also, the organ-grinders, yardkeepers, and other personages of their stories are typical not only of such classes in real life but also of the famed *narod,* or folk, who, the hope is, represent the best for Russia in its past, present, and future. Like the critics' understanding of the feuilleton, what Belinsky claimed for the Natural school can also be said for *Petersburg.* "If you would ask us what is the key strength of the new literary school," he wrote in 1845, "we would answer . . . that from the highest ideals of human nature and life, it appeals to the so-called mob, making it its exclusive hero and studying it with profound attention. . . . [Such a school] seeks, at long last, to advance the striving of our literature . . . to become truly national, Russian, original, and independent . . . to capture its expression in the mirror of Russian society, and to animate it with a lively national interest."[141]

The contributors to *Petersburg* make no apologies for who and what they are as citizens of both St. Petersburg and Russia. They are extremely at home in the city; the persistent foreignness, not to mention the trials and travails of the imperial capital that posed often life-threatening challenges to denizens and visitors (recall: Nekrasov), are nowhere present. Further, the charge by conservative thinkers and writers that St. Petersburg is alien to the past, or by liberal ones that it is enamored with the future, they greet

138. Virgil, *Aeneid* 2.65.

139. V. Dal', "Russkii denshchik," *Finskii vestnik,* no. 3 (1845), 14. Consider also this passage from an 1841 physiological sketch entitled "The Nurse" ("Niania"): "All our Russian nurses are cut from the same cloth. They are usually between the ages of forty and sixty and are almost always thin, since their cares and concerns for children do not allow them to get fat. Their faces are kind but pallid and covered with wrinkles; their hands are rough, but their attachment [to their charges] is exceptional." See Tseitlin, *Stanovlenie realizma,* 210.

140. Compare Belinsky's comment that "the task of true [literary] criticism is to seek out, in the works of a poet, the general and not the particular, the human and not the personal, the eternal and not the temporal, the necessary and not the fortuitous, and to define, on the basis of the universal, the value, worth, place and importance of the poet." See Belinskii, *Polnoe sobranie sochinenii,* vol. 3 (1953), 509.

141. Ibid., vol. 9 (1955), 388.

with attitudes ranging from bemused tolerance to outright contempt. The present in their city more than meets their needs, thank you.

Even would-be writer arrivals from the provinces bypass the difficulties associated with this type in both literature and life.[142] For instance, the future feuilletonist in Panaev's "The Petersburg Feuilletonist" begins life as a pampered child on an estate before he moves first to a boarding school in Moscow and then to the university there, where he publishes a translation for a journal. So emboldened, he seeks to take St. Petersburg by storm with vaudevilles and other hackwork. Revealingly, Panaev's hero does not spend his first days and nights in Peter's city as poor and sick, or as lonely and disenfranchised, or as trapped in a hit-or-miss approach to the Russian literary world. Indeed, the speed and facility by which he both subverts the conventional bildungsroman of a novice writer and accommodates the virtue (and vice) of urban and literary life speak volumes to his resourcefulness and pluck. Panaev's budding feuilletonist spends lavishly on clothes, attends the theaters, and works in civil service to climb the literary ladder as a writer of limpid, undistinguished romantic stories. Metaphorically speaking, he even acts as a barker-clown, advertising specious literary wares. Panaev's hero ends up embittered, alone, and lost; but, as the author makes clear, he alone is at fault. As his inner voice tells him, it is his lack of "thoughts, feelings, and convictions" which brings about his downfall and which casts him from the literary world of which he only recently has been a part.

The way the writers of *Petersburg* feel about their city, they also feel about their country. Although Nekrasov and company champion a stance of "love us or leave us," they also invite the world to follow their carnivalesque approach to life.[143] In *Petersburg,* there is no Gogolian sigh as to

142. For examples of literature of this type, see Nekrasov's 1840's poem "A Provincial Official in Petersburg" ("Provintsial'nyi pod"iachii v Peterburge"), and his 1843–45 piece "The Chatterbox: The Notes of the Provincial Inhabitant A. F. Belopiatkin" ("Govorun: Zapiski provintsial'nogo zhitelia A.F. Belopiatkina"). Also see I. Goncharov's 1848 work "Letters from a Friend in the Capital to a Groom in the Provinces" ("Pis'ma stolichnogo druga k provintsial'nomu zhenikhu").

143. Some things never change. In his memoirs, Alexander Benois noted that St. Petersburg, for all its European ambience, could never be mistaken for Paris or Berlin. "The masses of common folk in Russian dress . . . gave to streets in Saint Petersburg a unique 'national' appearance," Benois recalled. "The well-to-do public walking along the main streets of Saint Petersburg could be mistaken for those individuals whom they strove to copy—that is, western Europeans. . . . But one had only to glance from the pavement to the middle of the street for the illusion of western Europe to disappear completely. Here was a surging stream of the most extraordinary vehicles—sleighs in winter, droshkies in summer, harnessed in a strange way and driven by bearded coachmen, all wearing greatcoats and headgear of

"God, how sad our Russia is!" Neither is there a sense that national life is ludicrous and ominous, without character, purpose, and sense. Indeed, just the opposite is the case.

An additional distinguishing feature of *Petersburg* is its striking informality. The contributors to the work do not regard their writings as "high" in any sense of the word. In fact, judging by appearances alone, they style the work as unabashedly pulp: large-print text framed with pictures and illustrations—at once real, carnivalesque, and theatrical—of the characters and events in their tales. Their references to literature also show a special preference for popular fiction, histories, tales, and travelogues: a common cultural legacy with their audience. Additionally, the writers of *Petersburg* treat their readers not only as respected equals but also as intimate friends. They share anecdotes and jokes; they pass on gossip and news; they bring their readers to interact between their characters and themselves; they resort to imperatives and move at will among first-, second-, and third-person narratives. In fact, the only strain in the relationship between writers and readers in *Petersburg* is the often pronounced earnestness with which Nekrasov and company assert the truth of what they are saying.

In their works, the contributors to *Petersburg* also assert a profound authorial presence. They do not hide behind narrators or other fictional masks, nor do they don mock cloaks of modesty and shyness, bemoaning their ability to report on any and all that they see, hear, smell, taste, and touch. Rather, the writers of *Petersburg* step forth in bold first-person narratives, enamored with the limelight. In their selections, though, Nekrasov and his fellow physiologists are gentlemen. They speak their peace; but when they finish, they step aside to let their heroes and heroines assume center stage.

The focus on middling readers also means that the writers of *Petersburg* mix high and low styles with abandon. Like other fictional borders in the work, linguistic demarcations are for them items both to draw and, in carnivalesque fashion, also to override and deride. Masters of *skaz,*

---

fantastic shapes. . . . Another characteristic was the number of drunkards progressing along the street . . . some with arms around each other, singing loudly or drinking their bottles dry as they ventured forth from the public houses. The keepers of the peace—the police—eyed these rowdies with leniency; only when their behavior crossed the limits of decency did the police apprehend them, throw them into a cab, and lock them up for the night to get sober." See A. Benois, *Reminiscences of the Russian Ballet,* trans. M. Britnieva (London: Putnam, 1941), 19.

Nekrasov and his fellow physiologists move at will from the carefree ethers of circles and salons to the market-tinged midlands of newspapers and journals, and to the grimy depths of alleys and streets. Bracing archaisms and calques, dialects and diminutives join with vocational jargon, idiosyncratic names, and turns of phrase. In similar fashion, proverbs, gang slang, peasant speech, and Russified melds of German, French, and Italian take their place among the lexicon of fervid card games, intimate tête-a-têtes, and hack journalism. That the language of the selections in *Petersburg* often features malapropisms and errors in pronunciation, spelling, and syntax concerns its writers but little. (A favorite device is the so-called *oslyshka,* or "mishearing," a technique of folk theater in which, as shown in Grebenka's "The Petersburg Quarter," deaf or drunk characters spark a folie à deux by repeating a given line or sentence so often that it loses its original meaning and becomes comic or even obscene.) In fact, the physiologists in Nekrasov's work so delight in reproducing urban tongues for their readers that they often stop their narratives to probe etymologies, pose definitions, and conjure up suitable synonyms and metaphors for words and phrases that enter into their works.

The most decisive feature of *Petersburg,* though, the one that sets it apart from both European and Russian counterparts, is that its writers cast their subjects as living, breathing beings. Absent is Gogolian hyperbole and synecdoche, the obsession with noses, whiskers, and waists. Also missing are plot and action, intrigue and denouement. The goal, rather, is to present "one day in the life" of urban denizens and, within that time frame, to uncover as much as possible about their lives, thoughts, and deeds. What begins as a few broad brushstrokes moves quickly into iconic and woodcutlike *kleima,* or "episodes," detailing the prosaics of, on the one hand, everyday individuals and, on the other, early attempts at montage: kaleidoscopic pictures and planes which wreak havoc on conventional time and space and which as such offer new and often startling perspectives on individuals and their reality. Further, the stories of *Petersburg* remain open-ended and ongoing; frames that border mappings (fictional and otherwise), if not flexible, are ignored.[144]

144. "All you have to do," Wood writes, "is to ignore the way the window isolates one view at the expense of another, how it is open only at this or that time of day, how it takes in only so much terrain, how it obligates us to see it under this light . . . or that. . . . What is at stake is not latitude and longitude,

In further contrast to the fictional subjects of European and Russian physiologists or, for that matter, the urban denizens of Pushkin, Lermontov, and Gogol, almost all of the men, women, and children of *Petersburg* are not the poor and mute, ignorant and saintly folk so beloved by Russian intellectuals (and so necessary to their hopes and plans for national change). They do not inhabit the lowest rung of the societal ladder; rather, they are seen as perched in the middle and even as climbing to the top. Even more revealing, perhaps, the heroes and heroines of *Petersburg* welcome a dynamic and changing world. They care little for such static and vertical concepts as tsar and church; instead, they look to more vital and horizontal ideas: life abroad, current events, science and technology, even the latest fads.

They also take on life with no holds—or egos[145]—barred.[146] They are what Belinsky and his colleagues so wanted for Russia: as he wrote in "Petersburg and Moscow," citizens who, like Peter the Great, express the

---

measures to whatever degree of fineness imaginable . . . but *ownership* that is being mapped." See Wood, *Power of Maps,* 21, italics in the original.

145. Revealingly, egos were seen at this time as an acceptable and desirable part of Russian life. "To eradicate egoism from a man's breast," Herzen wrote in 1844, "means to eradicate his vital principle, his leaven, the salt of his personality. . . . I dare say that a *rational acknowledgment of self-will is the highest moral affirmation of human dignity and that all can aspire to it.*" A. Herzen, "Kaprizy i razdum'e," *Sochineniia v deviati tomakh,* vol. 2 (Moscow: Gosudarstvennoe izdatel'stvo khudozhestvennoi literatury, 1955), 382–83, italics in the original.

No less a personage than Dostoevsky agreed. In fact, as he saw it, the problem was not ego but the inability to express it in life. "When a man is dissatisfied," he noted in 1847, "when he is unable to express himself and reveal what is best for him (not out of vanity, but because of the most natural necessity to become aware of, to embody and fulfill his Ego in real life), he at once falls into quite an incredible situation." Frustrated ego, Dostoevsky concluded, was a key catalyst for human aberration and misery. How unwittingly, it was also the impetus for many of the characters in both his early and mature fiction. Because of unfulfilled ego, Dostoevsky wrote presciently on June 15, 1847, "one takes to the bottle in a big way; a second, a gambler and a cardsharp; and a third, a quarrelsome bully. Finally, a fourth goes off his head because of *ambition,* at the same time completely despising ambition and even suffering because he has had to suffer over such nonsense as ambition." F. Dostoevskii, "Peterburgskaia letopis'," *Polnoe sobranie sochinenii khudozhestvennykh proizvedenii v trinadtsati tomakh,* vol. 13 (Leningrad: Gosudarstvennoe izdatel'stvo, 1926), 29, italics in the original.

146. Consider Thomas Conley's claim that "in cartographic genres . . . the self is visible only when it achieves the effect of totality, of having engineered a world through its own labors. . . . The self's emergence is evinced where discourse and geography are coordinated, and the self becomes autonomous only when it is fixed to an illusion of geographic truth (often of its own making) . . . and [when it] experiences movement in space and language that redeems the labor of living" (Conley, *The Self-Made Map,* 6, 22).

The converse is also true: the fragmented characters amid the specterlike Petersburg of Gogol and Dostoevsky.

"thought and intellect, spirit and will of genius," that is, they know happiness and prosperity, they bristle with curiosity, energy, and ambition, and in so doing, they change society and the world. In their élan vital, most of the characters in *Petersburg* are successful; those who are not do something about it or fake it until they are. Indeed, there seems to be no obstacle the heroes and heroines in *Petersburg* do not overcome. If at first they do not succeed, they try and try again. Nowhere in Nekrasov's anthology, then, is there a sense of being à huis clos, a sense of closed worlds, of self-canceling conclusions. Many characters in *Petersburg* come into life with strikes against them—poverty, broken homes, and the like—but they do not accept their fate, lapse into solipsism, withdraw into fantasies, or bow before icons and God. It is not their way to rail against existence, to conjure up doubles, or to bargain with the devil. Neither is it in their ken to dally in intrigue, to reject society, or to plot revenge on the world. The characters in *Petersburg* do not have the desire or time to lead complicated spiritual lives or to engage in even more complex conversations about what they think and feel. They are too busy (and content) living life to lick their wounds in self-pity and regret or, as does Gogol's Akaky Akakievich, to cry out to tormentors for justice and brotherhood. Quite alien are they also to the vocabulary of mental illness that Vladimir Toporov sees as seminal to the Petersburg lexicon: they are not exhausted, lonely, hopeless, feverish, morose, anguished, anxious, depressed, insane, terrified, agitated, and alienated.[147]

If the urban masses in *Petersburg* are uncharacteristically at peace with their world, it is because the issue at hand is philosophical, not social or political. Unlike Bulgarin and other conservatives, they do not subscribe to the view that "only the poor are happy." Rather, they forge ahead, determined not only to make the most of what God and nature have given them but also to acquire the skills, property, and money to carve out a comfortable place in life. Their path is straightforward, internally and externally. Idée fixe and its subsequent *être fixe,*[148] that is, the frustration and failure to which such mental musings give rise, do not cloud their horizon. Kings of Spain, Don Quixotes, buffoons, rogues, and would-be beaux of the boss's

147. V. Toporov, "Peterburg i 'Peterburgskii tekst' russkoi literatury," in *Mif, ritual, simvol, obraz: Issledovaniia v oblasti mifopoeticheskogo; Izbrannoe* (Moscow: Progress-Iskusstvo, 1995), 313–14.

148. Fanger, *Dostoevsky and Romantic Realism,* 117.

daughter are the last people they want to be. Rather, the heroes and heroines in *Petersburg* set modest goals for a prosaic future: they seek not only overcoats but all manner of holiday dress. They also acquire the amenities of what they consider to be bourgeois well-being. No hermitlike ascetics are they, since, unlike many of their fictional confreres in London, Paris, and St. Petersburg, they succumb to a consumption that is economic, not physical. The homes of the men and women in *Petersburg* feature mounds of junk and debris—covered with grit and grime, but also with self-styled place and purpose in life. No matter how bizarre (or evil-smelling) the assemblage, the effect is to cast its owner as boss, as king of his realm. Further, whatever success, personal and professional, that the men and women attain in *Petersburg* does not ruin them; rather, they exit their stories as simply and sweetly as they entered.

Most dramatic in this regard are the various images of civic officials and clerks in the work. In contrast to both conservative and liberal renditions of this type, for example, Bulgarin's law-abiding citizens, Gogol's hapless Akaky Akakievich, and Dostoevsky's distraught Makar Devushkin and Golyadkin Senior, the *chinovniki* in *Petersburg* do not envy society; rather, they are the ones who are envied. Neither their bodies nor their actions and thoughts are little: sentimental, foolish, or romantic.[149] Rather, like everyone else in *Petersburg,* they loom large in their readers' imagination. In fact, if the officials and clerks in the work are reproached by their authors, it is for their success, not failure; it is because they appropriate too fully the physical and mental largesse of middle-class life. The officials and clerks in *Petersburg* hold for rank, capital, and marriage but without the *poshlost',* or "self-satisfied vulgarity" with which Gogol so informed his works. They give elegant parties and dinners; they engage in handicrafts and hobbies; they tend to flowers and gardens; like Peter the Great, they even embellish their homes with fountains. The officials and clerks in *Petersburg* are sometimes seen as venal and vain, obsequious and obtuse, conniving and hypocritical, with a special love for wine, women, and cards

149. "Everyone scolds the clerk," a reviewer for the *Finnish Herald* wrote in 1845. "The fool is a clerk, the deceived husband is a clerk, the good-for-nothing is a clerk, the rejected and scorned lover is a clerk, the bribe taker is a clerk. Indeed, it seems that the clerk is the only person in the world. And any writer and hack can ride the poor clerk as he sees fit." Quoted in V. Vinogradov, *Evoliutsiia russogo naturalizma: Gogol' i Dostoevskii* (Leningrad: Akademiia, 1929), 314.

(and an equally pointed hatred for satire that hits too close to home), but they are also judged tongue in cheek and as well in keeping with *l'âme russe* by writers who, in deference to their own failings and those of everyday readers, are lax to cast the first stone.

The characters in *Petersburg* are also at one with their surroundings. They assert their presence in life, but without skewing or jarring the urban landscape or its population. Unlike many of the fictional creatures of the northern Palmyra, they observe "unity and community."[150] In no way are the characters of Nekrasov's collection, as personal and professional successes, envied, excluded, or ousted by society. Nor are they ever warned about surpassing family and friends or about striving too high in life. Enemies and rivals (real and imagined) do not obstruct them; the mob supports, not swallows. Indeed, their inclusion into the life of St. Petersburg is accepted and even applauded. The men, women, and children in *Petersburg* are also not above, below, or outside the masses but on equal terms with them: community sans society. They talk and toil with other denizens; they stroll with crowds of all shapes, situations, and sizes; they make merry Russian-style on holidays and at carnivals (real and Bakhtinian). The men and women in *Petersburg* grumble and grouse at masters (and mistresses); but, with apologies to their Marxist critics, they do not suffer at their bosses' hands. They also do not deem the imperial city a haven of contrasts and contradictions, of haves and have-nots, of triumphant evil and suffering innocence, "of unimaginable wealth and wrenching poverty, of elegance and shabbiness, of cold, crystalline harmony and churning, burning disorder."[151] Their concept of society is rigid and hierarchical only in the most external sense; borders are for them malleable, if they exist at all.[152] Foreign to the yardkeepers, organ-grinders, and others who people *Petersburg* is a "poetics of the staircase";[153]

150. Fanger, *Dostoevsky and Romantic Realism,* 108.

151. Lincoln, *Sunlight at Midnight,* 121. Indeed, with such works as *Petersburg,* one must call into question other sweeping statements by Lincoln, that is, that in this period, "the entire fabric of Russian society was permeated with an arbitrariness which left subordinates at the mercy of their superiors . . . with no concessions to any individual elements of society." Lincoln, *Nicholas I,* 76, 78.

152. Compare Belinsky's 1846 claim: "In our time, it is no longer rare to come across a friendly circle which features a well-known *barin* and a *raznochinets* and a merchant and a bourgeois, in which everyone, forgetting all external differences, respects one another simply as people. Here is the true beginning of that educated communality which literature is creating in our country." See Belinskii, *Polnoe sobranie sochinenii,* vol. 9 (1955), 435–36.

153. Fanger, *Dostoevsky and Romantic Realism,* 173.

rather, the consensus is that there is enough to go around and that, with hard work and effort, opportunity is there for all. As already noted with the hero in Panaev's "The Petersburg Feuilletonist," the characters in *Petersburg* have a strong sense of capitalist-style justice: As they (and their creators) see it, those at the bottom of society have no one to blame but themselves. The heroes and heroines in Nekrasov's work look upward at "Excellencies" and "Very Important Personages"; but only as skewed and semiotic constructs, of clothes, mannerisms, and speech with which to model their own enlightened approach to the world.[154] They believe that in middling society it is the externals that make the man (and woman) and, more important, perhaps, manifest and even direct inner hopes and desires. Unlike their confreres in Gogol and Dostoevsky, though, the men and women in *Petersburg* keep things in perspective. They go into raptures over gold and china plates, and they drool over dresses of velvet and lace; but they also realize, as they do in Grebenka's "The Petersburg Quarter," that their betters are "people all the same and that they, too, cry more than laugh."

Further in contrast to the urban characters in Russia's literary canon, the heroes and heroines of *Petersburg* are productive citizens if not integral cogs in the workings of society.[155] They are staunch, rugged individualists. Unlike Gogol's or Dostoevsky's characters, they are men and women of thought *and* action.[156] Assertive and aspiring, they are never caught napping or sloughing off. They do not waste time as prowling lieutenants,

154. Indeed, if Nekrasov and company are to be taken seriously, one must also take with a grain of salt Lincoln's remark that "even though St. Petersburgers of the 1830s and 1840s shared the Nevsky Prospekt as the artery along which the life of the city flowed, they had very little else in common. Serfs, aristocrats, civil servants, and tradesmen all had their own special interests, and no group shared any sense of common purpose with any other.

"Those who lived in the squalid rear flats of an apartment building were of little consequence to the well-to-do nobles and merchants who lived in the front, nor did the poor clerks, artisans, and tradesfolk who shared those rear courtyard lodgings have any idea about the lives of those who came and went through the building's front." Lincoln, *Sunlight at Midnight,* 138–39.

155. Maps, Wood writes, "allow us to keep track of each other: the demands of specialization it requires to function." Wood, *Power of Maps,* 39.

156. It is thus significant to note that although Brooks locates the rise of folk individuality and initiative in Russia at the fin de siècle, such empowering largesse was well in place at least fifty years earlier. Brooks also writes: "It is remarkable that popular images of success developed so much later in Russia than in Western Europe and America, but it would have been more remarkable had a vivid popular imagery of success existed much before the emancipation of the serfs. Until that time the lives of the common people were sharply restricted by the system of hereditary castes and by the backwardness of the economy" (*When Russia Learned to Read,* 270).

dreamy artists, and lazy servants: "dead souls." Nor do they beat their heads against Russian walls as "superfluous" individuals caught between ideal and real worlds or as amateur philosophers with idiosyncratic (and often erroneous) views of the world.[157] (Such types, when they do appear in *Petersburg,* are given remarkably short shrift.) Rather, the characters in Nekrasov's anthology are always on the move: whirlwinds of activity. Yardkeepers, for instance, clean streets, answer bells, haul water and wood, chase away thieves, and report newcomers to the police. As petty capitalists, they trade, pay taxes, collect rents from lodgers, and lend money (at rates higher than those of the State Treasury). Many are also providers of extended clans who often hold down more than one job to take care of families in the village. The men and women of *Petersburg* do have their faults; they can be ill-tempered, knavish, and greedy. Such failings, though, are seen as part of their charm, as affirming that they are flesh and blood. Indeed, in both their strengths and their weaknesses, such individuals thrill philosophers styled after Schiller, Schelling, or Hegel. If they, as Belinsky insisted, specify and sustain both the national and the universal, then the world, at least from the Russian perspective, is very well off indeed.

Most striking about the heroes and heroines in *Petersburg* is that none of them is a shrinking violet.[158] Rather, they are seen as performers who so love the stage that only a hook can pull them off. Even in the "corners" of imperial life, they are in plain (and dramatic) view.[159] Not the inchoate

157. "One must turn all one's attention to the mob, to the masses," Belinsky wrote in 1847–48, "to depict ordinary people, not only those pleasant exceptions to the social rule which deceive poets toward idealization." Belinskii, *Polnoe sobranie sochinenii,* vol. 10 (1956), 294.

158. Consider Conley's claim that the connection between maps and literature came into relief during the Renaissance when a surge in cartographic activity underscored the growing importance of the self as a literary and theatrical construct set against new ideas of national space. See Conley, *The Self-Made Map,* 1–2.

159. In this, the characters of *Petersburg* draw directly from the heroes and heroines of the *lubok,* or woodcut. They, too, draw from all ranks of society, including lords and peasants, dandies and usurers and clerks. They also stand in iconic bas-relief, often one-on-one, face-to-face, with open mouths and outstretched hands. They dress in the latest fashion, engage in conversation and work, and delight in anecdotes and stories.

Further like the individuals in Nekrasov's work, the figures in the *lubok* are privy to idyllic order and calm, amid bright colors, rhythmic lines, and penetrating detail of everyday life. (Interiors of taverns and homes were particular favorites.) In all, the outlook was of a bourgeois-mercantile view of life, that is, of people in charge of their lives, with articulate and clear beliefs and tastes.

More important, perhaps, the *lubok* also was rife with the images and ideas of carnival. Parade and spectacle; irreverence for authority; worldly if cunning wisdom; bawdy slapstick and farce; all

and mute Akaky Akakievich are they. The slightest prodding of interlocutors moves the individuals in Nekrasov's anthology to discourse on a wide variety of topics. Like Grigory in "The Petersburg Yardkeeper" by Dal', they have "ideas and convictions . . . views and worldly experience—information that has been handed down from generation to generation." At will, the men and women in *Petersburg* expound upon likes and dislikes, professions and work, literature and art, society and politics, and—a must in Russian literature, whatever the genre or period—philosophies of life, reasons for existence, and the nature of law, order, and justice in life.

Although all the selections in *Petersburg* model one or more of the characteristics noted in the foregoing discussion, it is Dmitri Grigorovich's essay "The Petersburg Organ-Grinders" ("Peterburgskie sharmanshchiki") that best illustrates the far-reaching significance of the work.

As an initial strategy, Grigorovich makes it clear to his readers that he has done his homework. He fills his piece with a scholarly plethora of facts and figures on all aspects of his hero's life.[160] As a second tack, Grigorovich

---

these elements contribute to the aura of holiday and fair. Clowns, musicians, and bears mime, dance, sing, and invite spectators to join in the fun. Also noteworthy in the *lubok* is the idea of community, with professionals and peasants observing the goings-on and engaged in conversation and the like. See E. Ivanov, *Russkii narodnyi lubok* (Moscow: Gosudarstvennoe izdatel'stvo izobrazitel'nykh iskusstv, 1937), 31.

A key difference, though, between *Petersburg* and *lubki* is this: Whereas the latter stressed picture over text, the former emphasizes text over picture, itself an indication of the growing literacy of the reading public in Russia.

160. Such assertions are based in fact.

> Nekrasov whose practical mind was always on guard . . . asked me to write an essay [for *Petersburg*] . . . but having agreed, I, for a long time, did not know what to write about.
>
> Having passed through Obukhovsky Prospekt on a rainy autumn day, I caught sight of an old organ-grinder, dragging his instrument on his back. Up until this time, I had never noticed these people—for the most part, Italians—who made their living in such a way. One could meet every day in any of the big courtyards of Petersburg. They appeared with their barrel organs, their puppet comedies . . . their singers, dancers, and acrobats who walked on their hands and did salto mortale on the bare sidewalk. As I recall, they did not disturb the residents or the social order. Just the reverse, they enlivened the grey, mournful city.
>
> Following them with my eyes, I often asked myself by what routes they had come to Russia from Italy, how much deprivation and suffering had they had to endure along the way, how had they arranged their lives here, where did they live, were they content with existence [in Petersburg] or did they recalled their abandoned homeland with bitterness, and so forth.
>
> I set about my task with excitement. . . . For about two weeks, I wandered for days on end also the three Pod"yachesky streets where, at the time, the majority of organ-grinders

moves his investigation from the confines of his study out onto the street. He bids his readers to follow in his footsteps via carefully scripted—if unconventional—guided tours not only through the highways and byways of St. Petersburg but also through the hills and dales of its middling literature, through facets of anecdote, feuilleton, and sketch wedded to features from epistolary, travel, and dramatic literature.

Whatever the form, though, Grigorovich is always within speaking and listening distance of his readers. On one level, the teller of the tale of "The Petersburg Organ-Grinders" adopts a formal approach to his study; he is a teacher-scholar who, posing alternately as a sociologist, linguist, journalist, and ethnographer, asserts his views with judgment and authority. He probes the etymology of the word, "organ-grinder." He reflects on the origins and workings of the puppet show. With self-styled categories, he appeals to genus and species, with enthusiastic Italians holding sway—emotionally and aesthetically—over deadly Germans and dysfunctional Russians.

In line with this formal stance, Grigorovich also sees his listeners as well-heeled residents of St. Petersburg with limited perspectives on their city but also with ample curiosity about its people and environs. The stance is literature as "fact": direct, thorough, and concrete. Grigorovich sets his readers at ease by answering questions, posing issues, and even anticipating protests in a detailed and engaging way. With them, also, he ponders and provokes, admonishes and cajoles, challenges and projects. He even apologizes and pleads for patience and sympathy when he finds himself in uncharted waters, physical and otherwise. Further, as would any reputable scholar, Grigorovich considers the most minor characters and incidents with sophistication and seriousness. Also, with apologies to Gogol, he does not prattle, mystify, or frustrate with unresolved mysteries and loose ends; even his digressions are purposeful.

> had settled. I talked with them, poked in at all kinds of unimaginable slums, and, in the slightest detail, wrote down everything I had seen and heard. Having conceived the plan of my article and separated it into chapters, I began to write it with a timid and unsure feeling. (Grigorovich, *Literaturnye vospominaniia,* 77–78)

It should also be noted that Grigorovich, raised in a French-speaking household, learned Russian from yardkeepers and peasants and that as a young man, he had loved theaters, sets, and scenes.

On another level, Grigorovich recalls speakers of eighteenth-century letters and travel notes in his stops at urban way stations to confide his observations and views. Here the approach is intimate, whimsical, and chatty, the goal being to create new mappings of Peter's city with middling people, places, and events. Grigorovich enters into homes and exits onto streets and courtyards. He shares stories, eavesdrops on conversations, and waits his turn in crowds. Like the Deity, he looks upon life and finds it to be good. He even blesses urban denizens in a quiet, almost prayerful way, thankful not only for their existence but also for their impact on his and Russian life.

In "The Petersburg Organ-Grinders," Grigorovich also is well aware of tastes and trends in literature, particularly the penchant for so-called sentimental naturalism, that is, the portrayal of ordinary men and women in an overtly saccharine and lachrymose way. In his introduction to the piece, he gives a perfunctory if all-inclusive nod to the images and ideals of Bashchutsky, Bulgarin, and other conservative writers.[161] In fact, the opening lines of "The Petersburg Organ-Grinders" are so rife with the themes and motifs of sentimental naturalism that they move to parody and bathos. There is the organ-grinder, poor, solitary, and disheveled, burdened by familial woes and hoping for kopecks from indifferent and abusive spectators, annoyed by the squawks of his instrument. There is the organ-grinder's residence: a cellar or attic rented from a woman, also dressed in rags and living hand to mouth with a brood of her own. Further, as per the strictures of sentimental naturalism, integrity and pride are the only weapons in the organ-grinder's hopeless struggle with the world.

Immediately, however, Grigorovich turns his back on the sentimental scenario. As he tells his readers, he does not wish to present the organ-grinder as a model of virtue or an object of sympathy. Repeatedly, the teller of the tale in "The Petersburg Organ-Grinders" bids his readers to

161. Quite possibly, Grigorovich's introduction to "The Petersburg Organ-Grinders" was inspired by an 1839 piece in the *Northern Bee.* "Often on an early winter evening, when you draw close to a lighted stove, sit in your small room in a mournful frame of mind, and think about the boredom of our times . . . a street organ-grinder passes under your windows and plays a favorite aria from *Pretsioza,* making an immediate impression on you and rousing you to comforting memories." (*Pretsioza* was a musical spectacle written by Carl Maria von Weber around 1820.) "Ulichnaia sharmanka," *Severnaia pchela,* no. 284 (1839): 1.

look more closely at the subject of his study. Other goals, other images and ideals soon fill his narrative.

As his overriding principle, Grigorovich seeks to liberate his organ-grinder (and his colleagues) physically, socially, and spiritually. Although in reality, many in this group were poor, homesick, and hungry,[162] as well as harassed, abused, and even injured by both the authorities and the upper classes,[163] Grigorovich portrays them as winners in life. Uniformly, their trajectory is upward. Italian organ-grinders begin life as poor vagabonds, with St. Petersburg as a distant but attainable dream. Fate is on their side, though. All along the way, audiences shower Italian organ-grinders with so many kopecks that when they finally arrive in St. Petersburg, they hire workers immediately. With their earnings, they also begin several profitable businesses—enough to realize the middle-class Russian dream: home, family, and standing in the community. Even the initial, expected scene of unpleasant sights, sounds, and smells—the result of people and animals, slops and smoke—soon dissipates into a second picture of bourgeois order, cleanliness, and light.

Like Grigorovich himself, all the characters in "The Petersburg Organ-Grinders" embrace life. They are "resourceful, cunning, bold, and merry"; by their disposition, they "captivate, entice, and please" their public. Extroverts par excellence, their motivation is exceeded only by their mouths. Willingly, in a fractured but colorful mix of Italian, French, and Russian, they talk about themselves and their craft. To Grigorovich's physiological taste, also, the men and women in "The Petersburg Organ-Grinders" match their speech with substance.

162. In addition, entertainers in Russian carnivals often gave continuous ten-to-twelve-hour performances during the day and at night slept in unheated and highly flammable *balagany*. Their children had even more difficult lives, often being sold by their parents into effective slavery with circus proprietors where they were underfed, ill used, and regularly beaten, perhaps to death. Not surprisingly, some in this group were alcoholics by age ten. See C. Kelly, *Petrushka: The Russian Puppet Carnival Theater* (Cambridge: Cambridge University Press, 1990), 44–45.

163. Curiously, educated Russians regarded native puppet shows and other fairground entertainment with greater contempt than did their counterparts in other countries. Writers and memorists avoided such amusements studiously; and on the rare occasion when they took stock of such diversions, it was as puritans, not revelers, that is, they saw Russian carnivals either as pointed threats to civilized society or as crying examples of how the powers that be distracted, exploited, and hoodwinked the masses. Ibid., 140–41.

Whereas most of the characters in Pushkin, Lermontov, and Gogol, as well as lesser figures in homegrown romanticism and realism (liberal and conservative), are ungainfully unemployed, the organ-grinders and company in Grigorovich's work are "committed to their trade, body and soul." As "modest and serene artisans . . . with a passion for their noble art," they are quite proud of their talents, achievements, and possessions. The many and diverse tools of their trade, the growing numbers of crew and acts, they display proudly as the "eighth wonder of the world" and as signs of expertise, success, and advance from self-styled philistines to aristocracy. Further, as does Panaev in "The Petersburg Feuilletonist" (and Grebenka in "The Petersburg Quarter"), Grigorovich makes it clear that if his Italian organ-grinders come to rack and ruin, it is not society that is at fault; rather, it is they who bear the onus for their failings: poor decisions, reckless living, breaks with reality, or flawed doings in money and speculation. No matter, though, Grigorovich tells his readers, since such individuals invariably pick themselves up, dust themselves off, and begin life anew.

It is also within Grigorovich's physiological idea to cast Russian organ-grinders as being as engaging as their Italian counterparts. Indeed, what native musicians lack in initiative and talent, they more than make up for in simplicity and charm. At first glance, their lot is not a happy one. Moving from pillar to post and spending their last kopecks on drink, they hire themselves to the fellow Pietros in their craft. Nowhere in "The Petersburg Organ-Grinders," though, is there a sense of exploitation or unhappiness. Russian organ-grinders, it seems, are content with whatever arrangements life or their bosses throw their way. "Peaceful activities"—reading pulp fiction, a particular example—occupy their minds and souls.

Other Russians in Grigorovich's "The Petersburg Organ-Grinders" fare equally well, if not better. A would-be street clown surmounts such Dickensian obstacles as an attic home, an illegitimate birth, a Lovelacelike father, an abandoned mother who works as a laundress, and an apprenticeship to a rich workman to seek pleasure, excitement, and employment with a wandering troupe of acrobats and clowns. Indeed, the latter group are for the future street clown such "heroes and lords" that he can hardly wait for the day when he too can wear sparkled velvet camisoles and earn the friendship and applause of colleagues and spectators. As Grigorovich notes, the would-be street clown decides that "no matter what, he will attain a high goal in life." More important, perhaps, he realizes his dream. Having survived a perfunctory mention of the "most difficult school . . . the master's whip and stick," Grigorovich's street clown assumes multiple roles: bard, acrobat, mime, and devil, among others. Like the organ-grinder, he, too, faces periodic hard times; but, also like his Italian counterpart, he invariably sports a "self-contented smile . . . [and] is pursued by an enthusiastic public."

The linchpin in Grigorovich's "The Petersburg Organ-Grinders," though, is the puppet show at the end of the work. The Russian love for *balagan* and puppets (with, of course, Petrushka in the starring role) was key not only to such diverse personalities as those of Fyodor Dostoevsky,[164] Maxim Gorky,[165] Alexander Blok,[166] Andrei Bely,[167]

164. In his *Diary of a Writer* (*Dnevnik pisatelia*) for January 1876, Dostoevsky distinguished between the Italian-based Puchinella and the Russian-styled Petrushka, seeing the two puppets almost in terms of the doubles in his fiction. "Puchinella is something akin to both Don Quixote and Don Juan," Dostoevsky wrote. "How trusting he is, how merry and straightforward, how he wishes not to believe in evil and deceit, how quickly he gets angry and throws himself against unfairness, and how he exults as soon as he whacks someone with his staff." Petrushka, to Dostoevsky, though, was "a scoundrel who, though inseparable from Puchinella, both deceived and laughed at [his counterpart]." He was "akin to Sancho Panza or Leporello but was a completely Russified and folk character." F. Dostoevskii, *Polnoe sobranie sochinenii v tridtsati tomakh*, 30 vols. (1972–90), vol. 22, 180.

165. "Petrushka conquers everyone and everything," Gorky wrote in 1934, "priests, the police, even the devil and death." The writer also compared the puppet to Faust. See M. Gor'kii, "Sovetskaia literatura," *Sobranie sochinenii v tridtsati tomakh*, 30 vols. (1949–56) (Moscow: Gosudarstvennoe izdatel'stvo khudozhestvennoi literatury, 1953), vol. 27 (1953), 305.

Gorky also wrote in 1928: "Petrushka is the crude and naive image in which working people embodied themselves and their belief that in the end they themselves would have victory over everyone and everything." See M. Gor'kii, "O tom, kak ia uchilsia pisat'," *Sobranie sochinenii*, vol. 24 (1953), 494.

166. See Blok's 1906 lyric drama *Balaganshchik* (*The Fair Show Booth*).

167. For instance, in the chapter entitled, "Clown-Petrushka" ("*Paits-Petrushka*"), in his 1922 autobiographical novel, *Kotik Letaev*, Bely writes:

> Cockerel cry—
> krr–krr!
> cheeky crackle
> like cracker; crook-backed,
> cross, colored, splashly-flashly flibbertigibbet puppet:
> with witty ditties, rascal-king of the castle,
> with nozzle shrunken drunken sunken, with cap and
> shock of hair like mop, handheld he whacks and smacks
> for all he's worth—or why? who'll say—on
> the *balagan* corner—
> krr-krr-kr!—
> Catch me if you can!

See A. Belyi, *Kotik Letaev* (St. Petersburg: Epokha, 1922), 89.

Alexander Benois,[168] Igor Stravinsky,[169] Nikolai Evreinov,[170] Boris Kustodiev,[171] and Vaslav Nijinsky;[172] it was also seminal to Grigorovich. In fact, to Grigorovich goes the distinction of introducing *balagan* and puppet show into Russian literature and, by extension, into national art, music, and drama.[173]

168. "The *balagany* on the Field of Mars were a collection of village merrymaking in the city," Benois wrote in 1917, "a big, playful, uncontrolled village in which we, gentry children, were taken to 'learn about Russia' without realizing it." Later, Benois continued, "Here in one of the big wooden theaters were the traditional performances of the Harlequinades. . . . What I saw with my eyes surpassed all my hopes. I was almost dazed by this first experience of 'theater,' and, to this day, the memory [of it] has never lost its freshness and verve." See A. Benois, "Khudozhestvennye pis'ma. Novye balety. 'Petrushka,'" *Rech'* (August 17, 1911), 2; and *Moi vospominaniia v piati tomakh: Kniga vtoraia* (Moscow: Nauka, 1980), 293.

More tantalizing, perhaps, is Benois's assertion that he drew his costumes for the 1911 performance of *Petrushka* (in collaboration with Stravinsky and Mikhail Fokin) from the pictures by Vasily Timm and from caricatures of the 1840s. (Timm was an illustrator for *Petersburg*.) See R. Vlasova, *Russkoe teatral'no-dekoratsionnoe iskusstvo nachala XX veka* (Leningrad: Khudozhnik RSFSR, 1984), 148n172.

169. Stravinsky recalled, "Saint Petersburg was also a city of large open piazzas. One of these, the Champs de Mars, might have been the scene of *Petrushka*. The Mardi Gras festivities were centered there and, as puppet shows were part of the carnival entertainment, it was there that I saw my first 'Petrushka.'" I. Stravinsky and R. Craft. *Expositions and Developments* (London: Faber and Faber, 1959), 35.

170. Evreinov wrote: "And then *Petrushka*. . . . Good heavens, the excitement which the appearance of this street hero aroused in me! I nagged and nagged my parents until they gave me one of the sets of all the *Petrushka* puppets which were so popular at the time, a little book with a text, and a mesh 'squeaker' for my mouth, so I could talk like 'Petrushka himself.'

"What a strange scene the house looked! For entire days on end, the silken screen from my mother's boudoir was used to conceal the *Petrushka* player, until in the end it disintegrated; my brother, as the organ-grinder, turned the handle of the Ariston [windup gramophone] incessantly until my father fell on him foaming at the mouth; and our guests, under the threat of tearful scenes, had to watch the same thing a dozen times on end, applauding every time the devil took Petrushka off to hell. My poor parents! Our poor guests! Happy childhood! Magic puppets!" N. Evreinov, "Dan' marionetkam," *Teatral'nye novatsii* (Petrograd: Tret'ia strazha, 1922), 99.

171. For instance, from 1916 to 1922, Kustodiev did a series of paintings, entitled *Shrovetide* (*Maslenitsa*).

172. Consider the claim by Romola Nijinsky that her husband, in portraying Petrushka onstage, "amplified the crazy doll into the symbol of the spirit of the Russian people, pressed by autocracy, but resurgent and unconquerable after all its abuse and frustration." R. Nijinsky, *Nijinsky* (London: Sphere Books, 1970), 107.

173. Although puppet shows were popular throughout Russia from the mid-eighteenth century onward and also often the subject of commentary by such newspapers as the *Northern Bee* in the 1820s and '30s, it was in Grigorovich's "The Petersburg Organ-Grinders" that one finds the earliest reference to a glove puppet play in the homeland which, without a doubt, can be identified as a performance of *Petrushka*. (The work is also one of only about thirty surviving texts of the thousands of performances that took place in Russia during the nineteenth century.) Further, Grigorovich's text is invaluable because it provides the only known evidence for the intermediate stages in the evolution from the Western European prototype to the standard Russian version.

Much of what Grigorovich does with *balagan* and puppet show in "The Petersburg Organ-Grinders" is in sync not only with the rest of his essay but also with the other pieces in *Petersburg.* Just as Grigorovich draws the other characters in his essay sans caricature and grotesque, so does he withhold from Petrushka the physical deformities typically associated with this type. Grigorovich's Petrushka lacks the hooked nose, hunched back, and beady eyes of the stereotype. He also lacks the protruding chin, oversize teeth, short thorax, and spindly legs that recall his counterparts in Europe and elsewhere. Equally revealing, perhaps, Grigorovich's Petrushka moves about without the priapism that so titillated urban audiences in the West (as well as in medieval Russia).[174]

Also in his portrait of the puppet, Grigorovich bypasses the less-than-flattering features often identified with Petrushka's personality. Absent are the puppet's cowardice and cupidity, his crudeness and egoism, his womanizing and deceit, and, most distressingly, his frequent application of a huge *dubinka,* or "club," to anyone who gets in his way.[175] Rather, Grigorovich's Petrushka is seen as akin to his fictional organ-grinders, clowns, and the

---

It should also be noted that after 1842, references to street puppet shows proliferate and by the mid-1850s are a standard attraction of village fairs in Russia. "Then there is the never-failing Punch hard upon Judy," an anonymous English visitor to Russia recorded. "And there are also swings, hobby horses, shows, theaters, dancing bears, jugglers, and monkeys." H. Morley, ed., *Sketches of Russian Life Before and During the Emancipation of the Serfs* (London: Chapman and Hall, 1866), 273.

Also see C. Kelly, "From Pulchinella to Petrushka: The History of the Russian Glove Puppet Theatre," *Oxford Slavonic Papers* 21 (1988): 52, 60; A. Nekrylova, *Russkie narodnie gorodskie prazdniki uveseleniia i zrelishcha: Konets XVIII–nachalo XX veka* (Leningrad: Iskusstvo, 1984), 58; F. Bulgarin, "Nravy: Kacheli," *Severnaia pchela,* April 2, 1825, 2–4; and "Smes': Balagany," *Severnaia pchela,* February 1, 1839, 103–4.

174. Consider, for instance, this 1637 remark by the German traveler Adam Olearius: "But as [the Muscovites] are given up entirely to licentiousness, even to sins against nature, not only with men, but also with beasts. He who can tell most stories of that kind, and set them out in most gestures, is accorded to the bravest man.

"Their fiddlers put them into songs, and their mountebanks make public representations of them, and stick not to show their breeches, and sometimes all they have to their spectators. Those who lead bears about, jugglers, and puppet-players who erect a stage in a moment, by the means of a coverlet, which, being tied about their waist, is brought over their heads and within show their puppets, representing their brutalities, and sodomies, make sport to the children, who are thereby induced to quit all sentiments of honesty and shame." A. Olearius, *The Voyages and Travels of the Ambassadors, Rendered into English by John Davies of Kidwelly* (London: Thomas Dring and John Starkey, 1662), 81.

175. Consider Harley's assertion that maps "just as much as examples of literature or the spoken word . . . exert a social influence through their omissions as much as by the features they depict and overemphasize." Harley, "Deconstructing the Map," 290.

like in that he, too, enjoys life, swings with ups and downs; he even knows happiness.

Even in a brief performance, Grigorovich's Petrushka puts in quite a day. The puppet bypasses military recruiters, dances with "mam'selle Katerina," and is betrothed to ninety-year-old Matryona Ivanovna. He is seized on the nose by a dog and cured by a doctor. Petrushka is also a carnival type par excellence. To Grigorovich's taste, he is "a brawler, a madcap, and atheist" who delights the audience with his antics, particularly his infractions of the social order (which, in real life, often got the entire cast and everyone else in trouble with the powers that be).[176] Petrushka answers the doctor's kindness with a slap in the face. When handed over to soldiers for punishment, the puppet beats his superior "left and right." A struggle with the devil ends in a draw. Petrushka sits on top of the evil one, but his orders to the dark spirit go unheeded. The puppet eventually perishes and disappears offstage; but the ending lacks a tragic or final air. Rather, the final scene promises that Petrushka shares the same fate as all the characters in Grigorovich's "The Petersburg Organ-Grinders"—somehow, somewhere, he will rise and perform again.

Needless to say, puppet, puppeteer, and the other performers in Grigorovich's "The Petersburg Organ-Grinders" know both carnival and their audiences well; otherwise they would starve physically and aesthetically. In a sense, their task is an easy one. After all, Grigorovich's entertainers hail from the same déclassé, working-class backgrounds as the entertained. Outlooks and tastes on carnival and art are close, if not identical. The familiarity of Grigorovich's theatrical cast with the urban proletariat is also physical and verbal. Physically, contact is made at the very beginning of the spectacle. Actors appear onstage; they bow and greet their hosts; they ask for permission to begin the performance. The intimacy is maintained right to the end of the show when puppet, puppeteer, and fellow actors approach their viewers directly for remuneration and applause. Even after the spectacle is over, the group does not retreat into anonymity; rather, its members mingle again with the crowd to enjoy the festivities of the fair.

176. See Russell Zguta, *Russian Minstrels: A History of the "Skomorokhi."* Philadelphia: University of Pennsylvania Press, 1978, 114.

Verbally, puppet, puppeteer, and company not only address their spectators as old friends but also encourage them to be cocreators in the show. Grigorovich's entertainers bid the audience to answer questions, anticipate events, collude in the action, pose issues and plots, and register approval or dismay. As seasoned veterans, they know a crowd—startled, discomfited, or laughing at an ironic situation or at a third party's expense—often constitutes half the humor of the play. Master, marionette, and colleagues also intuit that the moods they convey must be as brash and bold as their mime. Subtle gradations in character and emotions are not for them. Anger, melodrama, and tears move in sync with slapstick, capers, and tomfoolery.

As is characteristic of carnival, folk theater, and orally transmitted texts, the actors and audience in Grigorovich's "The Petersburg Organ-Grinders" join in a performance that is part ritual, part impromptu; part recreation, part creation. The dynamic here is to safeguard and sustain but also to innovate and explore. On one level, Grigorovich's organ-grinders, clowns, and puppeteers work with traditional characters and scenes and with a particular focus on the moment. (On the average, real-life performances lasted between fifteen and twenty minutes.)[177] Puppet shows, along with the other acts in "The Petersburg Organ-Grinders," appear spontaneously anywhere anytime; readiness and relish for carnival, it seems, is a sine qua non of the Russian (and human) spirit. On another level, actors and audience improvise and exploit individual wit and talent to fashion a show that is impromptu, contemporary, and freewheeling, hence the rampant enthusiasm, the dizzying pace, the inspired nonsense, the high-pitched babble, and the steady stream of jokes, one-liners, and non sequiturs that inform the discourse between performers and populace. Hence also the veiled abuse, mischievous double entendres, and Aesopian references to sexual and social taboos that catch the ears of listeners—the issue of Petrushka's military recruitment, a key example—but that escape the eyes of outsiders or censors. Indeed, the implicit success of "The Petersburg Organ-Grinders" rests not only on the fact that spectators have the political and cultural wherewithal to understand the proceedings but also that, like their views on carnival and art, they share the political, social,

177. V. Krupyanskaya, "Narodnyi teatr," in *Russkoe narodnoe poeticheskoe tvorchestvo: posobie dlia vuzov,* ed. P. Bogatyrev (Moscow: Gosudarstvennoe uchechno-pedagogicheskoe izdatel'stvo ministerstva prosveshcheniia RSFSR, 1954), 394; Kelly, "Pulchinella to Petrushka," 67.

and economic outlooks of the performers. In truth, such agreement is a given: a certain that-goes-without-saying quality permeates the work.[178] In the unrestrained support between entertainers and entertained, all are determined to have fun at all costs; all are equally eager to find relaxation and respite from the grayness and cares of urban life. In the admiration and applause from both sides of the stage, all fashion a stirring model for the alliance of theater and literature in Russian culture and life.

Also important to Grigorovich in "The Petersburg Organ-Grinders" is that his "opera of the street-folk"[179] is both peaceful and pleasing to the senses. Like his portrait of Petrushka, Grigorovich avoids the raw seaminess that characterized much of Russian carnival life and that the artist Konstantin Makovsky captured so vividly in his 1869 painting *Folk Festivity During Shrovetide on Admiralty Square in Petersburg* (*Narodnoe gulian'e vo vremia Maslenitsy na Admiralteiskoi ploshchadi v Peterburge*).[180] The harsh sounds and smells typical of such gatherings are nowhere evident.[181] Also absent are incidents of drunkenness, shoving, fighting,[182]

178. Wood, *Power of Maps,* 77.

179. B. Jerrold and G. Dore, *London* (London: Grant, 1872), 175.

180. Consider Benois's remark that all of *Petrushka* "came as if out of Makovsky's painting." Quoted in M. Etkind, *A. N. Benua i russkaia khudozhestvennaia kul'tura kontsa XIX - nachala XX veka* (Leningrad: Khudozhnik RSFSR, 1989), 264.

181. "Good heavens, what goes on inside the circle [of the fairground]!" Ivan Shcheglov, an activist in the people's theater movement, recalled in the late nineteenth century. "You can hardly take it in, let alone describe it.

"First, the music—truly, the music alone could deprive someone who had just arrived of his senses, because the point is that it is not *the* music, it is all sorts of music—several kinds together, and your ears are deafened simultaneously by a satanic compound of winds and strings, steam and barrel organs, accordions, with the classic squeal of 'Petrushka' rising above all, in place, as it were, of a tuning fork. . . .

"And then there are the cries of the men and women selling things. . . . They are shouting now quite differently from the way they usually shout in streets and markets, with a sort of special frenzy, until tears come to their eyes and they go hoarse." I. Shcheglov, *Narod i teatr: Ocherki i issledovaniia narodnogo teatra* (St. Petersburg: P. P. Soikin, 1911), 108–9.

182. "At no other time are there so many accidents as in [Shrove] Week [in Russia], a German visitor recalled in the late eighteenth century. "Every instance drunks crash into each other so that the climax to the occasion is usually adorned by broken and bloody heads." Quoted in N. Simonovich-Efimova, *Zapiski petrusheshnika* (Leningrad: Iskusstvo, 1981), 119.

Similarly, Benois recalled, "These fairs . . . though modelled on the fairs in Western Europe, were imbued with a specifically Russian spirit; the gaiety was more violent, more elemental. . . . There were more drunks roaming about these fairs than anywhere in Europe.

"Towards evening, tipsiness of a boisterous, noisy sometimes frightening kind would spread among the simple folk who dominated the fairground in the square, giving an almost demoniacal character to the

and gross hedonism.[183] The carnival that is Grigorovich's "The Petersburg Organ-Grinders" does what politics, economics, and science cannot. The performances of puppeteers, organ-grinders, and the like merge not only actors and audience but people of all ranks and classes. All are welcome at Grigorovich's carnival-feast. Side by side, nurses and soldiers, workers and dandies, policemen and clerks, mothers and children watch and applaud the show.[184] As a measure of the new cosmopolitanism, even foreigners do well in the group.[185] (Historically, even tsars and aristocrats appreciated such performances.)[186] To his inclusive taste, Grigorovich also takes care

---

entertainment. This atmosphere is admirably reproduced in the fourth scene of Stravinsky's *Petrushka.*" See A. Benois, *Memoirs,* trans. M. Budberg (London: Chatto and Windus, 1960), 118–19.

Further, another reviewer noted that such carnivals-cum-*Petrushka* were often little more than "entertainment by hooligans for hooligans." See *Bemerkungen uber Russland,* vol. 2 (Erfurt, 1788), 193.

183. Compare Benois's comment: "Already along Millionaya Street one could hear a rumbling that immediately filled one's head with fumes. The carouse was a one even for those who did not take so much as a drop of poison into their mouths. But is drunkenness really that bad? The wide sea . . . of popular drunkenness, celebrating the turn toward spring, welcoming their ancient, Eternal Yarilo." (Yarilo was a Slavic god of masculine passion and power and also was one of the deities associated with Russian, Ukrainian, and Belarussian sun worship.) See Benois, "Khudozhestvennye pis'ma," 2.

184. In this, Grigorovich was well in sync with Belinsky and others who sensed a new integration in Russian society. "The hostility between the estates is disappearing," he wrote in 1842. "People are becoming reconciled in a realization of their mutual need for each other, as well as in their common importance for the whole of society." See Belinskii, *Polnoe sobranie sochinenii,* vol. 6 (1955), 92.

It should also be noted that puppet theaters-cum-*Petrushka* were more numerous than any other type of entertainment at Russian carnivals and also the greatest source of satisfaction for the crowds there. Indeed, the audiences for fairground and street theater ran into the millions, far outstripping the numbers who had access to printed material.

185. In this, Grigorovich and the other contributors to *Petersburg* saw what other Russian writers of homeland urban realism would or could not: the physical proximity of all social classes in Peter's city.

For instance, Bruce Lincoln writes:

> Every quarter of [St. Petersburg] housed its share of the carters, cleaners, and humble clerks who made up the ranks of St. Petersburg's less than fortunate. Set apart in terms of wealth and living standard, these people nonetheless crossed the path of the city's upper classes at almost every step, for even in the best parts of St. Petersburg, the downtrodden and disdained shared courtyards with the rich and famous. Generals, statesmen, petty bureaucrats, seamstresses, cobblers, and ladies of the night often called the same building home.
>
> The common practice of renting cramped rear rooms in St. Petersburg's larger buildings to the working poor while the well-to-do lived in the spacious, high-ceilinged splendor of apartments that looked out on the street made that inevitable. (Lincoln, *Sunlight at Midnight,* 8)

186. A. Alekseev-Iakovlev, *Russkie narodnye gul'iania po rasskazam A. I. Iakovleva; v zapisi i obrabotke Evg. Kuznetsova* (Leningrad: Iskusstvo, 1948), 12.

to admit both himself and his readers to the proceedings. Having come upon a puppet show in his travels, he bids his readers: "Why don't we stop in, too?"

Grigorovich ends "The Petersburg Organ-Grinders" on a strategic note. Ostensibly, he returns his organ-grinder to the introductory scene. Carnival, it seems, ends as quickly as it begins, grim reality again rising to the fore. The crowd disperses quickly, occupied more with the cries of children than with giving the organ-grinder his due. Scattered kopecks, ringing hollowly on the street, are his sole reward. Shivering dogs, scowling peasants, and thieving urchins join with dark skies, cold rain, and drenched hovels, completing the Dickensian picture. Stratification also returns: masters rise high over men. Against such a background, Grigorovich cuts to his organ-grinder, who again is poor and alone, tired and sad. The trouble is, the sentimental and naturalist picture no longer rings true. Indeed, it seems painfully, even annoyingly artificial and false. Grigorovich's readers now know too much about the organ-grinder's life, as well as about carnival, to accept this final portrait. Like his Petrushka, Grigorovich makes clear that urban merriment comes and goes, but its effects are lifelong—and infinitely preferable to the populace.

In light of all that has been said, Nekrasov's "The Petersburg Corners" seems to be a glaring exception. There is no joy in imperial Mudville, Nekrasov asserts, and his portrait of the humiliated and injured in the urban depths is seen as evidence for such a view. (Revealingly, the piece required special permission from the censors.) Close inspection, though, reveals that "The Petersburg Corners" accords well with the other pieces in *Petersburg*. The piece is rife with carnival allusions. Harshness assaults eye and nose.[187] The hero makes his way on fly-covered planks, through "rancid

187. Consider Grigory Kaganov's statement that "from the 1840s onward, tactile, motor and olfactory experiences began to shape images of urban space more than did visual experience." With regard to portraits of Russian carnival, he continues: "Images of festive crowding . . . surfeit all the senses in equal measure; it is so jammed with people that it can be assimilated only through incessant pushing and touching; in it one's hearing wearies from cries, laughter, and music; food and drink are sold everywhere; mouths are chomping; one's eyes fail to follow it all. . . . Here, in the crowd, surrounded on all sides by gaudy placards, grimacing harlequins, hawkers' trays, fleeting faces, and other hodgepodge, one keeps turning one's head, one's gaze leaps incessantly, working more like a frantically snatching hand than a quiet contemplating eye. Here, therefore, tactile and motor experience the tone." G. Kaganov, *Images of Space: St. Petersburg in the Visual and Verbal Arts,* trans. S. Monas (Stanford, Calif.: Stanford University Press, 1997), 123, 132.

water and cabbage," across "entire seas of mud and dirt," and alongside walls festooned with thick spiderwebs and covered with oblong and bloody stains: the thin and brittle shells of "sacrifices." Cacophony attacks the ear, the province of buzzing flies, humming crickets, howling dogs, creaking floors, and "crying and banging" workmen. Additionally, the characters in "The Petersburg Corners" show a theatrical and carnivalesque cast. A landlady is like a vampire or witch: her cheeks are "pitted with blood"; saliva splashes from her face. A down-and-out teacher-poet (aka the "green man") compares to a clown or puppet. Hiccuping and burping; looking and smelling like a "whiskey bottle"; and sporting a red nose, with red hairs protruding from facial warts, and a head topped by a thick black mop with several bald spots, the teacher-poet is not unlike an "actor . . . with a favorite and well-learned role into life . . . comic to the point of caricature . . . inevitable for a man unsteady on his legs." Conventional morality and fiction are also scorned and denied. In what is seen as a swipe by Nekrasov against Bulgarin and other literary conservatives, the teacher postulates that virtue is praiseworthy and evil, vile; but in a way that is incoherent and facetious. In what is also recognized as Nekrasov's gibe against both fictional romanticism and classicism, the teacher talks of his time with "a cavalier of some kind" as well as with Gavrila Derzhavin and Alexander Izmailov.

Even more damnable, perhaps, because the teacher-poet writes hack laudatory verse in the style of Vasily Tredyakovsky and Vasily Petrov, he is, deservedly, tormented by his colleagues. Further in the spirit of theater and carnival, Nekrasov seeks additional "slaps in the face of public taste" by presenting a drunken peasant girl who, notwithstanding the "full and youthful bosom of a Balzac heroine," screams and thrashes wildly until she is subdued by the house serf. In still another jab at Bulgarin and his ilk, sexual license is also given a light touch with Nekrasov's portrait of a pregnant girl who, not unlike Defoe's Moll Flanders, likes her trysts "pure and simple . . . putting her heart and soul into everything she does." Even the admittedly painful issue of a woman dying in childbirth is offset by a comment that another girl, in response to the kindness of strangers, steals their handkerchiefs.

Ostensibly, Nekrasov's "The Petersburg Corners" points the way to Gorky's famous 1902 play *The Lower Depths* (*Na dne*), in which urban workers take issue with their harsh lives. Here, though, personal difficulties do not impede the fun. Like other characters in *Petersburg,* the individuals in Nekrasov's "corners" stage modest dramas: they wine and dine, sing and dance, kiss and hug, quarrel and fight. As is the case with other pieces in *Petersburg,* responsibility is a key issue. Indeed, what Nekrasov shows in "The Petersburg Corners" are the consequences of not working, of not taking hold of one's life. Society is not the issue; drunkenness, laziness, and immorality are. The ne'er-do-well Kir'yanich is not only forgiven debts by his master but also refuses jobs offered to him by others. A house serf arrives from the village, but instead of looking for work, he polishes off five or seven bottles (accounts vary) at his self-styled housewarming. The teacher-poet, formerly a "gifted and capable man," ruins himself with drink and finishes his days as a "dog who keeps licking his tail . . . his hat in one hand and the bottle in the other."

The Russian interest in physiologies and physiological writing continued through the decade. In 1847, for instance, Dostoevsky, realizing that many residents of St. Petersburg "had not left their neighborhood for ten years or more and were familiar only with the route to their place of work," bid them to "scrutinize the city more attentively, to study its physiognomy."[188] As did the writers of *Petersburg,* he, too, saw the imperial capital as a living cell-like entity: "an enormous number of little circles, each with its own regulations, sense of decorum, law, logic, and oracle."[189] To his physiological taste, his 1847 *Petersburg Chronicle* (*Peterburgskaia letopis'*) featured sketches of a societal spinster, a debt-ridden husband, a spoiled son, a consumptive girl, and, of course, a hapless dreamer. Dostoevsky was not alone in his physiological quest. Articles on Lavater[190] and others took their place among such fictional physiologies as *Here Are Ours! From Nature* (*Vot nashi! S natury,* 1845), *The Petersburg Miscellany* (*Peterburgskii sbornik,* 1846), *The First of April* (*Pervoe aprelia,* 1846), *Nevsky Almanac* (*Nevskii al'manakh,* 1846), *The Illustrated Almanac* (*Illiustrirovannyi al'manakh,* 1848), *The Mocker* (*Zuboskal,* 1848) and *Yesterday and Today* (*Vchera i segodnia,* 1848). Of these, the most important was *The Petersburg*

188. Dostoevskii, "Peterburgskaia letopis'," 21.

189. Ibid., 13.

190. See "Trakat o fizionomike," *Literaturnyi sbornik s illiustratsiiami* (St. Petersburg: Sovremennik, 1849), 143–210; E. Littre, "Vazhnost'i uspekhi fiziologii," reprint from French journal in *Sovremennik* 1, no. 2 (1847), otdel. 2, 125–64. Compare Belinsky's remark: "Stat'ia o fiziologii Littre—prelest'" (*Polnoe sobranie sochinenii,* vol. 12 [1956], 323).

Miscellany because, as is well known, it was also published by Nekrasov and introduced a writer and his first work to the reading public: Dostoevsky and his novel *Poor Folk.*[191]

The era of Russian physiologies, though, was fading quickly, ceding to new Russian tastes and exigencies, such as the prolonged, agonized reflection over the so-called eternal questions (*vechnye voprosy*) that were beginning to bedevil national life and that found expression in the rise of the great Russian novel.

It is safe to say, though, that *Petersburg,* along with other Russian fictional physiologies, deserves an honorable place in the history of Russian literature. Indeed, it is not implausible to assert that without such works, the transition from Russian romanticism to realism would have been delayed by as much as a decade; that viable writing about St. Petersburg and urban themes would have been lost amid newspapers and journals; and that conservative writers and critics would have set an enduring agenda for official attitudes on the imperial city and its inhabitants. It is also safe to say that without *Petersburg* and works of its type, the borders of the Russian realism of Pushkin, Lermontov, and Gogol would not have been stretched to accommodate the aforementioned novels of Goncharov (*A Common Story*) and Herzen (*Who Is to Blame?*), with their focus on middling types, as well as of the loose baggy monsters of Dostoevsky and Tolstoy, specifically their characters and scenes of Russia's imperial city.[192] "We know which way Raskolnikov turns when he leaves the apartment," Donald Fanger notes of Dostoevsky's *Crime and Punishment.* "We know which street he follows; we know the color of the pawnbroker's wallpaper. The tavern in which he plays cat and mouse (or mouse and cat) with Zametov, like the amusement park to which Svidrigailov resorts on the eve of his suicide, is not just the symbol for a state of mind. . . . [*Crime and Punishment*] is crammed

191. *The Petersburg Miscellany* also featured works by Belinsky, Herzen, and Turgenev, as well as translations of Shakespeare, Byron, and Goethe.

192. See Fanger, *Dostoevsky and Romantic Realism,* 193. Consider Boris Meilakh's claim that "extremely substantive was the role of so-called secondary writers or ordinary talents [of the 1840s in Russia] not only in initiating new themes [into literature] but also as reworking various elements of genres." B. Meilakh, *Russkaia povest' XIX veka: Istoriia i problematika zhanra* (Leningrad: Nauka, 1973), 254. Compare also Fanger's remark that the "early sixties saw a flood of literature, sketches, and feuilletons as well as stories and novels, devoted to the city. This literature was related, of course, to the 'physiological sketches' of the forties." Fanger, *Dostoevsky and Romantic Realism,* 189.

with the sort of detail that is a physiological sketch par excellence."[193] The preferred neighborhoods of Dostoevsky's fiction, Fanger continues, are the "middle- and lower-class sections . . . full of lodging houses, narrow streets, and alleys . . . little worlds in themselves."[194]

The story of the Russian physiological sketch does not end there, though. Rather, like a living organism, it adapted itself successfully to a variety of fictional conditions and environments. With the 1847 publication of Turgenev's "Khor and Khalinych," the first vignette of what would be his 1852 work *Notes of a Hunter* (*Zapiski okhotnika*), Russian readers encountered ordinary men and women also from the provinces. Later they would see elements of fictional physiology in the works of such writers as Anton Chekhov and Vsevelod Garshin in the late nineteenth century and of Isaac Babel, Mikhail Zoshchenko, Il'f and Petrov, and Alexander Tvardovsky in the twentieth. It also can be argued that the content and form of the Russian physiological sketch was seminal to national painting, music, and dance. Slices of life of everyday heroes and heroines figured prominently in the art of the Itinerants (*Peredvizhniki*), in the music of Modest Mussorgsky in his 1874 work *Pictures at an Exhibition* (*Kartinki s vystavki*), and in the scenes of Sergei Diaghilev for Igor Stravinsky's 1911 ballet *Petrushka.* In fact, the claim can be made that even the often faux monumentality of early postrevolutionary and Soviet literature, art, and film had at its roots the Russian physiological sketch: the daily lives of everyday people making their way in a brave, new world.

If anyone was grateful to Nekrasov and the other writers of *Petersburg,* it undoubtedly was the people whom his characters represented in its works. For the first time in the national written expression, such individuals were not seen as appendages to aristocratic and gentry worlds. No longer were they portrayed as servants, valets, and nannies who kept their masters clean and fed, listened to their cares and concerns, and kept them from hurting themselves. Rather, in *Petersburg,* ordinary heroes and heroines appeared as individuals with minds and hearts of their own and with a grasp of life, its adventure and its possibilities—a sense of self and purpose far superior to those of the masters they served.

193. Fanger, *Dostoevsky and Romantic Realism,* 130.
194. Ibid., 132.

For all the divergent views and opinions expressed in *Petersburg,* there is a common theme: middling Russia, for all the darkness of the regime of Nicholas I, is alive and well. Its constituents are a vital, irrepressible force of ambition, energy, and fun, individuals who see the damned questions of "Who is at fault?" and "What is to be done?" as totally inconsequential and who get on with the prosaics of existence by living life in the fullest, most carnivalesque way.

In this new evaluation, *Petersburg* still deserves to be seen as a manifesto and seedbed of the Natural school in Russian literature. Such a claim, though, also argues for a more expansive and balanced assessment of Russian urban realism in the 1840s. The writers of *Petersburg,* as key figures in the Natural school, should no longer be seen as grim Gogollights who, on good days, provided an "honest treatment of 'ordinary' life among the lower classes of society . . . [as well as] a compassionate attitude toward the poor" and who, on bad ones, sowed the seeds for the "populist utilitarianism"[195] in the national written expression with "the correct presentation of Russian life: its poverty, social injustice, moral perversion . . . and extreme banality . . . without a breath of the positive spirit of existence . . . its vitality . . . [and] resilience."[196]

Like the great masters of Russian realism, Nekrasov and the other writers of *Petersburg* did not shy away from misery, physical or spiritual. They were careful, though, periodically to part the clouds and to show that life is a swirl of darkness and light, good and bad, and that, particularly in moments of carnival, it is very much worth living. That such a message appears in a fictional physiology rather than in a more extended work of Russian writing does not lessen its import or value. Just the opposite: it is something that all readers, middling or otherwise, Russian or not, in 1845 or later, always need to hear. It is particularly apt for the people of

195. V. Terras, *The Young Dostoevsky (1846–1849): A Critical Study* (The Hague: Mouton, 1969), 101.

196. Ibid., 205. Nor should the contributors to *Petersburg* be seen, again as proponents of the Natural school, as vaunting a "gray and depressing tonality . . . with the inclemencies of the Petersburg climate and the shabby squalor in whose midst its poorer inhabitants dwelled"; or as indulging in "muckraking . . . as delineating much of Russian life precisely in terms of the contract between a glistening surface of impeccable virtue and an underside of vicious corruption"; or, the ultimate, as bemoaning how "absolutism . . . strikes out self-respect and crushes inevitably the idyllic dream of a tranquilly mediocre private existence." J. Frank, *Dostoevsky: The Seeds of Revolt, 1821–1849* (Princeton, N.J.: Princeton University Press), 222, 322.

St. Petersburg: their triumphs and tragedies, political, social, and aesthetic; and most important, perhaps, their own strivings to realize carnival (and all that it means) in life. "The notion of freedom, perhaps phantasmagorical, but very full, inevitably arises in the consciousness of anyone living there," the Nobel laureate Joseph Brodsky once told a friend about Russia's northern capital. In this city, he added, "the individual is always going to strive to reach beyond."[197] In *Petersburg,* Nekrasov and his fellow contributors sought nothing less.

197. S. Volkov, *Conversations with Joseph Brodsky: A Poet's Journey Through the Twentieth Century,* trans. by Marian Schwartz (New York: Free Press, 1998), 273.

PETERSBURG: THE PHYSIOLOGY OF A CITY

Introduction

Vissarion Belinsky

Russian literature has often been reproached for its indifference to national themes. Such an accusation is both just and unjust. In actuality, does our country really have that many books from which one could study or simply come to know the many facets of the Russian way of life, of Russian society? We ask further: Where are these books on our country? They do not exist.[1] Russian literature hardly seemingly offers more on the historical and moral life of other countries than it does on Russia. We have in mind works that make up our *light literature,* so called because it occupies the spare time of most readers and satisfies their needs. In this light literature, we do not include aesthetic works, creations of art in the strict sense of the word. Thus, when we speak of the absence of literature which would acquaint Russians with their way of life, we do not have in mind those poetic creations which reflect Russian society and of which Russian literature can be so justly proud. For example: we have Fonvizin's comedies; Griboyedov's *Woe from Wit;* several of Pushkin's poetic works ("Count Nulin," *Evgeny Onegin,* "The Little House in Kolomna," and "The Genealogy of My Hero") as well as several of his novellas and stories in prose ("The Queen of Spades," *The Captain's Daughter,* "Dubrovsky," "A History of the Village of Goriukhino"); Gogol's comedies, stories, and his

1. Here Belinsky conveniently ignores the more than eight hundred governmental publications on life and mores in Russia, including Mikhail Zhdanov's *Travel Notes Through Twenty-Two Regions in Russia* (*Putevye zapiski po Rossii v dvadtsati dvukh guberniiakh*), which he reviewed in 1843. See V. Belinskii, "Putevye zapiski po Rossii," in Belinskii, *Polnoe sobranie sochinenii,* vol. 7 (1955), 25–26.

novel, *Dead Souls;* Lermontov's *A Hero of Our Time;* and finally, several other works of more or less remarkable talents.[2] Such writings, even if they were considerably fewer, would be in even greater demand. Nonetheless, we really cannot complain of the poverty of our literature because the appearance of great writers in our society does not depend on the will or wishes of its readers. We can, though, reproach or disapprove of the choice of subjects to which ordinary (and for that reason, more numerous) talents devote their pens. It is here that the public is most dissatisfied with our literature.

In truth, we have enough historical novels which acquaint the public with Russia's past, with its diverse epochs.[3] We have an even greater number of satiric and "manners" novels which enlighten the public about the mores of contemporary society—entire volumes of all kinds of descriptive, satiric, and humorous stories. But these sheer numbers do not resolve our dilemma in the least. For instance, we do not find anything in our historical novels besides historical names, much less anything resembling ancient Rus'. What we have, primarily, are crude attempts in imitation of the novels of Walter Scott,[4] sketches in which historical truth is sacrificed for a romanticism that has little to do with Russian life. Furthermore, our writers of historical novels have limited themselves to Karmazin's *History of the Russian State,*[5] perusing it for several days before they sit down to work.

2. Alexander Griboyedov wrote *Woe from Wit* (*Gore ot uma*) in 1822–23. Alexander Pushkin penned "Count Nulin" ("Graf Nulin") in 1825, "Little House in Kolomna" ("Domik v Kolomne"), and "A History of the Village of Goriukhino" ("Istoriia sela Goriukhino") in 1830, *Eugene Onegin* (*Evgeny Onegin*) in 1823–31, "The Queen of Spades" ("Pikovaia dama") and "The Genealogy of my Hero" ("Rodoslovnaia moego geroia") in 1833, "Dubrovsky" in 1834, and *The Captain's Daughter* (*Kapitanskaia dochka*) in 1836. Mikhail Lermontov's *A Hero of Our Time* (*Geroi nashego vremeni*) appeared in 1840, and Nikolai Gogol's *Dead Souls* (*Mertvye dushi*) appeared in 1842.

3. Belinsky reviewed the works of such Russian "historical" writers as Bulgarin and Polevoi, as well as of those of Nikolai Grech, Mikhail Zagoskin, Ivan Lazhechnikov (the "Russian Walter Scott"), and Alexander Veltman in his article "Russian Literature in 1843" ("*Russkaia literatura v 1843 g.*"). See Belinskii, *Polnoe sobranie sochinenii,* vol. 8 (1955), 52–57.

4. The works of Walter Scott were wildly popular in Russia from the 1820s onward. In fact, Belinsky so approved of Scott's novels that he not only placed them above the works of both Pushkin and Gogol but also insisted that they were more trustworthy than scholarly historical works. For instance, Belinsky wrote in 1843 that Scott's writings "read like history," whereas historical studies were often like "bad fairy tales, in which everything follows some strange magic, not the laws of rational necessity." See Belinskii, *Polnoe sobranie sochinenii,* vol. 6 (1955), 53.

5. Karamzin wrote his twelve-volume *History of the Russian State* (*Istoriia gosudarstva rossiskogo*) between 1818 and 1826.

The so-called novels of "manners" are no better. We do not know what is in them, but we do know that they do not depict the mores of Russian society. Everything that these works depict might just as easily have occurred—or not have occurred—in China, Abyssinia, under the water, or in the clouds, as in Russia. They neither satirize nor critique mores because they are without opinions, ideas, and significance for Russian society. Instead, these works contain only trifling gibes and schoolboy grumblings; they ignore provocative ideas as well as the striking contradictions between our European appearance and our Asiatic essence. Specifically, our novels of "manners" focus upon coiffures à la muzhik, eyeglasses, lorgnettes, mustaches, tufted beards below the lip, and similarly irrelevant accoutrements of fashion. They highlight paragons of virtue and malice whose names recall the proverb: *You can tell a dog by its fur;* and who let readers know what lies ahead. In these novels of "manners," there are no genuine people, no characters whose simplicity and actions ever transcend mere paper heroes of virtue. There are also no heroes and heroines who, from the goodness of their hearts and without any malice, inadvertently cause more evil than all the contrived monsters of vice in the world. "Manners" essays and articles are numerous but poor in quality. They tend to be descriptive, didactic, satiric, and humorous; they are also simple rhetorical expansions on some moral theme.[6] Because of the narrow focus of these "manners" essays, we are completely lacking in such artistic accounts of travel or excursions, essays, stories, and descriptions. Such works, however, would acquaint readers with the many regions of our boundless and diverse Russia. They would depict its many climates, its many people and tribes, its many beliefs and customs. They would portray the Russian population not as being one great mass but as having multiple, contradictory, and diverse strata—all striking the eye with their endless nuances.

Although writers have attempted works of this more informative cast, all of them—from Prince Shalikov's sentimental "Journey to Little Russia" to Marlinsky's turgid "A Trip to Revel"—can be considered inconsequential.[7] But our vast Russia offers so many materials for this type of fiction!

6. See, for example, Belinsky's stinging reviews of Bulgarin's feuilletons and his novel *Ivan Vyzhigin* (1828).

7. Pyotr Shalikov published "Journey to Little Russia" ("Puteshestvie v Malorossiiu") in 1803–4 and Alexander Bestuzhev-Marlinsky's "A Trip to Revel" ("Poezdka v Revel' ") in 1821.

Great Russia, Little Russia, White Russia, New Russia, Finland, the Baltic provinces, the Crimea, the Caucasus, Siberia—they are all entire worlds, distinctive in their climate and nature, in their languages and dialects, in their customs and mores, and especially in the mixture of the purely Russian element with diverse other elements, some indigenous, others completely alien! In addition, our great Russia abounds not only with variations in climate but also in social respects! The northern belt of Russia is quite different from the central, and the central from the south. If one crosses from Arkhangel'sk to Astrakhan, from the Caucasus to the region of the Urals, or from Finland to the Crimea, the differences are so vast that it is as if one is crossing from one world to another. Moscow and Petersburg, Kazan and Kharkov, Arkhangelsk and Odessa: What sharp contrasts they present! What food for the observant mind, for the humorous pen!

In France, for some reason, not a single book has focused on that country's outlying regions, fascinating though they may be in every respect. Writings on Paris, however, make up a large and independent literature. Who is not familiar with *The Book of the One Hundred and One,*[8] which has brought together the works of almost all the great, middling, and minor writers of France into an anthology and which depicts Paris in short fiction, stories, and humorous essays? Not long ago, Jules Janin published a splendid album entitled *A Summer in Paris;*[9] and now the recently published, illustrated work *The Devil in Paris* also focuses on the French capital. Just to count all the works of this type that are now being published in France would be difficult. The work *The French: A Self-Portrait* depicts the social mores of France in general. And, about twenty years ago, remember how many different *Hermits* there were—*Hermits* on Paris, *Hermits* on London, and God knows how many other types of *Hermits*! These older works were enthusiastically translated into Russian; and such individuals as

8. *The Book of the One Hundred and One* (more accurately, *Paris; or The Book of the One Hundred and One* [*Paris ou le Livre de Cent-et-un*]) was a highly successful fifteen-volume work that was published between 1831 and 1834 and that contained the works of 101 French writers, including François-René de Chateaubriand, Victor Hugo, Jules Gabriel Janin, Alphonse Karr, and others (including an essay by James Fenimore Cooper). The contributors to *The Book of the One Hundred and One* commented on the topography, population, and institutions of Paris, often from a satirical point of view.

9. *A Summer in Paris* (*Un été à Paris*) was a richly illustrated collection of essays that was compiled by Janin in 1844 and that contained pieces by Honoré de Balzac, George Sand, and Eugène Sue on Parisian urban and social life.

"The Luzhniki Elders" and "The Inhabitants of Gallery Row"[10] and others imitated them in this country. Unfortunately, the authors of these imitations limited their efforts to magazine-type articles, and Russian readers could hardly find anything uniquely Russian, that is to say, anything which would acquaint them with Russian society and consequently with themselves. In a similar way, the circumstances that led to the appearance of *The Book of the One Hundred and One* in Paris also gave rise to the publication of *One Hundred Russian Writers*[11] here in Petersburg. This undertaking is already in its second volume, but it has not succeeded in showing the public even twenty Russian men of letters. It sought to resurrect *A Discourse of Russian Writers;*[12] but it has come to an even more lamentable end than the original. *Ours, as Copied from Nature by the Russians* appeared after *The French: A Self-Portrait;* and, despite some awkward errors, it offered several more or less satisfactory articles. *Ours,* however, appeared slowly and now has disappeared altogether, God knows why.

What is the reason for all these failures? There are many, not one; but the crucial one is that these works do not offer a faithful view of the society they are trying to portray. More surprisingly, the contributors to these works could readily have found a truthful perspective on society in the works of several Russian writers who have grasped the mysteries of Russian reality. However strange it might sound, Russian literature is undoubtedly richer in works of genius than in works of ordinary talents. Who better than Gogol can acquaint readers with the peculiar character of Russians and Ukrainians? Do you particularly wish to investigate Petersburg? Have you read his "Nevsky Prospekt," *The Notes of a Madman,* "The Nose," "The Morning of a Businessman," "A Fragment," and finally, "Leaving the

10. "The Luzhniki Elders" (*Luzhnitskie startsy*) was the collective pseudonym for such writers as Mikhail Kachenovsky, Mikhail Pogodin, and others from the journal *Herald of Europe* (*Vestnik Evropy*) in the 1820s. Similarly, the "Inhabitant of Gallery Row" (*Zhitel' Galernoi gavani*) was the pseudonym for Orest Somov in his writing.

11. *One Hundred Russian Writers* (*Sto russkikh literaturov*) was the project of the famous publisher Alexander Smirdin to shore up the shaky state of his finances. Originally, *One Hundred Writers* was to consist of ten volumes, with each tome containing works by ten writers. Despite pieces by Pushkin, Bestuzhev-Marlinsky, Polevoi, Denis Davydov, Nikolai Nadezhdin, and others, *One Hundred Writers* was a failure. Only three volumes of the work materialized between 1839 and 1845.

12. *A Discourse of Russian Writers*—more accurately, *A Russian Discourse, A Collection of Works by Russian Writers* (*Russkaia beseda, sobranie sochinenii russkikh literaturov*)—was another venture by Smirdin; it appeared in three volumes between 1841 and 1843.

Theater"?[13] In these works you will find all the people whom God created nowhere else but in Petersburg. Do you wish to study Moscow, not only its mundane and incidental features but also its soul? Read *Woe from Wit.*[14] In *Dead Souls,* you will come to know the Russian provinces as you never would have known them, even had you lived there for fifty years. In *Onegin,* you will concentrate on Russian society in one moment of its development. In *A Hero of Our Time,* you will see the society from *Onegin,* but from a new perspective. Say you wish to known the Caucasus as if it were your homeland—read Pushkin and Lermontov.

One cannot say, however, that these geniuses stand completely alone; but neither are they surrounded by a sizable or brilliant retinue of talents who could act as intermediaries between them and the public. That is to say, there are few transitional writers who could adapt the ideas of these geniuses and thus travel closely on the road that these geniuses have paved. Such writers of middling talent are quite few in our country. Several are truly remarkable in their splendor and strength; others, though less forceful and gifted, are successful because they know Russian life well and portray it faithfully. Of this latter group we have only a few, even though our literature needs them most of all. Hence our fictional undertakings at present lack substance and offer our public nothing insightful to read. A great talent, especially a genius, is motivated by inspiration and capriciously follows his own road. He cannot be invited to collaborate in the publishing of a book, nor can he be told: "Write an article about life in Petersburg because what you propose for our book is unsuitable and something we cannot use." If great talents were to be absorbed thus, we would need many geniuses and great talents to satisfy the vital daily demands of the leisurely reading public and to ensure that they would never be lacking for artistic works. Sometimes a writer of genius appears only once in an entire century. But does this mean that society must do without literature during this time? Of course not!

13. Gogol wrote "Nevsky Prospekt" ("Nevskii Prospekt") and *Notes of a Madman* (*Zapsiki sumasshedshego*) in 1835, "The Nose" ("Nos"), "Leaving the Theater" ("Teatral'nyi raz"ezd"), and "The Morning of a Businessman" ("Utro delovogo cheloveka") in 1836, and "A Fragment" ("Otryvok") between 1840 and 1842.

14. Alexander Griboyedov published *Woe from Wit* (*Gore ot uma*) in 1833.

Literature, in the broad sense of this word, constitutes an entire lively world filled with diversity and nuance. It can, like nature, be classified into genus and species, into classes and subclasses, ranging from the enormous dimensions of an elephant to the minuscule proportions of a hummingbird. Poor is the literature that does not shine with the names of geniuses. Furthermore, a literature cannot be considered rich if all its fictional pieces are the works of a genius or if all its writings are commonplace and lacking in talent. Ordinary talents are indispensable to a rich literature; the more of them, the better. But—we repeat—we have too few of these, and thus our public has nothing to read.[15] Unfortunately, an ordinary talent does not possess sufficient intellect, knowledge, or education to sustain a more or less original and faithful view of things. He is thus completely unnoticed in the first stages of his career, or he stagnates. Equally regrettable, remarkable talents often appear, but they never amount to anything because, except for their native talent, they offer nothing of depth, even when examined under a microscope.

All this is especially relevant to our literature, and particularly to the surprising dearth of respectable works to satisfy the urgent demands of the public—despite the (relatively) striking wealth of truly sublime and artistic works already in print. The reproaches of the public are justified. Moreover, with the exception of journals, we are completely lacking in respectable publications that include the works of several individuals and which focus upon a single goal. Such compilations are common in French literature. Again, the reproaches of the public are in order. Readers fault our men of letters for their spirit of isolation and their inability to work together. There is a grain of truth in this. But what is to be done if this isolation is more often rooted in differences of education, motivation, and understanding than, as we have grown accustomed to believe, in mercenary schemes?

Profit binds as well as separates people; it cannot, therefore, be regarded as an insurmountable obstacle to congenial, collaborative activity. True, the disruptive and polemical attitudes which characterize our writers

15. In a review of *Petersburg,* Konstantin Aksakov could not resist the temptation not only to feign surprise at the great critic's concern over the paucity of "ordinary talents" in Russian literature but also to insist that Belinsky and the other contributors to the work had no cause for worry over such a perceived lack because *Petersburg* "was completely ordinary." K. Aksakov, " 'Fiziologiia Peterburga,' sostavlennaia iz trudov russkikh literaturov," in *Estetika i literaturnaia kritika* (Moscow: Iskusstvo, 1995), 110.

do militate against collaboration, but these attitudes arise from the indefinite, unascertainable, and variegated character of our very social life. In the social arena, one finds that advanced education clashes with crass ignorance, profound erudition with superficial half-knowledge, passionate assertiveness with an abysmal absence of any kind of opinion, and noble striving with mercenary calculation. Genius and banality, talent and mediocrity enjoy equal success. Even people who have an urge to collaborate—their talents and noble strivings—cannot get along. One is an Anglophile in his literary views; a second recognizes nothing besides German literature and particularly hates French fiction; a third wants to know nothing other than French literature. Just look at the differences that exist even among our men of letters in their attitudes toward Russian literature. One reverences writers of the old school and sees sublime models of literature only in Lomonosov, Derzhavin, and Karmazin. A second adds the name of Zhukovsky and looks askance at Pushkin.[16] A third coldly despises older writers and does so all in the name of Pushkin. A fourth, admiring the new writers, looks with hostility at the old ones. A fifth marvels at Pushkin's genius and does not understand how anyone can praise Gogol's "farces" (*The Inspector General* and *Dead Souls*).[17] In all this confusion, one sees social immaturity more than ignorance or narrow-mindedness, but in no way can mercenary motives be ascribed as the basis for these divergent opinions. And, truthfully, how can readers censure men of letters for the very differences that divide the readers among themselves? Literature, after all, is an expression of society, and its assets and liabilities are also the assets and liabilities of society itself.

The reasons for the inactivity of our writers and the consequential poverty of our literature—also include the hypersensitivity of readers, a shortcoming which arises from our amorphous and immature social life. Readers hastily identify real-life people and allusions in much that is playful, amusing, witty, and humorous. No matter what they read, such easily incensed readers exclaim: "How can such a thing be written? How can such a thing be published?" For instance, Gogol, in his fantastic story "The Nose," initially wanted to expound upon the subject of educated

16. The individual in question is Faddei Bulgarin.

17. Here Belinsky is referring to Polevoi. Gogol's *The Inspector General* (*Revizor*) appeared in 1836.

collegiate assessors; but he decided to say nothing at all about this interesting topic because, in his words, "Russia is such a marvelous land that if one were to talk about one collegiate assessor, then all collegiate assessors, from Riga to Kamchatka, would undoubtedly take offense. The same thing would happen with all ranks and titles." In *Dead Souls,* Gogol expressed himself even more sharply when he tried to justify why he had not given names to two of the women in the novel. He wrote: "The author finds it extremely difficult to name both women in such a way so as not to offend people as he did previously. To bestow a last name on a fictional character is a dangerous thing. It is a wonder to behold: No matter what name one thinks up, there can invariably be found someone in some corner of our kingdom who bears it, and he will become angry to the point of death. He will say that the author visited him on the sly to find out everything about him, for example, that he goes about in a sheepskin coat, that he calls upon some Agrafena Ivanovna, and that he loves to eat. And God forbid that a writer should name his character by rank! That is all the more dangerous. All ranks and titles are now so irksome to us that everything, no matter how it looks on the printed page, seems to have someone specific in mind. Such is the mood at present. Suffice it to say that if a certain town has a stupid person among its citizens, everyone knows who he is. Suddenly a man of respectful countenance will jump up and cry: 'After all, I am also a person, therefore I must be stupid.' In short, he is all too quick to get the point."[18]

In truth, the hypersensitivity of our readers is one of the most characteristic, most striking, and most comic aspects of our immature social life. Despite all our concerns for balls, meetings, clubs, street festivals, cafe-restaurants, concerts, and theaters—activities which often take up our entire life and fortune—we do not as yet have the slightest understanding of *public awareness.* That is why all our balls, meetings, festivals, and the like elicit such pedantic boredom and cause them to resemble stuffy ceremonial festivals. At such events, we chase after rank more than merriment. Pushkin said it so well: "We try to be humble but with dignity."[19] The French know how to live and make merry; but, for this ability, they are

18. In these citations, Belinsky is citing, with some license, from the second chapter of "The Nose" and the ninth chapter of *Dead Souls.*

19. Belinsky is citing from Pushkin's unfinished prose sketch, "The Guests Were Gathering at the Dacha" ("Gosti s"ezzhalis' na dachu"), written in 1828.

reproached as children. The French, though, do not think that only children know how to amuse themselves, nor do they fret that adults who wish to have a good time must necessarily be like children. Thus, if one credits the French for their ability to make merry, one may not fault them for the fact that they can be childlike. Indeed, they are children who are intelligent, dear, witty, and alive! Such a feature, by the way, does not prevent them also from being adults and extremely serious adults at that. The French have captured the secret of how to be important without pedantry and how to amuse themselves without pretense, with enthusiasm and ease. The French find it necessary to laugh at everything—even at themselves. In no way does this arise from the vulgar gaiety for which the French of the last century were so rightfully condemned; rather, it comes precisely from their absence of pettiness and pedantry. Show a Frenchman the funniest caricature of himself—and he will be the first to laugh at it good-naturedly. More than anything else in the world, the Frenchman loves the social and public life and to be amused at its expense. He knows that humor exists in everything and that one can laugh at the absurd. This inherent wittiness is why France is the source of so many sensible and important works and why it furnishes all of Europe and the entire educated world with light reading. This wittiness is also why we Russians are not alone when we follow everything, including the slightest ripples in the stream of French life, with such diligence. Indeed, we know the French light touch better than we do many things in our own country. Such an interest is understandable and natural. How can one not know his neighbor when this neighbor turns everything inside out and when he, so cheerfully and easily, reveals not only his good sides but also his weaknesses? Conversely, how can one know anything about someone who hides everything? From this point of view, therefore, we believe that for the public to reproach the inactivity of our writers and the paucity of our literature is hardly justified since the reasons for these shortcomings lie as much, if not more so, with readers as with writers.

It is hardly feasible, though, to sit, be calm, and do nothing over such a discomforting outcome. In such a case, it is more praiseworthy to write a "trifle," that is, to do what one can rather than merely to do nothing. Sometimes the attempt to do *something* (in the unlikelihood of doing something better) demands more courage and merit than the proud decision to insist on doing what one would like to do or to fail to do anything at all.

Be that as it may, while we wait for the long-hoped-for activity of our literary talents, we, for the lack of something better, ask the public's gracious attention to this book: an attempt to capture Petersburg in several essays on its characteristic features. The subject is entertaining and important. It takes great talent, observation, and ability to write. In a word, the subject demands more, perhaps, than the contributors to this book can give. So of what value would this book be? If our work turns out to be completely unsatisfactory, let others do something better. In such a case, our work will not be in vain if it will awaken the latent talent of our more gifted writers and motivate the appearance of a truly good book.

Our endeavor, meanwhile, has been made all the more difficult if only because, until now, no book of this type has appeared in Russia. True, Petersburg has been described time and again as regards its climate, topography, medical facilities, and the like. For instance, Mr. Bashchutsky, in his *Panorama of Petersburg,* attempted not only to describe the *external appearance* of our first capital (streets, buildings, homes, rivers, canals, bridges, and so forth, together with a historical overview of the construction and growth of the city) but also to give a glimpse of the characteristic features of Petersburg life and mores. Bashchutsky's undertaking was extremely useful and splendidly begun; but for some reason, it was not fated to be completed—not to mention the fact that since the time of its publication, Petersburg has changed a great deal. Furthermore, Mr. Bashchutsky's book had as its primary goal to *describe* Petersburg, not to *characterize* the city. Indeed, its tone was more official than literary. By contrast, the content of our book seeks not to *describe* Petersburg but primarily to *characterize* its mores and the distinguishing features of its population. Earlier we said that the moral physiognomy of Petersburg was portrayed with aesthetic fullness and depth in many of Gogol's writings. Many of its features and characteristics have also been captured, more or less successfully, in the writings of other authors, for example, Count Odoevsky, Count Sollogub, the Cossack Lugansky, and Mr. Panaev. In no way, though, do these writers make our book superfluous; for if all these other works were compiled into a single volume, they would not comprise an adequate whole, nor would they be written with the same purpose that we have put forth here.

Taken separately, the goal of each of these writers stemmed from a poetic thought that is brought to life by characters and events. The writings of Gogol, however, do not have a narrow or exclusive goal. They acquaint readers not only with the Petersburg citizen but also with humankind and the Russian. The natural compass of this goal is possible only for a great writer. Other more or less talented authors can attempt such a goal, but they cannot compete with an artist! As regards the individual contributors to this present work, they make no pretenses to poetic or artistic talent. Their goal is a most modest one—namely, to create a book of the type that so often appears in French literature and which, having momentarily captured the public's attention, gives rise to similar new books. The contributors to this work hope that readers will find in several if not in all our essays on Petersburg life accurate observations and more or less faithful renderings of the subjects which the authors have undertaken to represent. Concerning those articles in our work which have been signed by famous authors—these names suggest the merits of these works, but we offer them to the public for their judgment.

Moscow has been the subject of artistic renderings less often than Petersburg, but in certain regards, it has been more blessed than its sister-capital in characteristic representations of its physiognomy. Recently, there have appeared at least two complete physiological works on Moscow. One of them—*Moscow and Muscovites*[20]—was compiled by Mr. Zagoskin. To expound at length on this work is inappropriate. Let us only say that despite all its merits, ones that fully justify the fame enjoyed by its writer, the work has a glaring deficiency, that is, it describes neither Moscow nor Muscovites.[21] A second book, *Essays of Muscovite Life,* bears a new literary name, one Mr. Vistengof.[22] It occasionally reveals Mr. Vistengof's

20. Mikhail Zagoskin's *Moscow and Muscovites: The Notes of Bogdan Iliych Bel'sky* (*Moskva i moskvichi: Zapiski Bogdana Il'icha Bel'skogo*) came out in four parts from 1842 to 1850. It was reprinted in 1988.

21. In all fairness, Zagoskin's *Moscow and Muscovites* had its fans among conservative writers and readers. A reviewer from the *Northern Bee* praised the work for its "powerful Russian patriotism and fiery love for Moscow"; whereas a critic from *Literary Gazette* (*Literaturnaia gazeta*) vaunted it both as a "voice crying in the wilderness" and as a "conversation of a father or an honored elder with his children" about the patriarchal past and virtues of Russia as a fitting contrast to those of the "depraved West." "Smes': Zhurnal'naia viachina," *Severnaia pchela,* no. 12 (1843): 45; "Moskva i moskvichi," *Literaturnaia gazeta,* no. 23 (1844): 396.

22. Pyotr Vistengof wrote *Essays of Muscovite Life* (*Ocherki moskovskoi zhizni*) in 1842. Like many of the fictional physiologists of the era, Vistengof presented the denizens of Russia's ancient capital as colorful components of a carefree, ordered society in which all know their place and do not indulge in theft, drunkenness, and other vices. As might be expected, much of the work was superficial and tedious, with bland listings, hasty travelogues, and little sustained description, dialogue, or emotion. Characters

remarkable talent for observation and his ability to seize upon the characteristics of Muscovite society. Mr. Vistengof, though, lacks a definite perspective, which would have come to the fore had he not only observed but also judged his milieu.[23]

Thoughts that are one-sided, antiquated, or hackneyed—or, the absence of thought altogether—these are the shortcomings of our current light literature. Whether or not in the work submitted here we have managed to avoid these shortcomings (especially the latter), let the public judge. We can state that we have attempted only what has been within our power; and, if these two volumes find readers, then other volumes will follow.

—V. G. Belinsky

---

show little independence, change, or drive. Lower classes are typed by sickness and disease; bureaucrats are divided between those who drink and those who do not. Even in *Essays,* though, Vistengof was not alien to a sense of carnival, with scenes of balls, masquerades, and *gulian'ia* taking their place among portraits of clowns, magicians, and dancing dogs.

23. Concerning *Essays of Muscovite Life,* a reviewer from the *Northern Bee* was less complimentary. "If here you wish to see 'Mother-Moscow,'" the anonymous critic wrote in 1847, "with its golden cupolas, its revelry, and hospitality . . . you will be disappointed in the extreme. Mr. Vistengof's book depicts Moscow in the way that others depict Ivan the Great on snuffboxes and Muscovite mores in vaudevilles and comedies. . . . *Essays of Russian Life* . . . is merely a supplement of Muscovite life drawn from French physiologies and the novels of Paul de Kock." *Severnaia pchela,* no. 90 (1847), as quoted in Tseitlin, *Stanovlenie realizma,* 168.

Petersburg and Moscow

Vissarion Belinsky

Our ancestors were forcibly acquainted with *God's noblemen* in bloody battles on the shores of the Neva.[1] They never imagined, of course, that these wild, barren, low-lying, and swampy shores were destined to give rise to the Russian Empire, just as they never imagined that the Muscovite kingdom would someday become that very empire.[2] After all, how could they imagine such a thing? Who can know beforehand the birth of genius? And how could the masses discern the course of genius, even though this genius is nothing other than the thought, intellect, spirit, and will

1. Belinsky is referring to the Knights of the Livonian Order who, in the thirteenth century, waged war with the Russians on the shores of the Neva and the Baltic Sea and who were defeated by Alexander Nevsky and his troops on the ice of Lake Chud in 1242.

It should also be noted that Belinsky's "tale of two cities" received strong reviews from critics. A reviewer from the *Literary Gazette* wrote on April 5, 1845, that "by its profound thought, faithful outlook, and splendid exposition and goal, 'Petersburg and Moscow' occupies the first place in the work." Another from the *Finnish Herald* likewise acclaimed Belinsky's "extremely faithful and sharp characterization of both our capitals." *Finskii vestnik,* vol. 3, otdel., VI, 37; as quoted in I. Oksman, *Letopis' zhizni i tvorchestva V.G. Belinskogo* (Moscow: Gosudarstvennoe izdatel'stvo khudozhestvennoi literatury, 1958), 402–3.

Faddei Bulgarin, though, could not resist the opportunity to take a swipe at both Belinsky and his piece. "The well-known collaborator of *The Fatherland Notes,*" Bulgarin sniffed, "hailed for both his criticism and his noble, transcendental philosophy, has compared Petersburg and Moscow in sixty pages." F. Bulgarin, "Zhurnal'naia vsiakaia vsiachina," *Severnaia pchela,* no. 79 (1845): 314.

2. To such a claim, a reviewer from the *Northern Bee* wrote, "Belinsky begins [his piece] in surprise . . . that the shores of the Neva gave rise to the Russian Empire. Not the Russian empire, but Petersburg, Mr. Physiologist!" . . . 'Petersburg and Moscow' reads like the first essay of a schoolchild still in the gymnasium." "Smes'. Prodolzhenie razbora knigi: 'Fiziologiia Peterburga,'" *Severnaia pchela,* no. 235 (1845): 939.

of the very masses themselves? Moreover, how can the masses also grasp this incongruity, that is, everything that is nascently hidden within them today, and that impresses them as vague presentiments which will move to distinct consciousness?

For instance, by the end of the seventeenth century, the Muscovite kingdom contrasted markedly with the governments of Europe. Also, it could no longer move along on the rusty wheels of its Asiatic apparatus: that period of its history was over. But the Russian people had to continue, for in them was planted the seed of a great future. And so God raised from the masses a genius who joined them to Europe. As with all great people, Peter the Great appeared at the right time for Russia, but he differed from other great individuals in many ways. Peter's talents; his gigantic stature; his proud, majestic appearance; his vastly creative mind, and his overriding will were very much like the homeland in which he was born: a boundless expanse but not yet united organically. Such a shortcoming mirrored the people that Peter was destined to mold: a great people but with only a vague presentiment of its great future. Peter had to create himself, but the means for his self-development were not to be found in the social facets of his homeland; for them, he had to go outside. His first mentor was *negation.*[3] The utter boors and fanatics of Peter's time accused him of having contempt for his country, but they were wrong. Peter was tightly bound to Russia by an instinctive and invisible sense of his great mission in the future. He passionately loved the Rus', for whom his noble election by God made him spokesman. In the Russia of his day, though, Peter saw two nations—the one that he had acquired and the one that he would create. To the latter he gave his mind, his blood, his sweat, his labor, his life, and all the happiness and joys of his existence. Peter became a student of Europe, but he was Russian in his soul. He refuted the opinions of the feebleminded (many of whom still exist even now) who contended that the Europeanism of Russians would make them non-Russians—with the

3. Here Belinsky is borrowing from the dialectic of Georg Hegel, who understood "negation" as a necessary condition for progress. Consider also the great critic's remark: "Negation is my God." Quoted in H. Bowman, *Vissarion Belinski, 1811–1848: A Study in the Origins of Social Criticism in Russia* (Cambridge, Mass.: Harvard University Press, 1954), 124.

consequent implication that everything Russian could be sustained only by the savage and ignorant forms of Asiatic life.[4]

Moscow, the capital of the Muscovite kingdom—Moscow, by its very location in the center of Russia—could not conform to Peter's views, to his universal and radical reforms. Furthermore, Peter needed a capital on the sea. But he had no sea, since the northern and eastern oceans, as well as the Caspian Sea, could in no way facilitate the union of Russia and Europe. A new sea had to be won quickly. For conquest, Peter had two seas in the mind—the Black and the Baltic. For the first, he needed the full allegiance of the Ukraine, not just its external protection. Such a feat was accomplished only with the betrayal of Mazepa.[5] Peter also needed to seize the Crimea from the Turks and to take control of the vast steppe deserts surrounding the Black Sea. Occupation of these lands, though, meant their colonization: a task that was quite inopportune! Moreover, where would this strategy have led? A capital on the Black Sea would have joined Russia to Turkey, not Europe. Such a scheme would also have extended Russia's dominion to the point that we would have had a capital, so to speak, in another kingdom. The Baltic Sea, by contrast, did not present such difficulties. The countries on its shores were long familiar with the Russian sword and long splattered with Russian blood. If these lands had remained in foreign hands, and if the Baltic Sea had not become Russia's border, our country would have been forever open to hostile invasions and forever closed to intercourse with Europe. Such facts Peter understood extremely

4. Specifically, Belinsky is attacking the leaders of the Slavophiles as well as Pogodin and the other editors of the journal *The Muscovite.* For instance, in a letter to Pavel Botkin, penned on April 22, 1847, Belinsky wrote about Konstantin Aksakov: "Aksakov will sing hymns not to the Moscow that exists but to the one that is a figment of his imagination. And he will do so at the expense of Petersburg, the good and bad sides of which he knows absolutely nothing." Belinskii, *Polnoe sobranie sochinenii,* vol. 12 (1956), 356.

Similarly, Annenkov recalled, "*The Muscovite,* which had become the echo of the Slavophile school, went to the extreme of monomania in the defense of its basic stands—about the richness of the Russian national spirit, about its religious essence, about the elements of humility, meekness, endurance, and wisdom which made it unique—going so far as to assert, for instance, that the Russian land was fertilized for history with the tears of its inhabitants, not, as was true of Western nations, with their blood." Annenkov, "Zamechatel'noe desiatiletie, 1838–1848," 105.

5. In October 1708, Ivan Mazepa, hetman of eastern Ukraine, sought to free his country from Russia by switching allegiances from Peter the Great to Charles XII of Sweden during the Great Northern War between the two countries (1700–1721). Together with Charles, Mazepa was defeated by the Russians in the battle of Poltava in 1709, and he died the following year.

well. *Of necessity,* therefore, the war with Sweden became the key issue of his life, the governing stimulus for his activities. Revel[6] and especially Riga were practically begging to become the new capital of Russia: a site in which Russian traits would clash head-on with those of Europe but where these traits also would be accepted by other lands, not destroyed by them. Both Revel and Riga eventually became Peter's property;[7] though initially he did not wish for much—only a small corner of land on the Baltic. But Peter could never tarry; he felt compelled to hurry with his plans, to live, that is, to create and work. Thus, when Revel and Riga finally became Russian cities, St. Petersburg had already been in existence for seven years.[8] Much money had already been spent, much labor had been extended. Petersburg, situated on Kotlin Island[9] and on the Neva with its quadruple tributaries, was both charming and strategic; it so impressed its creator that it would have been regrettable if Peter had rethought his choice for his capital. It also was too late for him to do so.

Peter long regarded Petersburg as his creation. He loved it as the child of his own creative intellect, even though he found it difficult always to contend with the city's savage, severe nature, swamp-like earth, and damp and unhealthy climate. Perhaps, at times, he was also discouraged that St. Petersburg was almost like a desert—remote and removed from sources of food and materials. Peter's unbendable will, though, triumphed over all. Genius is persistent; that is why Peter was a genius. The more daunting the struggle, the more he enjoyed showing the world and himself his rich and inexhaustible powers. Solemn was the moment when the Great looked upon the wild shores of Finnish Gulf and conceived in his soul the idea of making these shores home to the capital of his future empire. In this moment, Peter provided the inspiration for a *poema* about that capital which only a great poet could capture in its splendor, gracefulness, and vastness:

6. Revel was the Russian name for Tallinn, the capital of present-day Estonia.

7. In 1710, Riga and Tallinn were captured by Russian forces in the Great Northern War with Sweden.

8. St. Petersburg was founded in 1703.

9. Kotlin Island, also known as Kronshtadt, was the site of a military fortress near the tributary of the Neva.

There by the billows desolate
Stood He, with mighty thoughts elate,
And gazed; but, in the distance only
A sorry skiff on the broad spate
Of Neva drifted seaward, lonely.
The moss-grown miry banks with rare
Hovels were dotted here and there
Where wretched Finns for shelter crowded;
The murmuring woodlands had no share
Of sunshine, all in mist beshrouded.
And thus He mused: "From here, indeed
Shall we strike terror in the Swede;
And here a city by our labor
Founded, shall gall our mighty neighbor;
'Here cut'—so Nature gives command
Your window through on Europe; stand
Firm-footed by the sea, unchanging!
Ay, ships of every flag shall come
By waters they had never swum,
And we shall revel, freely ranging."[10]

Petersburg was built in an instant. Things that should have taken a year were done in a month. The will of one individual triumphed over nature itself. It seemed as though fate itself, despite all right and reason, wanted to hurl the capital of the Russian Empire into this wretched region—a place where the sky is greenish white; where nature and the climate are hostile to humankind; where the plants of the north are thick grass, crawling heather, dry moss, gray tussocks, and swampy verdure; where sickly birch trees add to the pervasive monotony of prickly pines and sorrow spruce; and where the fumes from the swamp and the dampness of the air penetrate stone homes and human bones. Petersburg does not have spring or summer or winter; rather, it is host to a rotten and rainy fall which rages through the city all year long and which parodies first spring, then summer, and then

10. Belinsky is quoting from Pushkin's 1833 poem, "The Bronze Horseman" ("Mednyi vsadnik"). The italics are Belinsky's. The translation is from A. Yarmolinsky, ed., *The Poems, Prose and Plays of Alexander Pushkin* (New York: Modern Library, 1936), 95.

winter. It also seemed that fate wanted Russians, who until now had been sleeping the sleep of the dead, to work out their future in woeful struggle and bloody sweat, for victories endure only when won by hard work, and conquests last only when gained through suffering and blood! Perhaps, in a more favorable climate, amid a less-hostile nature, and without insurmountable obstacles, Russians would quickly have become proud of easy success; they would have gone to sleep again, never to awake fully again anew. But that was why he, who was sent to his people by God, was not only a sovereign and a tsar but also an individual who acted with authority, a person whose example disarmed an ignorance that was ingrained, and a cherished idleness that was centuries old:

> First a scholar, then a hero,
> Builder of ships, master of wood
> On the throne an endless worker
> Whose soul embraced all it could.[11]

Despite all his activity, a phenomenon that was quite unique in history, the Petersburg that Peter the Great bequeathed to Russia was far too poor and insignificant to be taken seriously. It seemed that the little city, which owed its turbulent existence to the will of one man, might not be destined to outlive its builder. The will of any one of Peter's successors could consign the city to eternal oblivion or to an insignificant and consumptive existence.[12] But here the genius of Peter the Great appeared in all its splendor: his outlines and plans ensured that the city would continue forever. Such is the power and prerogative of genius: Peter had not only laid the stone foundation of the new building; he also left behind its blueprint. His successors might have wished to move the building to a different place, but where could they obtain a similar stone for its foundation? The stone that had been laid by so great a genius was so huge that no one would dream of moving it.

11. Belinsky is quoting from Pushkin's 1826 poem "Stanzas" ("Stansy").

12. In fact, Peter the Great's grandson, Peter II, along with representatives from such noble families as the Dolgorukys, the Golytsins, and the Repins, sought to move the capital of Russia from St. Petersburg back to Moscow. From 1727 to 1730, this group destroyed many of the ornate buildings Peter the Great had erected in St. Petersburg, and in 1728, it forced the tsarist court to move from Russia's European capital back to Moscow. Peter II died of smallpox in 1730.

Petersburg could not but continue its existence because it was closely bound to the Russian Empire, the entity which had replaced the Muscovite kingdom. And Petersburg grew by hours, not by days.

> A century—and that city young,
> Gem of the Northern World, amazing,
> From gloomy wood and swamp upsprung,
> Had risen, in pride and splendor blazing.
> Where once, by the low-lying shore,
> In waters never known before
> The Finnish fisherman, sole creature,
> And left forlorn by stepdame Nature,
> Cast ragged nets—today, along
> Those shores, astir with life and motion,
> Vast shapely palaces in throng
> And towers are seen: from every ocean,
> From the world's end, the ships come fast,
> To reach the loaded quays at last.
> The Neva now clad in granite
> With many a bridge to overspan it,
> The islands lie beneath a screen
> Of gardens deep in dusky green.
> To that young capital is dropping
> The crest of Moscow on the ground,
> A widow in purple, stopping
> Before an empress newly crowned.[13]

Thus, Russia suddenly appeared with two capitals—an old one and a new one, Moscow and Petersburg. This unique situation was not without important consequences. At the same time that Petersburg was being beautified and built, Moscow was changing in its own way. On the one hand, Moscow was also host to the inevitable intrusion of Europeanism; on the other hand, it sought safety in preserving elements of its ancient heritage.

13. Belinsky is again quoting from "The Bronze Horseman." It should also be noted, though, that in the last lines of this excerpt, Belinsky is citing from a variant of the piece that had been rejected by censors because of Pushkin's comparison of Moscow to a "widow."

As a result, Moscow became a somewhat capricious place, a radiant city which stunned the eyes with its blend of European and Asiatic features. The city spread and stretched over a vast area. Indeed, it seemed that the city was without end! When you stroll through the city even now, you see that lengthy, extremely lengthy fences accommodate its vastness.[14] Moscow has no huge buildings. Its biggest structures are neither great nor small, nor do they flaunt architectural merits. Its architecture testifies to the genius of the ancient Muscovite kingdom in its faithful striving for family comfort. It is worth one's time just to walk through Moscow's crooked and slanting streets. You will immediately see that it is a town of patriarchal family life. The houses there are detached, private residences. Almost every one of them has a rather large yard that is covered with grass and surrounded by outbuildings. The poorest Muscovite, if he is married, cannot do without a cellar. In fact, even when he rents an apartment, he is more worried about the cellar where he will keep his foodstuffs than about the rooms where he will live. It is not uncommon for the poorest Muscovite to build his entire life around a most cherished dream, that is, he will someday stop *roaming from apartment to apartment* and take up life in his own little house. Indeed, his sorrow is cut in half when, having asked his parents for help and receiving a "perhaps" in reply, he buys or rents an empty lot in some remote place. Then for roughly the next five years, or sometimes even ten, he builds a little house with three windows, buying the materials on time or as they happen to come along in his path. Finally, there comes the longed-for day when he moves into his own house. The place is not nice, even if it is his, but it comes with a yard. Perhaps he could keep chickens there and even a

14. Here Belinsky is both tapping into and working against the increasing fondness of Russians for Moscow, the reason being that in the wake of ongoing political, social, and cultural change, citizens from all over the empire saw the ancient city as the repository of their spiritual strength and roots. Such emotions were well established even before the onset of Napoleon's invasion of the city. For instance, Alexander Radishchev, in his 1790 work *Journey from Petersburg to Moscow* (*Puteshestvie iz Peterburga v Moskvu*), was the first to point Russians in that direction when he criticized the empire and its empress in terms of a journey from Petersburg to Moscow, not the reverse. Other Russian writers followed suit. "O Moscow, darling daughter of Russia, where can your equal be found?" the poet Ivan Dmitriev had asked in his 1795 poem, "The Liberation of Moscow" ("Osvobozhdenie Moskvy"); in I. Dmitriev, *Polnoe sobranie sochinenii* (Leningrad: Sovetskii pisatel', 1967), 83.

As Russians grew more conscious of their history, especially after Nikolai Karamzin began to publish the first volumes of his monumental *History of the Russian State,* Moscow became for Russians the point of contact with the distant past upon which Peter the Great had turned his back.

calf. The main thing, though, is that his house has a cellar—what could be better? Moscow has countless homes like these, and they contribute to the city's expanse, if not its grandeur. Such homes can be found even on the best streets of Moscow in between the most lavish dwellings, just as good residences (two- or three-story edifices made of stone) are found among the poorest abodes and on the most remote and worst streets of the city.

Russians who have always lived in Petersburg are as astounded by Moscow as are foreigners. On the way to the city, our Petersburg citizens would, of course, see Novgorod and Tver, but these places would not at all prepare them for the sight that is Moscow. Although Novgorod is also an ancient city,[15] the only thing left of its antiquity is its kremlin, an extremely unprepossessing sight. Its Sophia cathedral[16] is very, very old, but it is neither graceful nor huge. The streets of Novgorod are not narrow or crooked; and the architecture and even the exterior of many of its homes remind one of Petersburg. Tver also does not give to our Petersburg citizens any preparation for Moscow. Its streets are straight and wide, and, for a provincial city, it is rather beautiful.

Thus, when our Petersburg citizens come to Moscow for the first time, they enter upon a strange, new world. In vain do they seek a main or best street which they could compare with Nevsky Prospekt. They are shown Tverskaya Street, but they are amazed to find themselves on a crooked and narrow thoroughfare that stretches out along a hill with a small square off to the side. They are also surprised to see that the largest and most handsome home on Tverskaya Street would in Petersburg be only a modest domicile, when compared to the other large and graceful dwellings there. When Petersburg citizens visit Moscow for the first time, they are also unnerved by the fact that, unlike the straight lines and corners of their own city, they see the following situation. One house protrudes several steps onto the street, as if it wants to see what is going on around it. A second retreats several steps back, as if, judging by its exterior, it does so from modesty or arrogance. A third is a run-down, wooden shack that finds a modest and comfortable place between two rather large stone edifices.

15. Novgorod, located 350 miles northwest of Moscow, dates back to the eleventh century.

16. The Novgorod Cathedral of Saint Sophia (Novgorodskii Sofiiskii Sobor) was built between 1042 and 1065.

Although the walls of this shack rest solidly against those of neighboring homes, it seems unhappy that its sturdy supporting structures will not let it collapse completely or do not shield it from the rain and cold. Finally, when our Petersburg citizens first encounter Moscow, they are surprised to find a tiny tobacco stand, or a dirty tavern or bar, standing alongside a splendid modern home. They are deeply chagrined, however, when they realize that the strange grotesque which is Tverskaya Street has its own type of beauty. And, they are completely taken aback when, going down as far as Kuznetsky Bridge, they encounter—with the exception of wooden hovels—everything that they have already seen. They see stone houses next to modern ones; but before they come to these, they see tiny dwellings as well. Indeed, our Petersburg citizens suddenly wonder if they have not turned into some new Gullivers who have entered the kingdom of Lilliputians.[17] Although our Petersburg citizens refrain from expressing surprise or rapture, they cannot keep from loudly uttering some interjection when they transverse the circle of avenues girding Moscow—its best adornment and one that our Petersburg citizens have full right to envy. They also cannot restrain themselves when, first going down one hill and then up another, they see themselves surrounded by an amphitheater of roofs and the verdure of gardens. Moreover, if our Petersburg citizens imagine that they are seeing minarets instead of churches, they find themselves transported to some Eastern city, something akin to what they have read in Scheherazade.[18] They love such a sight. In fact, as spring moves to summer, they choose not to seek out the capitals and cities of the East but to enjoy the picturesque landscapes they find there in Moscow.

Many streets in Moscow, for example, Tverskaya, Arbatskaya, Povarskaya, Nikitskaya, and the two lines that go along the sides of Tversky and Nikitsky avenues, are graced primarily by "lordly" (a Muscovite word!) homes.[19] Here, on these Muscovite streets, you will see more comfort than

17. Jonathan Swift wrote *Gulliver's Travels into Several Remote Nations of the World* in 1726.

18. More accurately, Belinsky is referring to a character in *The Thousand and One Nights,* also known as *The Entertainment of Arabian Nights,* a collection of Oriental stories that are of uncertain authorship and date and that includes the tales of such well-known figures as Aladdin, Ali Baba, and Sinbad. Earliest references to the work date back to the mid-tenth century; its stories draw from the cultures of India, Iran, Iraq, Egypt, Turkey, and possibly Greece.

19. These streets are roughly one mile west of the Kremlin. Moscow had both a Tversky Street (*Tverskaia ulitsa*) and a Tversky Avenue (*Tverskii bul'var*).

grandeur or grace. Everything bears the mark of family life: a comfortable home, spacious, but nonetheless suitable for one family, a wide courtyard, and countless servants poised at the gates during summer evenings. Everything in Moscow is also separate and private. Everyone lives in his own house and keeps a firm distance from his neighbor. Such separateness is even more noticeable in the area of the Zamoskvorechie,[20] a purely merchant and petit bourgeois part of Moscow. There the windows are covered with curtains, and the gates are under lock and key. Should someone knock on them, he will hear the angry barking of a chained dog. Everything in the Zamoskvorechie is dead or, more accurately, asleep. The house or hovel resembles a fortress, prepared to sustain a prolonged siege. Everywhere there are signs of family life, but the city is almost nowhere to be seen! . . .

Moscow has many eating houses that are frequented primarily by people who drink only tea. We need not explain what kind of people we are talking about: They are individuals who take their tea from fifteen samovars a day, who cannot live without the stuff, and who drink it five times a day and at taverns and inns, God knows how many more times after that. And if you were to examine such individuals, you would be not surprised to see that tea does not upset their nerves, nor prevent them from sleeping, nor ruin their teeth. You would even think that such individuals could smoke tons of opium with impunity—perhaps even for their health. Moscow, though, has few confectioners' shops. People visit them infrequently; but when they do, they buy a great deal. The hotels in Moscow exist primarily for travelers or for unmarried youth who love to carouse. In Moscow people dine more at home. Even poor bachelors do not care to eat out, since they, too, enjoy the family character of their city. When such individuals do dine outside their homes, they usually do so with some family who are acquaintances of theirs, especially *relatives.* Generally speaking, Moscow is famous for its hospitality and generous spirit; but it is alien to the urban or social life. For instance, the English Club[21] in Moscow is known for its

20. The Zamoskvorechie (or literally, "beyond the Moskva river") is located just south of the Kremlin. One of the oldest parts of Moscow, it was initially an outpost against the Mongols and housed artisans serving in the court. Beginning in the 1820s, the Zamoskvorechie was home to merchants, petty officials, and members of the bourgeoisie.

21. The English Club (Angliiskii klub) was founded in Moscow in 1772 and included both foreigners and aristocrats living in that city. It was operated by Englishmen as a cultural haven for British expatriates,

sumptuous dinners; but if you try to eat there, you will invariably be dining with relatives, even if you are seated among five hundred or more people. The actual members of the English Club also love to eat there, because, as they see it, they are dining at home, with their families. Everything that is Muscovite bears the imprint of family life!

Even now, kinship plays a great role in Moscow. There no one can live without relatives. If you are born a solitary soul and come to live in Moscow, you are immediately married off and become host to a family seventy-seven times removed. In Moscow, not to love and esteem relatives is considered worse than freethinking. You must know the birthday and name day of at least one hundred and fifty people, and woe betide you should you forget to acknowledge even one of these. True, such an endeavor gets a bit burdensome and boring; but after all, kinship is a sacred thing. Wherever there is a developed sense of family, kinship cannot but be held in high regard.

With the death of Peter the Great, Moscow became a haven for high-ranking nobility who had fallen into disgrace, as well as a place of repose for grandees who had retired from active life. As a result, the city acquired a kind of aristocratic character which took particular hold during the reign of Catherine the Great. Who has not heard of the grand, unbridled life of the grandees in Moscow? Who has not heard stories of how they open their lavish gardens for everyone or of how they entertain, on a daily basis, the famous and the unknown, friends and strangers, urbanites and villagers? Who has not heard stories of their banquets—stories that sound like excerpts from *The Thousand and One Nights*? You see that Moscow has always remained faithful to its ancient character: arrogance, conceit, and unbridled amusement have always found refuge here! Beginning with the previous tsar's reign, Moscow has also, little by little, become a city of industry, manufacturing, and trade. Moscow dresses all of Russia with its cotton goods, and its distant environs are dotted with factories, big and small. In this regard, Petersburg is no match for Moscow, since Moscow's location almost in the middle of Russia has made it a center of industry. Furthermore, Moscow will continue to prosper, once the railroad connects

as well as for the indigenous social and literary elite of St. Petersburg. At this time, membership in the English Club was limited to 500 men. (Women were not admitted.) The English Club was the site of various entertainments, political discussions, and solemn occasions and celebrations. In 1924, the English Club housed the Museum of the Revolution.

it to Petersburg[22] and the highway links it, like an artery of the heart, to Yaroslavl', Kazan, Voronezh, Kharkov, Kiev, and Odessa.[23]...

Moscow is proud of its historical antiquity, its monuments. It is itself a most historical antiquity, both externally and internally. How strange a sight Moscow offers in its mix of old and new. In fact, there is hardly one map of the Kremlin, since it is constantly under repair or undertaking a new building. The spirit of the new wafts over Moscow and little by little washes away the city's ancient imprint.

We began talking about Petersburg and expounded upon Moscow, but in no way did this digression depart from our main focus. We have two capitals. How can one talk about one without comparing to the other? Indeed, only through such a comparison can we learn the peculiarities and characteristics of each. Nothing in the world exists in vain. If we have two capitals, it means that each one is necessary and rooted in an exclusive *idea.* Petersburg exemplifies one idea; Moscow exemplifies another. It is because of this principle also that when we resume talking about Petersburg, we will turn our attention to Moscow as well. So far we have found that the distinguishing characteristic of Moscow is its family life. We now turn to Petersburg.

We have grown accustomed to thinking about Petersburg as a city situated not on a swamp but somewhere in the air. Many people actually assert that Petersburg is a city without sacred historical places and without ties to the homeland, that is, a city that was built on pile dwellings and calculation.[24] These opinions are already outdated, and it is high time to abandon

22. The building of the Nikolaevsky (now the Oktiabr'sky) railroad, which covered the four hundred miles between Moscow and Petersburg, took place between 1843 and 1851. From the beginning of its construction, Belinsky was greatly interested in the project. For instance, Fyodor Dostoevsky, in his 1873 *Diary of a Writer* (*Dnevnik pisatelia*), quoted the critic as saying, "I often go and see how the work is progressing.... At long last, we will have at least one railway. You cannot believe how such a thought often brightens my day." Dostoevskii, *Polnoe sobranie sochinenii,* vol. 21 (1980), 12.

23. Moscow is approximately 150 miles southwest of Yaroslavl, 250 miles north of Voronezh, 400 miles west of Kazan, 400 miles north of Kharkov, 500 miles northeast of Kiev, and 700 miles northeast of Odessa.

24. Here Belinsky is polemicizing not only with the Slavophiles but also with Herzen, who, in his 1842 article "Moscow and Petersburg" ("Moskva i Peterburg"), affirmed that St. Petersburg was a "city without history" and that it lacked "a heartfelt tie to the homeland." A. Herzen, *Sobranie sochinenii v tridtsati tomakh,* vol. 2 (Moscow: Izdatel'stvo Akademiia nauk SSSR, 1954), 31, 36.

Of course, both before and after *Petersburg,* comparisons between Moscow and Petersburg were a mainstay of Russian literature. See, for instance, D. Burlaka, ed., *Moskva-Peterburg: Pro et Contra; Dialog*

them. True, they contain a grain of truth, but how much more falsehood. People say that Petersburg is an ahistorical city, without tradition. Such a view is an absurdity that is not worth refuting! Petersburg's misfortune arises from the fact that it is not only a young city, but it is also simply a child when compared to old lady Moscow. But following this logic, does it make any sense to say that a young man who has begun his life with some great achievement is not a historical individual because he has lived for so short a time? By the same token, can one also affirm that an old man is a historical being merely because he has lived for so long? Ancient Moscow, the capital of the Muscovite kingdom, has not only lived a long time, it has also experienced a great deal. Moscow has its own history—no one can argue this. But what is all its history when compared to the great epos that is the life of Peter the Great? Is not Petersburg closely tied to this life? And if one refutes the historical importance of Petersburg, does this not also denigrate the role of Peter in Russian history? People also ask: Where in Petersburg are those monuments and historical holy places which time has not destroyed?[25] It is true, my respected sirs, that Petersburg has no such places, nor can it have, since it is only *one hundred and forty-one* years old. But Petersburg itself is a great historical monument. Everywhere in the city one can see the living traces of its Builder. Indeed, Peter's little house in the Petersburg Quarter, his palace in the Summer Garden, and his palace at Peterhof are worth not one but many Kremlins. What can one do? Everyone has his own taste! But can it be that human calculation is inferior to blind chance? The wisdom of the ages says that an iron nail fashioned by the coarse hand of a village smithy is more valuable than any flower;[26] the nail, after all, is the work of a *conscious* spirit, but the flower is the creation of a *spontaneous* force. Calculation is also a conscious process. The

---

kul'tur v istorii natsional'nogo samosoznaniia; Antologiia (St. Petersburg: Khristianskii gumanitarnyi institut, 2000).

25. Belinsky is paraphrasing lines from Konstantin Batyushkov's 1813 poem, "To Dashkov" ("K Dashkovu").

26. Belinsky is again citing from Hegel here, specifically, Hegel's idea that work done by the creative subjective spirit (humankind) is more valuable than the fruits of the elemental intellect in nature. Bulgarin, believing such an idea to be Belinsky's, wrote in a review of "Petersburg and Moscow": "Imagine! A smithy is higher than nature because he is conscious. . . . Oh, my dear public . . . what people won't tell you! Even worse, there are individuals who see such ideas as serious matters!" F. Bulgarin, "Zhurnal'naia vsiakaia vsiachina," *Severnaia pchela,* no. 79 (1845): 318.

wisdom of the ages also says that Petersburg has nothing that is original or authentic, that it somehow resembles an urban capital, and that it looks like other capitals of the world. But which capitals precisely? In no way does Petersburg recall Rome, London, and Paris, and any attempt to liken it to these old metropolises would be an absolute untruth. If Petersburg resembles any cities at all, it would most likely be the big urban centers of South America, which, like it, were also built according to a calculated plan. But can it be that none of these cities has anything personal or original about it? Can it also be that because each wall and stone of these cities bear witness to the *future*—that they do not see something original, and moreover, splendidly original? But Petersburg is more original than all the cities of America because it is a new city in an old land. Indeed, it is the new hope, the new future of this country.

In line with this, we must say: either the reforms of Peter the Great were a great historical mistake or Petersburg is of immense, important significance for Russia. We must also say: either this new formation of Russia is something that is transparent or false and will completely disappear without a trace or Russia will, forever and irrevocably, be torn from its past. In the first case, Petersburg is the accidental and ephemeral outcome of an epoch that has taken a wrong turn in history. It is like a mushroom that springs up during the night but dries up the following day. In the second case, Petersburg is a necessary and enduring phenomenon, a sturdy and majestic oak, one that draws upon all the life juices of Russia. Some of our homegrown politicians, people who consider themselves profound thinkers, reason that since Petersburg appeared in an instant and owed its existence to the will of one individual, then some other person with power from above can abandon it and build a new city in another part of Russia.[27] This is an extremely childish opinion! Such matters are not so easily undertaken and brought to fruition. Two things are needed: an individual who possesses not only the power but also the energy to create a miracle, and a moment when such power and energy can realize something in life. Arbitrary rule can produce nothing great. Great things issue forth only from rational necessity and consequently from God himself. Arbitrary rule alone does not create a great city in a short period of time. If anything,

27. Belinsky is again attacking the Slavophiles.

arbitrary rule can create only a *Tower of Babel,* not a reborn nation with a great future. To abandon Petersburg is easier said than done. "Language is without bones," the Russian saying goes, which means that one can speak a tongue as one wishes, but empty words cannot accomplish anything. Only the Messrs. *Manilov,* in their idle fantasy, can build bridges over ponds, with benches on both sides.[28]

The foreigner Algarotti said: "Petersburg is the window though which Russia looks out upon Europe"[29]—a wonderful pronouncement in which a few words successfully capture a great thought! Indeed, such a pronouncement underscores the firm foundation of Petersburg—more so than the piles upon which it is built and from which it cannot easily be removed! In this assertion also is the idea behind Petersburg and consequently the city's great significance and sacred right to everlasting existence! People say that Petersburg expresses only a superficial Europeanism. Let us assume that such a thing is so. But in the development of Russia, a development that was completely antithetical to anything European—a development that went from the top down and not from the bottom up—*externals* have a much more *noble* significance than most people think. For instance, what does one see in the poetry of Lomonosov? Only externals. For example, squeezed into Latin and Greek constructions were Russian words, together with fragments of thoughts which had no bearing for the Russian society for whom Lomonosov wrote his rhetorical verse! Not without foundation, though, was Lomonosov called the father of Russian poetry; not without foundation does such poetry boast of producing such a great writer as Pushkin. Must we prove, therefore, that if our country had not *begun* its literary tradition with verse that was dead, imitative, and purely external, there never would have come into being the lively, original, and personal poetry of Pushkin? No, for even without proof, such a premise is clear, like a day from God. So, sometimes the *external nature* of an item also counts for something. We will say further: the external nature

28. Manilov is a character in Gogol's novel *Dead Souls* (*Mertvye dushi*).

29. Francesco Algarotti made this statement in his 1760 work *A Sampling of Letters About Russia* (*Saggio di lettere sopra la Russia*) about his visit to the homeland in 1739. It should be noted that it was Pushkin who first made use of Algarotti's assertion, having read it in a French translation of *Letters* and using it as a line in "The Bronze Horseman": "Here fate told us to cut a window on Europe" ("V Evropu prorubil okno"). Francesco Algarotti, "Letters from Count Algarotti to Lord Hervey and the Marquis Scipio Maffei," Letter IV, June 30, 1739 (London: Johnson and Payne, 1769), 70.

of an item sometimes influences its inner cast. For instance, the fact that someone wears a jacket and tailcoat—instead of a sheepskin coat, a blue *armyak,*[30] or a dark caftan—does not make him a European. But why is it that in Russia, the people who dress like Europeans are the only ones who read, study something, or exhibit a taste and a love for the fine arts? No matter if people say that a jacket and a tailcoat are items that seem to be completely *external,* these items nonetheless influence the *internal* well-being of the individual. Peter the Great grasped this relationship extremely well; hence his opposition to beards, caftans, peasant-style blouses, fur hats, and all the other cherished accoutrements of Muscovite fashion.[31]

There exist wise people who are suspicious of everything that is an external. Give them such concepts as *idea, love,* and *spirit;* but facts, things of the practical world, and everyday slices of life, these are items that they do not wish to see. There are other wise people who do not want to know anything but facts and causes and who see *idea* and *spirit* merely as dreams. As their special mark, the members of the first group—people who choose love over daily life—are irked whenever others talk about railroads in their presence. To depend on such a mundane item to elevate the moral dignity of the nation seems to them trivial, even false. Members of this first group keep waiting for a miracle, hoping that one fine day education will fall from the sky and the folk will take to learning—even though they have never been able to endure books and the like. Wise sages of this type have long been hailed by the name of *romantics.*[32] The wise sages of the second group—people who choose the practicalities of life over love—eat and sleep highways, railroads, manufacturing, trade, and banks, and they believe that society should indulge in various kinds of pragmatic speculation. This is their ideal for the well-being of the government and the folk. Such concepts as spirit and idea are for them useless—even harmful—dreams.

30. An *armyak* is a peasant coat of heavy cloth.

31. Here Belinsky is again poking fun at Aksakov and such other Muscovite Slavophiles as Alexei Khomyakov, as well as Ivan and Pyotr Kireevsky, who loved to parade about Moscow in tall fur hats, floor-length caftans, and the like. For instance, Alexander Nikitenko recalled of an 1856 meeting with Khomyakov, "He appeared . . . without a tie and in an *armyak.* He also was wearing a red shirt with a slanting collar and carrying a tall fur hat under his arm. Despite his pretensions to Russian nationality [*narodnost'*], he spoke constantly in French." See Nikitenko, *Moia povest' o samom sebe,* 429.

32. Again read: Slavophiles.

Individuals who espouse such views are the *classicists* of our times. We do not belong to either of these two groups. In the latter we see if only something, but in the former—we are guilty—we see nothing. In our opinion, there are two ways to introduce new life into a stagnant social organism. As a means to spread enlightenment, the first is science or study, as well as the publishing of books in the wide sense of this word. The second is existence itself, meaning the various forms of normal, everyday life, customs, and mores. Reading and ideas are important and genuine only when they enter into existence and become, so to speak, everyday and usual. There is nothing stronger or more powerful than custom. Indeed, it is far easier to convince people of the logic of some convenient truth than, if custom tells them otherwise, to incline them to the practical application of this truth. It seems to us that it is the fate of Petersburg to choose the second way of reviving the social organism: to use existence itself, the various forms of normal, everyday life, customs, and mores, to extend and affirm European influence in Russian society. Petersburg is the model for all of Russia in everything that touches upon the various forms of life, from fashion to an enlightened bearing, from the way of laying bricks to the sublime mysteries of architectural art, from graceful typography to journals that command the attention of the public.

Compare life in Petersburg with that of Moscow—compare their differences or, better to say, their contrasts, and one will immediately see the significance of each city. For instance, although Muscovite streets are narrow and flanked by sidewalks only about a foot wide, they appear crowded only in the afternoon, and then not all of them at that. And the reason the streets there always seem crowded is precisely because of their narrowness rather than because of the number of people on them. From about ten in the evening on, Moscow is already empty, and particularly in winter, its crooked streets with its even more crooked alleyways are deserted and boring. By contrast, the wide streets of Petersburg are almost always alive with people who are rushing off somewhere. Even at midnight, these avenues are rather crowded, and stragglers can be found here and there right up until early morning. The confectioners' shops in Petersburg are generally filled with people: Germans, French, and other foreigners as well as natives and visitors who eat, drink, and read the newspapers. In the shops of Petersburg, Russians eat and drink even more than their European colleagues do. They also scan *The Bee* and *The Invalid;*[33] sometimes they pore over the thick journals that, for their convenience, have been bound by sections into special kinds of books. These people are the lovers of literature. (In general, devotees of politics are relatively few in any part of our country.) The eating houses and restaurants in Petersburg are also always filled with people. Here it is the same thing: people eat, drink, read, smoke, play billiards—but mostly in silence. If they do talk, their conversations are hushed and tête-à-tête. Occasionally, however, one also hears very loud voices that talk openly about things that are in no way of interest to passersby, for example, how Ivan Semyonovich was without a deuce and played a seven of hearts; how Pyotr Nikolaevich got a job and Vasily Stepanovich moved up a rank, and other literary and political news. As everyone knows, the homes in Petersburg are huge. The Petersburg citizen does not worry about cellars. If he is not married, he dines in taverns; if he has a wife, he buys all his basic foodstuffs in shops. If he rents, the building where he has an apartment is a veritable Noah's ark in which one can find pairs of all kinds of animals. It is rare for the Petersburg citizen to know who is living alongside him because above him, below him, and to the left and right of him dwell people who are just like he is. That is, they are preoccupied with their own affairs; they do not have the time or interest to know about their neighbors or their neighbors to know about them. The key attraction of an apartment in Petersburg, one that everyone in the city pursues, is that it is close to everything—to one's place of work and to stores where one can get everything better and cheaper. The Noah's ark that is the residence of a Petersburg citizen must be near a small cellar, a confectioner's shop, an eating house, and fashionable stores; it must also be close to tailors, shoemakers, and everyone else in the world.

The idea of a city arises mainly from the fact that it has abundant conveniences compressed into a very small circle. By this measure, Petersburg is an incomparably greater city than Moscow. Moscow, on the other hand,

33. *The Bee*—more accurately, the *Northern Bee* (*Severnaia Pchela*)—was published by Bulgarin and Nikolai Grech in St. Petersburg from 1825 to 1864. Originally a liberal publication, it adopted a reactionary line, both politically and aesthetically, after the Decembrist Revolt of 1825. The *Northern Bee* catered to military officers, provincial landlords, civil servants, and members of the urban bourgeoisie. *The Invalid*—actually, the *Russian Invalid* (*Russkii invalid*)—was a military newspaper published in St. Petersburg from 1813 to 1917. The incomes from this patriotic and philanthropic publication assisted disabled war veterans and the widows and orphans of casualties in war.

is perhaps the one urban center in all of Russia where everything is separated, scattered about, and imprinted with a feeling of family life. If Petersburg has no public spirit in the genuine meaning of this term, it is primarily because it lacks a sense of domestic or family privacy. Specifically, Petersburg loves the street, the carnival, the theater, the coffeehouse, and other places of public merriment and fun; in sum, it loves all social institutions. At present, the city has relatively few such places, but it will increase their number in time.

Another trait of Petersburg is that it cannot live without newspapers, posters, and advertisements of every kind. For a long time, the city has been accustomed to seeing the *Police Gazette*[34] as both a city newspaper and a necessity of life. No sooner does a Petersburg citizen awaken than he immediately wants to know what is playing today in the theaters or whether there has been scheduled a concert, a horse race, or a carnival with music. In a nutshell, he wants to know everything that makes up his world of diversions and pleasures. To do such a thing, he need only run down to the first confectioner's shop or, if he is receiving all the newspapers in town, simply stretch out his hand to the table. In Moscow, many people subscribe to the *Moscow News,*[35] a publication that comes out three times a week (on Tuesdays, Thursdays, and Saturdays), but such individuals go out to get it only on Saturdays, so that they will have all three issues at once. Such a custom they find convenient especially during the holidays when they can catch up on world news. Also, if a Muscovite does not have a city post office or a distribution service, he usually sends a servant to the publishing house at the university, though such a luxury is not possible or convenient for everyone. For the Petersburg citizen, a daily glance at *The Bee* or *The Invalid* is as necessary and as *customary* as drinking tea in the morning. . . .

In contrast to Moscow, the huge homes in Petersburg are not closed in the afternoon but are accessible through gates and doors, and at night you can always find the doorman or ring the bell. Consequently, you can always get into the home that you—invariably—need to get into. The door

34. The *Police Gazette*—more accurately, the *Gazette of the St. Petersburg Municipal Police* (*Vedomosti Sanktpeterburgskoi gorodskoi politsii*) was published from 1839 to 1873 and featured personal advertisements as well as information on events and cultural life in the capital.

35. The *Moscow News* (*Moskovskie vedomosti*) was published from 1756 to 1917. At this time, the *Moscow News* was an important literary and social publication.

of each apartment has a doorbell, and it usually has not only the number of the residence but also, on an iron or bronze nameplate, the name of the occupant. Although the streets in Moscow are not very long, each of them has a special name, and almost every one of the them there is home to one church, and sometimes more than one. It is easy to find someone if one knows the address; otherwise, it is a genuine torment, especially if a building houses more than one person. Usually, you enter into a rather large courtyard, which is deserted except for a dog or two. If you need help, you have to knock on a door and ask—"Does So-and-So live here?"—because in Moscow, doormen are rare and doorbells even rarer. In no way can one merely stroll Muscovite streets, which are narrow, crooked, and crowded. You have to be a Muscovite to stroll bravely down them, just as you have to be a Parisian to know where to walk to avoid getting splattered from the muddy streets. Incidentally, Muscovites do not like to walk. That is why cabbies there have so much to do. Fares are cheap, but people must ride in dull-looking carriages and the most wretched sleighs. The carriages are uniformly awful because that it is the way they are made. Simply put, they are instruments of torture for inquests of the guilty.

Petersburg, by contrast, has no poor sleighs. Even the most wretched of them are made in the manner of good ones. The passengers are covered with a traveling rug made from calfskin but which looks as though it came from a bear. In Petersburg no one can get in a sleigh without his "bear"! Incidentally, very few people ride around in Petersburg. They prefer to walk, and such a practice is good, if only because movement is the best and also the cheapest way to prevent hemorrhoids. Moreover, it is easy to walk anywhere in Petersburg. There are no mountains or hills, everything is sleek and smooth, and the sidewalks are made from flagstone and sometimes granite. No matter the season, they are wide, flat, and clean as house floors.

To become better acquainted with our two capitals, let us compare the people who live in them.

In any city, the highest stratum, the highest circle is something that is quite exclusive, and in Petersburg this stratum is larger than anywhere else in the world. This circle is a genuine terra incognita for anyone who does not claim citizenship in it. It is a city within a city, a state within a state. Those who are unaware of this stratum's mysteries gaze upon it from afar, or at least from a respectful distance. They look upon it with envy and torment, much as a traveler who, lost in the sandy deserts of Arabia, looks at a mirage and thinks that it is a flowering oasis. People outside of this top circle cannot enter the paradise of high society because it is guarded by porters with clubs and by crowds of waiters who, dressed like eighteenth-century marquesses, do not even steal a glance at the Edenic luxury surrounding them. People who belong to the middle social strata or circles, from the highest to the lowest, listen with strained attention to what is going on in the distant and incomprehensible roar of high society, and they interpret, each in their own way, the curt phrases and speeches wafting over them. With ecstatic looks, they tell and retell each other the latest anecdotes, which they distort in their simpleheartedness. In short, individuals who belong to the middle social strata are so enthralled by high society that they cannot breathe without it. But this is not enough. These poor souls struggle so greatly to mimic the customs and mores of high society that—*à force de forger*—they achieve a sweet assuredness that they too are part of this group. Of course, genuine high society would laugh at them in a genial way if it found out about their endless pretensions to close kinship with it. Nevertheless, the passion to see oneself as belonging or attached to high society has gripped the middle social strata in Petersburg to the point of frenzy. As a result, the city is host to countless circles of "high society." From the top down, members of these circles distinguish themselves in a pompous way or with slyly humorous glances; but from the bottom up, they exhibit irritated and injured pride, assenting testily that they are no different from anyone else and taking care always to be seen in bon ton. This bon ton has moved to genuine lunacy among Petersburg citizens. The most petty class of bureaucrats earns no more than seven hundred rubles a year, but for the sake of this bon ton, a member of this class will occasionally let drop a garbled French phrase—the only one that he has happened to memorize from his *Self-Teacher*. Also, for the sake of this bon ton, this individual will acquire his clothes from a respectable tailor and wear yellow gloves, even if they are dirty-looking. Even the girls of the lower classes love to embellish an illiterate note in Russian with an equally illiterate French phrase. And, if one should happen to write to such a maiden, he will find that there is no better way to flatter her than to mix French phrases with the Russian that is spoken in Nizhni Novgorod.[36] In so doing, he can show her that he considers her an educated woman as well as one who holds herself in "bon ton."[37] The young women of Petersburg are also fond of verse, especially couplets from vaudevilles; some even have enough taste to appreciate the poetry of Benediktov.[38] (Such lasses hail from the most aristocratic, the most bon ton circles of the bureaucratic class.) Don't you see? Petersburg has a very assured opinion of itself; it strives for the highest form of social mores. Moscow, though, is not like this at all. The high society of the city has its own special character, true, but anyone outside its circle does not care about such a thing because he lives securely in his own social rank.

The elemental core of the Muscovite population is its merchant class. Following their ancestors, 90 percent of this populous stratum wear huge, Orthodox beards, full-length frock coats made from blue cloth, and velveteen or cloth trousers tucked into tasseled boots. The other 10 percent are clean-shaven, and by their clothes and way of life—by their *externals*—they resemble unwashed intellectuals and even middle nobility. How many of these ancient noblemen's houses, these grand monuments to the customs and mores of another time, are now the property of the merchant class! (The old gentry homes that the merchant class does not own have, almost without exception, become government institutions of higher learning.) How this "rispicted" merchant class lives and arranges its affairs in these palaces and mansions—the curious can read about in Mr. Veltman's "A Traveler from the District, or Chaos in the Capital."[39] But it is not only in kingly or princely places that the merchants of Moscow do well; they also parade their status in expensive carriages and droshkies that rush off in

36. Here Belinsky is paraphrasing, somewhat inaccurately, a line from Alexander Griboyedov's *Woe from Wit.* Nizhni Novgorod is 250 miles east of Moscow.

37. Muscovites of the period, even the Westerners among them, agreed. The consensus, Annenkov recalled, was that "all a man of Petersburg's efforts consisted in being *reputed* a clever man, with such things as point of view, convictions, tendencies being considered by him various points of tomfoolery interfering with one's making a career; and then, once reputed a clever man, the Petersburger slept and dreamed of ways of selling himself, bag and baggage, as dearly as possible." See Annenkov, "Zamechatel'noe desiatiletie, 1838–1848," 153.

38. See Belinsky's harsh 1835 review of Vladimir Benediktov's poetry in Belinskii, *Polnoe sobranie sochinenii,* vol. 1 (1953), 355–71.

39. Alexander Veltman published "A Traveler from the District, or Chaos in the Capital" ("Priezzhii iz uezda, ili sumatokha v stolitse") in 1836.

whirlwinds and are led by splendid horses in blazing harness. Such carriages feature a "rispicted" and extremely self-satisfied [merchant with a] "beard." Next to him is his wife—a dense, voluminous mass with a shaking middle, all powdered and rouged and ringed with pearls. Sometimes this wifely mass has braids about her temples and a kerchief on her head. More often, though, she wears a hat with feathers. (Even among the merchant class, the fair sex far outstrips its male counterparts in the pursuit of European manners!) There is also an attendant who stands on the footboard of the carriage and who wears a full-length, Jewish-style frock coat, tassled red shoes, a down hat, and green gloves. The petit bourgeois, together with other passersby, look at these dashing steeds, cluck their tongues with satisfaction, and proudly pronounce: "Well, look at how well some of our group are doing!" The nobility, though, think with annoyance, "That damned peasant! He's gone crazy! God knows what the hell he thinks he's doing!" For the Russian merchant, especially one from Moscow, a fat, portly horse and a fat, portly wife are the first blessings in life. In Moscow one meets merchants everywhere, and everything there testifies that Moscow is primarily a city of the merchant class. Muscovite merchants live around Kitai-Gorod;[40] they are the exclusive masters of the Zamoskvorechie; and, they swarm over the most aristocratic streets and places of the city, such as Tversky Avenue and Tverskaya, Prechistenka, Ostozhenka, Arbatskaya, Povarskaya, Myasnitskaya, and other streets.

Alongside the numerous Russian merchant class has arisen a still more populous group: the petit bourgeois. The petit bourgeois have adopted a mode of dress made up of national Russian and infidel German styles. They deck themselves out in green gloves, down hats, and peaked caps—vulgar and ugly things taken from both Russian and foreign types of male headgear. They also wear colorful, often dirty kerchiefs; red alexandrine or cotton shirts with slanting collars; nankeen or cloth trousers tucked into calf-leather boots; and something between a full-length Jewish-style frock coat and a merchant's caftan. The women of this petit bourgeois group distinguish themselves with a wild mix of Russian and European clothing. Women of this stratum generally go about in dresses and shawls that,

40. Kitai-Gorod is the region directly east of the Kremlin and, beginning in the eighteenth century, was the commercial center of Moscow.

although of the poorest quality, still mark them as respectable ladies, but they hide their hair under hats made from flowery silk kerchiefs. The characteristic features of this group also include powder, rouge, and hair dye, together with glassy eyes, lifeless faces, and black teeth. The petit bourgeois are found in all Russian cities, even in large villages. They are brilliantly portrayed by the Petersburg actor Mr. Grigoriev the Second. Indeed, much of his success at the Alexander Theater[41] he owes precisely to this group.

In Moscow, though, there exists another type of middle stratum—the educated middle class. We do not consider it necessary to explain to our readers what we have in mind when we speak about educated classes. After all, who in Russia does not know that a sharp line separates the educated classes from the uneducated ones and that this line manifests itself, first, in customs and clothes that decisively suggest Europeanism; second, in a love for playing preference;[42] and, third, in a more or less sustained pursuit of reading. Regarding the last item, we can say with assurance that faithful readers of *The Moscow News* belong to educated society, assuming of course that their customs and clothes bear a Western stamp. Among the necessary differences separating "educated" and "uneducated" groups in our country, there is also the distinction of rank. (Although for some time now, we have realized that one can be an educated person without a rank, just as one can be an ignoramus with it.) Incidentally, the general views on what constitutes educated society in no way have penetrated into the lower classes. The millionaire-merchant may smooth his beard and boldly pretend to intelligence (he is a master at fooling friends and enemies alike) but never to education. Furthermore, the degrees and differences among the so-called educated people in our country are many. Some read only the calendar, *The Moscow News,* and the business letters and briefs that affect them personally. Others go further, being regular readers of the *Northern Bee.* Still others choose to read only Russian books and journals—nothing foreign, even if they know another tongue. Finally, there are those *esprits forts* who read a great deal in foreign languages but decidedly nothing in their own. Without a doubt, though, one must also respect as "educated"

41. The prestigious Alexander Theater (Aleksandrinskii teatr), home to Russia's oldest theater company, was built in St. Petersburg in 1832.

42. "Preference" (Russian: *preferans*) was a popular card game in Imperial Russia. Similar to bridge, it is still played in post-Soviet Russia and the Balkans.

those among us (and they are not few in number) who *sometimes* glance at Russian journals, *regularly* look at foreign ones, *occasionally* read the few good Russian books that exist, and *often* scan foreign ones.

The many nuances of being educated can also be seen in clothes, customs, and cards. In our country, some people wear European clothes only on official occasions, but at home, without guests, they go about in Tatar robes, Moroccan shoes, and all kinds of skullcaps. Some even prefer bizarre caftans made of colored silk or wool and gathered at the waist—the preferred mode of dress of dandyish provincial lackeys. Others, even when they are at home, remain faithful to the European model and wear a suit coat in which they can receive guests simply, without breaking any rules of propriety. Certain members of this group are constant followers of fashion; others are carried away by dolman jackets, wide Cossack trousers, and similar daring and devil-may-care accoutrements of provincial elegant taste. As regards the various lifestyles of the so-called educated people in our country, the essential difference is this: while one group keeps to the old ways, another group rises late, eats no earlier than four o'clock, drinks tea in the evenings no earlier than ten, and goes to bed late—the later, the better. Still another group holds on to the ways of old. Furthermore, the social nuances of our educated society are so varied that there is no way we can even begin to talk about them, but all its members, from the very highest to the very lowest, are equally faithful to externals that have nothing to do with anything internal, that is, they all wear the same fashion in their clothes. Our educated society shows its love for cards in three ways: some play preference, others faro, still others both; preference and faro. That there is a difference in the stakes goes without saying. In Petersburg, people play preference by suits and never buy more than seven cards at a time; in Moscow and the provinces, they buy ten cards at a time but without regard to suits.

The educated class in Moscow is numerous and varied. Not disputing the fact that all Muscovites look alike, the learned ones of the city recall a line uttered by that most famous Muscovite, Famusov:

> From head to toe,
> All Muscovites have a special stamp.[43]

43. Belinsky is again quoting from *Woe from Wit.*

Muscovites are truly sophisticated people. They are genuine Athenians, only in the Russian-Muscovite way. They love to live well, and in their view, they do so very well. Who has not heard of the Muscovite English Club with its ample dinners? (Besides the English and German clubs, there is also another one—the Nobleman's Club.) Who has not heard of Muscovite hospitality and friendliness? In what other city of the world can one find it so convenient to marry and dine as in Moscow? Where, besides Moscow, can one work and carry on trade, write novels, and publish journals, and not for any other reason other than for one's own pleasure and relaxation? Where else can one better rest and regain one's health, if not in Moscow? Where, if not in Moscow, can a man speak at length about his labors, present and future, pass for one of the most energetic people in the world—and at that same time, do absolutely nothing?[44] Where else can one be more content in being idle but also in spending time in a most pleasant way? Why is this so? Because Moscow is where so many joy seekers from the provinces wish to go to carouse, make merry, lead a happy life, and get married. Because Moscow has so many dressing gowns, dolmans, official-looking trousers with stripes on them, and jackets with braids, something so unheard of that, when they appeared on Nevsky Prospekt, they were regarded with horror by the entire population of Petersburg. Moscow even sports round fur caps, the type that, its citizens insist, Ryurik used to wear. Finally, Moscow is a place like no other because only there could a gypsy choir like Ilyushka's flourish.[45] The Muscovite's face never has a concerned look: it is kind and open and looks as though it wants to ask one: "*And where are you dining today?*" Anyone who is even minimally familiar with Moscow cannot help knowing that besides English comfort, there is also something called *Muscovite comfort,* or, as it called there, "life in the grand style." Muscovites are very different from non-Muscovites. For example, a Muscovite *barin,* a Muscovite lady, a Muscovite lass, a Muscovite poet, a Muscovite thinker, a Muscovite writer, and a Muscovite youth who works

44. Belinsky is again mocking Ivan Kireevsky and Alexei Khomyakov.

45. Belinsky is referring to the famous gypsy choir of Ilya Sokolov, which in the 1830s and '40s performed not only at street festivals and in theater and concert halls but also in the homes of merchants and nobles and in the literary, artistic, and dramatic circles of Moscow. It was in the latter places that Sokolov and company thrilled such individuals as Pushkin, Herzen, Ivan Turgenev, and the young Leo Tolstoy.

in the archives[46]—these are all types, these are all technical designations that are absolutely beyond the understanding of anyone who has never lived in Moscow. Such types and designations originate in the exclusive situation of Moscow, the city from which Peter the Great initiated his reforms. Moscow embraced the threefold idea of Oxford, Manchester, and Reims.[47] It is also an industrial city. It is also home to not only the oldest but also the best university in Russia, an institution that attracts the brightest youth from all parts of the homeland. Although a significant number of these students, when they finish their course of study, leave Moscow to accomplish something in the wider world, all of them would rather stay in the city. Those who do remain, together with those who are still students, make up a special middle group that embraces people from all social strata.

Education, or at the very least the striving to be educated, unites and brings these people together. A middle group of the student type is an oasis in the sandy soil of all other groups. Such oases are found in many if not all Russian cities. In one urban area, such an oasis may comprise five people; in another, two; in still another, only one person. Several Russian cities, though, have no such oases at all; they are only all pure sand, or black earth, covered with nettles and weeds. To Moscow's very great credit, one cannot but agree that the city has more of these oases than any other place in Russia. The reason for this is twofold. First, despite the fact that Moscow is a capital

46. Here Belinsky has in mind "archival youths" who, in the idea of Sergei Sobolevsky, worked in the dungeons of governmental institutions but who, in their love for German philosophy, romantic theories, and literary creativity, renounced societal pleasures and expressed an ironic attitude toward society.

The image of "archival youths" also appears in chapter 7 in *Eugene Onegin.* As Pushkin writes:

Arkhivny iunoshi tolpoiu
Na Taniu choporno gliadiat
I pro nee mezhdu soboiu
Neblagosklonno govoriat.

In swarms around Tatyana raging
The modish record office clerks
Stare hard at her before exchanging
Some disagreeable smirks.

A. Pushkin, *Polnoe sobranie sochinenii v shestnadtsati tomakh,* vol. 6 (Moscow: Izdatel'stvo Akademii nauk SSSR, 1937), 160.

47. That is, Oxford as home to a university, Manchester as a locale for industry, and Reims as the site for the coronation of kings.

of our country as well as a huge administrative center for the surrounding region, it has not cultivated an administrative, bureaucratic, or official character. Second, the city is influenced by Moscow University.[48] That is why on questions of science, art, and literature, Muscovites exhibit more breadth, knowledge, taste, tact, and education than most of the reading and even writing public of Petersburg. This intellectual life, we repeat, is the best side of the Muscovite way of life.[49] Everything in this world, though, is so ingeniously structured that the best side of this everything must also contrast with a weak side. As everyone knows, there are no more educated people than the Germans, and in science, Muscovite students are no match for their German counterparts. But then the Germans have their weak side: they are *students* until age thirty; then, for the last half of their lives, they are self-contented, limited hypocrites with a *philistine* outlook on life. They thus have no time to be *people.* The situation is the same in Moscow. The people there set education as the goal of their lives and begin their lives with great hopes, but if they do not leave Moscow before it is too late, they settle into becoming Muscovites and abandon their dreams. They are like people for whom the time to make promises has passed but for whom the time to fulfill these promises has not yet come. Even the young people in Moscow "who have big hopes for themselves" have a common failing: they often lump together disparate and contradictory notions, for example, poetry and business or idle fantasies and genuine thought. Many of these individuals (the exceptions are rare) see it as worthwhile first to conjure up some theory or fantasy, or more often to resurrect ones that are already made, and then to make up their own minds about the justification of this theory or fantasy when compared to reality itself. And, the more that life contradicts their favorite dream, the more stubbornly convinced they become that it is the unequivocal interpretation of genuine life. Hence

48. Moscow University was founded in 1755 during the reign of Empress Elizaveta Petrovna. At that time, it was host to the competing ideologies of Russian conservatives, liberals, and radicals, with Westerners, Slavophiles, and proponents of "official nationality" seeking a voice in the homeland. Distinguished alumni of Moscow University included such writers as Lermontov, Griboyedov, Turgenev, and Goncharov, as well as such thinkers as Belinsky, Herzen, and Nikolai Ogaryov.

49. Others agreed. For instance, in his memoirs, Annenkov wrote: "At that time, Moscow was truly the focal point for newly born talents and powers. With special force, Muscovites formulated philosophical systems, seeking to discover particular principles [of life]. They did not fear sharp polemics or abstract discourse to express their own thoughts and experiences." Annenkov, "Zamechatel'noe desiatiletie, 1838–1848," 145.

the playing with words that these young people let pass for something real, and the playing with notions that they treat as facts. Such things, though, are innocent if not amusing. No matter what the young people who leave Moscow for Petersburg do in life, they do something. Muscovites, by contrast, limit themselves to their conversations and arguments about what needs to be done, to conversations and arguments that are often intelligent but always fruitless. The passion to deliberate and argue invigorates the lives of Muscovites, but nothing ever comes from these deliberations and arguments. Nowhere else are there so many thinkers, poets, talents, and even geniuses (especially "exalted natures") as there are in Moscow. And such individuals become known outside of Moscow only when they move to Petersburg. There, willingly or unwillingly, they fall into the mob that they have always abused and become simple mortals, or they find an actual outlet for their talents—which are sometimes remarkable, if not the stuff of genius.[50] Nowhere do people talk so much about literature as in Moscow; but it is precisely in Moscow that there is no literature of life, at least not right now. If a journal would suddenly appear in that city, it would contain nothing but high-flown views on Moscow's mystical significance. (It would take for its cue the Tsar Cannon and the great bell tower,[51] as if the city of Peter the Great stood outside of Russia and as if the giant who stands on St. Isaac's Square were not the greatest historical and sacred object of worship for the Russian people.[52]) This journal would also be filled only with numerous mediocre poems to maidens, the moon, Ivan the Great, the Sukharev Tower,[53] and sometimes—however unbelievable it may sound—to

50. Belinsky is, in part, talking about his own experiences in St. Petersburg, having come there from Moscow in 1839.

51. Belinsky is again deriding the editors of *The Muscovite,* who in 1841 published a poem by Fyodor Glinka entitled "Moscow" ("Moskva"), featuring these lines: "Who will lift the tsar-bell? Who will turn the tsar-cannon?"

Also, the Tower of Ivan the Great (Kolokol'nia Ivana Velikogo), built between 1505 and 1600 and rising some 250 feet, was once the tallest edifice in Russia—and also one of the most enduring. When Napoleon, in his retreat from Moscow in 1812, ordered that the tower be destroyed, only the contiguous belfries on the top of the structure were lost. (The entire tower was restored in 1814 and 1815.)

The Tsar Cannon (Tsar-Pushka) is another fine example of Russian craftwork. Cast in 1586, the Tsar Cannon weighs over forty tons and was designed to fire grapeshot, not cannonballs.

52. Belinsky is referring to Étienne Falconet's famous statue of Peter, *The Bronze Horseman* (*Mednyi vsadnik*), created between 1768 and 1778.

53. Belinsky here is poking fun at Evgeny Mil'keev's 1843 poem "The Sukharev Tower" ("Sukhareva bashnia"). Further, the Sukharev Tower was constructed between 1692 and 1701 by Peter the Great and

sparkling wine as if such a thing were the source of all that is great in the Russian national character. There would also be lackluster stories, belated judgments on literature, enduring hostility toward the West, and direct and indirect attacks on the immorality of anyone who does not hail the coming of this journal or who is indifferent to the genius of its collaborators. If a pamphlet were to appear, it, too, would contain either sophisticated-sounding outbursts attacking the rotten West or childish fantasies with arrogant pretensions to truths, such as that Gogol can be seen, seriously, as our Homer and that his *Dead Souls* is the only genuine epic after *The Iliad*.[54]

Although we have been talking about the problematic sides of Russian life, we do not negate the possibility of some splendid exceptions. Everywhere there exists something good but also something weak and insignificant. Petersburg and Moscow are two sides—or, better to say, two one-sided realities—whose collective brilliance simultaneously constitutes a splendid and harmonic whole. Each brings its best to the other. And the time between them is becoming shorter: the railroad has become a reality. . .

Let us now turn our attention to Petersburg.

The lowest stratum of any population, the simple folk, is the same everywhere. Nonetheless, the simple folk of Petersburg are somewhat different from their counterparts in Moscow. Besides strong vodka and tea, the simple folk in Petersburg love coffee and cigars; even peasants on the outskirts of the city are fond of such things. The fair sex, however—cooks and servant girls of all kinds—do not see tea and vodka as a necessity, but they definitely cannot live without coffee. Peasant lasses living on the outskirts of Petersburg have forgotten native Russian dances and have substituted

---

initially housed his newly founded school of mathematics and navigational science. From the eighteenth century on, the district around the structure was a thriving marketplace for foodstuffs, handicrafts, and other artifacts of popular art and culture. In 1934, the Sukharev Tower, along with hundreds of important sites in Moscow, was demolished by Soviet urban planners seeking to reconstruct areas of the city.

54. Belinsky is again taking issue with Aksakov, particularly his 1842 pamphlet *A Few Words About Gogol's Tone Poem, "The Adventures of Chichikov; or, Dead Souls"* (*Neskol'ko slov o poeme Gogolia "Pokhozhdeniia Chichikova ili Mertvye dushi"*). It should be noted that Belinsky and Aksakov were already engaged in a bitter polemic over *Dead Souls.* Belinsky's caustic review of *A Few Words* triggered an angry retort by Aksakov, which in turn prompted a final response by Belinsky, "An Explanation on the Explanation of Gogol's Tone Poem, *Dead Souls*" ("*Ob"iasnenie na ob"iasnenie po povodu poemy Gogolia 'Mertvye dushi'*"). Belinskii, *Polnoe sobranie sochinenii,* vol. 6 (1955), 253–60, 410–33; K. Aksakov, "*Ob"iasnenie po povodu poemy 'Mertvye dushi',*" *Moskvitianin,* no. 9 (1842): 220–29.

the French quadrille, which they perform to the sounds of a beloved concertina. Again, anyone can see the influence of the cunning West and the calculated consequences of its hellish intrigues! Petersburg seamstresses—and, generally speaking, all simple women who have adopted European dress—prefer hats to bonnets. It is just the reverse in Moscow, however. Again generally speaking, seamstresses and simple women dress with greater taste than Muscovite women, even those who are not of their rank and station. The same thing can also be said about the men. One knows the social stratum of an office or factory worker only by his manners, not always by his dress. Again the cunning influence of the West! Later on in our book, respected reader, there will be a story about so-called servants' balls,[55] an event about which the common folk can still only dream. When we spoke about Moscow, we purposely went on at length about the merchant and petit bourgeois classes as well as about the distinguishing characteristics of both groups. Without a doubt, the petit bourgeois of the type that Mr. Grigoriev the Second portrays so successfully on the stage of the Alexandrine Theater can be found rather frequently in Petersburg, too. They are rarely at home; rather, they are always out visiting someone as if they were aliens or foreigners passing through. The Petersburg German is more of a native of the city than they.[56] The petit bourgeois appear on the streets of Petersburg less than they do in Moscow, but one can find them on Shchukin Court[57] and in the vegetable stands, meat markets, and various petty stalls and stores strewn throughout the city.

The petit bourgeois men in Petersburg, like their civilized brethren in Moscow, are salesmen and merchants who work in the stores located on the more visible streets of Petersburg. Generally speaking, they blend into the city's population so well that they do not strike the eye as their confreres do in Moscow. We will even say that in Petersburg, these men somehow pass completely unnoticed. That is why we think that Mr. Grigoriev the Second would not have the success on the Muscovite stage

55. The piece on "servants' balls" was apparently intended for a third part of *Petersburg* that never came to be. Servants' balls, however, were a theme in an article entitled "Literary and Journal Notes" ("Literaturnye i zhurnal'nye zametki") that was published in *Otechestvennye Zapiski* in 1844. Belinsky may have been its author.

56. The life and mores of Petersburg Germans, as well as other foreigners of the city, was a special feature of Bashchutsky's *Panorama of Petersburg.*

57. Shchukin Court (Shchukin dvor) was a commercial center in the center of St. Petersburg.

that he enjoys in Petersburg. The type that Grigoriev portrays, of course, is not something unheard-of in Petersburg; but this type is also not such an everyday phenomenon that it sharply contrasts with the prevailing mores of the city or could arouse loud and merry laughter at its own expense. The merchant class in Petersburg is also quite unlike its counterpart in Moscow. In Petersburg, very few merchants, especially rich ones, have beards; indeed, bearded merchants seem like aliens in this Europeanized city. The merchants in Petersburg have even chosen special streets for their exclusive place of residence: Troitsky Lane and the streets that border on the so-called Five Corners near an Old Believer church. The majority of the merchants in Petersburg are German, even English. A large part of the city's native Russian merchants are therefore not seen as merchants at all but as wholesalers, undistinguishable from the unbroken mass that makes up the middle stratum of Petersburg.

Finally, we have reached a group who, by virtue of their numbers and common physiognomy, are known merely as the "Petersburg stratum." It is well known that no other city in the world has so many young, middle-aged, and even elderly homeless people as Petersburg has. Nowhere else, also, are domestic and family individuals so unlike the homeless as in Petersburg. In this regard, Petersburg is the antithesis of Moscow. This sharp contrast is explained by the peculiar location and circumstances of each capital. Petersburg is the center of the government; it is a city that is primarily administrative, bureaucratic, and official. Almost a third of the population in Petersburg is composed of military men, and the number of government workers almost exceeds that. In Petersburg, everyone works, everyone pleads for a job or for some designation in work. In Moscow one often hears the question: "What do you do?" But in Petersburg, this question gives way to another: "Where do you work?" In Petersburg, the word "civil servant" is as typical as the words "lord," "lady," and the like are in Moscow. The civil servant is a native, a true citizen of Petersburg. If a lackey, a boy, or a little girl, even if she is only five years old, is sent as a messenger, that person, when looking for one's apartment in some building, will ask the doorman, "Does the *civil servant* So-and-so live here?"—even if this individual does not possess any rank at all, has never worked, and has never had any intention of working. Such are the "ways" of Petersburg! The Petersburg citizen is usually "sick" with the fever of activity. In truth, he often has *nothing to do* (unlike the Muscovite who *does nothing*); but the "nothing" that engages the Petersburg citizen is for him always "something." At the very least, he always knows why he is bustling about. The Muscovites, God love them, have discovered the secret of how to do everything in the world so that the people in Petersburg can rest and do nothing. In truth, the Petersburg citizen even goes about a visit, a stroll, or a dinner with an anxious air, as if he is afraid that he will be late or lose valuable time or that he will not always accomplish everything unless he calculates or has a goal. In Moscow, even solid people are silent only when they are sleeping, but the youth there—especially those who "have given themselves over to grand hopes"—talk even when they are asleep. They sometimes even publish their more worthwhile sleep-filled ideas (which must explain some of the literary currents going on in Moscow today). But a Petersburg citizen, if he is a solid individual, is sparing with words that do not lead to a positive goal. The face of the Muscovite is open, happy, good-natured, carefree, and cordial. The Muscovite is already ready and willing to strike up a conversation or argument on any topic one may wish, and in this dialogue, he is most direct. By contrast, the face of the Petersburg citizen is always preoccupied and overcast. The Petersburg citizen is usually polite and kind but, for some reason, cold and restrained. If he strikes up a conversation, it is usually about the most ordinary things. He talks preferably about work, and he detests arguing or debating about anything. One can see from the Muscovite's face that he is satisfied with people and the world. The face of someone from Petersburg, though, shows that if he is satisfied, it is with himself, and then only if his affairs are seemingly going well. He has a meticulous sense of observation and an enduring flair for delicate irony. The Petersburg citizen will notice if one's shoes are well polished, or if one's pants have a torn cuff, or if a button is about ready to fall off one's waistcoat. He will notice these—and smile a sly and self-contented smile, one that, incidentally, reveals his entire ironic stance to the world. The Muscovite tolerates all kinds of dress and is generally oblivious to everything that has to do with external appearance. What he wishes is that one be a good old chap or a person with a heart and a soul. When the Muscovite first meets someone, he will start an argument with this individual and will only smile an ironic smile when he sees that this person's opinions do not coincide with the opinions of the circle in which he declaims at length, or in which he listens to others declaiming at length, and which he invariably considers a literary or philosophical "party." Generally speaking, any Muscovite, no matter what his calling, is completely satisfied with Moscow and can enjoy life in his own way because, in his own way, he lives in a grand, expansive style. What constitutes the Muscovite's enjoyment of life? That is another question. Everywhere, intelligent people have long agreed that a good sleep, a healthy appetite, a ruddy complexion, a strong stomach, a healthy respect for the size of the abdominal cavity, and, finally, the enviable ability to remain in a good frame of mind are the essence and the most solid foundation for genuine happiness in our sublunary world. Muscovites, being intelligent people, are fully in accord with such views. They even think that the less a person worries about something, the less he will do about it, and that the more he talks about everything, the happier he will be. And are they, happy sages, not right in this regard! For this reason, one look at a Muscovite will stimulate an individual's appetite to speak a great deal, passionately, with conviction—but decidedly without any goal or result! But the casual observer's soul remains unmoved when he looks into the face of the Petersburg citizen. The object of his scrutiny rarely has any color in his face. He is often pale, and his visage suggests the hemorrhoidal coloring peculiar to the Petersburg sky. The face of the Petersburg citizen almost always registers anxiety. It communicates something that is anxious and unsettled, but, together with this, there is also a slightly discernable pleasure with self and a sense of the person's unshakable faith in his personal worth. The Petersburg citizen never goes to bed before two in the morning, and sometimes not at all, but that does not prevent him from being at his department or place of work at nine the next day. After dinner, he invariably goes off to the theater, a party, a ball, a concert, a masquerade, a card game, or an outdoor gathering, depending on the time of the year. The Petersburg citizen manages to be everywhere, and whether he is at work or relaxing momentarily, he often keeps his eye on the clock because he fears that he will not have enough time to do everything that he wants or needs to do that day. The Muscovite is a most kind individual: trusting, talkative, and especially inclined toward friendship. By contrast, the Petersburg citizen is taciturn and regards others with distrust, projecting his feeling of his own personal worth. In his mind, at least, he is busy with business affairs or with preference, and as everyone knows, such important activities demand both silence and attention. The Petersburg citizen contrasts markedly with the Muscovite even in the way he seeks enjoyment. With food and drink, the citizen of Petersburg seeks elaborate gastronomic delights but not oceans of spirits and drinks. In society, he thinks that it is better to be bored than to give himself over to the art of gentle conversation or to risk spoiling ceremony and decorum in which he traditionally expects propriety. The exception is bachelor parties: the Russian *carouses* in the same way throughout all corners of the homeland, and in his *carousing* he always vents a steppe-like freedom reminiscent of the mores of ancient Novgorod.

Unlike Saint Petersburg, Moscow has no civil servants. To their credit, respectable Muscovites, when they are not at their place of work, can simply be people. No one need guess what they do for a living. The lower-ranking bureaucrats there still pass under the name of "petty officials," and they are considered little or insignificant by those who do not do business with them. They come to the fore, however, for those who need them. Moscow also has few military men. Those they have are there only for a period of time, on vacation. Simply put, Moscow has hardly anything official about it, and a Petersburg civil servant in Moscow is as strange and surprising a phenomenon as a Muscovite philosopher is in Petersburg. The Muscovite is, generally speaking, more original (or seemingly so) than the Petersburg citizen, and he gets accustomed to Petersburg very quickly if he moves there to live. So where do all his high-blown dreams, ideals, theories, and fantasies fly off to then? Petersburg is a solid rock, an anchor for the individual. Anyone who lives in the city does not get carried away by the whirlwinds of holiday life. He can preserve heart and soul, but not at the expense of common sense; he can sustain his human worth; he can even become a Don Quixote. To this individual, one can bravely extend his hand, from one human being to another. Petersburg has a sobering effect on several types of people.[58] Initially, its atmosphere makes one's most vibrant convictions and beliefs drift down around one like leaves falling from a tree. The same individual, though, will quickly notice that such views were not really convictions and beliefs as much as they were dreams born of a holiday-style

58. Belinsky is speaking from personal experience. For instance, he wrote to Vasily Botkin on February 3, 1840, "Petersburg was for me a terrible cliff which my starry-eyed idealism (*prekrasnodushie*) knocked up against in a painful way. This was something that was necessary and improved my life. . . . I will always thank fate for driving me to this vile Finnish swamp." See Belinskii, *Polnoe sobranie sochinenii,* vol. 11 (1956), 437.

life and a probable ignorance of reality. He may feel a momentary deep grief, but he will also embrace much that is sacred and humane. After all, what are these dreams, really! In the eyes of a *practical* (i.e., "judicious") person, the most enchanting of them are worthless alongside the most bitter reality because the happiness of a stupid person is a falsehood, and the suffering of a practical person is a truth and consequently something that is fruitful for the future.

To complete our picture, we are including an excerpt from an excellent article about Petersburg and Moscow which still retains its relevance despite the fact that it was published seven years ago:

> Petersburg is always on the move, from its cellars to its attics. For instance, from midnight on, it begins to bake all kinds of French breads, which its various peoples will devour entirely the very next day. All night long, Petersburg first keeps one eye open, then the other. By contrast, all of Moscow sleeps soundly during the night, and on the next day, it crosses itself, greets everyone in sight, and heads off to the bakery and market. Moscow is a feminine city; Petersburg is a masculine one. In Moscow, everyone is a bride; in Petersburg, everyone is a groom. Petersburg observes strict propriety in its dress, for it does not like gaudy flowers or sharp and bold departures from fashion. Moscow, however, demands that whatever is fashionable must be on display everywhere. If a dress fitted at the waist is long, then Moscow lets it be still longer; if the lapels of a jacket are large, then Moscow insists that they must look like the doors of a barn. Petersburg is an exacting individual, a most absolute German. It looks at everything in a calculated way, and before it even begins to think about giving a party, it takes a look into its pocket. Moscow is a Russian nobleman, and if it decides to make merry, then it will do so until it drops and not worry about whether it needs more funds than it finds in its pocket. Moscow does not like the middle way. It always travels wrapped up in a bearskin coat and, most often, out to dinner. Petersburg wears a banker's suit, has both its hands in its pockets, and flies off at full speed to the Exchange or to its "place of business." Moscow is out on the town until four in the morning, and

on the next day, it does not rise from bed earlier than two in the afternoon. Petersburg also is partying until 4:00 A.M., but by nine the next day, it acts as though nothing has happened and rushes off to work in its banker's suit. In Moscow, Rus' dawdles along with money in its pocket and returns home in a free and easy manner. In Petersburg, people go about the city streets without any money at all but travel to any corner of the globe with a sizable amount of capital. In Moscow, Rus' jaunts along in winter carriages over winter potholes to buy and sell. In Petersburg, though, the Russian people go about on foot in the summer to build and work. Moscow is a pantry; it piles up packages and goods and does not want to look at the petty buyer. Petersburg is divided and broken up into little pieces. Everywhere it features shops and stores, and works to lure everyday customers. Moscow says, "If and when I need to buy a thing or two, I will go out and get it." Petersburg peeks from under a sign, burrows under a floor with its Rhinelike cellars, and places a cabbie's exchange in front of the very doors of a home. Moscow does not consider its own citizens first but sends its goods throughout all of Rus'. Petersburg sells ties and gloves to its civil servants. Moscow is a huge arcade. Petersburg is an enlightened store. Russia needs Moscow; Petersburg needs Russia. In Moscow one rarely sees a waistcoat without a family coat of arms. In Petersburg there are no waistcoats without such adornments. Petersburg loves to make sarcastic remarks about Moscow and its awkwardness and lack of taste. Moscow jeers at Petersburg, claiming that it does not know how to speak Russian. On Nevsky Prospekt in Petersburg, people go walking at two in the afternoon and look as though they have emerged from the fashionable pictures of a journal that has been displayed in a store window. Even the old ladies wear such narrow-waisted dresses that they look ridiculous. At street festivals in Moscow, a fashionable crowd always includes some motherly types wearing kerchiefs on their heads and dresses without any waist at all.[59]

59. Belinsky is quoting, somewhat inaccurately, from Gogol's 1836 work "Petersburg Notes" ("Peterburgskie zametki").

We have omitted several lines from this excerpt because they are already obsolete and because they need additional interpretation. But we cannot pass over the phrase "Russia needs Moscow; Petersburg needs Russia" without comment. Such a phrase is more witty than fair-minded. Russia needs both Petersburg and Moscow, and both Moscow and Petersburg need Russia. One cannot diminish the historical importance of Moscow, even if one cannot say precisely in what it consists. The importance of Petersburg is, at this point in its history, clearer a priori than a posteriori. That is why we say that we are living in a genuine moment of our history.

Our past is not so great that we can only guess about the future and not talk about it with confidence. We are in a period of transition. That is why we think it wise to seize upon, in a truthful and determined way, the characteristics of both cities. Discoursing about what they are now, one must always keep in mind what they can become in the future. Perhaps the significance of Moscow lies in the fact that the city preserves our national beginnings (the essence of which, like the essences of many things in this world, is impossible to define) and that it counters foreign influences that could remain decidedly external and thus fruitless if they did not encounter and struggle with national elements. Everything living is the result of struggle; everything that makes its appearance and is affirmed without struggle is dead. Despite the evident passion of Moscow for new opinions, or more accurately, new ideas, it is—Lord help it—still living in the old way and is perfectly content to do so. It receives ideas like a German: ideas are one thing, and life is another. Clearly, Moscow embraces a personal *conservative* beginning that only now, slowly and little by little—is admitting new ways of doing things but refusing to submit totally to them. The representative of new images and ideals is Petersburg, and this is of great significance for Russia. Petersburg does not get carried away by ideas: it is like a positive and thoughtful individual. It never calls a banker's suit a Roman toga; it prefers playing preference to worrying about the impossible; it cannot tolerate dreams, and it is not in awe of theories and speculation. Petersburg does not find it pleasant to be situated in a swamp, but it prefers this to being suspended in thin air, without any supports at all.

The law of Petersburg is the accumulating force of circumstances, and it is ready to do whatever needs to be done. Thus, it finds it wise to act on the basis of what it was and what it is. Not a single Petersburg citizen passes himself off for a genius or dreams of transforming reality. He knows life too well not to be reconciled to its sheer force. Geniuses are born by the hundreds only in those places where circumstances permit a pervasive ignorance of what is called reality, where everyone takes his own measure of the world, and where the dreams of idle fantasy are accepted on a par with the indisputable facts of history and of contemporary life. In Petersburg everything has its own place because if someone there has pretensions of being better or more elevated than others, he will be told, "Well, go ahead, give it a try!" Simply put, Petersburg does not believe in ideas; it demands action and the realization of ideas. There everyone strives toward a goal, and no matter what it may be, he attains it. This has its own advantage, and a great one at that, for no matter what reality may be, customs—generated by the acquired ability to make things happen—are a marvelous thing. An individual who sits idly by, twiddling his thumbs as if he has nothing to do, may be able to act when the time comes; a city is not like an individual, though. Even though a hundred years may pass by, the city will have no concept of time. Simply put, we think that Petersburg has always been fated to work and do things and that it is Moscow's task to prepare doers. This can be seen even now. How many young people, after they have finished the course of science at Moscow University, come to work in Petersburg! Notwithstanding the influence of Moscow University and the quiet *provincial* location of Moscow, the people there do not read any more than their counterparts in Petersburg. In the areas of science, literature, and art, though, Muscovites acquire more breadth, knowledge, taste, tact, and education than do the majority of the Petersburg reading and thinking public. As a result, the young people of Moscow are more capable of action than those in Petersburg, but they accomplish things only if they come to Petersburg. In Moscow, the people—even the young—only talk about what they would do, if they ever got around to doing something.

—V. Belinsky

The Petersburg Yardkeeper

Vladimir Dal'

Outside the weather is fair to middling. Visitors would call it nasty, but natives would find it tolerable and even hope that it will still rain buckets in the evening. The cabbies are completely content with the situation: rides in their covered carriages will cost more.

One yardkeeper sweeps the flagstone; and across from him, a second varnishes iron posts with oil and soot: a great boon to the coats and capes of the pedestrians who pass by.

"Hey, Ivan, that oil you got there—is it the raw kind?" asks the yardkeeper with the broom.

"What?"

"You can smell it clear across the street."

"Yeah, it's raw. It ain't thickened, so I'm smearin' it on so I don't get hauled in before the police."

Civil servants walk along at a pace somewhere between an amble and a half run. The clip-clop of their shoes brings to mind the assured walk of a horse trader. The first yardkeeper catches each and every one of them with his broom; he does so vigorously, sweeping right up to their legs. The civil servants take their turn jumping over his broom. One of them, though, stops and swears.

The yardkeeper keeps right on working, as though he has not heard what the civil servant said. He grumbles to himself, but loudly enough to be heard across the street:

"So you won't go around me, huh? Don't you got eyes in your head?"

The other yardkeeper (for whose benefit he is speaking so loudly) merely laughs. He straightens up, rolls up his sleeves, and scratches his side with his elbow. He shifts the black oily broom to his left hand, resting and freeing up his right to scratch his head.

A respectably dressed man stops at the gate, looks at the sign, and asks, "Hey, pal, can you tell me where the yardkeeper is here?"

Grigory keeps silent, as though he has not heard. The gentleman repeats his question, this time a little more loudly and insistently.

"There. Ask inside."

The gentleman passes through the gate. The second yardkeeper, Ivan, laughs and says, "How come you didn't answer him?"

"Many of his kind pass through here!" Grigory answers, continuing to sweep.

A cabbie for hire passes by at a trot. He is asleep, sitting sideways in his carriage. His horse is broken down; his carriage is all in tatters. The leather between his splashboards is torn, and straw sticks out from the cushion. Suddenly, a bolt falls from the wheel.

The yardkeeper with a broom keeps an eye on the cabbie for quite some time. He then rushes out into the middle of the street, picks up the bolt, and puts in into his pocket. By this time, though, the wheel has fallen off the carriage, and the cabbie has almost smashed his nose on the pavement. He jumps out, stops his horse, and rushes back. Having seen the yardkeeper walking back to the sidewalk, the cabbie asks him, "Did you, by chance, pick up anything, my friend?"

"Anything or anyone?"

"Why, like that there bolt. Give it back, please!"

"You saw me pick up something?"

"How could I not? Give it back, please!"

"Give it back? What should I give back? Better you give me a two-kopeck piece before you start saying 'give it back.' "

Little by little, the quarrel becomes more heated. The cabbie first pleads; then he swears that he does not have even five kopecks, since he had only just now left the garage. The abuse and cries begin. Along with the usual invectives, one only hears, "Give it back, I tell you, give it back!" on one side, and on the other, "What should I give you back? Did you see me pick up something?"

With warlike cries, the enemies set upon each other. The yardkeeper, Ivan, brush in hand, takes advantage of the pleasant spectacle, and, smiling, he takes a rest from his chores. A crowd begins to gather, forming a circle. A rather hefty fellow also stops. Having found out about the entire affair, he says to the cabbie, "Why start a brawl? Why talk to him at all, the dog? You hit him in the snout, and I'll smack him on the back of the head."

Hardly has he said this when the two, as if on command, put such practical advice into action. All around the crowd begins to laugh loudly. The obstinate Grisha is stunned by the sudden resolve of the cabbie and his friend. He fishes the bolt from his pocket and gives it back to the cabbie with this advice: "Don't you lose it again, 'cause you ain't gonna get it back again. No'un else won't give it up, no matter how much you hem and haw! Next time you'll have to pay a ruble to a smithy for a new one. There's lots of the likes of you out there!"

The spectators enjoy the shameful spectacle. They now go their separate ways, occasionally glancing back. The cabbie puts the wheel back on the carriage and tightens the bolt, cursing all the while. The yardkeeper Grigory again takes up his broom and confines himself to repeating the advice he has just offered the cabbie. The yardkeeper Ivan teases his friend. He laughs quietly, "Why did ya let the cabbie go? Wasn't the lad's fist good and sound?"

Meanwhile, the gentleman has been searching for a yardkeeper in all the corners of the courtyard. He now comes back out through the gate, and, rather insistently, he addresses our friend: "So you're the local yardkeeper, right?"

"Who ya lookin' for?"

"The titular counselor Bylov."[1]

"Go left after the gate, top floor, door on the left."

"But why didn't you tell me that when I had asked you before? You were also the local yardkeeper then, weren't you?"

"The yardkeeper, indeed? Not 'nuff yardkeepers 'round here, if you ask me! Why some, the rich masters, have three apiece, livin' right there with them. But ours gets along with only one."

1. A "titular counselor" (*tituliarnyi sovetnik*) or "staff captain" (*shtabs-kapitan*) occupied the ninth step in the so-called Table of Ranks (*Tabel' o rangakh*) established by Peter the Great in 1722 for service in the Russian army, navy, guards, civil service, and court bureaucracy.

The visitor has to accept such logic for an answer. He shrugs his shoulders and sets out, following the yardkeeper's directions.

Two ladies pass along the side of the street. One has a small dog in her hands. She kisses it and slobbers all over it profusely.

"Now would ya look at that," says the amused yardkeeper Ivan. "Them ladies over there won't kiss their own kids, but they'll slobber all over their pets!"

The two ladies glare at the smiling yardkeeper, staring at him as though he had said something impertinent and unforgivable.

Meanwhile, a slovenly servant girl darts out of the building in Grigory's charge. Her hands are covered by a greasy calico which she has sewn at her own expense. She is quite annoyed: Her mistress, you see, has taken it into her head to present her with two kitchen aprons, one made from canvas, the other from ticking. "Grigory!" she begins to scream. "Hey there, you, Grigory! Good Lord, what a bunch! Did you done bring today's water?"

"Keep your shirt on! What's yer rush?"

"'Keep your shirt on,' he says! That's what you always say. The mistress is swearin' up a storm; this is already the third time she chased me out for water. I've run aroun' the entire house, and there's ain't no water nowhere. And here he is, cool as a cucumber, as if for the love of Christ the water is to get there all by itself. You'd really like that, wouldn't you? Get a move on, damn it, and bring us some water!"

"So it's bring you water? Well now, you take your pick: either I go for water or I sweep the street. And what if the master should happen to pass by? Why, then we'd both be in for a holiday, wouldn't we?"

"Holiday? What do I care about holidays! It seems that you're always on a holiday! Just bring us some water!"

Grigory turns around and, slow as a bear, heads for the gate. The servant girl sees that her eloquence has vanquished his obstinacy, and she runs quickly back through the gate. Grigory, with a powerful wave of his hand, flings the broom behind him. Ivan, though, cries out, "Well now, our fancy lady has left! She almost got it that time. She really must find it hard to walk about so fancy-like!" And alluding to her bare feet, he adds, "You'll get your socks frostbit, my lady!"

Between such diversions, Ivan and Grigory do their chores (if only because no one else will do them). You get up at dawn, tidy the yard, sweep around the gate, carry water for as many as ten families, and carry wood to the top floor—all for about forty kopecks a month. (Grigory usually hoists an extra pile of logs on his shoulders because he wants to do it all in one trip. To do so, he puts on his hat and stretches the rope across his head, securing the load with his hand.)

You scrape ice off the walk, sweep it, and throw sand over it; next you sweep the street and take away the garbage. You then tidy around the well where the cabbies stand and pile up everything in the yard. For a cartload of manure, foreigners pay him a ruble (willingly, by the way). Germans, you see, have need of such things. Next you glance around—if not rain, then snow; again you sweep the walk, doing so day after day. During the entire time, you also guard the apartment building and frequently run down to the police station to report about a new occupant. You are up and down the entire night. You hardly sleep, much less oversleep. The doorbell, you see, is located right over your very head. You cannot get away from it (but you would if you could). Almost all the living space in his cellar room is taken up by a huge stove. Go down about half a dozen steps, stop, and blow away the heavy air and clouds of steam. If, by the third step, you have not fainted from the sour and rancid fumes, you will catch a glimpse of the various objects lying amid the endless gloom of the cellar.

Beyond the forbidding hefty-sized stove, you will see a bench, lacking legs at one end and propped up there by a barrel; a table with legs protruding a full two inches from the tabletop; and, between the stove and the wall, a bed that leads a most perverse life. During the day, it rests like a spark slumbering amid the ashes; but at night, it comes alive, supporting the corpulent body of our hefty yardkeeper. (Grigory, by the way, envies no one and speaks in such a way as not to offend his colleagues.) Remarkably, the animals that share Grigory's quarters have grown accustomed to the doorbell. They are like fish bred for sale, only in a reverse sense. Such fish come together whenever the master rings a bell; the yardkeeper's animals, by contrast, immediately scatter in all directions once the wicked doorbell sounds over the head of sleeping Grigory. They patiently await his return and bravely retake the field only when he lies down to sleep. (One of the lapels of his sheepskin coat covers his head). Grigory's room also features three very short shelves standing next to the stove. They hold two wooden cups and one clay one, spoons, a pitcher for seltzer, a quart bottle, a half-quart bottle, a small carafe, some kind of opaque and empty glassware, and a golden china cup bearing the crown of a count. Under the bench are a storm green samovar with three legs; two broken bottles filled with lard and soot (for smearing posts); and, most likely for the sake of a full and pleasant smell, a pile of scorched oil lamps. Pots and pans are not part of Grigory's housekeeping; instead, two cast-iron vessels, one for *shchi,*[2] the other for kasha, stay permanently on the stove or, at the very least, are never removed from the hearth. To wash these vessels occasionally is a task that Grigory sees as completely superfluous because he knows from experience that no matter how many times he cleans them, they still get dirty. (Incidentally, Grigory once assured me that he washes all his dishes once a year—during Holy Week, but, as he himself said, not for the sake of cleanliness but for his sins.)

In Grigory's cellar room, also, a sheepskin coat and a caftan hang over the bench by the window so that Grigory, when he is having dinner with friends, can amuse both himself and his guests by wiping his face on his clothes. In the corner is an icon surrounded by willow branches. Inside the icon case are a small egg that has been saved from Easter and a small piece of the *kulich*[3] with which he broke the fast this year. Under the icon case are a bottle with holy water that has been blessed on the feast of the Epiphany and a pair of porcelain eggs. One should also mention the hand towel that hangs under the mirror in the corner, next to the shelves and alongside the pictures of Platov and Blücher—if only for the item's scarlet embroidery. This hand towel has been greased and fattened with all kinds of things. Indeed, it could not possibly hold any more. Most likely, it has lasted this long only because the mice have not yet managed to get it off the nail, and also because Grigory does not keep dogs. It happened, though, that a hungry dog once quietly made off with this tasty towel, and it would have disappeared without a trace if the dog had not gotten into a fight with another stray over the tasty morsel. The quarrel attracted the yardkeeper's attention to the prize at stake (which, since neither of the litigating

2. *Shchi* is a soup made with cabbage or sauerkraut, winter vegetables, and sometimes meat.

3. *Kulich* is a Russian cake that is made at Easter. Studded with candied fruit, almonds, and raisins, and flavored with saffron and rum, it is baked in a tall and cylindrical pan, and drizzled with white frosting. On one side, spelled out in candied fruit are the letters XB, representing the Cyrillic letters for *Khristos voskres* or "Christ is risen."

criminals had claimed it, had become quite damaged in the fray). Grigory kicked one hound in the leg, shook the towel several times, and hung it back in its place. In cases such as these, Grigory does, in fact, love order.

You might ask: Why does Grigory always sweep the yard and street, when he himself cannot boast that his own kennel is particularly tidy? Well, to tell the truth, Grigory is not so much responsible for such activities as is his master who never lets him out of his sight. That is why matters of cleanliness have become so hateful and wearisome to our yardkeeper. In his own cellar room, though, Grigory gets even for it all. There he is his own boss. There—and only there—can he breathe freely, delighting in the soft and dirty exterior of all the objects in his household, sustained if not intoxicated by the heady fragrance of its homegrown atmosphere.

The next morning, Ivan and Grigory, brooms in their hands, again greet each other from opposite sides of the street.

"What's with you? You OK?"

"I'm down with something," Grigory says. "I can hardly move and my stomach is upset."

"You should drink a spot of *kvas,*" answers Ivan, "and eat some cucumbers with lots of salt."[4]

"No, I've already drunk some water mixed with ashes in it; maybe it'll go away."

Ashes do not cure him completely, however, and so Grigory decides to visit his physician, that is, a shopkeeper, for help. The physician-shopkeeper does not question him for long, but, having learned all the chief symptoms, he has Grigory lie on his stove. He orders his patient to lie on his stomach and to press down tightly against some freshly baked loaves of bread. The physician-shopkeeper then covers the sick man with a sheepskin coat and gives him something hot to drink. At dinnertime, he has the yardkeeper stand up. Grigory thanks his "physician," at the same time thinking that it would not be a bad idea if, after all this, he should take care of himself and satisfy his hunger with a light Lenten meal: sauerkraut, cucumbers, a piece of rotting fish, and some lamp oil.

Grigory sometimes loves to yell at and abuse people, but he is also quite willing not to raise a fuss. He is content merely to turn away, grumble, and

4. *Kvas* is a fermented, mildly alcoholic beverage made from black or rye bread.

berate someone behind the person's back. He has told Ivan a hundred times that today would be his last day at his master's and that he would leave the next day without fail—only to return to work the next morning, armed with broom, shovel, or buckets. Grigory's master is, though, quite pleased with him, in particular for his honesty and meticulous tending to his job. Grigory also has a flair for spotting suspicious characters on sight, and he usually sends them packing. He begins by plying them with questions—why have they come and whom do they want to see—and then he demands their passport and place of residence. From past experience, Grigory knows that these people are most unwilling to disclose such things. They usually do not prolong the conversation but seek a place to stay elsewhere. Grigory will sometimes meet a man with a half-shaven beard and wearing a greasy-colored kerchief and a small, down overcoat. Quickly and assuredly, he will explain to this man, "Well, old boy, fellow, there's nothin' for you here. You best be on your way." Without further ado (so he thinks), he grabs the uninvited guest by the hair and hustles him away by the scruff of his neck. The cheerful yardkeeper Ivan deals with such cases in a different way. He forces a thief to take flight through an opening under the gate, driving him on from behind with frequent swats of his broom.

Sometimes, a lucky scavenger brings Grigory a piece of clothing he has happened to come across somewhere, which he now conceals under his arm. Grigory, with an absolutely clear conscience, either barters for the thing or buys it outright if he can get it cheaply enough or if it can be easily repaired. "What's it to me?" he says. "What do I know? I didn't steal it, did I? Sure, it's stolen, but not from around here."

During the holidays, Grigory loves to dress up as a cabbie. In summer, he wears a velveteen coat; in winter, he dons a dandyish caftan, velveteen trousers, and a sheepskin coat thrown over his shoulders. He even puts on a foppish, wide-brimmed hat. Thus decked out, Grigory often sits outside the gate. With arms folded, he whistles through his teeth or treats himself to some peas that he fishes out of a fiery red kerchief. Such kerchiefs, by the way, are now rare. They are called "diamond kerchiefs" because a white pattern was etched on a scarlet field with some kind of acid. These diamonds, however, quickly become little holes, which now cause Grigory to pick up the peas that fall to the ground, blow the dirt off of them, and eat them one by one. Ivan, sitting alongside or across from his friend, prefers cabbage stalks; otherwise, he turns to turnips. Their tastes merge in summer, however, because both men delight in gooseberries that are still unripe—green, bitter, and no bigger than a pea. Almost daily, both yardkeepers stock up on two or three pomade jars full of this delicacy; they buy them from a twisted and misshapen woman who walks through the streets, screeching like a rooster: "Gooseberries, ripe gooseberries, home-grown gooseberries, the finest ones around," and so forth. The woman does not raise her head to the windows above; rather, she looks downward to the cellar apartments, and, for a kopeck, she gathers the pomade jars from below.

Grigory cannot stand nuts, though, since he believes that it is proper only for girls to eat such things!

Grigory spends an entire holiday on the following: From time to time, he really goes and ties one on, having some countryman take his place for days on end. He never makes arrangements in advance, though, and he never goes out of town. Indeed, if anyone mentions that a holiday is coming, he usually replies, "But what kind of a holiday is it for the likes of us?" Grigory agrees completely with a certain worker who responds to all holidays, even Christmas, with a touch of philosophical depression. This workman, for instance, once remarked with a sigh, "Yes, what kind of a holiday is it for the likes of us? Why, the fun lasts only three days in all. You hardly have time to make merry when, before you know it, you wind up in the clinker."

"But, my friend," replies the slow-witted Grigory, "you never know where you'll be."

"No one really gets picked up," the worker retorts, shrugging his shoulders. "For the first three days, they leave everyone alone."

The holidays, despite their insignificance to Grigory as days of feasting, are nonetheless special to him because on these days, he goes to all his occupants to collect his rents. Grigory's apartments are like those of his master: they are all assessed by their occupants' income. They range from the ten kopecks he receives twice a year from an absolutely wretched bookbinder who smells of moldy paste to a red assignat for two apartments on a second floor. Imitating Ivan's wit, Grigory gives nicknames to his tenants according to the number of rubles that he receives from them during Christmas and Holy Week, for example, "the twenty-kopeck bookbinder," "the three-ruble bureaucrat," and so forth. Grigory even once raised the tax on vodka, thereby moving one occupant from the three- to the five-ruble category. (Rumors about Grigory's classification have reached the ears of his tenants.) Whenever a new tenant arrives, Grigory always manages to inform him well in advance (and before the holidays) how much he normally received from his previous lodger. Moreover, those rowdy dwellers who return home at all hours of the night Grigory sometimes (and insistently) charges a top rate (*for tea*), contending that there is much more bother with them.

Grigory also has a small business on the side. He is tied up with a small circle of speculators from a small domestic bank, and he will lend them, with full guarantee and collateral, up to a hundred rubles on interest. On a loan of a hundred rubles, Grigory rarely succeeds in making more than eight or nine rubles a month. From time to time, someone will reproach him for overcharging, claiming that the State Treasury takes only five or six rubles for a similar amount. In reply, Grigory will wave his hand and say with the utmost calm, "Well, then go to the treasury." Grigory does warn them, though: "Whatever you do, don't go to the count's valet. That one will charge you twenty rubles a month. What's more, he'll take the receipt showing that he bought your pledge, and if he can find a good buyer, he'll sell that, too, even before the repayment date is due." Grigory sees no sin in such deals as these. He will say, "I don't force no one, I don't stick my nose into other people's business. But fifty rubles are no good just lyin' around in my trunk."

That such transactions have to be conducted in secret, though—this Grigory understands very well. After all, if such dealings were not done in secret, they would be considered very corrupt affairs indeed. It is a well-known fact in Grigory's world that one must guard against complaining in public and keep everything to himself; otherwise, one can get caught up in all kinds of trifles and will be indicted for everything. Grigory is, after all, an old yardkeeper and a citizen of Petersburg's streets. It often happens, then, that he will encounter and become friends with all kinds of people. Grigory not only knows the tricks of Petersburg's rogues, but he also understands their language; and Ivan sometimes takes lessons from his streetwise friend. For instance, "to wipe something out" means "to pilfer a hat"; "to grind down a rogue's skates and rakes" means "to furnish a young helper with slippers and gloves"; "to get hold of a tag" means "to acquire a passport"; and "to make off with a bench" means "to steal a horse." Such expressions Grigory understands without a translation. Grigory even makes the bemused Ivan laugh. Once during a holiday, both yardkeepers were sitting side by side outside the gate and were becoming giddy from the fumes of some stinking oil lamps. Apparently, the theater had just closed for the evening, and a sizable gang of rogues was passing by. These rogues caught sight of a colleague who had been stationed there to observe life *behind the scenes,* that is, to pick the pockets of the passersby. They asked their friend, "How's the glue these days?" meaning, "How's business"? Grigory interrupted quite calmly, "*Knucklebones, freckles, and rags,*" that is, "Money, a watch, and a kerchief." The rogues looked at Grigory in a bewildering way. Was he a swindler, too, they wondered, and if so, was he friend or foe? Ivan also learned from Grigory how to scare off such scoundrels and how to recognize them in a crowd. Grigory only had to say, "Easy does it!" that is, "Look out!" and any swindler would suddenly look around.

Like all his fellow yardkeepers, Grigory knows such people. Sometimes he catches them red-handed. He even knows, through word of mouth, who they are and what and where they steal. So why, you might ask, does Grigory not set a trap for them or report them to the police as he should? Why does he regard them with indifference, as harmless individuals who do not concern him? Why? Because when all is said and done, Grigory has his own ideas and convictions, his own views and worldly experience—information that has been handed down from generation to generation. It would indeed be difficult to refute such deeply imprinted and accepted views. Grigory is firmly and logically convinced that he who gets caught is guilty but that he who gets away is not. He believes that only public crime warrants investigation and that the guilty are those who are openly mixed up in a dangerous affair. To back up such views, Grigory has a hundred absurd reasons in reserve. For instance, as he sees it, a person becomes guilty for informing on a thief, another for being implicated as a witness, and still another for getting dragged through interrogations and depositions. Grigory also has little use for the individual who gets sentenced for giving *conflicting* testimony about an affair of which he has absolutely no knowledge, that is, one time he says that he knows nothing, another time he says that he does not know anything. Grigory has similar disdain for people who are seized and imprisoned because they have stopped in passing to glance at a floating corpse or a so-called dead body, or for those who get involved, written up, and convicted because they have taken it into their heads to intervene when someone was being robbed. In short, Grigory considers himself an experienced individual and habitually judges cases rather cold-bloodedly.

Grigory knows by heart the way each of his tenants rings the bell. The sounding of the thing immediately causes an uproar among the occupants of the building as well as the visitors in his own apartment. Having awakened, Grigory usually grumbles to himself, half asleep. "That's the twenty-kopeck master, no doubt," he says. "Now, then, don't get so bent out of shape, you still have time." Then he turns slowly, combs his hair, yawns, and throws on his coat. Taking the keys in his hands, he next sets out barefoot on the snow, shoving his right hand into the left sleeve of his coat along the way. Since Grigory is still half asleep, he cannot find the other sleeve. He stops again under the gate and mutters, "What devil sewed these sleeves on so tight?" Then he will cry aloud, "I'm coming!" and grumble (this time, by the way, not altogether to himself), "These people tell you, 'Hurry up, get a move on!' I'm frozen through, what a business!" But, having opened the gate, though, Grigory usually becomes more civil and polite. He lets the lodger in without a word, but sometimes he mutters, as if unwittingly and half with a yawn, "Be so kind, dear sir." Ivan, though, handles things in a different way. A lively and cheerful individual, he does not force his lodger to tarry at the gate. If it is late, however, he exchanges bows with the newcomer, and, dressed only in a nightshirt and standing barefoot in the snow, he says to him, "We just had another person, sir, who also came home late. He's a good master, thank you, and just like your grace, he always gives a little something for tea." Note: *for tea,* not vodka. (Ivan has a countryman who polishes floors, a man of rather refined manners, and from him Ivan learned to express himself a bit more precisely.)

One must also say several words about our Grigory's domestic relations, that is, his family and household.

Whether Grigory is good or bad, whether he is honest in *his way* or *ours,* or whether he earns a lot or a little, he does take care of his family in the village. He, like others, will talk of his life in one and the same way: "You see, the times are hard, the Good Lord does not give birth to bread, the land we have is little, and then there's the poll tax, the levy on the land, and the assessments of the village councils. . . . I also have to pay taxes for my father because he is blind; well, for my father, that would be nothing. But I also have to pay for my grandfather because he's still alive. He isn't blind, mind you; but he sits on the stove just like Il'ya Muromets.[5] . . . I also have to pay for my two small children, one deceased, the other living."

Grigory will live for ten, perhaps fifteen more years. When he returns to the village for good, he will also sit on the stove, having gotten rid of all his businesses; or, if his money is not tied up in mortgages, he will take up trading. Grigory will come to the village with about three or four hundred rubles. He will çut open a window for a shop near his hut, prop up some shutters with a pole, and hang about ten bundles of branches (bast and hemp), together with halters, horse bridles, and three garlands of turnip-shaped onions. He will also have two barrels, one with pitch, the other with honey, and they will stand side by side, according to the well-known proverb.[6] Grigory will also have ten belted knouts, hewn ropes, bast shoes, gingerbread cookies, braids, and several knitted lambskins. Here will be all his reserves, all his trade.

And if one thinks that Grigory will not make a go of it, he is mistaken. Grigory is an experienced man. The tar in his barrel will be so endless that he will fill two or three barrels more. Grigory will cut and spread his honey so masterfully that if, during tea, one does not lick the thick paper on which it has set, he will never really know its true taste. Finally, Grigory will have ropes . . . ropes without end. He will measure them by the turns of his flywheel, unwinding for his patron as much as he wants. Indeed, the customer will be amazed; he will only raise his hands in a hopeless gesture. Rope, however, is expensive, and as one cannot get it everywhere, one takes as much as one can.

Ivan, I think, will not go back to the village. Rather, he will decide to become a cabbie. Otherwise, he will break ice in the winter and sell apples

5. Ilya Muromets is a hero of the Russian *byliny,* or heroic folk epics.

6. That is, "a spoonful of tar in a barrel of honey" (*lozhka degtia v bochke meda*).

in the summer; and, in spring and fall, he will buy and sell whatever happens to appear in the market. Ivan's ambition makes him feel constricted among yardkeepers and bored at home; after all, a man with an urban education finds it difficult to live in a backwater . . .[7]

—V. Lugansky

7. Ludicrous is the assessment of L. Kozlov, who insists that "the portrait of the Petersburg yardkeeper [in Dal''s work] underscores the darkness, ignorance, and lack of culture [in such an individual] and arouses a feeling of responsibility in society for the situation for this poor soul." Quoted in V. Dal', *Povesti, rasskazy, ocherki, skazki* (Moscow: Goslitizdat, 1961), 13.

The Petersburg Organ-Grinders

Dmitri Grigorovich

Introduction

Look at this person, moving slowly along the pavement; examine his figure attentively. His long hair is black as pitch; it sticks out in disarray from under a torn cap, overshadowing his thin, sunburned face. Also notice his jacket, without color or buttons; his worsted scarf, carelessly wound about his swarthy neck; his canvas trousers and tattered slippers; and finally, a huge musical organ, bending his figure with its weight. These items make up the property of one of Petersburg's most abused artisans: the organ-grinder. Particularly observe this individual as he works the street. His left hand laboriously turns the bronze handle of his organ. The sounds, first mournful, then cheerful, burst forth and fill the street. Meanwhile, its owner fixes his eyes on the windows above. He listens attentively for the slightest cry or call, and should he meet a friendly face, he stands his street organ upright and begins to play the best piece of his repertoire. Each time, however, one of the pipes of the organ forgets all respect for human ears and starts to squeal in a loud and annoying manner. Look again. Look at the painstaking care with which the organ-grinder turns the handle. He thinks that, in so doing, he will make amends for his harsh-sounding instrument and that he will not create an unpleasant situation for his listeners. A small window opens, and, a half- or five-kopeck piece, wrapped in paper, falls at the organ-grinder's feet. It is a reward for his efforts. All too often, though, the organ-grinder exhausts his repertoire in vain. He withdraws slowly—sad, downcast—without murmur or complaint. He has lông grown accustomed to such a life. No matter what the weather—rain, sultry heat, or hard frost—one will always see the organ-grinder in the same clothes, with the same street organ on his back. All this so that he can earn a copper half kopeck. It is more often the case, though, that when the organ-grinder plays, he receives only a "fitting rebuke" from a janitor (dispatched by some registrar who has returned home from work, eaten an ample meal, and settled down for a long nap). A single street organ often feeds an entire family, so one can well imagine how the poor organ-grinder suffers whenever he attempts to move a crowd. (His attempts are often in vain, I might add, because a large part of his audience usually takes a dislike to him.)

Of all the professions, of all the possible means by which to earn one's daily bread, the most pitiful, the most uncertain is the calling of an organ-grinder. All artisans have profit as a goal. A half-destitute woman, dressed in a dirty coat (and marked with small patches from top to bottom), sells boiled potatoes on Haymarket Square.[1] She keeps them warm in a well-known way—only with the rags that make up her undergarments. The woman entices invalids and peasants by crying, "Potatoes, get 'em while they're hot! Soldiers, soldiers, come and get 'em! Spuds . . . get your spuds . . . men for your ladies, get 'em while they're hot." Such a woman is certain that she will return home with a thick piece of bread. With it, she will feed two or three imps of either masculine or feminine gender. (It is difficult to guess which, judging by clothes alone.) The organ-grinder, by contrast, climbs down from an attic or up from a cellar. Unlike an artisan or the potato woman, he is rarely sure if his meager trade will earn him enough to eat. He is equally uncertain as to whether he will have enough money to pay his rent at the end of the month. (The organ-grinder's apartment is typically a corner rented from the very same potato woman, and for late payment of the rent, she would have the full right to chase him from his yard.)

If you examine well the moral side of the organ-grinder, you will find that his rough exterior often conceals a sound inner power—his conscience.

1. Haymarket Square (Sennaia ploshchad'), now called Peace Square (Ploshchad' mira) and located right in the center of St. Petersburg, came into being in the 1730s and enjoyed an unenviable reputation as the focal point of prostitutes, beggars, and thieves. Not surprisingly, Haymarket Square was the site of a cholera outbreak in 1831. Much of the area was destroyed by Soviet urban planners in the 1930s.

As do other poor men, the organ-grinder could beg for alms. What would stop him? After all, why should he carry a street organ on his back all day long? Why should he give up his freedom, spend month after month training dogs, and exhaust his patience teaching a monkey how to do all kinds of tricks? What spurs the organ-grinder on to such achievements if not an inner voice that says that bread earned by begging or trickery is dishonorable? I do not wish here to exalt the organ-grinder as a model of virtue. I am even less inclined to show that virtue in our time is the exclusive province of organ-grinders and that, consequently, if one considers himself virtuous, he must arm himself with an organ and head for the streets. Moreover, although I portray the organ-grinder as an abused individual, I am far from eliciting your sympathy. I only wish to say that the organ-grinder's personal and social life (read: "street") offers many things that are worthy of attention. And, if the reader agrees, I need not ask you to read on. That you will do yourself . . .

I now take up my hero with all proper zeal . . .

Categories of Organ-Grinders

The origin of the Russian word for "organ-grinder" is difficult to determine. The task is made all the more burdensome because the word, it seems, originated in old Russia and was tied to the life of the folk. A Russian is peculiar in that he often gives a name to an unfamiliar person or object without any basis and, more often, without apparent thought. Sometimes, however, his labels are characteristic and precise, for, as you know, "Russians have a way with words."[2] A Russian does not bother with reasons, the how and why of things. Suddenly and without warning, he will just let something slip out of his mouth. Later, one wracks one's brains (or thinks up an excuse) as to why the Russian expressed something in one way and not another, for example, why he called the object in question a "street organ" and not a "carriage shaft." But it is all quite the same to him. Now, if I belonged to that esteemed group of people who call themselves etymologists, I would venture some educated guesses as to the origin of the word

2. Grigorovich is citing from chapter 5 of Gogol's *Dead Souls.*

"organ-grinder."[3] "Most likely," I would say, "the original word was 'screen stager,' the root coming from the 'screens'[4] behind which Puchinella[5] (even now the eternal companion of the organ-grinder) summons both the idle and the curious with his ringing voice." I would add with great assurance, "Such a supposition is all the more valid since the first street organs that appeared in our country were indistinguishable from the puppet shows that have existed in Italy from time immemorial." I fear, however, that I would bore you with such suppositions, and so I will let the origin of the word rest and pass directly to the organ-grinder himself.

At first glance, it seems that all organ-grinders make up a uniform and distinct class of street artisans. In reality, however, they fall into numerous categories and are sharply defined by both their activities and their nationality. In general, the organ-grinders of Petersburg are one of three nationalities: Italians, Germans, and Russians.[6] Among them the Italians

3. Discussions of etymologies were frequent lead-ins for European physiologies. See, for instance, Balzac's 1844 *Monograph on the Parisian Press.*

4. In reality, the word "screen-stager" (*shirmanka*—or, more accurately, *sharmanka*) derives from the German song "Charmante Catarine," which musicians performed on special music boxes.

5. Punchinello (compare Italian, Pulcinella) is the most popular of marionettes and glove puppets. Punchinello traces his roots both to the Roman clown and the comic country bumpkin, as well as to the Italian commedia dell'arte of the seventeenth century.

Italian puppeteers carried Pulcinella, as well as the assorted plots and characters of the puppet's repertoire, throughout Europe. By the mid-seventeenth century, he was known as Polichinelle in France, as Don Crisobal Pulchinela in Spain, and as Punch in England. (Punchinello is thought to have been brought to Russia via Germany by the *skomorokhi,* or wandering minstrels-cum-clowns, of this period.) In Russia, a similarity between the antics of Punchinello and of Pietro Mira, a famous clown in the court of Anna Ivanovna and known in Russian folk pictures as Petrillo, Pedrillo, or Petrukha, rechristened the character "Petrushka," paving the way for the figure to achieve even greater fame as the subject of a 1911 ballet by Sergei Diaghilev and Igor Stravinsky.

It should also be noted that not only the figure of Petrushka but also the plots, settings, and dynamics of the puppet repertoire drew their inspiration from their counterparts in Western Europe. Particularly recognizable are the violent encounters with which Petrushka outwits his enemies; his distinctive, high-pitched squeaky voice produced by a strange instrument (known as a "swazzle" in England) which the puppeteer inserted into his mouth to produce his hero's voice; Petrushka's chatting with the audience as well as the musician (fiddler or accordionist) who accompanied him; and finally, the brightly colored or striped boxes in which the performances took place.

Further, it must be stated that investigators into the puppet show in Russia also posit that it draws upon Eastern influences as well as upon the legacy of medieval minstrels and buffoons in the homeland.

6. The fictional classification of groups according to nationality and the like was a common feature in Russian physiological writing. "Not only every people," Dal' wrote in his 1846 sketch "Finns in Petersburg" ("Chukhontsy v Pitere"), "but also natives of well-known places who look for work in the capital keep to their own way of life and trades. For instance, the Kasimovsky Tatars are almost always

hold the primary place. They are the undisputed master of their trade, the scion of their craft.[7] The Russians and the Germans are nothing more than followers: they take to the street organ only to escape death by hunger (or, as is more often the case, because they are unwilling to take up a different and more practical trade). Organ-grinders rarely begin their profession by owning the instrument from which they take their name. To own one's own hand organ or, as it is pleasantly called, a street organ, is already a sign of an improved condition. A flute or a clarinet; a viola with a large bow; a seal in a cage with the inscription, "Look, ladies and gentlemen, at the sea monster"; and a tall box, covered with green cloth, called a "fortepiano anglaise," and filling the air more with the tinkling of broken glass than with music—equip the organ-grinder to make his debut. His stage is vast and richly decorated: the streets of Petersburg. Two or three years later (if he has not found another means of earning his bread), the organ-grinder lives to see a most happy day: a splendid, long-awaited moment which shines likes a beacon light on his unsteady horizon. On this day, the organ-grinder takes his savings and buys a street organ. With this purchase, he achieves his hopes and dreams.

Hoisting his treasure on his back, the organ-grinder thinks only about how he can attract attention to himself and be rewarded for his efforts. First, he embellishes a waltz by Lanner with whistles and trills.[8] Then he hires two small children from a destitute laundress or chimney sweep and has them dance a foolish step of his own making.[9] If luck is with him, he eventually exchanges his scraggly-looking street organ for one which, while

---

yardkeepers. People from Ryazan are bricklayers and tax collectors; from Belarus, exclusively excavators; and so forth. You will never see a Finn among yardkeepers, nurses, or even deliverymen. . . . The highest circle of this artisan or working class . . . is the silversmiths, next the chimney sweeps; last black people, who wander in Petersburg, who from youth are either chimney sweeps or sometimes cabbies." V. Dal', *Polnoe sobranie sochinenii v desiati tomakh,* vol. 3 (1897-98) (St. Petersburg: M.O. Vol'f, 1897), 369.

7. It is of interest to note that in 1794, Italian organ-grinders, shadow players, and acrobats were seen as standard entertainment in St. Petersburg. I. Georgi, *Opisanie rossisko-imperatorskogo stolichnogo goroda Sankt-peterburga i dostoprimechatel'nostei v ego okrestnostiakh* (St. Petersburg: Pri Imperatorskom Shliakhetnom Sukhoputnom Kadetskom Korpuse, 1794), 656.

8. Two of Lanner's works, his *Steyerische Tanze* (1841) and *Die Schönbrunner* (1842), were among the folk and popular melodies that Stravinsky used in *Petrushka.* See R. Taruskin, "Stravinsky's *Petrushka,*" in *Petrushka: Sources and Contexts,* ed. A. Wachtel (Evanston, Ill.: Northwestern University Press, 1998), 70.

9. An organ-grinder, a music box, and two street dancers were also the basis for an episode in Stravinsky's *Petrushka.* Ibid., 72.

incomparably smaller, nonetheless presents his most honored public with a truly wondrous spectacle: a figurine of Napoleon, dressed in a blue coat and a three-cornered hat, twirling about the figures of ladies who are without noses and who are covered from head to foot with shiny foil. If the owner of this treasure is Italian, he will invariably engage you in conversation. He will explain to you the significance of each and every puppet, and for your benefit, he will not restrain from scolding Napoleon and the Austrian ladies who twirl about him. (God knows why.)[10] Should the organ-grinder accumulate still more money, he will purchase additional or improved equipment. He has probably been longing for a tall organ with brilliant tin pipes, horse brass, and golden tassels. The organ will ride atop a green cart and be pulled by a brown nag. Such an acquisition is truly worth any sacrifice he has to make. In the first place, the organ-grinder no longer has to carry his instrument, so there is less work. In the second place, he can transport the organ to dachas where, as everybody knows, people are kinder. There, solid families are more inclined to innocent and bucolic pleasures. They are there for a holiday and are thus particularly disposed to spend money. The key advantage of the dachas, however, is that they are always host to numerous children, who, generally speaking, love puppet theaters and street organs. Such things have a significant (and salutary) effect on the income of the organ-grinder, especially if he can take up a good position and occasionally delight his audience with a serenade. Fortune does not smile on every organ-grinder, however. One can find poor souls who, until advanced old age, are condemned to playing the same aria on the clarinet or to dancing the trepak on a cobblestone street, to the accompaniment of a viola.

So begin the "philistines" in this class of artisans. By contrast, the "aristocracy" among the organ-grinders begin their careers with greater pomp and circumstance. The aristocratic organ-grinders rarely go out alone but travel about in groups. One carries an expensive street organ, decorated with little bells; another has a monkey in a hussar's costume and a Tyrolean hat; a third is equipped with street screens and a chest filled with puppets that are dressed in multicolored rags and covered with sparkles. The procession comes to an end with an old, saddled poodle who takes the place of

10. In 1810 Napoleon divorced the childless Josephine and married Marie-Louise, daughter of Emperor Francis I. As a result, the Austrian court had little choice but to submit fully to Napoleon's many prescriptions and demands.

a horse (for the hussar in the Tyrolean cap). Other groups roam about as orchestras, and still others add a clown who, on a tattered rug, does salto mortale to the howling of a street organ. Musical romances accompanied by harps, trained dogs, two or three violins, and a clarinet (all playing one and the same tune)—such trappings, in their own way, display the prosperity of their owners and place the group high above the numerous "philistines." Occasionally, however, the differences between "classes"—the "aristocrats" and the "philistines"—are smoothed over by money. For example, a modest lifestyle may allow a philistine organ-grinder to amass a small sum. The "aristocracy" starts off incomparably richer as a group, but sometimes some of the members fall into extreme poverty because they have become deeply involved in speculation. (This we will see later.) When members of the "aristocracy" lose money in this way, they come down from their heights and (as if motivated by a kindly feeling) draw close to a philistine-outcast. These "aristocrats" may even accept him into their company. And, if this former philistine-outcast has more money than was thought initially, these fallen "aristocrats" bind him with the most durable of ties—kinship. Note that money is the sole condition which brings these otherwise vying parties together.

Italian Organ-Grinders

The origins of Italian organ-grinders are extremely obscure. For the most part, they are born under wooden, tumbled-down roofs, in hovels somewhere in the picturesque Apennines (which they now call the Perpi Mountains). Their parents are half-destitute mountain dwellers who, due to insufficient land or the laziness native to all Italians, aspire to the modest vocation of shepherds. Since they cannot feed their own numerous children, they hand their offspring over to an old organ-grinder. (This organ-grinder has returned to the homeland only recently, but after some time, he must again take up his organ and roam the entire world.) In this way, a small boy abandons his home, his mother, and his father, and, trusting fate, he comes down from the hills, hoping someday to see them again. Switzerland, France, Germany, the Tyrol—everywhere he plays the five or six songs of his repertoire. (There does not exist a single hamlet, burg, or settlement which had not heard him at least several times.) Finally, rumors reach the lad that somewhere in the north, in Russia, organ-grinders are few and that he might make a profit there. "Onward! *A Pietroborgo!*" the poor soul exclaims, and so he undertakes the difficult trip. He has not been deceived because the difficulties of his travel are well rewarded by the half kopecks tossed out on courtyards and streets. Sometimes the Italian organ-grinder chooses a path that does not lead directly to the capital but which makes the rounds of the provinces instead. He visits fairs, villages, and towns, and, having saved some money, he appears in the capital and hires several colleagues of his calling. Little by little, the Italian makes a profit. He eventually gives up the wandering life and forms a circle of acquaintances: fellow artisans, clowns, rope-dancers, and sellers of figurines (whose wares include rose-colored Napoleons, angelic cupids with arms and hands folded in a cross across their chests, cats that dangle their heads from left to right—in short, all conceivable forms, species, and likenesses).

Finally, the Italian organ-grinder marries the daughter of one of his friends. Having begun a household, he (for some unknown reason) chooses a residence on Pod'yachie and Meshchansky streets. His haven is a small, two-story wooden home, painted dirty green and rising in the corner of a dark yard. The exterior of the building is usually plastered with landings, which you get to only with difficulty. You climb a shaky staircase, and on the corners of each landing there is, at each door, a tub swimming with eggshells, fish innards, and several heaps of charcoal. In general, the staircases of these domiciles have the dank odor that is customary of all of Petersburg's dark staircases, and they show an utter lack of respect for the tenants who are forced to go up and down them. The apartment of an organ-grinder is almost always found at the end of one of these landings (the rent is cheapest there). The place consists of two rooms made from one. If you wish to know the details of what they are like, take the trouble to stoop down and enter the first room. Your eyes are already dimmed by tears (the effect of the staircase). When your vision clears, the first object that you will notice will be a Russian stove of incredible size, covered with soot and surrounded by rags (the wardrobe of the tenant). The walls and the ceiling are covered with amiable insects, which have a name identical to that of well-known European people.[11] (I would express myself more simply, but I fear that

11. Compare *prussak* (Prussian) and *prusak* (cockroach).

I would offend those readers who *blow their noses with a handkerchief*.[12]) Along the walls of the organ-grinder's apartment are long benches. On them lie workers in extremely unflattering positions—Russians, Germans, Italians, all of whom have been hired by a certain Signor Charlotto Bonissi. Chests filled with straw stand in the middle of the room. Three or four monkeys scamper about them, squeaking in a most unpleasant treble. Several screens, boxes of puppets, and knapsacks of flour and macaroni lie scattered in the various corners of the room. A tub full of slops gives off an especially unpleasant odor from under the stove. Smoke, fanning out from small, short pipes (a necessary accessory for Russian workers), occupies the space not taken up by the trash. Voices and guffaws, squeaking monkeys, howling dogs, and screaming children combine to drown out the snoring of organ-grinders who are sprawled out on the stove, the benches, and the floor. Finally, a small window lets several rays of light into the room. This is not a typical feature, though. If there is but one Russian in the troupe, the window is invariably plastered with various types of figurines, cut out from writing paper with great skill. Among them, the picture of a goat with unusually large horns and a beard strikes the eye. The second room of the organ-grinder's apartment offers a completely different spectacle. Here one immediately notices the presence of women. This second room distinguishes itself not only by its cleanliness and order but also by a certain pretense to luxury: drapes, a wide bed, a chest of drawers, enormous wall clocks (suitable for any tower, but with hanging bricks instead of weights), flowerpots with scraggly-looking plants, and a table with a samovar as bright as the sun. Street organs of various shapes and sizes are lined up along the wall, giving witness to the trade of the master.

Hardly has the clock struck twelve when the entire population of the apartment rises and tosses off a cup of either *shchi* or macaroni. The men hoist their organs on their shoulders and go down to the street. Once there, they separate into parties and go off in different directions.

The distinguishing feature of Italian organ-grinders is the puppet show.[13] Such a spectacle delights not only mothers, children, and

12. Here Grigorovich is parodying the affected manners of the provincial ladies in the eighth chapter of Gogol's *Dead Souls*.

13. It is of interest to note that as early as 1813, the British traveler Edward Daniel Clarke encountered Calabrian puppeteers in Russia who first gave shows in Petersburg and then toured as far as the Don (Kelly, "From Pulcinella to Petrushka," 53).

apprentices but also adults. What the Italian performs in our Russian courtyards, however, is quite different from what he has imported from his native land.[14] The Russified Italian has accommodated (as best as he can) his puppet show to the language of the Russian worker. The language of the puppet show resembles that of a profligate who, having gone through fire and water, can talk nonsense nonstop and season it with his own witticisms. The Italian has reworked the puppet show in his own way. Indeed, nowhere do the qualities of Russian humor appear so forcefully as in these reworkings. Nowhere can a poor man reveal himself so poignantly or earn a kopeck with such abandon. Listen to the dialogues of Puchinella and his friends in a Russian adaptation; study each dramatic act and its location in the play. One thing that comes to mind is those Russian songs whose words are chosen only for their rhythm (and in fact contain nothing but that). You will also detect a similarity with those fairy tales in which everything is done in jest and in which the narrator confounds his listeners and, at times, even himself. For example, no matter how much I have tried, I have never figured out why a well-known (and beloved) comedy always has a character who is clearly expendable. Yet, why is it that not a single street performance of this comedy can do without this individual who, as you know, bears the name *Petrushka*? In these comedies, also, I have never understood why it is that before a devil (who looks very much like a goat) captivates Puchinella, two Arabs appear, play with a stick, and disrupt the action of the play. Why is this so? Try to find out from the organ-grinder! "It has always been that way," he tells you. "First the Arabs must come on stage, and only then can the devil carry off Puchinella. That's the way it's done, and that's the way it

---

Four years later, a Russian commentator, recording a comic battle between a marionette puppet and his wife, noted how German and Italian puppeteers distorted Russian words. See A. Konechny, "Peterburgskie narodnye gulian'ia na maslenoi i paskhal'noi nedeliakh," *Etnografiia Peterburga-Leningrada: materialy ezhegodnykh chtenii* (Leningrad: Nauka, 1989), 23; Kelly, *Petrushka,* 48.

It is also thought that Italian puppeteers brought *Petrushka* to Russia sometime between 1810 and 1840 and that Russian showmen performed *Petrushka* from that time on. See A. Bragaglia, *Pulcinella* (Rome: Gherado Casini Editore, 1953), 410; Kelly, *Petrushka,* 47, 60.

14. Such a statement is typical of the brashness that the contributors to *Petersburg* exhibited toward cultures other than their own. Undoubtedly, Grigorovich had never seen an Italian puppet play and thus was ill qualified to compare Russian renditions of the phenomenon with more indigenous ones. Direct comparison between the two, though, shows that what Grigorovich recorded is close to the original. See Kelly, *Petrushka,* 53.

should be done," he concludes, thereby leaving you as confused as before about why either Petrushka or the Arabs appear.

The puppet show, though, is not the only resource of the Italian organ-grinder. For many in this group, trained monkeys and a street clown are also part of the entourage. The organ-grinder's wife and daughters (if they are on hand) further contribute to his efforts. His wife makes little cherubs out of wax, which, when hung from willow branches, play an important role in their own right. His daughters, sweet little Italian lasses with small oblong faces, sew dresses to order or paint fashionable pictures on the tops of pomade jars. Generally speaking, therefore, Italian organ-grinders are not dissolute wanderers but modest and serene artisans. They consider their craft a noble one and love it dearly. I remember that when I once asked one of them, "How are things going for you in Petersburg?"—he replied in broken French, "*Oh, mon signore, nous povero artisto pas bien vivera a Pietroborgo, a Pietroburgo o n'aime pas beaucoup ces artisto. . . . Le publico ne pas aimer la musica, signore . . .*" A passion for his noble art often causes the Italian organ-grinder to spend entire months refurbishing his street organs. He decorates them with various figurines and ornaments, for example, triangles, cymbals, Turkish drums, even little bells. He rings them all with a cord tied to his leg, and when he does so, he proudly distinguishes himself from his colleagues, imagining that he now owns the eighth wonder of the world. Imagine a landowner who shows off his newly built home without omitting the slightest detail and even bragging about the construction of those items which no one would deem as particularly important. Even he, though, would extract from you the praise that an organ-grinder would for his new street organ. He will open it several times, unscrew the sides, ask you to look inside, stroke it, turn its handle, and, finally, acknowledge its cost—all so that he and his modest craft will rise in your estimation.

With so many resources, Italian organ-grinders could easily, in the course of several years, return to their native hills and be secure for the rest of their lives. An innate attraction for speculation and money, however, often drives them to ruin. First, their stock of plaster figurines sells poorly. Then, the construction of a booth on Admiralty Square (where they show trained monkeys, Chinese ghosts, and a puppet show) costs the master more in expense than the profit he takes in. Next the attempt to establish an institution to further their craft does not pan out in the way he hoped. Sooner or later, one of these undertakings ruins a poor organ-grinder completely. It forces him again to roam the streets with a street organ, to gather half kopecks one at a time, and to feed a family with a piece of dry bread, the reward for his labor and sweat.

Russian and German Organ-Grinders

Although the street organ is rarely the lot of Germans, the wide interest in this craft draws them into this class of artisans at times. German organ-grinders fall into two types. The one, from Switzerland, Germany, or the Tyrol, has earned a living since childhood. The other starts here in Petersburg, after one or more personal calamities. Generally speaking, the personal details of either type are of little interest. German organ-grinders live in small groups on Haymarket Square and Gorokhovaya Street, and in the most pitiful and unenviable of situations. They themselves are to blame for their plight. An Italian organ-grinder is committed to his trade, body and soul. He is resourceful, cunning, bold, and merry, and by his cheerful disposition, he captivates, entices, and pleases his public. The German organ-grinder, by contrast, is dry and phlegmatic, flaccid and careless. He cannot spark any response in a Russian audience (who loves to be entertained at all costs). The German organ-grinder does not try to amuse you or create a good impression. On the contrary, he tires you with the same boring arias, earning money only when a listener, having lost patience, finally wants to be left in peace. Although German organ-grinders do not often reap a profit, they have equipment and variety. For instance, an organ, giving off squeaky sounds to the tune of "Katen'ka goes throughout the village,"[15] accompanies the mournful singing of the master. A thin German woman plays a harp while, at the same time, her husband does lightning variations on his violin. (It should be noted that the German woman has a shining red face and an unusually sharp nose; she also wears a huge cap and a black shawl.) Trained dogs dance on their hind legs to the

15. Grigorovich is referring to an 1836 vaudeville-comedy, *Katen'ka, or Seven Seek Marriage, But One Gets the Girl* (*Katen'ka, ili Semero svataiutsia, odnomy dostaetsia*).

tune of Mal'bruk's famous journey to the campaign[16] and look fearfully at their broad-shouldered owner (who is armed with a whip suitable for an elephant). A little Tyrolean, dressed in national costume, dances, whistles, and plays a viola. Finally, wandering orchestras made up of trombones deafen the unsuspecting inhabitants of the courtyard and drown out two or three clarinets and the violin.

Similar to the Italians, German organ-grinders have businesses on the side. They make powders, matches, and smoking candles; they train puppies, which, after they have completed the course, are consigned to an invalid with a swollen lip. (The invalid in turn sells them either to sensitive and languid ladies who wear ringlets and carry handbags or to petty officials, fathers of families who love nothing better than to surprise their daughters with shaggy lapdogs or snub-nosed pugs.)

Petersburg has few German organ-grinders because for the most part, they do not remain long in a calling so ill suited to their character.

A lackey on a perpetual binge; an apprentice of humble origin who has been ousted by his master; a shop assistant who has lost his boss's money in games of pitch-and-toss and cards; and sometimes a poor soul who has been fired unjustly—these make up a large part of the Russian organ-grinders who pound the pavement of Petersburg daily. The overwhelming urge to spend the last half kopeck in an institution marked by the sign DRINKS SERVED HERE sooner or later forces a Russian to offer his services to an Italian who keeps organ-grinders. Rarely, extremely rarely, a Russian organ-grinder strikes out on his own and makes a living with his organ. Invariably, though, he needs the "company" of friends, for he is, generally speaking, drawn to the social life. Russian organ-grinders settle in the Petersburg Quarter, in modest little shacks enclosed by kitchen gardens on three sides. The fourth side usually looks out on a narrow lane and has a motley shed. Misfortune often brings the Russian organ-grinder to such a situation that

16. More accurately, "Mal'bruk" is the Duke of Marlborough, John Churchill (the great-grandfather of Winston Churchill). Grigorovich is citing a Russian version of a French song, "Malbrough is Going Off to War" ("Malbrough s'en va-t-en guerre"), which was well known during the reign of the French king Louis XVI and which concerned Churchill's victory over the French in the War of the Spanish Succession nearly a century before. (The French called Marlborough either Malbrough or Malbrouk.) In Russia, the song "Mal'bruk" became wildly popular after the war with Napoleon because it was seen as mocking the French emperor. Incidentally, the original version, "Malbrough," is still sung by French children today.

he may even lie down and die of hunger. Despite this possibility, as long as he is alive, he works at his "art" (as does every one of our common people). The organ-grinder invariably covers the walls of his hovel with interesting pictures: *The Triumph of Mordecai; Aman at the Foot of His Lover; The Peasants, Dolbilo and Gvozdilo, Beating the French;* and *A View of the City of Syzran.*[17] (Landscapes of this type usually have small regular hills in the form of sugar mounds placed one on top of the other, with grass on each peak and crooked cupolas atop the whole.) *The Frightened Tailor* and other creations of native fantasy stand out like bright red, orange, and yellow spots on the sooty walls. For instance, a portrait of a field marshal on a horse takes up the whole surface of one picture; alongside, one might see the top of a pomade jar with the inscription *à la violette* or the portrait of a Circassian landlord. Any of these is plastered right above a touching scene, *Mice Burying a Cat,* and a glued-on portrait of a kislar-aga.[18]

There is no one more carefree than the Russian organ-grinder. He never worries about the next day. If he happens to come into enough cash that would take care of his needs for several days, he does not hesitate to take his friends to the nearest café-restaurant. There, for a reasonable price, he can get beer, herring, and tea sold in pomade jars. Like a Neapolitan *lazaroni,*[19] the Russian organ-grinder does not work if the money that he has earned in the morning will suffice for the evening. Whenever our virtuoso has indulged until he is reeling, he returns home. If exhaustion does not lead him to the thin mattress that serves as his bed, he engages in peaceful activities that are compatible with his tender soul. He listens as one of his friends (the literate one in the group) reads pamphlets, purchased at the flea market. He is particularly enraptured by excerpts from

17. Syzran is almost five hundred miles to the southeast of Moscow.

18. In Constantinople under the Ottomans, the "kislar-aga" was the chief black eunuch supervisor of the harem. After the sultan and the grand vizier, he was also the third highest-ranking man in the empire, with multiple duties and responsibilities. For instance, it was the kislar who executed a woman if she displeased the sultan. The titles that Grigorovich lists here were standard fare in the pulp pictures and editions of the time. For instance, *Mice Burying a Cat* was a well-known folk illustration that was inspired by Old Believers and directed against Peter the Great and his reforms. Generally speaking, the pulp pictures (*lubki*) that adorned Russian walls featured portraits of biblical figures, epic heroes, and Russian and historical leaders, as well as scenes of nature, historical events, and Russian and foreign cities. The goal of pulp pictures was part entertainment, part education. Indeed, they were a seminal factor in cultivating literacy, patriotism, and mass taste. It is also of interest to note that Benois, in his rendition of *Petrushka,* hung crudely stylized *lubok*-like folk prints on the left-hand side of the stage.

19. More accurately, a *lazzarone,* or "ruffian," "scoundrel," or "slacker."

such books as *The Life of One Avvakumovsky Hermit in the Byrne Woods Where He Resided, and the Humorous Conversations of His Soul, While Traveling Across the River Styx; Balakirev's Anecdotes; The Adventures of Van'ka Kain with All His Investigations and Searchings for Criminals, and His Extravagant Wedding; The Story of the Brave Knight, Frantsyl Ventsian, and the Beautiful Queen, Rentsyevna; The Goat-Rebel and Masha's Wedding* (a marvelous piece, beginning with the epitaph "All Works Are Dust, But This One's a Must"); *Kandrashka Bulavin;* and, *The Perils of Drunkenness.*[20] Such books, especially the last, are extremely edifying, even if they are of little use to readers or listeners. Surprisingly, the Russian organ-grinder is not social-minded when he is out in public. He pays little attention to his listeners. He is almost always gloomy and dissatisfied with himself, except when he strikes a friendly blow on the shoulder of a familiar cabbie, greeting him, "And how's my friend Vanyuka doing?!!!"

The Street Clown

The attic of a huge home on Haymarket Square usually is his place of birth. Some laundress, a maid of the third class, deceived by a lackey and dividing her love between a tavern and a greenhouse, brings a future street clown into the world. The baby's first glance at his half-hung-over father is often his last. Indeed, such a man is fickle and unstable. He deserts the woman and her attic soon after his pledge of love is born, and he resolutely intends to play the Lovelace[21] in different and more suitable places. The poor woman is thus abandoned in a dwelling that even a Spartan would find bare. Convinced that her lover is unfaithful, she immediately takes up

20. The various editions that Grigorovich cites here were enormously popular with lower-class readers and enjoyed numerous reprintings. For instance, Matvei Komarov's *The True and Detailed Stories of Two Russian Swindlers: The First Is the Famous Russian Thief and Legendary Muscovite Detective Van'ka Kain with All His Investigations, Inquiries, His Extravagant Wedding and His Various Amusing Songs; and the Second Is the French Swindler Cartouche and His Colleagues* (*Obstoiatel'nye i vernye istorii dvukh moshennikov: Pervago Rossisskago slavnago vora, razboinika i byvshago Moskovskago syshchika Van'ki Kaina, so vsemi ego suskami, rozyskami, sumozbrodnoiu svad'boiu i raznymi zabavnymi ego pesniami*) was published at least twelve times between 1777 and 1835. (It is also enjoying renewed popularity in Russia, with at least five printings since 1991.)

21. Lovelace is the villain in Samuel Richardson's 1744 novel *Clarissa; or, The History of a Young Lady.*

work. Her maternal instincts give her new strength, and she quickly makes up for lost time. Meanwhile, her baby grows. He is already running about the room, babbling disconnected words, and eating the coal and clay he has taken from the stove—an infraction for which his mother cannot punish him too severely. A bird leaves the nest and, barely aware of it strength, flies high into the sky. Having glided through the heavens, it descends into a fragrant limewood grove. It lights onto a sandy shore alongside a gurgling stream and fills the airs with its resonant chirping. In exactly the same way, our hero leaves his native attic. Having felt the strength of his arms and legs, he goes down the dirty staircase to the street below. While squirreled away in the attic, he had devoured the sidewalks and pavement with greedy eyes. They now lie before him in all their splendor, presenting him with a thousand distractions and pleasures. He finds a throng of boys just like himself, organ-grinders, a puppet show, grandmothers, hawkers' stands laden with oranges and gingerbread, soldiers passing through the square to the accompaniment of music. All these so capture his young imagination that he haunts the streets for days on end. He particularly loves to be out in the rain and would rather admire the water gushing out of a gutter than go home.

Everyone knows, however (even those who have not read copybook maxims), that happiness is fleeting and filled with disquiet. Hardly has the little boy turned eight than his solicitous mother is already thinking about how she can attain for him an honorable and lucrative profession. She shoves him into the usual lines of industry. Around his neck she hangs a wooden box, filled with matches; she also supplies him with walking sticks, sealing wax, and green apples. If the woman is a person of some means, however, she seeks a more enduring trade for her child and hands him over to a rich workman. The boy is now an apprentice in a heavy, striped robe, the wide flaps of his which can accommodate three youths his size. But, having tasted freedom and feeling constricted by such apparel, he shakes off his yoke as quickly as he can. Spoiled friends tempt the novice. Each Sunday they set out for Krestovsky Island for the entire day. There they conjure up the idea for a spree. Over time, they progress from gingerbread and nuts to pipes and wine. The poor soul gets more and more carried away. He becomes a scoundrel and usually ends his career at the master's by stealing or by flight.

Driven away by the master (or having run away from him), the boy accidentally runs into a wandering troupe of acrobats and clowns. It may be that his mother washes their laundry, or he himself might strike up an acquaintance. In either case, the former apprentice soon becomes a member of the company. At first, he works as a tailor, mending well-worn rags or putting soles on boots. Except for earning his bread, though, his avocation brings him misfortune and woe. The clowns, the acrobats, and the ropedancers are his heroes and lords. His wounded pride does not give him peace day or night. He dreams of a velvet camisole, sewn with sparkles. He yearns for applause and, from the clowns, hopes for friendship and cordiality (rather than contempt). He decides that, no matter what, he will attain a high goal in life. The shrewd master of the troupe sizes up the boy's suffering, and with no thought of ever paying the lad, he offers him training rather than money. The poor soul accepts the offer with delight and entrusts his body to the master's whip and stick. He has entered a most difficult school, and if he endures to the end, he will, within the course of several years, be awarded entry into the troupe. In time, his demands for a salary are seen as impertinent, so he moves on to a different group, now a performer in his own right and with full billing to boot. In such companies, our hero performs all kinds of theatrical roles. He is subject to some entrepreneur—a Mr. Caspar, Weinert, or Dobradini. He plays every part, beginning as a lamplighter and ending as an acrobat. He appears before the most esteemed public in this order: a clown, a Cassander,[22] a mime, and a devil. He swallows swords and lighted flax. He lifts weights and does pantomime[23] (which usually ends with the entire cast disappearing into the gigantic mouth of a canvas devil). His activity is sometimes legendary.

22. Historically, Cassander was a Macedonian king, but here, Cassander was first a comic personage in the Italian theater in Paris and then an enduring figure in street presentations and puppet shows in both Western Europe and Russia. Specifically in these presentations, Cassander is an old crusty burgher who opposes the marriage of his daughter, Columbine, to Harlequin. He seeks to keep the lovers apart through the services of his foolish but good-hearted servant, Pierrot, who himself is in love with Columbine. Not unexpectedly, and via numerous comic pranks, Cassander and Pierrot suffer defeat, and Harlequin and Columbine together live happily ever after.

23. It is interesting to note that, at this time, pantomime was quite popular with audiences in both theaters and the streets. A reviewer from the *Northern Bee* wrote in 1831:

> Pantomine is an art in which the gifts of the word are replaced by the movements of the body. Pantomine even gives a certain pleasantness to these movements, even in the most vulgar comedy. In the days of the Roman Empire, not only plebeians and senators

At one and the same performance, he summons the spectators and sells tickets at the entrance; does somersaults and frolics on a tightrope; and jumps from a trampoline over twenty soldiers, dances on a horse, and plays a part in a pantomime. He often ends the show by executing a caper he has copied from a first-class troupe. This epoch of his life is short-lived, however, coming to an end with Mardi Gras and Holy Week. As a result, he is forced to "dishonor" (so he expresses it) his noble craft: He performs as a clown for a rich organ-grinder, receiving only twenty-five kopecks for each ruble earned in the streets and yards. In contrast to organ-grinders, the street clown is almost always Russian.[24] His colleagues at the fairs are foreigners; and as they go abroad immediately after the holidays are over, they leave him to the mercy of fate. The former Hercules now climbs down from the stage and onto a sparse carpet in the street. He performs to the howling of a street organ and the din of a tambourine. A street clown thus spends a large part of the year with organ-grinders; it is an unhappy time in his life.

A street clown's earnings hardly pay for his upkeep; and, since after work, he loves to play the sybarite, his savings quickly disappear in taverns. With each passing day, his situation becomes worse and worse. By the end of the year, he has only the clothes on his back. As is the Russian custom, though, the street clown continues to entertain his friends, even if he must sell his last camisole with the sparkles. Happily, though, the street clown is rescued by the owner of a fair booth who hires him for the next group of holidays. Without such fortune, it would be farewell both to the camisole and to the man who wears it. Everything would perish! Yet, despite

---

had a passion for pantomine, but also Caesar Augustus himself loved this type of dramatic presentation.

As far as we are concerned, we give priority to a good pantomime over all the *merry* tragedies and *mournful* comedies. The heroes of pantomime are far more engaging for us than tragic ones whose only virtue in declamation consists in screaming, stamping their feet, and waving their arms. The deft pantomine of Columbine is a thousand times more pleasant than all the comic ladies on stage who, playing princesses and countesses, seem to be disguised servants!

If our readers love to laugh, we advise them to visit Leman's productions: the spectator will hear neither foolish verse, nor illiterate prose, nor good poetry mangled by behind-the-scenes heroes. He will not frown where he is supposed to smile. (Smes': Pantomina g. Lemana," *Severnaia pchela,* no. 38 [1831]: 3)

24. It is a fact that many young Russians worked in foreign troupes. See Alekseev-Iakovlev, *Russkie narodnye gulian'ia,* 10.

his meager life, the street clown does not become melancholy or downcast. True, his exterior is sullen: he growls constantly and looks distrustfully from under his brows. Such dourness, however, lasts only until he enters a courtyard to give a performance. A friend unfolds a thick rug on the sidewalk which serves as his arena, and the clown looks proudly at the crowd who has hastened to see him. Look at his self-contented smile as he removes the jacket hiding his poppy red camisole and wide white trousers. A tambourine and a street organ play an introduction. The clown raises his curly head, takes several steps backward, and, in a running jump, stands on his hands. Somersaults follow one after another. The public applauds, and half kopecks pour out from all the windows.[25] But the clown does not note such things because, for some seconds now, he is balancing, on his nose, a chair holding a little girl whom he has chosen from the crowd. The mournful sounds of *Luchinushka* signal the end of the performance. The clown again puts on his coat, pulls his tattered hat over his disheveled hair, and leaves the courtyard, pursued by the enthusiastic public.

But not all street clowns come upon such solid work by chance. Some have been committed to it since childhood. The children of an old acrobat or clown follow (often unwillingly) in the footsteps of their father. They usually end their life either in this calling or during an unsuccessful somersault. Their situation is most unfortunate; from cradle to grave, they are doomed to incredible difficulties. Many find clowning burdensome. Some have no other means of support, while others, after having spent several years in this calling, return to a previous trade. So do not be greatly astonished when you see that the clown who was so admired in the courtyard, who went about so deftly on his hands, who balanced a chair on his nose,

25. The street clown was indeed a favorite with the Russian public. "Have you noticed," a reviewer for the *Northern Bee* wrote in 1839, "that [at a carnival] the waves of people quiet down little by little, and that you find it impossible to move forward or backward? The crowd is waiting for its darling—the Russian clown . . . our folk Paskvino. Here he comes out on the balcony, in clownlike attire, with clownlike grimaces. The loud laughter does not stop for a minute; it grows with every one of his lines. Look at the way he grimaces: what could be funnier? . . . We hear that for Shrovetide, there will be a Russian presentation . . . in which this clown will play a key role. Undoubtedly, it will be a success: our pale imitations of Italian pantomime always enchant the public. But our Russian tales about the Firebird, Prince Bova, and Baba-Yaga make up an inexhaustible treasury by means of which such actors as our Paskvino and his brothers will create original renditions of this type of production." "Peterburgskaia maslenitsa," *Severnaia pchela,* no. 32 (1839): 126.

and who twirled a tambourine in his fingers—also holds an awl or scissors in his hands.

The Organ-Grinder's Public

On an autumn evening, around seven o'clock, a party of organ-grinders turns from a dirty canal into a narrow alley surrounded by tall homes. The organ-grinders are noticeably tired. One of them, a tall man with a phlegmatic air, hardly moves his legs as he lazily turns the hands of his street organ. Another, having loaded up the screens, bells, and well-made sawhorses, can no longer even think from sheer fatigue. A singularly red-haired boy with a box of dolls has exhausted all his energy.

Organ-grinders, it seems, are about to enter the gate of a certain familiar and prosperous home.

Well, now! No doubt about it! There will be a comedy! The organ-grinders enter the courtyard and strike up a waltz. The penetrating cry of Puchinella issues forth.[26]

26. Until 1874, the Russian carnival-cum-*Petrushka* in St. Petersburg typically took place on Admiralty Square twice yearly, during the week of Shrovetide and the week after Easter, the former being the more popular. Along with puppet shows, the carnival featured European-inspired ice hills, menageries, acrobatics, pantomines, peep shows, pageants, swings, roller coasters, merry-go-rounds, sleigh rides, and seesaws. It was also host to dancing bears, clowns, and mummers in strange animal masks. In fact, resources for the fairgrounds in St. Petersburg were often so abundant that carnival showmen often lived very well and fashioned new repertoires every year, if not each season.

The carnival-cum-*Petrushka* was a frequent item for discussion in Russian newspapers, particularly the *Northern Bee.* Revealingly, Belinsky approved of such entertainment. "Have you sometimes happened to see the antics of circus clowns and listen to their witty jokes? It has happened to me because I sometimes love to look at our kind folk in their happy moments so as to learn about their aesthetic directions. . . . I cannot wait for Shrovetide and Easter. . . . Look: Here is a clown on stage, that is, on the boards of a *balagan;* before him is the shadow of the aesthetic folk who seek *their own* gracious art. The buffoon's witticisms flash forth like sparks from steel. Everyone laughs with good-natured laughter. In the crowd I see a Tatar. 'Hey, my lord, come here,' the clown cries to him, 'I'll burn your curls for you.' The earth and sky shake with laughter." Also see Belinskii, *Polnoe sobranie sochinenii,* vol. 1 (1953), 349–50.

As Benois and others make clear, though, the Russian carnival departed markedly from its counterparts in Western Europe. Benois wrote in his memoirs:

> The Russian fair did not resemble those one saw in Paris, Vienna, or Rome. The whole atmosphere was different; the gaiety more intense, the revelry more spontaneous and wholehearted.

Meanwhile, a ragged urchin has been sitting idly on the curbstone. He has been playing with pebbles, teasing both his sister and the two small brothers whom she holds in her arms. He suddenly jumps up, makes a face at his brothers, leaps over the entire group, and dashes at breakneck speed through the yard.

The local baker, standing in a booth attached to the wall, smiles condescendingly and takes some snuff. Two soldiers, engaged in a fascinating conversation, notice the organ-grinders entering the yard. They stop, and, after a moment's indecision, they also enter. An old woman with an unusually red face and a broom of twigs under her arm follows. In short, the arrival of the organ-grinders has produced the desired result.

Why don't we stop in, too?

The yard is wide and spacious; a hundred windows look down upon it.

Screens are set up in the middle of the yard. The phlegmatic owner of the street organ has set his burden on the sawhorses and now plays an introduction. The performers need not delay their show. They cannot complain for lack of an audience today because, from all sides, people are rushing into the yard. The organ-grinder does not cease surveying the windows from which the curious heads are beginning to protrude. He expects more from them than from the crowd of idlers that surrounds him.

The cry of Puchinella echoes for a second and a third time. The upper stories are settled and become quite lively. Rows of the most diverse heads lean over the windowsills. One sees a bureaucrat, a pipe in his teeth and wearing a colorful robe and a red skullcap. Next to him a group of workers have taken up six windows in a row. A lovely-looking woman and a lapdog are seated on a morocco pillow. Here and there, several made-up faces look out, only momentarily attracting attention to themselves.

> I was frightened, for instance, by the noise—menacing, almost, rather than gay—that hung over the grounds and vibrated through the thin winter air for miles around. [I recall] the noise of innumerable brass bands playing simultaneously; the dull rhythmic beating of the Turkish drums; the squeaking of the swings; the chatter and cries of the thousands of people assembled around the "ice hills" or in the decorated lanes between the various pavilions and merry-go-rounds.
>
> I was frightened, too, by the enormous swing-boats, as they flew high up in the air, their brightly colored wagonettes filled with laughing and shrieking girls. There seemed to be a foreboding of evil in the strong smell of cooking pancakes and "Berlin" doughnuts, as it mixed with the rising vapors of vodka. (Benois, *Reminiscences of the Russian Ballet,* 27, 28)

For an excellent survey of the carnival in St. Petersburg, see Konechnyi, 21–52.

The petty official, Fedosei Ermolaevich, is awakened from his afternoon nap by the calls of Puchinella. (Fedosei Ermolaevich is an extremely honorable man. He has a very good job, and the director himself once patted the man on the shoulder.)

"Tereshka!" Fedosei Ermolaevich calls to his servant, yawning and stretching. "What's going on out there, old man? What's all the noise about?"

"It's organ-grinders, sir," Tereshka answers, his head and arm bent toward the window.

"But why are they out there, old man? . . . Why?"

Another cry of Puchinella wakes up Fedosei Ermolaevich completely. He stretches one more time, gets up from his bed, and with sleep-filled eyes looks out onto the courtyard.

"Papa, there, there they are . . . down there . . . Will all of them be playing?" asks little Ermolai Fedoseivich, dragging his father to the window with all his might. (The child, speaking in a nasal, whining tone, utters the last words as if in a refrain. Such mannerisms, though, do not affect his excitement and curiosity.)

"But there is only one organ-grinder, little one."

"No, no, there they are, all of them. Will all of them be playing?" answers the little boy, demanding an explanation.

"But there is only one organ-grinder, my dear . . ."

"No, no, all of them are there . . ."

We too are not satisfied with Ermolai Fedoseivich's answer, so we also had better go down to the street below. We are accompanied by Ermolai Fedoseivich's nurse, who impatiently carries off the child. (His chatter has denied her any peace for a full three hours.)

The comedy must begin right away, for the public has no more room to move.

The two soldiers have refrained from interfering with the crowd. They now take their places in the forefront. They are hemmed in by a horde of workmen dressed in torn peasant coats, their faces dirty with soot. Mothers, nurses, and wet nurses (together with children of all ages and sizes) stand out in the crowd with their bright sarafans. An army orderly, having returned with some tobacco, anxiously awaits a newly promoted officer; for the moment, though, it seems that he has forgotten all about his superior. A barefoot street girl, her hair cropped in a circle, stands in a thoughtless trance, holding a basket of half-kopeck rusks in her arms. A portly gentleman wearing glasses, having gone out for a breath of air, shares the overall impatience. Three clerks mock the organ-grinder with their clever jests. (The organ-grinder has already sung two refrains and, dissatisfied with the attendance, has moved on to a third.) A mob of riffraff pours in from the street. Two dandies stop at the entrance gate, turning their right legs back a little and propping themselves up with canes in a picturesque way.[27]

The crowd becomes excited and noisy. Everyone is waiting, everyone is calling for a performance. A little boy runs about in a circle, chasing a dog. He pokes his nose at some, sticks his tongue out at others, and pinches the children on the sly. He is all set to swipe a rusk from a street girl when suddenly Puchinella appears on top of the street organ. Puchinella is received with rapture. As a character, he is loud and noisy, a squabbler and a crank; in short, he possesses all the charm which endears him to the public. "Hi, there, ladies and gentlemen! I am here to amuse you (and to pocket anything you'd care to give)." So Puchinella begins. His greeting is especially welcome. The soldiers come closer; the boy makes another face. One of the workers scratches the bald spot on his head and says, "Well, will you look at that!" just as another, a friend of his, clutches his sides and bursts out laughing at the top of his lungs.

The laughing soon dies down, however. Puchinella questions the musician; all eyes are focused on his phlegmatic friend.

"And what can I do for you, Mr. Puchinella?" asks the organ-grinder.

Puchinella asks him to play the song "Along the Bridge." The musician bargains: "Well, how much will it be, monsieur? Twenty-five ruble-assignats!"

Puchinella: "I've never seen twenty-five rubles in my entire life. I think two rubles would be enough."

27. This leveling of caste, which Grigorovich saw as such an important facet of the puppet show, was so striking that it brought no less a personage than Bulgarin to note in 1834: "Can one look coldly upon these ice mountains, at this collection and rabble of any and all kinds of people (*sbor i sbrod vsiakoi vsiachiny*), of young lads and old men, of carriages and sleighs, of peasants and masters, of nuts and gingerbread cookies, monkeys and horses, magicians and quacks. . . . Good Lord! What these mountains do not have on them! Is there naught on these mountains!" V. V. V., "Maslenitsa 1834 g. v Peterburge (stat'ia vtoraia)," *Severnaia pchela,* April 4, 1834, 3.

The Musician: "Well, all right, Monsieur Puchinella. You've got a deal." The musician then begins to turn the handle of his street organ.

The sounds of "Along the Street Bridge" find a warm response in the hearts of the spectators. A sturdy fellow shrugs his shoulders; the snapping of fingers merges with the stamping of feet.

A new [puppet] face now appears above the screens: it is the police captain of the provinces. He needs to recruit someone. The musician introduces Monsieur Puchinella.

"What can I do for you, Your Excellency?" asks Puchinella.

"Why, you seem to be a good man. How would you like to come to the recruiting station with me?"

Puchinella tries to bargain with the police captain; for some reason, he does not trust the captain's politeness. The public becomes extremely sympathetic to Puchinella's plight.

The Police Captain: "Hey, old man, now what's the point of you bargaining with me? Sooner or later, you're bound to lose!"

Puchinella: "I'm not worried about losing. I'll fight to the end."

The Police Captain: "But I'm offering you a good deal, my friend: a very good salary, excellent food, three pounds of chaff, and ten liters of ripe berries; and, if you go off to Mam'selle Katerina and take her this note, you'll get twenty-five rubles as a reward."[28]

Puchinella: "Very well, Your Excellency. I'll not only bring her the note, but I'll bring her back, too."

The public laughs as the naive Puchinella runs to get Mam'selle Katerina. She now appears on stage, dances with the police captain, and leaves.[29] The crowd takes it all in, mouths agape; several even slobber.

New complications arise: Puchinella wants to marry. The musician suggests a bride; the spectators are completely enthralled with Puchinella's intended: the ninety-nine-year-old Matryona Ivanovna, who lives "in the Semonovsky Regiment, in a small room belonging to the Fifth Company of Goat Swamp." Although Puchinella does not want such a bride, his curiosity has him knock on the screens and call upon his betrothed. Instead

28. The affair with the note compares favorably to standard Italian scenarios in which servants assist in the intrigues of their charge-lovers. See Kelly, *Petrushka,* 60.

29. Mam'selle Katerina is thought to have been drawn from the original Columbine. Ibid., 56.

of Matryona Ivanovna, however, a dog jumps out, seizes him by the nose, and pulls him with all its might.

The public is in a frenzy: "Pull him, pull him . . . that's it! Pull him, pull him!" resounds from all sides.

Puchinella rolls to the edge of the screen. Plaintively, he calls for a doctor. But he does not forget to ask the price for such a visit.

The doctor appears and cures Puchinella. Instead of gratitude, though, the doctor gets a slap in the face.

The police captain is indignant over such an infraction of etiquette and breach of social tranquillity. He hands Puchinella over to the soldiers.

"Well, then, on your feet, monsieur," says the corporal, furnishing him with a stick. "Look sharp, attention!"

Puchinella first obeys the command. Then he begins to beat his master left and right—all to the great amusement of the spectators. Clearly, such a brawler, madcap, and atheist can no longer live in this world, but there is no way that he can be punished: Human power alone cannot stop Puchinella in his tracks. So hell itself disgorges a devil to vanquish the criminal.

The comedy is coming to an end. Petrushka is now onstage; but his appearance is unsolved, mythical, and inappropriate. He does not save Puchinella from a fatal end; he only arouses bewilderment in the crowd. The staunch Puchinella sits on top of the devil, but the devil refuses to obey his commands. The horseman calls Petrushka for help, but it is too late. Sentence has been pronounced, and Puchinella perishes, a pathetic figure. He disappears from the stage.[30]

30. Of such native street performances of *Petrushka,* Benois recalls:

> When I look back on my life, I consider it a remarkable stroke of luck that I had the opportunity of seeing these traditional pantomimes before they disappeared. Thanks to them . . . Pierrot, Harlequin, and Columbine are for me not characters constructed by learned research into the commedia dell'arte but real figures that I have seen with my own eyes.
>
> The charming Harlequin, whom I first saw in 1874 (when I was four years old) in Yegarev's *balagan,* I accepted wholeheartedly as a kind of deity, and to him I lost completely both my curly head and beating little heart. That visit to Yegarev's *balagan* was my *first* experience of the theater, and to this day I consider it to have been a most wonderful beginning to my artistic life, a beginning which had the greatest significance for the whole of my existence . . .
>
> [I remember that] I left the *balagan* in a daze, intoxicated, euphoric. The four-year-old child understood at that time that he had been considered worthy of becoming part of something utterly beautiful, utterly significant. . . .

A final aria resounds; the show is over. The public is extremely pleased, but when the organ-grinder takes his tambourine, twirls it in his fingers, and begins to make the rounds among the spectators, the crowd disperses. The first to desert are the two soldiers and the lady with the broom of twigs under her arm. The cries of the children arise anew with even greater force, compelling their mothers to leave quickly. In a nutshell, the crowd shrinks rapidly. The organ-grinder is in complete despair. Even the portly man wearing glasses merely stares at the tambourine as if not understanding what the suppliant wants. Grief-stricken, the organ-grinder turns to the theater boxes: the windows from which curious heads still protrude. Finally, a five-kopeck piece falls to the pavement, ringing and jumping about.[31] After it, there is another and then a third—this one, tossed out by the hand of the son of Fedosei Ermolaevich, who has instructed him: "Throw it into the tambourine, little one."

"No, no, there they are, all of them. Will all of them be playing?" repeats the persistent little boy.

A five-kopeck piece falls awkwardly among the stones. The official in the red skullcap has not given so much as a kopeck, even though he has

---

> [I also recall that when I first saw these pantomimes] my delight was truly unbounded and that I was entirely engrossed in the performance. I ceased to feel even the biting frost—the *balagany* were not heated—and when the time came to leave began to cry, so unwilling was I to part from what seemed to me to be the height of bliss. . . .
>
> All this was certainly not a ballet in the proper sense, but it impressed my unspoiled child's imagination as a spectacle so wonderful and enchanting that the innumerable ballet performances I have since seen on the stages of St. Petersburg, Paris, and London are nothing in comparison. (Benois, *Reminiscences,* 30–32, 35)

31. In his memoirs, Grigorovich recalled that Dostoevsky, with whom he had been living at the time, objected to an earlier version of the incident with the five-kopeck piece.

"No, not like that, not at all like that!" Dostoevsky interrupted Grigorovich, who had been reading his piece aloud. "What you have written—'the five-kopeck piece fell at the organ-grinder's legs'—sounds so very dry. . . . You should say: 'the five-kopeck piece fell on the pavement, *ringing and jumping about.*' "

"Dostoevsky's comment opened up an entire world for me," Grigorovich continued, "Truly—'ringing and jumping about' sounded much more picturesque. . . . Indeed, these two terms were enough for me to understand the difference between a sterile expression and a living, literary-artistic device." Grigorovich, *Literaturnye vospominaniia,* 78–79.

Revealingly, Dostoevsky heeded his own advice, using such phrases as the "money clinked" and the "button jumped . . . and jingled" in his 1845 novel *Poor Folk* (*Bednye liudi*). The image of the organ-grinder also captures the momentary attention of Makar Devushkin, the hero of Dostoevsky's first novel, but only to feel his own poverty in life.

bustled and fussed more than anyone else. He now becomes singularly interested in the fate of the organ-grinder.

"Right, to the right," he exclaims, pointing to where the five-kopeck piece has fallen. "Still more to the right . . . what's with you, old man? Not there! I told you more to the right!"

"To the right, now a little to the back," echoes a voice from another window.

"That's the way it is with you all," thinks the organ-grinder. "All you're good for is bustling about. You're all masters at that, but when it come to giving something, it's nothing . . . Such is my life, such is my lot!"

The organ-grinder again takes up his street organ and, accompanied by his plaintive music, leaves the courtyard. The crowd is dispersing; it seems that all must come to an end. An event occurs, though, which is impossible to omit. Until the end of the play, there had been a slight drizzle. Now it begins to rain cats and dogs. The official wearing glasses (as is his prudent custom) reaches into his pocket for a handkerchief to wrap around his new hat. To his utter amazement, he pulls out a hand which, at that very moment, has also dived in for the very same handkerchief.

The official turns his head, but the boy (it is our old friend from before) breaks loose with a quick movement of his hand. He darts forward and disappears into the crowd.

"Catch him! Catch him!" the official begins to cry. "Catch him! Hold him!" echoes from everywhere. "Catch him!" the workmen cry.

The courtyard continues to empty until only one person is left. A peasant, who has laughed enthusiastically from the beginning of the performance to its end, remains in his place. The smile of pleasure is still on his face. He glances around and looks at the place where the street organ stood. He does not forget to look up at the windows, which are now locked because of the downpour. He makes a discontented face and heads for the gate.

There, the peasant meets a wretched little dog, shivering from cold and huddled against the wall. He stops, looks fixedly at the dog, bends over to it as closely as possible, and says: "Why, you're frozen through!" after which he immediately leaves the yard, extremely satisfied with himself.

Conclusion

Have you ever happened to stroll along Petersburg's far-flung streets late at night in the fall?

The high walls of homes, illuminated from time to time by the dim light of streetlamps, seem even bleaker than the sky. In places, the buildings and the gray clouds merge into a single mass, and the small lights in the windows shine like moving stars. The rain falls on roofs and pavements with a monotonous tone. A cold wind blows forcefully and wails mournfully through the gates. The streets are empty. Here and there, a rather late pedestrian makes his way, or a night cabbie drags himself along, cursing the bad weather. But soon all quiets down. Now and then one can hear only the prolonged whistle of a watchtower or the creaking of a barge, swaying in the gusting wind. All again becomes silent.

The weather profoundly influences the disposition of the spirit, and so one somehow becomes sad quite unwillingly.

Gradually, one recalls long-forgotten sorrows, one after the other. A sad and uncomfortable feeling fills one's soul, and an inexpressible melancholy possesses one's entire being.

One enters a remote, dark alleyway, and the heart contracts more powerfully than before. The tall fences disappear in the darkness. A half-ruined hovel is without a sign of life. All is empty, without a single living soul. Only a wet dog runs by, snorting and sniffing, hoping in vain to fall upon a trace of its master.

Suddenly, one hears a street organ amid the silence. The sounds of *Luchinushka* reach the ear, and, very shortly, the figure of the organ-grinder passes by.

You somehow come to life. Your heart begins to beat strongly. The anguish momentarily disappears, and you set out cheerfully for home. The mournful sounds of *Luchinushka,* though, continue to hover over you. For a long time there flashes before you the pitiful figure of the organ-grinder whom you have met in the dark alleyway, and instinctively you think: Perhaps, at this very minute, he is tired, shivering from the cold, exhausted from hunger, and alone in a lifeless world. Perhaps, also, he is recalling his native hills, his aging mother, the olive trees, and his black-eyed mistress. And again instinctively you ask: Why and by what wind has the organ-grinder been carried to God-knows-where, to a foreign land where he meets neither a kind word nor a friendly smile and where, as he rises in the morning, he does not know how his day will end, and whether he will end up wretched and cold. . . .

—D. Grigorovich

The Petersburg Quarter

Evgeny Grebenka

"Study, my son," my now deceased grandmother often told me when I was a boy. "Study, and you'll grow up to be wise. You'll go and work in Petersburg. You'll wear an embroidered uniform. And you'll live in the Petersburg Quarter itself, right on Dvoryansky Street. You're nobility, after all."

I do not know why my grandmother had such a high opinion of the Petersburg Quarter. (She had never been to Petersburg, you see). Perhaps it was because our village priest had a son who worked in Petersburg.

Perhaps you find this strange. But just wait, there's more. This priest often dined in our home during the holidays, and each time, he spoke of his son: how he was getting on in the capital and how he often had the good fortune to converse with the generals who lived there. My grandmother (for all her respect for the priest) never seemed quite convinced of his stories, and she almost always said to him, "God grant, Father Peter, that I see your Ivan Petrovich before I die."

The old lady's wish came true.

One fine summer, Ivan Petrovich came home on leave to see his father, Father Peter, and, *one equally fine day,* he came to our house for a visit. He was wearing a uniform, complete with a sword, never before seen in our region, and holding a cocked hat under his arm.

My grandmother and I kept looking over our Petersburg guest as though he were a rare beast. Finally, she could not restrain herself any longer. She sat down next to him and plied him with various (and timely) questions about the capital, its footmen, and so forth. . . .

(I thought that I had long forgotten this episode, but recently, while reading about the travels of Dumont d'Urville,[1] I suddenly recalled that my grandmother's questions were not unlike the simplehearted queries the queen of the Oceanic Islands had made of some traveling European.)

"A real edicated person," my grandmother said, after Ivan Petrovich had left. "The priest's son has seen a lot of the world, even if he made up a little as he went along. 'I,' he says, 'live in the Petersburg Quarter, and on Bol'shoi Dvoryansky Street, to boot!' . . . And just what kind of nobleman is he, may I ask?! . . ."

"It's nothing to joke about," she added, sighing from the depths of her soul. "Just look at what the world has come to!"

The old woman immediately began to wring her hands.

(All this happened very long ago. Yet, to this very day, one still finds people in the provinces who think that Petersburg is a grand place and that the Petersburg Quarter must be a veritable paradise. After all, they reason, if the nobility holds the highest rank in the state, what must life be like on Dvoriansky Street or, for that matter, in Petersburg itself?)[2]

My grandmother and the official, Ivan Petrovich, led me to believe (however childishly) that the Petersburg Quarter was a kind of El Dorado: magical and fantastic. For instance, I was once immersed in *The Thousand and One Nights* and came across the description of a legendary castle (the product of some Eastern fantasy). I imagined it in Petersburg, in the Petersburg Quarter, and invariably on Bol'shoi Dvoryansky Street where

1. Dumont d'Urville's highly popular *A Picturesque Voyage Around the World: A General Summary of Travels and Discoveries* (*Voyage pittoresque autour du monde, resumé général des voyages de découvertes*), published in Paris in 1834, had been translated into Russian by Polevoi two years later. (A second translation of the work by an unknown author appeared in 1843.)

A Picturesque Voyage included the observations and impressions not only of Dumont d'Urville but also of such foreign explorers as Ferdinand Magellan and James Cook and of such Russian navigators as Faddei Bellinsgauzen and Ivan Kruzenshtern. Vissarion Belinsky highly approved of the work. Belinskii, *Polnoe sobranie sochinenii,* vol. 2 (1953), 68–70.

Incidentally, among the "simplehearted queries" the queen of the "Oceanic Islands" (read: Hawaii) addressed to the "traveling European" were questions as to whether European women had pretty dresses and used good oil on their hair.

2. Such a view was enduring. "We provincials somehow turn our steps toward Petersburg," Mikhail Saltykov-Shchedrin wrote in 1872. "It's as if Petersburg, with its name, its streets, and its fog, rain, and snow, could solve life's problems or shed new light on them." M. Saltykov-Shchedrin, *Sobranie sochinenii v dvadtsati tomakh*, 20 vols. (1965–77), vol. 10 (Moscow: Khudozhestvennaia literatura, 1970), 271.

every inhabitant (or so it seemed to me) was a nobleman whose greatness was beyond words! Such an individual, I thought, first visited his neighbor in a golden carriage. He then went hunting on dashing steeds, accompanied by the sounds of trumpets and horns, and surrounded by hundreds of huntsmen and dog trainers. God knows what my childish fantasy did not conjure up at that time!

Since then many years have passed. My inquisitive grandmother has been lying in the village graveyard for quite some time now. The birch saplings that had been planted on her grave are now huge trees. The priest, Father Peter, has also passed on. I do not know if Ivan Petrovich is alive or not. I also do not know if he still lives on Dvoryansky Street or if he has moved to Liteinyi Prospekt, having settled into an existence requiring a carriage, connections, a sense of his own importance; not to mention the probable appearance of a bald spot on his head. For my part, however, I now live in Petersburg and have seen both the Petersburg Quarter and Dvoryansky Street.

Having compared reality and my previous fantasy, what I saw and what I had heard from my grandmother and Ivan Petrovich, I confess that I have learned, the hard way, the truth of two sayings. One of them belongs to Father Peter: "*Seeing is believing.*" The other is a folk proverb: "*Glorious are the tambourines beyond the hills.*" (Inexplicably, I again recall that having read a rather eloquent description of Alexander the Great in Kaidonov's history,[3] I very nearly doubted the greatness, wisdom, and courage of this hero. I am very sorry to say that I was even ready to see him as a myth in my heart.)

If you have a lot of money, and if you will live in the center of town, you ride along the parquet pavement of Nevsky Prospekt or the Sea Streets. And if your eyes have grown accustomed to the bright gaslights and the luxurious stores, you (as becomes your status as an able person) will sometimes grumble about your fate or exaggerate your misfortunes. When such a thing happens, I advise you to stroll to the Petersburg Quarter, the poorest section of our capital. Look at the long rows of narrow streets (many of them unpaved) and the wooden homes that line them. The

3. Grebenka is citing Ivan Kaidanov's work *A Short Outline of World History* (*Kratkoe nachertanie vseobshchei istorii*), the ninth edition of which appeared in 1839.

farther you travel from Bol'shoi Prospekt, the more desolate, gloomy, and impoverished the Petersburg Quarter becomes. Remember that here live thousands of poor but honest workers who are cheerful in their own way, and believe me when I say that you will be ashamed of your grumblings. The terrible darkness of a narrow, dirty alleyway (barely lit at one end by a dim lantern) makes you appreciate the almost sunlike brightness of a gas lamp. The uneven pavement continually throws a passenger from side to side, causing you to breathe peacefully only when your carriage reaches a road paved with wooden blocks. The sight of a pastry shop with broken windows makes you yearn for the mirrored displays of stores laden with luxuries.

Each to his own taste, true. But it is sometimes to me very enlightening to walk through the Petersburg Quarter.

At one time, the Petersburg Quarter really was the best part of town. Here was the palace of Peter the Great (now a priceless artifact on the bank of the Neva).[4] Here, distinguished citizens once lived (as can be seen from the names along Dvoryansky Street). With time, however, people built their palaces on the other side of the river, and, since Petersburg traded with Moscow and the central regions of Russia, it began to expand southward toward the Muscovite gates. The Petersburg Quarter, though, was cut off from the center of the city by the Neva, and because it faced north (out upon the Finnish hills and swamps), it began to decline and became a haven for poverty. An impoverished clerk who can scarcely set aside several rubles at a time can buy a piece of swamp in the Petersburg Quarter almost for a song. Little by little, he builds a cheap wooden hovel, and, having worked until he receives a pension (and gray hair), he moves to his new home to live out his remaining years. In this way a large part of today's Petersburg Quarter came into being. Should one wish to be convinced of such a thing, one need only explore the streets there and read the inscriptions on the gates of the homes. Here all ranks, from the collegiate registrar to the councillor of state, stand out vividly on yellow plates. Most of the residences in the Petersburg Quarter are currently owned by titular councillors and clerks of the eighth class. Homes belonging to councillors of state are few,

4. The so-called Peter's Cottage (Domik Petra) was Peter the Great's first residence in the city. Built initially from pine logs in 1703, the now brick-encased "cottage" consists of two rooms and is one of the old structures in St. Petersburg.

and those of de facto councillors fewer still. In the Petersburg Quarter, one finds more the homes of retired clerks, noncommissioned officers, retired chamber musicians, stokers, court lackeys, and even court Negroes. Homes owned by merchants are rare and are found more in the area of Vasilievsky Island, near the Church of Saint Nicholas of the Sea.[5] In the summer, the Petersburg Quarter also houses many of the runners for the stock exchange as well as merchants from Pskov and Ryazan who deal in hemp and flax.

One old man (an acquaintance of mine) told me the following story: Some fifty years ago, when he was a young man, he was looking for an apartment in the Petersburg Quarter. He happened to read the inscription on the gate of a rather pleasant-looking home: THE RESIDENCE OF THE RETIRED ARAB N.N. So he knocked on the gate.

(Note: At that time, the Petersburg Quarter had no bells on the gates of its homes; even now this luxury is not everywhere to be seen.)

A gray-haired old man came out and greeted my friend. He was wearing a white dressing gown and a hat which, along with the unusual pallor of his face, made him look very much like an albino.

"What can I do for you?" the pale old man asked.

"I wish to see the master of the house," my friend answered.

"I am the master, at your service, sir," said the albino, raising his hat slightly.

"You are . . . the master?!"

"That is correct."

"Excuse me, I thought . . . you see, I have been accustomed to think . . ."

"Don't worry about it. What can I do for you?"

"I'm looking for an apartment; it seems that you have one."

"At your service, sir."

The white Arab took my friend to see the apartment. The apartment, though, did not so much engage my friend as the question: How did this Arab become so white? His head, let's suppose, could have gone white with age. But his skin should have stayed as black as soot, yet why was it also white? So my friend thought and thought, as he went from one room to another. Finally, beating around the bush somehow, and with great

5. The Church of Saint Nicholas of the Sea was built in 1743 not far from St. Isaac's Square in central St. Petersburg. It no longer exists.

difficulty, politely and subtly, my friend conveyed to the albino his amazement at the latter's white skin.

"You are not the first to be surprised," the old man noted calmly. "I became an Arab solely by favor of the authorities."

"The authorities?"

"That is correct. Allow me to explain. I was working as a simple stoker when the time came for me to retire. 'Grigory Ivanovich,' my wife said to me, 'ask them if you can retire as an Arab. After all, an Arab's pension is twice as large.' 'Why, I never thought of that!' I said, and off I went to the authorities. I petitioned as was proper, put forth my reasons, you know how it is, the wife, the children. . . . And here the boss—he was a kind man, thank you—put me down on the rolls as an Arab and retired me on an Arab's pension. But my face is as God created it, my kind sir. . . . Why, after me, three others also retired as Arabs."

"And were they also white?"

"That is correct, sir."

"And where are they now?"

"Why, they live not far from here."

The poor (and for the most part, inhospitable) homes in the Petersburg Quarter are owned by people of modest means and are occupied by tenants who also do not live life on a grand scale. Imagine that there once lived a man with a job. This job was not much by way of significance or salary; nonetheless, it was a so-called cushy job. That is, it was sanctioned from above and attained for the man the various blessings indispensable to life. This man, a clerk, held this job for quite some time. He married and settled down to a large family. He lived recklessly, though, without a goal—neither glancing back at the past nor looking ahead to the future. He was friendly with the higher-ups, gave magnificent parties and dinners, played handily at preference and the like—and, quite unexpectedly, overate one day and died. A new clerk promptly appeared in his place. As was customary, he asked the family of his predecessor to vacate the state-provided apartment. The ever-solicitous government endowed the wife and children of the deceased with a pension in accordance with his former salary. Such largesse, however, was hardly sufficient for people accustomed to luxury, and neither the mother nor her children had ever bothered to learn anything useful (like needlepoint, for example). Finding it expensive to live in the city proper, they now load their belongings (the remnants of their previous splendor) on horse-drawn carts and roam about—(a pitiful) crowd in the Petersburg Quarter.

The Petersburg Quarter also harbors the poor clerk-dreamer who has quit his hometown and who hopes (as they say) to find happiness in the capital. He now looks at his situation in horror and beats a hasty retreat to the Petersburg Quarter—there he can find an apartment within his means; there everything reminds him of his small town in the provinces.

The actor who has been hissed off stage, the poet who remains unacknowledged, the girl who has been hurt by the wide world flee to the Petersburg Quarter. There they settle in attics, and, in silence, they lapse into fantasies.

The Petersburg Quarter also sustains the unfortunate merchant who went bankrupt either because of stupidity or excessive trust of people.

(Note: The so-called fraudulent bankrupts do not live in the Petersburg Quarter, for they love noise and splendor.)

In the Petersburg Quarter you will also encounter the temporary clerk as well as the junior one who did not want to study and who thus lives on a salary of four hundred rubles. There you will also meet the poor (but noble) provincial parent who has brought a pack of sons to the city so that they can study at an official institution of higher learning. You can spot such an individual by his important bearing, his healthy red face, his military uniform (without epaulets), his tricornered hat adorned with feathers, and three or four minors in nankeen suits and service caps who follow him single file. It is always interesting to see that while this creature is filled with a sense of his own worth, he—politely, kindly, and almost shyly—lets pass anyone he meets along the street. In this way, he shows to his sons his desire for societal manners as well as his political desire not to offend a stranger he might need someday.

In the Petersburg Quarter, you will find foremen without apprentices or workers, servants without masters, masters without servants, gardens without trees, and trees without gardens (which, incidentally, do not grow well here). God knows how and why all this chaos came about. As a further example, a stream, the Karpovka, sometimes runs dry; but alleyways are constantly covered with puddles. There, ducks swim amid flourishing algae and swamp grass.

You can also come across in the Petersburg Quarter people who have wasted their lives and fortunes in litigation. Such individuals rarely come out into God's world. While others slosh and tramp through the mud-filled streets and alleyways (tracking the dirt in on painted floors at house parties), these unfortunate souls sit at home over papers and painstakingly practice their handwriting in an empty silence.

You will not meet these people in the street. They do not stroll about; they take refuge in their own thoughts and dreams. One can, however, catch a glimpse of them at Mytnyi Ferry at about nine in the morning. There they gather to cross over to the senate (burdened with bundles and sheaves of papers). One of my acquaintances told me that long ago, he often met there a sickly and consumptive little man who laboriously carried a birch log under his arm. This birch log was heavy, thick, and wrapped painstakingly in a checkered cotton kerchief. After getting into the boat, the old man would place the log carefully on his knees; he would look at it and rewrap it lovingly, just as a mother would her child.

"Take care of your log, take care of it, Ivan Ivanovich," the young driver often teased the old man. "Your log might catch a cold, after all. It'll begin to cough and not let you get any sleep."

"That'll be enough," the little old man always answered. "My log keeps me up all night as it is!"

"Now, why is that?"

"You mean, I haven't told you?"

"Why no, indeed no! . . ."

"Oh, come now, I must have told you! . . ."

"No, no, you've never told us. Perhaps you told Petr Petrovich, but not us."

"Well, perhaps I did. I distinctly remember that I told Petr Petrovich. It's an interesting story. Why, my entire life has depended on this log. You must understand, my dear sirs, that this is no ordinary log, but one that is dear to me: a most exemplary log, if you will . . .

"You see, in the year 17—, I worked as a supplier of wood . . ." and the old man would (for the thousandth time) tell his captive listeners how he once somehow supplied wood on contract; how he was not paid for it all because the wood was allegedly shorter than was specified in the agreement; how he, together with the deputy mayor A. and the provincial secretary B. (whom he had called as witnesses), took a log from a pile of wood into his own hands; how, without rhyme or reason, he had hid it and set up a business . . . and so forth. Now as proof of what he had done, and also in case anyone should ever accuse him of anything, he sets out each day for the senate, taking along his log, and calculating how many handkerchiefs it has worn out, and so forth. In a word, the old man keeps on talking until the boat comes to the other shore and his audience scatters in different directions. Then, breathing a sigh, he gives a copper coin to the boatman, puts the log under his arm, and heads for the senate.

In the Petersburg Quarter you also come upon unlucky speculators, that is, individuals who have been ruined completely and do not know where next to turn. In the quarter, they silently plot the possible schemes by which they can escape, break loose from, or simply crawl out of their difficult situation.

(Note: As soon as a speculator gets on his feet again, he immediately leaves the Petersburg Quarter. He says that the climate is unhealthy and the situation awkward.)

So far, I have been talking about the overall population in the Petersburg Quarter. I now take up some of its local color. The Petersburg Quarter intersects with the clean and splendid Kamennostrovsky Prospekt. There one can find the elegant Alexander Gymnasium[6] as well as the splendid but small homes owned by private individuals, of which more are being built year after year. (The side adjacent to Tyuchkov Bridge features military schools and other huge stone buildings.) The former patriarchal life of the Petersburg Quarter has all but disappeared. Now, instead, you will see a carriage, general's epaulets, and a dandyish droshky belonging to a doctor or a steward. Sometimes you will also hear regimental music and glimpse into rooms with drapes, elegant bronze, and comely pictures. In such homes, people drink champagne, eat truffles, and smoke cigars. (Although most of the food there is local, one can always find foreign provisions wrapped in red paper.) People in the Petersburg Quarter also discuss opera (though often dishonestly), read journals, and critique French performances at the theater (many times, it is true, on hearsay alone). In short, the Petersburg Quarter is an enlightened place.

6. More accurately, the Imperial Alexander Lycée (Imperatorskii Aleksandrovskii Litsei), founded by Alexander I in 1810 to educate sons of the nobility for government service, had moved from Tsarskoe Selo to the Petersburg Quarter in 1829.

In summer, the entire Petersburg Quarter comes alive with nature. Dachamania (i.e., the passion for dachas) rages fiercely among our Petersburg citizens and drives them all from the city.[7] In the words of one poet, they:

> "Both gallop and crawl
> Ride and swim."[8]

Away from Petersburg. The richer one is, the farther he goes. The not-so-fortunate, though, go to the Petersburg Quarter. It is (so to speak) a village in its own right. The air is clean, homes are wooden, and gardens are numerous. Most important, the Petersburg Quarter is not far from the islands or the center of town, for some, three miles from work; for others, four.

Such selling points cause the entire Petersburg Quarter—its homes and its hovels, its attics and cellars—to be taken up by *dachniki* (visitors to the country). Small shopkeepers buy up twice their usual amount of reserve supplies. Droshkies thunder along the clavichord-like thoroughfares that lead to the Krestovsky Ferry. Highways and byways become filled with merchants and artisans. Every evening, the streets and alleyways of

7. Petersburg dachas were regular subjects for social satire, burlesque, and farce in Russian vaudevilles and sketches throughout the first half of the nineteenth century. They were also the ideal breeding place for middle-class urban culture. As Stephen Lovell declares, "If the tag 'middle-class' refers to anyone in Russia, it is to the dachniki, in their creation of a hybrid cultural zone that combined intelligentsia, merchant, and petty [*sic*] bourgeois values." See S. Lovell, "Between Arcadia and Suburbia: Dacha in Late Imperial Russia," *Slavic Review* 61, no. 1 (2002): 87.

Like everything else in Russian literature of this time, Petersburg dachas entered into the struggle between conservatives and liberals for control of the national written expression. For instance, Faddei Bulgarin, in an 1837 article entitled "Dachas" ("Dachi"), expressed conflicting views on such residences. On the one hand, he saw the widespread growth of dachas as a "barometer of a people's strength, prosperity, enlightenment, civic spirit, and communal life." On the other hand, Bulgarin questioned the cost of such progress. "You might die ten times over before you find your doctor in the dacha region, or before he could be brought back from his dacha," he complained. "And don't bother," Bulgarin continued, "to look for a merchant in his shop, an apothecary in his drugstore, a German tradesman in his workshop, or a clerk in his office! All of them are at the dacha!" F. Bulgarin, "Dachi," *Severnaia pchela,* no. 176 (August 9, 1837), 703–4.

Not to be outdone, Nikolai Nekrasov, in an 1844 cycle of six feuilletons entitled "Petersburg Dachas and Environs" ("Peterburgskie dachi i okresnosti") added, "How many dramas, how many vaudevilles play out until finally the residents of Petersburg divide among themselves . . . these airy, quick-growing structures with which the environs of Petersburg are strewn?" Nekrasov, *Polnoe sobranie sochinenii,* vol. 12 (1955), 87–88.

8. Grebenka is paraphrasing Ivan Dmitriev's 1794 poem "Seekers of Fortune" ("Iskateli fortuny").

the quarter come alive with strolling groups of colorful ladies and their escorts. . . . Follow the sidewalks of the Petersburg Quarter. They are not very level (and they are a little wobbly), true, but they are lined by cellar apartments. Glance down and you will see family scenes, touching and diverse. In one, a man plays a violin while his wife feeds kasha to an infant in her arms. In a second, an angry father boxes his son's ears. In a third, a family is sitting down to tea. In a fourth, another family welcomes or sees off a guest. In a fifth, a face looks out absentmindedly onto the street. Now look at the middle stories. There you hear a piano playing or someone's legs clicking in a quadrille or a gallopade. If, by chance, the blinds are lowered, you can (for lacking of nothing else to do) ask yourself: "Now who can that be dancing there? Is it, perhaps, a young girl who thinks that life is one uninterrupted and merry dance? An old maid who has set her cap for some man, wishing to captivate him and make him her husband? A plump baroness, the matriarch of a large family, who jumps about in a sweat and looks very foolish? A young man who clicks his heels in a quadrille before a horrid and rouged old woman (his boss's wife)?" You may ask further: "Is this, perhaps, his first time out in society? . . . What should one call him?" . . . Well, let's just say that he has a talent for getting on in the world: he will go very far in life, and someday one will greet him as a very important and significant person. . . . If you are not intrigued by lowered blinds—then go further. One will hear from an attic the soft sounds of a guitar and a song:

> "You will not believe me, you will not believe me,
> You will not believe me, when I tell you
> How dear you are! . . ."

Sometimes, high up in one of the attics, someone will sneeze very loudly, and he will be greeted from the street: "God bless you!"

Everywhere there is life!

But how the Petersburg Quarter comes to a standstill in the winter! No sooner do the leaves turn yellow than the *dachniki* (like birds of passage) move back to the center of town. The population diminishes, and the quarter becomes noticeably deserted. Day by day, it becomes gloomier and more desolate. The streets are covered with mud: Truly, they are a wonder unto themselves! . . . Anyone who, by chance, merely passes through the Petersburg Quarter from Troitsky Bridge to the islands along Kamennostrovsky Prospekt does not even guess the existence of its miserable side streets. Turn either right or left, and such a chance visitor will discover a maze of streets, all varying in width, length, and importance, and bearing the most diverse and incomprehensible names. One will see several Grebensky streets; a few Dvoryansky, Raznochinnyi, and Zelenyi streets; and, at least one Teryaev, Podrezov, Putalov, Odnostoronnyi, Barmaleev, and Gul'yarnyi street.

One even finds a Dun'kin Lane, as well as others with the strangest of nicknames. There is even a street with a first name and patronymic: *Andrei Petrovich* Street! Some of these streets are superbly paved in stone, but others drown in mud, and in the fall and spring, a cabbie will not drive down them, no matter what one offers to pay. Several of these streets have cobblestones strewn about (as if for fun). They either protrude from the mud or are concealed in it, thereby causing carriages to give the most unpleasant jolts. Still other streets are covered with planks of wood. You travel on these as if along the keys of a clavichord. It is all very amusing.

One spring day, at about five in the morning, two friends are conversing warmly on Bol'shoi Prospekt. They have just stepped out of a home where the lamps are still burning, even though it is already light outside.

Our friends are young men, dressed neatly in tailcoats with bright buttons.

"Well, so long," one says to the other.

"No, no. I don't want to say good-bye. I really don't want to. . . . We certainly tied one on, didn't we? The host is an extremely generous man; there was all the champagne one could want."

"Just a second here. You thought that *that* was champagne?"

"Well, and what did you think?"

"I thought that it was so-so for champagne."

"Why, I almost thought the very same thing . . . truly I did! . . . and did you notice how that brunette was giving me the once-over? Huh? . . ."

"Yes, I noticed . . . But back to the subject. What was served was simply a *Chablis mousseux* . . ."

"Yes, yes, that's it exactly. It was precisely a Chablis. You know, how fortunate I am to have met such a marvelous fellow like yourself so unexpectedly."

"The feeling is mutual. Farewell . . ."

"No, no, wait a minute. Where are you off to? I don't want . . ."

"What don't you want?"

"I don't want a farewell from you; a good-bye is better! Surely a good-bye is better? Isn't a good-bye better?"

"All right, it's better. Well, then, good-bye."

"This means, of course, you'll visit me sometime? You'll come and visit me?"

"Yes, I'll visit you. Now good-bye!"

"Wait a minute. Where are you going? . . . It's always good-bye with you!! . . . And where are you going to visit me? . . ."

"Why, at your home, your home, I guess."

"At my home? . . . Very well, and just where is my home, huh? Where is it, my home, you tell me, where?"

"It's on street . . . Er, you'll excuse me, I forgot. It's such a difficult name and I really do have a bad memory. I forgot the street. I'm at fault, you see. Forgive me, I forgot!"

"Well, now, so there you are. You forgot. I live on Polozov Street. Understand? Got it? Now good-bye! But you will come and visit me? You're coming?"

"Yes, I'll come. Good-bye!"

"Good-bye. And where will you come and visit me?"

"At your home on Podrezov Street."

"You did it again. You forgot! You've got one wretched memory there. You'd have a really difficult time of it if you were back in school! Am I right?! . . . One really difficult time."

"I guess you're right."

"You guess I'm right? I should say so, I'm right. Now just wait a bit. So you won't forget the street. Just listen. Polozov, Polozov, Polozov. Got it?"

Suddenly, one friend starts to crawl on all fours.

"You won't forget now?"

"No, I won't forget . . ."

The men go their separate ways. For my part, I thought that the one on all fours had made up his home address. So I purposely set out to find Polozov Street. I did. I asked many of the residents there why the street had such a strange name. As if having agreed in advance, they all replied: "Why, such a name is most usual when you get right down to it. Besides, what else would you call it, if not Polozov Street?"

Now when I asked about Andrei Petrovich (or Andrea Petrovna) Street, I was more fortunate.

The story goes that there once lived a happy couple (as if taken from the novels of Lafontaine).[9] The husband, Andrei Petrovich, loved his wife to a degree impossible to imagine, whereas his wife, Aksinya Ivanovna, loved her husband to a degree impossible to express (so one storyteller of Andrei Petrovna Street put it succinctly). Suddenly, from neither one thing nor another, Andrei Petrovich died. Aksinya Ivanovna was left behind, but she was never the same after that. The poor thing went out of her mind from grief, you see; she imagined that she was not Aksinya Ivanovna but Andrei Petrovich and that Andrei Petrovich had not died but had become her, Aksinya, and that now only Andrei Petrovich remained in existence.

Aksinya Ivanovna did not respond to her former name, but when she was called to, "Andrei Petrovich!" she would always respond, "Who's calling?" She even went about in men's clothing.[10]

9. The sentimentalist novels of August Lafontaine were quite popular in Russia in the first two decades of the nineteenth century. Russian adaptation-translations of his works included such titles as *Alexandra and Maria; or, Love and Honor on Trial: A Novel in Letters* (*Aleksandra i Mariia, ili Liubov' i Chestnost' v Ispitanii. Povest' v pis'makh*), *The Vestal Virgin* (*Vestalka*), and *Prince Fyodor D-ky i Kniazhna Maria M-va; or, Loyalty and Death: A Russian Event* (*Kniaz' Fedor D-kii i Kniazhna Mariia M-va ili Vernost' i Smert': Russkoe Proisshestvie*).

Others of Lafontaine's works that were favorites of Russian readers included *Blanka and Maria; or, Mores of the Bourgeois* (*Blanka i Mariia, ili Meshchanskie Nravy*), *Alexander Mikhailovich the Great, Prince of Tver: A Historical Novel* (*Aleksandr Mikhailovich Velikii, Kniaz' Tverskoi: Istoricheskii roman*), *Amalia Gorst; or, The Secret of Being Happy* (*Amaliia Gorst, ili Taina Byt' Schastlivym*), *Agnes and Bertha; or, Women of Earlier Times* (*Agnessa i Berta, ili Zhenshchiny Prezhnikh Vremen*), and *Louisa and Duvalle; or, An Unhappy Love* (*Luiza i Diuval', ili Neschastnaia Liubov'*).

10. Grebenka is drawing his anecdote from the saint's life of Blessed Ksenya Peterburgskaya, who was born in St. Petersburg sometime between 1719 and 1739. Like Aksinya in Grebenka's story, Ksenya was also widowed at age twenty-six with the death of her husband, Andrei Fyodorovich Petrov, a singer in the court chorus. She too lost her sanity with his passing. For the next forty-five years, she wandered through the Petersburg Quarter, where she wore her husband's clothing, answered only when called by Andrei's name, and insisted that her husband was alive but that his wife was dead.

Unlike Aksinya, though, Ksenya gave all her earthly possessions to the poor and rambled the city as a "god's fool" (*iurodovaia*), suffering insults and abuse from the mob until she cured the sick and disclosed the inner life of the people she visited. Even greater fame came to Ksenya when she predicted the future, for example, the 1764 overthrow of Ivan VI and the 1761 death of Empress Elizaveta Petrovna.

Further, Ksenya's passing in her seventies (dates of her death vary) was the occasion of numerous miracles and divine intercessions for people of all social classes who prayed to her on their behalf.

Still more remarkable in the Petersburg Quarter is one of the Zelenyi streets. It is wide and lined with trees; it also has a gate at both ends so that the entire street can be put under lock and key just as if it were a courtyard.

Despite their different names, the streets in the Petersburg Quarter bear a common stamp. They are all lined with identical (or almost identical) hovels with or without attics; front gardens with two lilac bushes or yellow acacia; and small shops with the inscription NO. 1 in which merchants sell tea and silk not by any standard weight or measure but by various combinations of coins: twenty-five-kopeck pieces, five-kopeck pieces, or some other amounts of change. . . . Such weights leave natives not a little surprised.

The inhabitants of the Petersburg Quarter usually dine at home; the so-called tavern life does not exist here. Every unmarried man keeps a cook who feeds him, buying provisions at Sytnyi Market[11]—so named because, with the exception of beef, flour, and vegetables, one need not go anywhere else.

"Can you get honey, mushrooms, and other things?" asks a resident of the Petersburg Quarter.

"We're stocked full, my dear sir. What else would you like?"

"Well, I need some pieces of glass, a couple of buckets, all kinds of wooden dishes, nails . . ."

"You can get all of these at Sytnyi Market."

I once asked a well-known etymologist about the word *Sytnyi.* In response, he said, "I once knew a brave man who, after drinking a wineglass full of vodka, also consumed the glass itself. That is to say, he ate the glass too; or, speaking rhetorically, having drunk the contents, he also ingested that which contained it. He suffered no ill effects. I also had this horse which used to nibble on buckets and all kinds of wooden dishes. The

During the prerevolutionary period, as many as five thousand people visited her grave; in 1988, during the millennium anniversary of Russia's conversion to Christianity, there were even more. For more on Ksenya Peterburgskaya, see V. Toporov, "Teksty blazhennoi Ksenii Peterburgskoi i ee kul'ta (po materialam Smolenskogo kladbishcha 70–80–e gody," in *Mif, ritual, simvol, obraz: Issledovaniia v oblasti mifopoeticheskogo; Izbrannoe* (Moscow: Progress, 1995), 369–76. Also see Buckler, *Mapping St. Petersburg,* 124–26.

11. Sytnyi Market is located in the center of the Petersburg Quarter. Initially, the place was called Glutton Market (*Obzhornyi rynok*) and later, Goat Swamp (*Koz'e boloto*). In fact, to residents of the area, the phrase, "to go to Goat Swamp" (*idti na Koz'e boloto*) meant "to buy a bottle of cheap port wine at any time of the day." Also, in the eighteenth century, Sytnyi Market was a place for public executions and punishment.

animal found some of the nails to be inedible, but then there are no rules without exceptions!"

I consider as an exception, though, several bachelors in the Petersburg Quarter, bachelors who keep cooks and take their meals at home. They usually rent a room (with a servant and board) from a married couple for thirty (or sometimes twenty-five) rubles a month. For this, they give you a rather humble room either on the first floor (with access to the kitchen) or in an attic, which you climb up to on a dark, steep, wooden staircase that creaks. Every morning, a girl or an old lady furnishes you water to wash. She also sets out the samovar, sometimes cleans his boots, sometimes sweeps his rooms, and almost always, at some appointed time, serves him *shchi,* and something else after that, and something else after that.

For the most part, though, lodgers dine together with their proprietors. They grow quite fond of their landlords and often make up one happy family. Dinner usually consists of three dishes. The dining room is usually papered in violet or storm green colors, with various scenes from mythology.

(Note: This is the cheapest kind of wallpaper. The proprietors buy it in a small shop on Sadovaya Street not far from Shchukin Market.[12] They pay two and a half, sometimes two kopecks per piece, and with it, they decorate all the rooms of their lodgers.)

Sometimes, modest fellow lodgers (of a certain type) inhabit the cracks under the wallpaper. Sometimes, the wind blows too strongly from the windows; sometimes, the walls freeze through, or, for some mysterious reason, it is simply cold in the room. These, however, are incidentals—personal incidentals, true, but incidentals all the same.

The residents of the Petersburg Quarter, however, rarely receive their lodgers for tea. "Tea is expensive," the proprietors usually say. "Guests come and visit you, and, my dear sir, they dearly love their tea. But at these prices, I need not use it so quickly, and so I don't serve it. So there you have it. But I can't win. When I do serve it, first with sugar and then without, dissatisfactions always arise! . . . Good Lord! And I have such a disposition, you see, that dissatisfaction is like a sharp knife going right through my heart. I

12. Shchukin Market was a commercial and produce center on Sadovaya Street, roughly a mile south of the city.

love to treat refined people in a cordial manner, you see. And so, Avdotya will set the samovar for you at my expense, but I cannot put out anything for coal. . . . Nowadays, coal has become so expensive and hard to get. . . . Well now, my good sir, here's your room, you'll be satisfied with it, a nice room it is. . . . The windows don't look out onto the street, but you will be so kind as to notice that it's right in the sun, very good for flowers, you know, and for a bird, that is, if you have a bird—it'll sing the whole day long. I'll very likely take you on as a boarder. The food is decent, without any of those French bouillons and artichokes and things like that. Why, my dinners are fit for a staff officer, if I do say so myself. I myself love to eat, and in my house, my boarders eat what I eat. The only thing I ask is that you bring your own tea, for it will make the meals happier for you and more agreeable for me."

Speaking about residents in the Petersburg Quarter, I should also note that not far from the military schools in the area live the wives of the junior officers. In addition to keeping cows, they also take in lodgers or "paying guests" for fifteen or seventeen and a half assignats a month. For this the individual receives a place for a bed in a common room that he shares with the proprietors. He is also given lunch and dinner daily: for the most part, dairy items. Such apartments are almost always occupied by young men.

People who are elderly, with graying hair and a reddish hue to their cheeks, face a different situation. They typically despise such dairy fare. They say that they have long abandoned the cradle, and so, paying a silver ruble for a corner somewhere, they usually eat at a shopkeeper's for ten kopecks a day. Strangely, not a single shopkeeper will offer to feed you on a monthly basis, and to such a suggestion he will always answer, "No, sir, we're not allowed to do so. We have no *riggerstration.* Besides, you call this dinner? We ourselves eat what God sends us."

But if you go to his home on a daily basis, he will (and with pleasure) serve you *shchi* or pie, and aspic with horseradish and *kvas,* and for it all he will charge only ten kopecks.

People who have recently moved to the Petersburg Quarter and have not as yet found a job (or grown accustomed to the customs of the inhabitants there) usually dine at some lonely eating house. They pay a ruble assignat for a dinner of four courses. No matter how one counts them, four courses are always served, whether starting with soup and ending with pastry or starting with pastry and ending with soup (inclusive). And if a person does not fall ill from overeating, he will, by some quirk of nature, feel starved and think, "How and where can I eat again today?"

Go along one of the large streets of the Petersburg Quarter and you will see an alleyway at one end. Here you will come upon a large pole with a blue, green, and gray board nailed to it. The sign says (in large yellow letters): THE COOK, —OV, IS TODAY PREPARING . . . and nothing more. Perhaps the size of the board did not allow for a full inscription, or old man-god Saturn, flying over the Petersburg Quarter, hit the sign with his scythe and knocked off the interesting item: what is *the cook preparing*? No matter what, the thing or things which Mr. —ov cooks remain a mystery for the public. Nonetheless, a person, endowed with thought and reason (especially if he is hungry), easily guesses that although it is not forbidden for a cook to *prepare* lacquer, wax, fireworks, and so forth, he is probably also *preparing* food. As a result, the shrewd reader turns off a street and into a narrow alleyway and, more by smell than sight, finds the quarters of the cook. This dwelling is typically a wooden log cabin with two stories. The host, that is, the cook, meets him in a waiting room with two windows that face out onto a yard. The guest sees two cages, one with a chirping canary, the other with a singing Danish lark; a table covered with a tablecloth (which is not what one would exactly call fresh); two chairs, covered in leather; a leather couch; and a mirror. Amid such decor, the cook receives his customers. He assures them that in the Petersburg Quarter, one should dine only at his place, that he will cook circles around the French, that the French only boast of their accomplishments but that the Russians will beat them every time. (He cites the War of '12 as an example.) The language and mannerisms of the cook are deft, gentle, and assertive—just what one would expect from a person who wishes to call upon the health of one's pocket. If a guest should pay for dinner in advance, though, the cook will express himself more brusquely, just like any Russian who has maneuvered an unsuspecting individual into his hands. Suppose, for example, a person sees a cockroach in his soup. Undoubtedly, he will show it to the cook with the comment that this is something extra and that he is not about to pay for it. The cook will answer, "Ah, so what?"

"What do you mean, 'so what'? It's simply vile!"

"Why, what do you mean, 'It's simply vile!'? Good God, we do not take money for vile things."

"But there's a cockroach in my soup!"

"What cockroach?! Come now, we should all see a cockroach. That's not a cockroach. Why, it's simply a servant at your beck and call!"

If the argument continues, the cook will become rude. He will remark that he is not at fault if cockroaches have taken up in his kitchen and that he is not about to seek new quarters for anyone. After a while, though, he will calm down a bit and whisper softly, "If it happens again, send it back. I'll bring you a new serving."

"And what will you do with the old one?"

"I'll pass it along to someone in my household. See that old blind man sitting on the stove? He's my father; he'll eat anything. You just send it back next time."

At the end of the month, the cook serves up better dishes, and the portions are larger. In fact, he sometimes astounds his guest with an unexpected chicken, a fine pastry, or a dish of cold game that he calls a "galantine." Our cook is quite eager to win his guest over for yet another month of meals.

The Petersburg Quarter (as any poor part of town) has neither theaters nor magicians nor a zoo of its own. In short, it does not offer those amusements whereby one can kill time or spend money. People also say that the residents of the Petersburg Quarter do not like the stage and rarely visit the Alexander Theater. Such an assumption is unjust, though. The truth is that even the most fervid desire to attend the theater would grow cold in the journey from the quarter to the Alexander. In autumn, there is dampness and slush; in winter, there is storm and frost. Petersburg citizens (like all people) like to spend their time laughing or crying over another's woe. The residents of the Petersburg Quarter are no exception. Until recently, they (or so they say) always tried to get tickets—no matter what the cost—to performances at a theater founded by a convivial old fellow right there in the Petersburg Quarter.

There once lived (or so they say) in the Petersburg Quarter an old man with money and rank, a most cheerful character with a most kind soul. God had not blessed him with legitimate children, and so the old man kept his house full of wards whom he loved as his own (and upon whom he never tired of feasting his eyes).

Once on the old man's name day, his wards gave him a *surprise.* They dressed themselves not as shepherdesses or goddesses but as women from ancient mythology. With wreaths on their heads, they presented the man with a gift, a purse of their own making. They then began to sing some poetic lines (which had been written by an old teacher precisely for such an occasion):

That which is yours has come back to you.
The ardor of our hearts, accept as your own
A gift from Pindar draws close upon you,
Like the dream of maidens, accept what we have sewn.
Although we are dressed as goddesses,
Do not reproach us, O father thine,
For we love you like your children,
For what other maidens could you pine?

The old man greatly enjoyed the purse, the singing, and the costumes of his wards. Such novelties pleasantly aroused his already awakened emotions, and, having exchanged kisses with his goddesses, he gave his word to found a theater. The theater was built not far from where Malyi Prospekt intersects with the street leading to Krestovsky Ferry. A wide grain barn was cleared out, a stage was raised, and an orchestra pit was fashioned from cheap wallpaper. Decorations were made, and curtains were cut from white canvas. When lowered, they depicted a single huge lyre, but without the usual clouds, laurel wreaths, or flowery garlands. Long white benches were made from planks. They were not sectioned into seats but had numbers (up to a hundred) painted on them instead. Opposite the stage was placed the box of the theater's founder (plastered with cheap wallpaper). A wooden star with six candles hung over the pit. This was the chandelier. Besides the chandelier, four candles burned brightly in the orchestra. The orchestra consisted of two violins and a bass; sometimes the bass was replaced by a flute or a clarinet. The musicians were amateurs. Actors included the founder's wards, some well-known clerks, and an old teacher, who, they said, was an inimitable comedian. Initially, the theater was a purely domestic affair. With time, however (or so they say), patrons paid for tickets.

Free or not, the theater was always full. The loud applause and bravos clearly testified to the pleasure of the spectators. The theater brought life to the monotony of the Petersburg Quarter. The public often spoke and argued about the place, and when, with the owner's death, the performances ceased, everyone bemoaned the loss. With the flood, however, the theater was forgotten (as was everything else then in the world). In my opinion, the Petersburg Quarter should have a theater which is not expensive but accessible to the common man. Its plays should match the local demands, tastes, and attitudes of its inhabitants. Nowadays in the Petersburg Quarter, army musicians sometimes stage vaudeville in their barracks. The quality of these performances is not for us to judge. All the seats in such "theaters," however, are always taken, and many would-be patrons sadly return home, having been unable to get tickets. Usually the best seats go for thirty kopecks silver, and the cheapest go for ten. Personages such as the cook who has cheated the "master," the lackey-scoundrel, and the like find a warm response whenever they appear on stage.

Right next to the theater, a speculator once built a wooden arcade in the Petersburg Quarter. The building (on Malyi Prospekt) still stands to this day. It is surrounded by a colonnade and still preserves its grandeur from the outside. The building, however, gives one a sad feeling. It stands (or better to say, is collapsing) amid small hovels and dirty streets. Everything in it is dead and black. The windows and doors have darkened terribly and look like the socket hollows of a dead skull. Inside, it is terribly blackened, run down, and stripped to the frame. One finds neither life nor sound in these ruins. Sometimes, however, when the wind passes through, one will hear a cautious breathing or a quiet rustling. Sometimes, from behind a door, a girl in tatters appears, stealthily pulling out a half-rotten plank or log; or, from under a floorboard, a dog begins to bark at a passerby.

The Petersburg Quarter has few residents who own horses and carriages. The individuals who own such things live along Bol'shoi Prospekt toward Tyuchkov Bridge and near the military academies. Our Petersburg citizens do go about in cabs, although by preference they love to walk. That is why so few cabbies live or work in the Petersburg Quarter. At nine o'clock in the evening, in spring, fall, or winter, one will not find a single cab—well, perhaps on Bol'shoi Prospekt, but not always. (In winter, however, one can catch a sleigh on Malyi Dvoryansky Street, right by the house of Peter the Great; from there it will take one to the other side, to the Gagarinsky Wharf or the Marble Palace.)

The Petersburg Quarter has absolutely no taverns or cafe-restaurants where one could have breakfast or dinner. True, Bol'shoi Prospekt (near Sytnyi Market) and Bol'shoi Dvoryansky Street have several signs which read THIS WAY TO EAT, but these places serve only tea, and their customers are only the common people. One of these establishments, located by the Samsonovsky Bridge, is called the Cape of Good Hope. Here, long ago, students in their final year at the Medical Academy used to drink and carouse.

Several years ago, suddenly and without warning, the corner of Malyi Prospekt and the street to Krestovsky Ferry sported a sign that read CONFECTIONER'S SHOP. This sign stood out quite vividly, attracting the attention of riders and pedestrians who traveled to Krestovsky Island on Sundays. After the sign had hung there several months, however, it suddenly vanished. The story goes that a lame veteran of Napoleon's service was the proprietor of the shop. He would praise Napoleon to his visitors, and, with tears in his eyes, he would point to his idol's portrait (which hung in the corner of the shop). Needless to say, he sold very few of his wares.

I think that many people would recall this remarkable portrait (it was actually a woodcut about two and a half inches tall) which depicted Napoleon at full height, his hands absurdly stuck in his narrow trousers. Once, after dinner, on a hot summer day, I was strolling through the Petersburg Quarter and dropped by this shop. I asked for some ice cream. "At your service," said a small boy standing at the counter. He then rushed headlong out of the room.

Ten minutes passed. In that time I examined the portrait of Napoleon quite thoroughly. I was astounded by the assurance with which he had thrust his hands into his pockets. The boy did not return. Finally, the door opened and out came an elderly woman in a cap. She looked at me with questioning eyes.

"Will the ice cream be coming soon?"

The woman went out without saying a word.

After a while, the door opened again. This time, there appeared the bald head of the proprietor, also an elderly individual. I again asked for some ice cream. The head disappeared, but the boy reappeared, announcing that the ice cream had not yet frozen and that it would not be ready before two o'clock. I then asked for some lemonade. The boy disappeared. The same lady again came out and told me that they were out of lemonade.

"Well, then, could you give me some orgeat?"

The woman again left; the bald head of the proprietor reappeared, and, after that, a torso dressed in a gray nankeen jacket. Frowning, the proprietor approached me and uttered some strange sounds—like those street urchins make when they entice dogs to go under a gate.

"Now what's the problem?"

"The orgeat is kind of sour. It got soured and so forth . . ." From this, I gathered that the milk had spoiled and that the proprietor (speaking an absolutely unintelligible Russian dialect) was offering to pour me a cup of chocolate or a glass of water with sugar in it.

With such a debut, the new confectioner's shop could not last long. Here is what happened. The sign that disappeared from Malyi Prospekt turned up suddenly, like a faithful bird, on Bol'shoi. Everything was in its place. The same engraving hung behind the door; on it was Napoleon in uniform, his hands thrust into his pockets. There, too, was the lame, old proprietor doing what he had done before: selling little but talking a lot about Napoleon.

Besides the usual holidays and holy days, the majority of the residents in the Petersburg Quarter—clerks who work in the Senate, provincial posts, and the like—enjoy a personal holiday that lasts several days, the time being prolonged or cut short depending on the cold. The holiday is known as the river-freeze.

If sometime in autumn, down around First Street on Vasilievsky Island, you will see crowds of people who are properly dressed, who are laughing and conversing merrily, whose ranks extend from Isakievsky Ferry to Tyuchkov Bridge, and who carry notebooks and papers under their arms—you can be assured that the river-freeze has begun (or that if the Neva is not frozen, then it will, at the very least, allow people to cross over to the other side). . . . Sometimes this holiday will last an entire week or more. This is the time that the inhabitants of the Petersburg Quarter begin their social season: visits, parties, friendly games at preference, dances, and other diversions—just as if it were Christmastide and expense was no object.

The price of food, especially beef, rises during the river-freeze. Several years ago, when the river froze (and before the construction of a permanent Tyuchkov Bridge), game was cheap in the Petersburg Quarter. This was because the villagers who brought game into town were unable to carry it to the other side and had to sell it here, and because the merchants of the Petersburg Quarter refused to charge higher prices. Such a thing does not happen, now, however. The island buys up everything in sight and pays dearly for it.

Talking about festive occasions, for example, weddings, name days, and the like (that is, about occasions where there is music), the inhabitants of the Petersburg Quarter generally make merry to the music of a piano. Here, in the Quarter, you will not find the German dandy who has been hired to play for three rubles a night (as is the case in Kolomna, for example). Instead, one will encounter some old maid who is somebody's relative, acquaintance, or friend (perhaps all three) or who is there only to receive an old dress, a pound of coffee, or half a ruble. Whoever she is, this elderly individual serves as a go-between for young men and women alike. Maidens tell her all kinds of secrets; escorts whisper confidences under their breath. For her part, she will first threaten a rose-colored dress with her finger; next she will frown or shake her head at a civil uniform; then she will look over to a blue jacket, direct her eyes to a boss's daughter and strike up a gallopade.

Dances in the Petersburg Quarter often do without even such a cheap musician as this, and instead of an old maid–pianist, one finds the hostess herself or her daughter or her sister, who, in turn, is relieved by relatives or friends. In cases such as these, the girls finish the quadrille and immediately hurry over to the piano to thank the musician. One pays her reverence; another presses her hands; still another, for one reason or another, kisses her fingers all too fervently—such girls, you see, have just danced with the escorts of their dreams. The escorts also thank the musician. Some make witticisms when the opportunity arises; others state good-naturedly, "Please excuse us, my dear madam, we must have completely worn you out."

"Au contraire, I am finding it all quite pleasant," she answers in a still more jovial frame of mind.

In homes without a piano, girls dance to the music of a violin. (In these situations, however, one never strikes up an acquaintance with the violinist.) Sometimes people even dance to a guitar, but such an occurrence is likely to happen only at bachelors' parties. There, one often hears a ribald song, the woeful chords of a guitar, whistling, and the sounds of shattered glass. God be with them! Such parties we will not even begin to describe!

The lowest rung of dances in the Petersburg Quarter are done simply a cappella. I say such a thing quite seriously. Man is a strange animal. When he is happy, he will even dance to his own music, capering about as he hums a tune. An acquaintance of mine, a native of the Petersburg Quarter, told me about one such evening:

"We once got together on the feast of Saint Dmitri[13] to celebrate the name day of our very dear Dmitri Dmitrievich . . . Perhaps you know him?"

"No, I don't."

"What a pity. Everyone knows Dmitri Dmitrievich. He's a good soul, an old bachelor who loves our Petersburg fountains dearly. We arrived at his place for a little party. There happened to be five of us, including his dear old friend and godfather (one could even say his very special friend), a police officer with his wife. Since Dmitri Dmitrievich was, in turn, the godfather of all the police officer's children, the officer (you know how it is with relatives) also brought along his three daughters, the godchildren of Dmitri Dmitrievich. By this time, though, the lasses were grown maidens. Although Dmitri Dmitrievich lives as a bachelor (he is an elderly gentleman and a godfather to boot), it was certainly no sin for him to be visited by young women on such an important occasion. The officer's wife presented Dmitri Dmitrievich with a teapot with an inscription in gold: *as a token of our love.* The godfather was delighted with the gift. He set the teapot on the dresser in the parlor and showed it to everyone. In turn, everyone examined the teapot, read the inscription, and wished the name-day celebrant well with his gift.

"Dmitri's neighbor, Ivan Ivanovich, placed the teapot on his lap, tapped it lightly on the cover with his index finger, and, having listened

13. The reference is to the early fourth-century saint and martyr Dmitri Solounsky, whose feast day is celebrated on November 8 in the Russian Orthodox calendar.

attentively to the sound, announced that the gift was indeed valuable and that it would probably last a hundred years, if no one broke it before then. Everyone was quite amused by such a pronouncement. Ivan Ivanovich is quite a character, the life of the party. The host next ordered tea to be served. Tea was followed by a glass of Madeira—not any Madeira, mind you, but from Butsev's wine store on the corner on Bol'shoi Prospekt. We then began to play cards, while the women ate sweets.

"Dmitri Dmitrievch loves it when his home is all astir. But just then he sees that the ladies have devoured the sweets, that there is nothing else for them to do—and that they are quite ready to go home. The old lady is already putting on her gloves. 'But where are you going? But where?' he asks. 'Why, I will not let you go! I've got an eel and sturgeon pie for you!' The grandmother begins to dissuade him, but the godfather begs. Everyone was raising such a fuss that I cannot tell you who was the first in this chaos to take up talk about dancing. I recall that Dmitri Dmitrievich asked Ivan Ivanovich to play something on the violin. Ivan Ivanovich went home for his violin but came back without it. The cook, he told us, had gone visiting and had locked the apartment, making off with the key. Ivan Ivanovich was sent off to someone else's house but again returned empty-handed. The officer's daughters began to grumble: 'We could have (so they say) danced the whole night away.' Ivan Ivanovich then showed his true colors. He put together four couples, arranged them as for a quadrille, and just started singing things from, well, you know, some Tyrolean songs. Everyone just laughed and laughed. They exclaimed, 'Now isn't this funny! Isn't this so terribly funny!'—but they danced just the same. Dmitri Dmitrievich was delighted to see the godmother and her three daughters prancing about the drawing-room. In the sixth turn of his song, Ivan Ivanovich made up a completely new refrain, singing without pause:

> But to carouse, oh, but to carouse,
> But I'm married and chained to the house.

"Dmitri Dmitrievich did not dance but, hearing how Ivan Ivanovich led the ladies from one side to the other, cried, 'Change partners, now cross!!!'—and, caught up in the excitement, he joined in singing in the same tone of voice:

Godmother turn, godmother cross,
Godmother turn, godmother cross.

"Suddenly, without losing the beat, he cried out this refrain:

Godmother, poor will be your lot,
Godmother, if you break my teapot!!!

"With both hands, Dmitri Dmitrievich pulled her away from the dresser, but it was too late. Having gotten up to dance, the godmother had forgotten about the crowded room (and the dresser). Having taken several steps, she kept moving backward toward the dresser until her back crashed into the teapot.

"Needless to say, the quadrille ended badly. The host saw the accident with the teapot as a bad sign. He even got a little sick over it (but recovered by the end of the week). I should note, however, that friends now greet Dmitri Dmitrievich by saying, 'Hey, you, old godfather, cross and turn!' "

Early in this story, my friend noted that Dmitri Dmitrievich loved fountains dearly. Recently, I saw in the Petersburg Quarter a small garden with summer houses partially covered with hops and other creeping plants. In front of each house (and also at the path crossings themselves) were fountains or, better to say, parodies of fountains. They were splashing no higher than several inches from the ground: one stream is a thread, another is a lacelike pattern, just like those which tie sugar mounds together. The story goes that these hydraulic toys were put there by the master of the house himself, without skilled mechanics—simply through Russian ingenuity. The master, it seems, was a titular councillor, an adjunct of some accounting department. Apparently, he had seen a great many fountains at Peterhof, and, himself having a small home and garden, he wanted fountains for his residence too. But for such a thing, he needed water, and to make matters even more difficult, water at a higher level than the garden itself. The poor householder could not afford to have water brought in, so there was only one thing left for him to do: to build a great reservoir, dig a well, and pump the water from there. But such a plan also would have meant outlandish costs for constructing a well, not to mention the continual expense for pumping the water. The titular councillor, however, so wanted the fountains that he became quite inventive. He had all the drain pipes from his home, the stables, and the barns empty into an enormous barrel which, standing on some elevated floorboards, served as a reservoir. He then installed tin pipes throughout his garden. The fountains were ready. The usual Petersburg rains (the scarcity of which we can never complain to God), allowed the fountains to splash continually. The master is pleased, and his guests never cease to be amazed by his cleverness.

By the way, speaking about homemade fountains, one must also note the many handicrafts of the Petersburg Quarter. In idle moments, poor clerks engage in various activities: one pastes splendid pictures from cardboard; another etches engravings; a third fashions various figures from wax; a fourth cultivates flowers. Such innocent activities, together with a salary from the state, allow insignificant clerks to live a comfortable life.

For instance, in the Petersburg Quarter there lives a clerk who maintains a splendid collection of cacti in his home. Most likely, it is the only assortment of its kind in Petersburg. This clerk tends to his hobby with a special love, and he pays a good price for rare cacti, importing them from abroad. He grows them here in the Petersburg Quarter and sells them very cheaply.

Until recently, we have nourished an absurd prejudice and a false shame, that is, bureaucratic officials saw it as degrading to sell their handicrafts openly on the market. Although these individuals would never admit such a bias, they are sometimes forced by need to sell their wares on the sly (and for a song) to stores where a buyer will pay ten times more than what the store purchased them for. Would it not be better for buyer and seller to deal with each other directly? Suppose that one is not on intimate terms with the official in question. He might say to the man, "Would you bind my book, Ivan Ivanovich, and I will pay you what such a task is worth." Ivan Ivanovich, though, is quite offended; he is even ready to scold you or to complain that he has been insulted. So the customer goes off and pays a bookbinder, let's say, five rubles for a book, whereas Ivan Ivanovich would have charged only a ruble copper. That is why a bookbinder wears a knee-length overcoat in winter (with a five-hundred-ruble beaver collar) and Ivan Ivanovich runs around in a cold greatcoat he has bought for fifty rubles in Apraksin Market.[14]

14. Apraksin Market exists to this day and is located about a mile to the southeast of the city center.

(Why is it that people are ashamed to sell the fruits of their labors but that they do not blush when they buy or sell the works of their neighbors?)

The Petersburg Quarter closely resembles provincial towns in both its structure and the mores of its inhabitants; as a result, it is not immune to a common provincial pest: *gossip.* This disease has become an epidemic in the Petersburg Quarter. Of course, one can cite sufficient exceptions, but they are exceptions nonetheless.

(Note: I am speaking about the inhabitants of the Petersburg Quarter, in general, and in particular, about the women there.)

The petty shops and stores in the Petersburg Quarter are the junctions where all gossip starts, the reservoirs where it flows in and out. Here gather cooks with news—market and domestic; the widowed scandalmonger who buys five kopecks' worth of sugar and leaves a hundred rubles' worth of bile (which she heaps upon her neighbors); the lackey who has overslept and who, having sold some stolen papers for a song, now decides to tell the truth. Meanwhile, a clever merchant-proprietor buys and sells, weighs and hangs, all without uttering a word. He needs the peace and quiet to think about his trade, knowing well in advance to whom he can give credit and for how much he can trust the borrower.

Initially, it also seems all the more surprising that in the Petersburg Quarter you can quickly find out—that is, of course, assuming that one wants to—all the secrets, liaisons, and heartfelt joys and sorrows of the residents who live in the splendid palaces there. The reason for such a free flow of information is that the servants and valets of the nobility have their own small homes and friends in the quarter. Here they have their own ties and acquaintances, societies and clubs in which, like crows in peacocks' feathers, they plume and preen themselves according to the importance of their masters. These valets and servants parade their gossip if only to impress their poorer brethren, amazing them with stories of life in a different sphere: a world in which people eat on gold and china plates, dress in velvet and lace, and breathe a most aromatic air. They confess, however, that such individuals are people all the same and that they too cry more than laugh.

The residents of the Petersburg Quarter listen to such secrets of the salons greedily, with great pleasure, and they in turn rush off to tell (and overawe) their relatives and friends.

The servants of the nobility are sometimes very discreet about what they say because they see themselves as living abroad, in a different land, in a different part of the world than the Petersburg Quarter. At other times, though, they give full rein to their tongues and often, for effect, embellish the facts.

In my opinion, such playing with the truth is the cause for much of the gossip in the Petersburg Quarter, particularly its beau monde.

The Petersburg Quarter is bordered on one side by Krestovsky Island. The embankments facing Krestovsky are taken up by respectable homes (in reality, cottages) with gardens, which, during the summer, are the scene of various and unpretentious entertainments. One has Chinese paper lanterns; another has music playing, and so forth. I will describe this region another time because it has much in common with Krestovsky. I hope that we will meet again and talk about this region. Indeed, one could say a lot about Krestovsky, if anyone would care to listen.

—E. Grebenka
September 19, 1844

The Petersburg Corners

Nikolai Nekrasov

From the Notes of a Certain Young Man

FER RENT: KORNER TO LET, SECOND YARD,
CELLAR; PRICE, ASK FOR APERT'MENT
LADY, AKULINA FEDOTOVNA.

(From a notice on the gate of an apartment house)

I entered a yard and came across a building that was extremely large but quite tumbledown and unsightly. I was overwhelmed by the unbearable smells as well as by all kinds of crying and banging. The house, you see, was filled with men who worked and sang at every window. My eyes lighted upon various dog-eared inscriptions. They read: COFFINS AND WIDOW'S WEEDS FOR SALE OR HIRE; COPPER TINNER HERE; LOOKING FOR FOREIGNERS, TROFIMOV; KATERINA BRAGADINI, LICENSED RUSSIAN MIDWIFE; BOARDING SCHOOL; PRIVATE: ALEKANDROV, KUPRIANOV. Each sign had a hand which pointed to the entrance of a ship or an apartment, along with a picture that helped explain the sign itself, such as uniforms, shoes, scissors, sausage, a samovar with a broken handle, and a ham surrounded by laurel leaves. (Pictures to illustrate texts were used much earlier than we think; they entered literature directly from the signs posted on streets.) I also came across a rouged (one could say reddened) figure of a woman, about thirty years old, poking her head out of a corner window on the fourth floor. At first, I also took her for a sign, and to tell the truth, I was not that far off. The yard itself was absolutely filthy. A puddle had gathered at the gate. It had spilled into the yard, joined forces with the puddles that were standing at each and every door, and now, replete with gurgling and noises of all kinds, was flowing majestically into a cesspit. There, two pigs and a dog were busy digging holes, while a group of clothes dealers loudly took up this song:

> Enough, my lady, don't get smug!
> Get a move on, wash your mug!

What I saw now, though, was nothing compared to what awaited me. The notice had said that the corner for rent was located in a rear court. So I went through a second gate and came upon a courtyard that was smaller than the first but a thousand times more untidy. This time entire seas of mud and dirt opened up before me. Looking at my shoes in horror, I wanted to turn back. It seemed that I could not step anywhere without getting stuck up to my ears in mud. I clung as close to the wall as possible, if only because the periphery of the yard seemed higher than the middle. Such height proved illusory, however, since it was made up of mounds of garbage, poured (or thrown down) from the windows by the residents who live there.

Having stepped on one such mound, my leg sank up to my knee, while my nose was assaulted by a most sharp and unpleasant smell. I decided to take the advice of a well-known proverb, and leaving the periphery of the yard in peace, I set out for its middle. I followed my instinct for about twenty steps or so and came upon a door with an awning that was right across from the gate. I noticed that my leg, with each step, got stuck less and less. A few steps more and I found myself in front of another door leading to a cellar. I slipped and flew headlong—more accurately, I sailed through the air—downward, it seemed, much like sledders who take to the hills during Mardi Gras.

My shoes struck the steps of the staircase like a drum. I did not sail downward for long because I soon knocked up against something with my foot. I jumped up and took a good look around. It was dark, and the air smelled of rancid water and cabbage. I suddenly realized that here was the vestibule. I looked for the door and stumbled up against a washtub, spilling some water in the process. I then crashed into a pile of wood and almost fell. Something creaked. Something else bumped me on the forehead, but the foyer suddenly became lighter. A woman's figure appeared behind the half-opened door. An old, twisted hag asked me what I was doing. Then, without waiting for an answer, she announced that she had seen many rogues in her time, that she had nothing for anyone to steal, and that she herself would go and rob someone if it were not a sin and would cause her shame. (You do not as yet know me, dear readers, but if you examine me thoroughly, you will see that I am a most refined man, and that to take me for a thief is a mortal insult to my dress and physiognomy.) I thus could not restrain myself and called the old lady a fool. Now, there are many people in this world, dear readers, who can tolerate being called a "scoundrel" better than being called a "fool." My old lady was apparently one such type. At the very sound of the word, she shuddered terribly and let out a ghastly cry. The dimples of her pitted cheeks became filled with blood.

"A fool, you say?" she exclaimed in a fit of temper. "Me, a fool? No, my dear sir, you are still a bit wet behind the ears to call someone a fool. . . . Why, when I lived in Danilov,[1] the entire province there knew that I was no fool. . . . The sexton's wife herself often came and visited me. . . . Me, a fool, you say? Me, a fool?"

The old lady then set out to prove that she was no fool, not forgetting, in the interim, to call me both a fool and a swindler. Saliva flew from her mouth, splashing my clothes and face and making her look very much like a mad dog.

At first I thought to calm the old woman down, but then I weighed several things in my mind: Time was dear to me, and she might go and complain to my supervisor. I would then have to wait in somebody's office (and perhaps in the clinker itself) until the matter was resolved. So I thought that, for peace of body as well as of mind, I should leave as quickly as possible.

I had already gotten halfway across the yard when the old lady suddenly called out after me and forced me to turn around.

"Well . . . Why have you come? If you're not a thief, tell me why you have come, and to a fool like me, no less! Have you come to visit? I didn't invite you here, after all . . . So, tell me, why have you come?"

I explained to the old woman the reason for my presence, and she immediately became quite sympathetic. What's more, she even fished a copper five-spot out of her pocket and told me to rub it against the bruise

1. Danilov is a town near Yaroslavl, about two hundred miles northeast of Moscow.

on my forehead. I could hardly refuse, if from gratitude alone. (My heart is such, dear readers, that I cannot nurture hatred for long.) I thus forgave the old lady for her fit of temper and set out with her to look at the apartment (the entrance to which, by the way, was through a door right across from the one that had struck me on the forehead).

The old woman led me to a rather large room that was bathed in a suffused light (the kind artists love). The light came from five small windows, which were level with the ground outside but which were also quite removed from the floor inside. The room itself was about thirteen feet high, not unlike a wine cellar or a burial vault. A huge, dilapidated Russian stove stood to the left of the door. What space remained was filled up with various kinds of rubbish and trash. The floor creaked and groaned from my weight. The cracks in it were huge; several planks were so warped that if one stepped on one end, the other end jumped up at you. The walls of the room had once been plastered, and here and there one could still see the cruciform laths that accompanied such work. Some of these laths were now broken and stuck out from the wall. The chief adornment, however, was neither the decorations nor the remnants of plaster but the oblong, bloody (but innocent) stains that bore the traces of fingerprints as well as the thin and brittle shells of sacrifices that had perished long ago. Thick spiderwebs hung in curtains and garlands about the room. Their strands went out in all directions, entangling my face and even getting into my mouth. From under a middle crossbeam, a plank in the ceiling, black and covered with flies, had jumped out at one end and now stuck out at a slant—to the delight of the cellar's tenants, who hung their shirts and towels on it. There was also a rope that extended the entire length of the room. One end was secured with a hook above the door, the other by the upper loop of a wardrobe—or so one could call the oblong hollow thing with several small shelves which stood along the back wall of the room. At one time (so the old lady told me), the object in question had doors, but one of the tenants had torn them off, mounted it on two logs, and thus made himself a bed. Of course, the old lady was quite upset by such rashness but otherwise spoke quite well of the tenant.

"And what does he do?" I asked.

"Who the hell knows what he does," she replied. "But he's a good chap, and with a passport to boot. That's the way I am, like it or nor, even if you'd give me two rubles silver. You think that ain't much 'round here? Why, there are some places where you can stay the entire night for only ten kopecks. . . . My tenant, it seems, is out for the morning. Look around you: there's his slippers; there's his shirt; there's his collar. . . . Most likely, he went off to the baths; his soap is missing. . . . He's a good tenant, really. He's rarely at home; he only comes here to sleep and to yell at the spiders, so he puts it. I say to him, 'Now look here, Kir'yanych. . . . Don't you ever wish . . . with all this rubbish about . . . don't you wish that you ever get a hold of yourself?'

" 'Why should I?' he answers, 'can't make me what I ain't. . . . Just 'cause I see a spider doesn't mean I could kill it.'

" 'Well, all right, Kir'yanych,' I say, 'so long as you don't bother anyone.'

"My tenants are good people, God bless them, and my house will last longer because of them. But I'm so glad that he finally got rid of all those spiders. But one will never find a ruble on him—not even for medicine! Just like he lived in a palace or something. . . . There's one thing I don't like about him, though—I can't stand all this rubbish about."

The old lady then pointed to a small, ash-colored, half-shaven mongrel, which had, in the meantime, crawled out from under Kir'yanych's bed (located in the corner to the right of the door) and which was now ruthlessly biting its dirty feet, its teeth abruptly jumping from paw to paw.

"It wouldn't be so bad if he had only one mutt," the old lady continued, "but one time he suddenly had five of them here . . . and did they ever raise a howl. You know why, don't you? They were always hungry, of course. But whether he feeds them or not, he loves them just the same. He says that he cannot live without his dogs. . . . I say to him, 'You can't be serious, Kir'yanych! You must be joking!' but that's the way I am, like it or not. . . . You yourself see what is going on here, but in my own house I see nothing . . . I know nothing. . . . It's better that way . . ."

The old lady waved her hand in such a way that I felt compelled to assure her that I did not raise dogs for a living. She continued:

"I don't know how all this will end. Everyone takes care of himself, and God takes care of all. He has a passport, so I'm not responsible for him. So I just throw up my hands. . . . 'Let him have his dogs,' I say to myself! 'I'll not turn away a good tenant because of that. . . .' And is a dog really so bad? Such an animal, God forgive me, is just like a man. Sometimes a man is worse; his sins are greater. You yourself should know. Take a man's tongue, for example. A trained dog's got one, too. What's more, it'll hand over whatever it has in its teeth. It'll grovel, too. . . . Like I said, it'll do anything a man will do. Indeed, one's better off with a dog. Well, I see you ain't too fussy about things" (I was petting the little gray dog), "but there are other people, you know. . . . Is it true that dogs can think? . . . Now, that's rubbish as far as I'm concerned.

"I once had this hooligan here. He had been running wild and just plumb burned himself out. Then he shows up here. He takes a look at the apartment, turns around to me, and says, 'I'd really be going to the dogs if I had to live in a kennel like this!' . . . Imagine, 'a kennel,' he says! . . . It takes a real blowhard to say something like that. You know the type: Ambition by the ruble, ammunition by the kopeck. . . . A small apartment is more than it seems. It's cool in the summer, but in the winter, it's so warm that even an official could live here, and look at all the space . . ."

"How much?"

After some haggling, the old lady and I agreed on four rubles a month. She swore that no one had ever gotten off so cheaply and begged me not to tell the other tenants what I was paying.

"I admire your type, my good man," the old lady told me. "True, you have nothing . . . but then where would you get anything at your age! You're still young, true, but you have nothing just the same . . . "

I had no idea what the old lady was leading up to, but I bravely answered, "That's right, nothing."

"But you have to have some furniture. After all, only the real down-and-out sleep on the floor. I'll get you a little bed. . . . I'll bring you some water, too. . . . The bed is wide, built for two" (here the old lady grinned). ". . . So don't you worry, don't you worry at all. I think I'll put it a little farther from the wall . . . yes, yes, I'll put it there myself."

I gave the old woman a deposit and went back for my things. A cabbie charged me about ten kopecks to move it all. When I arrived back at my home—dressed in my winter coat and carrying a small parcel and all my pipes—the bed was already in its place. It stood in a corner on the left, opposite the window and the aforementioned wardrobe. The old lady had somewhat exaggerated the amenities. The bed could indeed accommodate two people, but only if they took turns. She had also gotten hold of a recently sanded table that she had placed in front: an opening on one side had apparently held a drawer. The cellar, which had somehow lacked something in the morning, now seemed to present a full and completely furnished picture.

There are times when one unwittingly becomes pensive if only because the mind is idle and the soul secure. The new year, a birthday, a sudden funeral, the day one moves to a new apartment—such occasions, I believe, make a person reflective even if he is not accustomed to think at all. It was about nine o'clock in the evening. The Petersburg "white nights" were in full swing, but it remained dark in the cellar. Flies, like swarms of industrious bees, were flying about the ceiling, buzzing shrilly. A grasshopper was singing behind the stove. Something was crawling up my face, while something else was prickling my hand. I sat motionless on the bare boards that made up my bed . . .

The door creaked open, and the room was suddenly filled with sounds much like the clicking of castanets.

Startled, I raised my head.

A gray figure was slowly making his way to the right corner of the room, all the time clicking his fingers and tongue. With an air of complete unconcern, he nodded to me.

I remained silent, however. The gray figure reached the bed, sat down, and, having put his left leg over the thigh of his right, stared for a long time at his shoes, saying slowly and deliberately, "The shoelaces on these things have really had it. . . . I guess it's because I get around a lot. . . . And the shoes aren't much good either. . . . They've even give me corns. . . . Hey, you, you there, you from around these parts?"

"I am."

"Is that so? Your name?"

"Trostnikov."

"I know that name. Beat me, he would, this Trostnikov.[2] Every day we'd go hunting with the master. Sometimes you got unlucky with the

2. The individual is picking up on the word *trost',* or "cane" in Russian. Nekrasov is also echoing a similar event in Gogol's 1842 play *The Marriage* (*Zhenit'ba*), in which the character Zhevakin (Chew-Man), having heard the name of the administrator, Yaichnitsa (Omelet), replies without thinking, "Yes, I also have had a snack."

rabbit, or you unleashed the dogs too late. Yes sir, he'd go straight up to you, he would. He galloped on his horse once too many times, though. He died right on the spot, that he did. . . . After his death, people said he died before his time! . . . Ha! Served him right! You don't get into fights with people you don't know. Yes sir, Estafy Fomich Trostnikov . . . How could I forget him? Hot-tempered, he was. No doubt you got something from him after he died?"

"I don't know any Trostnikov other than myself."

"Well, now . . . then excuse me, my good sir. . . . And here I thought that you were one of the gentry. . . . Stupidity on my part, sheer stupidity . . . You see, I left the village only three weeks ago. . . . I wouldn't be here at all if it weren't for a certain young lass. . . . 'Dogs and people are bringing us to ruin, dear boy,' she says. 'Don't expect any love from me, dear boy, so long as you've got all these dogs runnin' 'round this house.' We argued and argued. Finally, we decided to hang all the dogs and get out from under our debts." The house serf began to whistle. "And so for about a year afterward, I roamed the towns and villages of our Rissian Empire. . . . And now I've washed up here. . . . One time I was on this big boat. . . . Eighteen days we were at sea. . . . People sang all the time. . . . We even took turns at the oars. . . . What else was there to do, I ask you? . . . And now here I sit like a crab on a pile. But you've got to have a place to call home, I guess. I'm sick of my own grub, but I got to pay for this here 'partment, you see. My shoes are completely worn out; the left one has really fallen apart."

The house serf lit a wick that stood in a pomade jar filled with tallow. Then, from under his bed, he dragged out a small wooden box from which he took out some thread, a small awl, and a hammer. He next took off his left shoe, and commenced repairing it, all the while humming something to himself.

A half hour later, the door opened again. A tall, strapping peasant walked in, carrying a little dog in his hands. He was about fifty years old, with a gloomy face and thick beard, and dressed in a weather-beaten fur half coat. His countenance, movements, and gait revealed that he was an angry man and highly irritable by nature. The peasant went straight to his corner (to the right of the door) and angrily threw down the dog, which had begun to howl. Having crossed himself before the icon that hung over his bed, the peasant sat down, stretched, and yawned. He yelled to the dog, "Quiet down, or I'll break your neck!" But then he picked it up to pet it. The dog, though, scratched the peasant on the hand, jumped down from the bed, and scratched at the door. The peasant threw the dog a piece of bread, but the latter only sniffed at it. He then called for the dog with all the usual canine names but for some reason distorted them terribly in the process. With each name, the peasant stopped and looked fixedly at the dog. The dog did not quiet down, though, causing the peasant to lose patience. He stamped his foot and soundly cursed the dog for over a half hour (observing no proprieties whatsoever in expressing his indignation). Finally, the dog quieted down and took refuge under the bed. The peasant sprawled out, yawning terribly and repeating in a greatly drawn-out voice, "Lord have mercy! Lord have mer-r-cy!"

"Tell me, Kir'yanych," the house-serf said, "tell me, if you suddenly got hold of, say, ten thousand rubles . . . what would you be doing now?"

"And what would you do with such a sum, may I ask?"

"With ten thousand rubles?! Why, ten thousand rubles is an awful lot of money. You'd probably drink yourself silly, but any house serf worth his salt would want to be wined and dined till his eyes pop out. Everything else could go to hell as far as he'd be concerned! But, then, why talk such nonsense? Only innkeepers take credit these days."

"And your master? Does he take credit, too?"

"Master, what master? He let me off my debts; beyond that, I don't want to know any more about him. . . . And if he didn't let me off, well, what can I say? God be with him. He'd only beat me and then load up my wagon anyway. . . . Ten thousand rubles! Now that would suit me just right. . . . Ten thousand rubles! But, again, why talk such nonsense? Twenty-five kopecks would do splendidly right now. . . . Boy, would they do splendidly . . . if only for a half-pint to chase away the blues."

"Well, then" (the house-serf yawned), "go-o-o buy-y-y some, for God's s-a-ake, go buy some."

" 'Buy some,' you say? And just where should I go out and buy some? And with what, may I ask? One pocket is empty, the other has nothing in it. . . . Well, that's not quite true. I've got these here fifty kopecks. . . . (Some poor orphan got a bit close, you see.) . . . You know how it is, after all. You've got to have something to eat. You don't want to die from hunger.

It would be another thing altogether if I could find a job. . . . But, just today alone, I went to five places, and there was nothing. . . . Beggars beware only when masters appear, as the saying goes . . .

"For instance, at one place, this guy comes out, all sickly and thin . . . and looking like he could use a good meal. The room's got these three chairs, with this wretched robe on one of them, one hole on top of another. . . . 'The only thing I ask, my dear sir,' he says to me, 'is that my man be honest, punctual, and polite, and that he neither drink nor steal.' . . . 'Now then, sir, why should I steal?' I says to him. . . . 'You think that I think that it's all right to steal, my good sir? . . . God forbid that one does not look after his own, but he'll not be happy with another's.' I then says to him, 'Is the pay any good?' . . . 'Fifteen rubles,' he says.

"Why, I got so damn mad. . . . 'Fifteen rubles! Is that so, my kind sir,' I says. . . . (Imagine! He has the nerve to tell me, 'don't drink, don't steal.' . . . 'What could I steal from you,' I says to myself, 'it'd be slim pickings for sure!') . . . So, hat in hand, I says to him, 'Much obliged . . . but I'm not going to be kicked around anymore than I am now!' . . . I got out of there as fast as I could. . . . I just bowed and left . . .

"Then I go to this other place. . . . The guy is so fat, you'd think that his mug would burst, that's how red it was. . . . 'I pretty well do everything myself,' he says. 'I don't need no help. . . . Mornings, it's vodka to the clerks, then a run to the cook's for a quick bite to eat. Afternoons, it's vodka to the merchants. After that, I go to bed. . . . As I always say, "off with the shoes, but still pushing the booze." . . . That's about it. That's my life 'round here!' And then he says, 'See what I got here?' and shows me this devil that he's got here right on his shoulders. . . . A devil, a real devil, I tell you . . . but it's not all that strange, I guess. . . . Who's a man, who's a devil, who the hell knows these days? . . . Now this devil, it just sits there, staring into space and smacking its lips. 'Take a good look at him,' the guy says. Then he starts prancing up and down the room, this scarecrow-looking thing all the time on his shoulders. . . . Why, it even made faces and flipped me off, would you believe it? . . . 'Look how much he loves me,' the guy says. . . . 'You'd do well to go get yourself one,' he says. 'They're a lot of fun to have around,' he says. . . . 'But they get sick awfully easy or hurt themselves somehow. . . . But as for a salary, you won't get a penny here, and besides, I have friends and neighbors to help me.' 'Thank you most humbly,' I say. . . . 'Much obliged to you . . . but I'm not about to kowtow before highbrows or anybody else for that matter, and as for devils like the one you got there, there's nothing to say 'cept I ain't gettin' one.' 'This, my good man,' he says, 'is no devil; it's a munkey.' "

Kir'yanych yawned loudly.

"Hey there, hedgehog head! You sleep all day, but I got some money. . . . I'll give you some, no strings attached. Untie that purse over there. Someday we'll settle accounts in the poorhouse."

"That's just where we'll wind up," Kir'yanych said with a sigh. "I'm ashamed to say we're all sinners, we've angered the Lord God. . . . It's a rotten business, to be sure! Not a penny for tobacco. . . . I'm really in a bind this time. I ate up my last penny in the eating house across the way. . . . It was so long ago that it would hurt my nose just to smell food now . . ."

"No tobacco nowhere!" repeated the house serf sadly. After some silence, he added, "But then, I ask you, who among our kind ever has any money? Everybody knows how much we've got. It's not worth even sewing a purse for—we just roam the world. Now I'm sure it's another thing altogether with the *master* over there."

Apparently, the last remark was meant for me. My suspicion proved correct. The house serf had wound up in these unhappy depths quite unwillingly. Full of hope, he had just arrived from the village and had rented a "corner" before he started looking for work. The day was solemn in the full sense of the word: Seven bottles were polished off at his housewarming.

"We drank only five," said Kir'yanych.

"Seven, hedgehog head!"

"I said five! I remember it as though it was yesterday. The flies and mosquitoes were biting like mad!"

Kir'yanych and the house serf argued hotly about the number of bottles.

"Well, no matter how many bottles there were," the house serf concluded, "I only want to say that we Russians have this custom: We'll spend our last kopeck to celebrate a housewarming; otherwise, a new apartment will not be a happy one."

"And the Good Lord will not forget who does what is proper," remarked Kir'yanych.

"Listen here, pal," I said.

The house serf jumped up and bowed respectfully.

"What can I do for you, my good sir?"

"Here's some money, my man. Go buy me some wine."

"Yes, sir. Now that's a fifth you'd want to be ordering, sir?"

"Get a fifth."

The house serf wound some thread about the shoe that was falling apart. He put it on his left foot, seized his cap, and took off at a run. Within five minutes, the table in front of my bed held wine, two herrings, half a dozen cucumbers, three pounds of black bread, and four packages of snuff. The house serf gave me back the change, respectfully excusing himself that he had incurred some additional expenses along the way. Kir'yanych meanwhile went to the landlady to get some glasses.

"First, the host," said the house serf, pouring the wine.

I refused, however.

"Now you're not going to say no!" exclaimed the house serf with a mock horrified air. "What kind of a guy are you who don't drink? . . . As the proverb says, 'Hit the tavern, smoke some tobacco, drink some wine, beat up some beggars . . . and you'll wind up either in hell or a foreign kingdom.' Don't you want to wish us well, after all!"

"Now then, you wouldn't be insinuating something, would you, now?" added the phlegmatic Kir'yanych. "Why, your face is as ashen as a scorched birch."

But I again refused.

"Well, there's nothing much you can do about him," said the house serf, smiling slyly. "After all, if he don't want to drink, he shouldn't have to." And with that, the house serf drank his wine, held his glass over his head for a moment, and said in a drawn-out voice, "God grant that my soul get to heaven, right to the pearly gates themselves! Hey there, Kir'yanych!"

Kir'yanych heard nothing, however. He was looking down at the floor, stamping his feet, hopping from place to place, and shouting, "Someone get me a light! Someone bring me a candle!"

Finally, he stamped his foot with terrible force, wheezed solemnly, and returned to the table. His face was also solemn.

"Enough of you killing spiders, Kir'yanych. Better they crawl the walls. They won't let you sleep as it is. . . . Now then, let's hold off on the vodka until it's really cold!"

"It wouldn't be a sin to drink it now," Kir'yanych said smugly. "May the Lord grant health to the kind man!" He then crossed himself and drank down his glass.

After a second round, the house serf reached for his balalaika, struck up a trepak, and began to sing:

On Monday
Savka mills the seed.
On Tuesday
Savka saddles the steed.
From Wednesday to Thursday
Savka serves his lord.
And also every Thursday
Bakes bread flat as a board.
On Friday
Savka grooms the master's dogs
But eats worse than his hogs.
On Saturday
Savka scratches his snout
Enduring the blows of the master's knout.
But on Sunday
Savka is lord and king,
Drunk as a skunk
And ready to sing!

There was a knock at the door, followed by loud grumbling.

"Well now, master, you're really in luck today," the house serf exclaimed.

"Now we'll have some fun. The teacher is coming!"

"What kind of teacher is he?"

The door flew open and banged against the wall with a deafening sound. Something akin to a whiskey bottle entered the room, swinging from side to side, a human head taking the place of a cork.[3] This is how

3. Compare Gogol's description of the departmental director in his 1835 piece *Notes of a Madman* (*Zapiski sumasshedshego*): "He was a cork, not a director. . . . A simple everyday cork, nothing more."

I first thought to describe a man in a light green coat that was without a collar but which he wore draped about his shoulders. The collar, it seemed, had been used to repair the other parts of the coat and had been missing since 1819. There exists a vast difference between people who are drinkers and those who are genuine drunkards. The former reek of wine in well-known situations, their smell being tolerable even to those who see themselves as proper people. Such drinkers are typically the souls of discretion. They know (and do not forget to use) the tried-and-true measures by which they can dull the stinging sharpness of their breath. They choose cloves, tea (minimal strength), Hoffman drops, peppermints, violet root, and finally onions or garlic. The "drunkards," however, constantly reek of wine even though they haven't touched a drop for a week. Their smell is easily distinguished. It is not so much an odor; instead, one feels as if one's nose sniffed a wine barrel that has been plugged up for quite some time and which has suddenly been popped open. Such a reeking smell attended the green man, and I immediately sensed that he belonged to the second class of drinkers. In fact, as I looked intently into his face, I saw that he was not altogether unfamiliar to me. I had once passed a building with a sign that read PUBLIC HOUSE. A man lay outside its entrance. He was stretched out, flat on his back, and wore a dilapidated jacket with white buttons. His eyes were closed; obviously, he was asleep. The hot summer sun shone directly on his face, etching fantastic designs on his glassy but terribly haggard face. A thousand flies were strolling up and down his face, while a thousand more were circling his head, humming incessantly and waiting their turn. For a long time, I looked at the man's face with a heavy heart. (As you have already guessed, dear readers, I am a sentimental soul.) It engraved itself sharply on my memory. Now the new arrival in our room was dressed somewhat differently and seemed a little older. His coat was torn from behind, about three quarters of the way. Beyond this, his apparel included some reddish brown slippers with patches in three layers, and a dirt gray object that stuck out whenever his coat flew open. He was about sixty years old. His face had nothing special about it. It was yellow, glassy, and wrinkled. His chin had several warts, which doctors call "mouse moles." These, in turn, had red hairs crawling out of them in a circle just as sextons and noncommissioned officers sometimes grow for good luck. There was a scar on his nose, and his eyes were gray and lackluster. His hair (what a strange thing that was!) was black, thick, and almost without a part. One could almost call it handsome, if it were not for two or three bald spots, which were the size of a penny but which had been the doing neither of Mother Nature nor of goodwill. In general, however, the green man presented a sharp picture to the eye. He was not unlike an actor who has carried some favorite and well-learned role into life. His movements were comic to the point of caricature, inevitable for a man unsteady on his legs. There was also something staid about them, though, akin to a feeling of personal dignity and worth. Even when he spoke about complete trifles, he had the stance of a person who is ready to state for all to hear that virtue is praiseworthy and that evil is vile. There was a certain incoherence in the green man that made him extremely funny.

The house serf, already laughing, hailed him with his usual greeting:

"Hello, there, red-nosed one!"

From all indications, the green man became quite angry but checked his anger right away. He gestured toward the bottle and said in an affectionate voice, "Greetings, Egorushka. Won't you pour me a little glass?"

Slyly and without raising any suspicion, the house serf poured a glass of water from a clay mug that had been standing on the table. He gave it to the green man. The green man downed it in one gulp. The house serf and Kir'yanych guffawed loudly, stamping their feet on the floor. The green man stood motionless for a moment; then, opening his mouth wide and with glass in hand, he began to rail at them.

"Now look here, pal, don't you go around joking with me! Who gave you the right to poke fun at me? Why, just today, I was at a house . . . an honest-to-god gentleman, a cavalier of some kind, he was. . . . You hear me? A real cavalier. They wouldn't let the likes of you into that house; you'd never get past the foyer. But I got into the study. This cavalier, he says to me, 'I feel for you, Grigory Andre'ich (you hear that, he called me by my patronymic!). You've turned into a real drunkard. Look out or you'll let wine ruin you completely,' he says to me. 'This I did not expect from you,' he says. . . . 'Now sit there,' he says, 'and we'll talk about the good old days.' . . . Then he ordered a small carafe to be brought . . .

"So I began to talk. . . . I know what to talk about. . . . I was acquainted with Izmailov, after all.[4] . . . I was always welcome at Gavrila Romanovich

4. Nekrasov's "green man" recalls Gogol's Khlestakov, who, in his 1836 play *The Inspector General* (*Revizor*), says, "I was acquainted with famous actors . . . and vaudevillians. I was on friendly terms with Pushkin."

[Derzhavin's]. I used to live at Yakolev's. . . . Now there was a great man, in case you didn't know! . . . Besides tea, Yakolev and I would eat together and drink some vodka. So that's where I've come from. So, brother, don't you go around playing tricks on me. . . . Why, you know what kind of students I've had? . . . I once had one. . . . Whew, was he an ace! . . . He was just a little boy when he came to me. . . . I used to call him my 'watchman,' I really did. . . . He wouldn't let anyone get away with a thing. . . . Now, when we start recalling old times, we always wind up laughing. . . . Once he says to me, 'It's about time for me to make my way in the world. . . . You've certainly whipped me enough for things.' . . . 'I,' he says, 'will never forget you,' and then he shoves twenty-five kopecks into my hand. . . . 'One fights a man when he's young,' he says, 'but thanks him when he's old.' . . . So now you know how I get my money, pal . . .

"But you . . . you who go to work everyday. What do you get? Five rubles a year, but five slaps a day, that's what.[5] . . . I once had many talents. I used to take snuff, pal, not from a thing like this (he tapped a birch snuffbox). . . . No sir, it was gold . . . indeed it was. . . . Just a pinch from it cost eight hundred rubles . . . and all that for nothing, mind you! . . . And then there was my poetry. . . . Let me tell you about the poetry I wrote, pal . . ."

I was so intrigued by the green man's story that I had to know more about him. Undoubtedly, he made up a lot as he went along, but there was an element of truth in his words. Long ago, some forty years past, the green man had graduated from the seminary and began teaching in some remote institution. He did his job well. True, he sometimes indulged in an extra glass or two, but he always smelled more of cloves than of wine. The morals of his charges were never in any danger. The school administrators were rather lenient toward him because they sensed that he was a gifted and capable man. They also tried desperately to restrain the young teacher's passion for drink. But such passion was stronger than the green man's superiors, no matter how noble and supportive they were. After some time, people noticed that when the green man appeared, the classroom was invariably filled with a smell that might serve as a bad example to the students. To complicate matters, the green man once came to class

5. The "green man" is quoting from Denis Fonvizin's 1783 play *The Minor* (*Nedorosl'*).

without a tie and hardly able to stand on his legs. Then, instead of greeting his superior, who happened to be sitting at the edge of a bench, the green man turned to him with this question: "Hey, you there, which verbs take the genitive case? . . . Aha! So you don't know! Well, then, on your knees, sir!"

Needless to say, the green man was dismissed, and his place was given to a young man who fully restored the respect due to the position of a teacher. His successor did not miss a class and was respectful to his elders. Also, he very soon rejected the disquieting characteristics of the single state by marrying the boss's sister. Although the green man had been dismissed from his post, he received a small pension, the patronage of a certain kind man who respected his previous service. What followed was not surprising, however. Idleness strengthened the green man's passion for wine and brought him to the situation we have just now seen. The green man led a most interesting life in the cellar. Several days before the first of each month, the landlady dutifully kept track of his presence, taking care that on the last day of the month, he always got drunk at home. The morning after, she set out for him and counted out the money that was due her. The green man would take what remained and disappeared—God knows where, for several days at a stretch. When he returned, he was usually battered, filthy, and penniless. For the rest of the month, the green man would, almost on a daily basis, make the rounds of his former colleagues and students (who by this time were adults). . . . Everywhere, he got a glass of wine, sometimes two. On those rare occasions when he got nothing, the green man left, raining down curses on one and all, and long thereafter, he would lie on his bed, angrily expostulating about human ingratitude.

Regarding poetry, it is true that the green man did write verse. Such a phenomenon is not at all that surprising in our Russian Empire, since almost everyone writes (or has written) poetry. No one is banned from doing such a thing, you see. The green man did not delay in proving this final part of his tale. From under his slippers, he pulled out two very thin and shiny pamphlets (each consisted of twelve pages). He put them before the eyes of the house serf and, moving his index finger down each line of the title page, said with a triumphant air, "You see, you see that there, you see it? . . . Huh? . . . Right there, see that too?"

But the house serf angrily pushed the pamphlet away from him, saying heatedly, "Don't poke that thing in front of me! What the hell are you poking it at me for?! I'm not one of the gentry, pal. I can't read. Since when can people like me read? 'Learn to read, forget your feed.' . . . that's what we say 'round here. . . . You want to show me something, fine; well, go get a ribbon or some other decoration for it! I daresay that if you ever got such a thing, you probably lost it or gave it away. . . . I doubt if you're that good, though. . . . Knowing you, if you couldn't eat it, you'd sell it. . . . By the way, while we're on the subject, who ate my loaf of bread the other day?"

"I sold it, it's as simple as that," the green man answered dolefully. "After all, do you think we take snuff from golden boxes or wear precious stones on our fingers?"

He then waved his hand, poisoning the last bit of fresh air with a prolonged sigh.

Meanwhile, I glanced at the green man's pamphlets. One of them joyfully commemorated the name day of an important person of the time; the other celebrated the marriage of the same person. Both pamphlets were written in a high-flown verse and sang the praises of the green man's patron. I read aloud the following:

> In the good old days, pamphlets such as these inundated Russian literature. Indeed, one could say that Russian literature began with eulogistic hymns for solemn occasions. At that time, the poet always had to have an official inspiration in mind. When he was successful, he was fed; and when he was not, he was beaten—often unmercifully. Everyone knows the anecdote about Tredyakovsky whom Volynsky punished with his own hand because the poet did not prepare an ode for some great holiday.[6] The poet Petrov served as the official bard for the feats of Potemkin. That is why he always

6. Most likely, Nekrasov is repeating the incident as told by Pushkin and published by Belinsky in an article in 1843. The story is not true, though. Vasily Tredyakovsky was punished by Artemy Volynsky, the cabinet minister under Anna Ivanovna, for complaining about him to Ernst Biron, a leading figure and personal favorite of the empress. Actually, the event was of minor significance because both Volynsky and Tredyakovsky opposed the so-called German yoke—the entourage of German statesmen and the like—who held sway in Anna's court. Also see Belinskii, *Polnoe sobranie sochinenii,* vol. 7 (1955), 16.

> marched at the rear of the army during the general's campaigns.[7] Petty bigwigs and swaggering lackeys soon followed the example of the greats. They too had their poets. They were delighted to receive odes on their birthdays, name days, marriages, christenings of their children, the attainments of ranks or decorations, and, in general, all other solemn occasions of their lives. For such verse, they allowed the poet to sit at the far end of the table. They let him eat with the "master" and not the servants (as was customary or ordinary those days); they even let the poet kiss their hand. The powers that be also gifted the poet with a ring, a snuffbox, or money, or they made the bard drink until he got drunk and then ordered him to get up and dance. The poet, in turn, wrote to honor such individuals as benefactors, patrons, protectors, father-commanders, and even gracious well-wishers. This type of writing began to decline in the beginning of the nineteenth century. The year 1812 dealt it a mortal blow, and the romanticism that appeared in the twenties finished it completely. So-called ceremonial poetry is now considered synonymous with "versemongering." So do our customs and mores change. A pamphlet filled with doggerel, replete with pompous, senseless, and base flattery, is no longer rewarded with a ring, a snuffbox, fifty or a hundred rubles—not to mention the title of poet. Indeed, the decline of such verse is probably one reason why our old boys, those belated remnants of the good old days, are so angry at our times, and why, with rapture and melancholy, they recall their own era in which, they insist, everything was so much better than it is now.

"What a heap of nonsense!" said the house serf, noticing that I had become engrossed in my reading. "That you should even want to dirty your hands with such tripe!"

"Nonsense! You say nonsense!" shouted the green man so loudly that I dropped the pamphlet and looked him squarely in the face. "You should be as stupid as this nonsense! Why, when I presented verse like this to his

7. The enterprising poet Vasily Petrov—often the butt of ridicule, lampoon, and parody—also wrote hymns to Catherine the Great and others in her court. Additionally, he served as General Potemkin's secretary.

excellency, he kissed me on the lips, sat me down next to him on the couch, and bade me read it to him, yes he did. . . . As I was reading along, he took some snuff and said to me, 'Here, take some.' 'No, thank you,' I said, 'I don't take snuff and much less from the snuffbox of your excellency . . .' 'Take some!' he replied. 'An educated man must always have some snuff!' and then he gives me some from his own snuffbox. . . . Why, I've been taking snuff ever since. He even ordered me to be a guest at his table. . . . You should have seen how I was treated, taken in. . . . And what guests they were! . . . Even his excellency's boss came over and kissed me. . . . I wrote for him, too. . . . I used to drink myself silly. . . . I spoke to them as if we were equals; but they, for their part, did nothing but laugh. . . . I got invited everywhere. . . . So, take that for 'nonsense,' my dear sir!"

Something akin to emotion flashed in the green man's eyes. He stood there (in the middle of the room) for a long time, his hand raised. Suddenly, he shook his head and said in a voice that recalled Manfred begging relief from heaven.[8] "Pour me one, Egorushka, my good fellow. Please, I beg you, just a small glass!"

The house serf poured a glass of wine and called the green man over to him, but he now embarked on a new (and cruel) farce. He brought the glass close to the lips of the green man, but when the latter extended his lips, all ready to drink, the house serf suddenly pulled the glass away and drank the wine himself. The green man did not get angry, however. The smell of raw vodka had vanquished his dignity and put to rest what little sense of self-respect he had had the moment before. Humbly, he begged the house serf "not to joke around."

"Dance a bit and I'll bring you a new glass!"

The green man began to dance without delay. The house serf, though, kept repeating, "More! More, I tell you! You're quite spirited today! Even better than yesterday! Still a little more!" The house serf then poured some salt into a glass, added some dirt from around the room, filled what space remained with wine and began to mix it altogether . . .

I begged the house serf not to give the horrid mixture to the green man, saying that he was drunk enough already.

8. Nekrasov is referring to Lord Byron's 1817 play *Manfred,* in which the hero asks the spirits for oblivion.

"Drunk, you say? Well, will you hear that now—he's drunk, you say! That's a remark I would expect to hear only from lasses or learned people," answered the house serf, all the time mixing the contents. "Just because a man falls down doesn't mean he's drunk; just because he's got a loose tongue doesn't mean he's drunk either. Now, if two people have to help a man get about, and a third has to get his legs moving, now that's what I'd call drunk!"

"And if he lies there without breathing—that too means he's drunk," Kir'yanych chimed in, having been awakened by the capering of the green man. "Whew-i—i-ee! Lor-r-r-d hav-ve mer-er-cy!" he intoned.

The green man drank down the glass the house serf had prepared and then praised its contents. Kir'yanych and the house serf did the same. Not surprisingly, the cellar was becoming noisy. The green man graciously offered to dance again, but this time he insisted on music. The house serf again reached for his balalaika, struck up a song, and, tapping his feet, even thought up a little dance for the green man to perform. Meanwhile, Kir'yanych had crushed yet another spider. He was in unusually high spirits and greeted each caper of the green man with grunting and guffaws. The green man did not need any accompaniment, however, because he was accompanying his dancing with the hiccups, curses, and cries typical of Russian burping. More interesting for the moment, was the house serf's song:

> At age fifteen, not more
> Little Liza made for shore
> And wandering though an open grove
> She met a beetle, black as a stove.
> This beetle had a mustache
> and black curly hair.
> "I'll take him home," said Liza,
> "And give him my care.
> Perhaps he'll eat sugar,
> Eat, eat, my beetle fair."
> But when her evil aunt
> Saw Liza's friend,
> She grumbled at her niece,

"Just what do you intend?"
She sternly ordered Liza,
"Throw it out the door!"
"But I didn't obey her order,"
Liza later swore.
"I put it in my bed instead,
And kept it warm, content, and fed,
And by this time next fall
I'll count my beetles one and all."
. . .
And so here's the lesson, lassies,
For it has forever been said:
Never go to the shore alone,
Or put a beetle under your bed!

Suddenly, a penetrating, inhumanly savage cry was heard outside our room and put a momentary halt to our merrymaking. It was a cry the likes of which I had never heard before. It was like the caw of a raven sensing a storm; the chatter of a wood grouse running through a field; the neighing of a proud steed, escaping the lasso and sensing freedom and the field; the squeal of a piglet that is being roasted alive; and the yell of a man who is being lynched. We hardly had time to exchange glances when an old woman rushed in. Her face was so frightened that I hardly recognized her as our landlady. She was wringing her hands, crying, "Help me, my dear sirs. Help me, I beg of you!"

"What's going on?" I asked in bewilderment.

"Ah, it's nothing," the house serf answered coldly. "Is she drunk again?"

"Yes, she's done it again. . . . Boy, is she drunk this time. She's got froth around her mouth and everything. . . . She's even grabbed a knife. 'I'll kill myself!' she says, 'and stab you all to boot.' Good sir, Egor Kharitonych, what am I to do with her?!"

"She should go ahead and do it."

"I couldn't agree more. It would serve her right. One couldn't hope for a better ending, but I'm afraid it will never happen. . . . And it wouldn't be good for the tenants. . . . The police would come. She must have drunk up whatever money she had. Her coat alone was worth fifty rubles. . . . Look around, it seems that's what she's done. She doesn't worry about her soul, that's for sure. She won't even have a shroud to bury her, if she keeps this up. My dear sir, Egor Kharitonych, she won't be buried with anything at all."

The house serf, Egor Kharitonych, and Kir'yanych left with the landlady, Fedotovna. My curiosity compelled me to follow after them. We passed through a door (the very one with which, if my readers will remember, I had become well acquainted earlier) as I entered the quarters of the landlady. Her room was exactly like ours but furnished somewhat differently and better. Beds stood in two corners of the room, while the other two corners were fenced off by screens that had been glued together with paper from an old journal. (One could still read the pages.) There were also narrow shelves that resembled those in peasant huts. They hung down about a foot from the ceiling, extended the length of the walls, and held all kinds of clay and wooden dishware. What was going on there is worthy of a precise and skillful description. A woman was rolling on the floor in the middle of the room. She bore the full and youthful bosom of a Balzac heroine. Her cheeks were puffy and as dark red as a beet. She kept crying out in a choking and shrilly penetrating voice, "A . . . a . . . a . . . oi . . . My dear sir! . . . A . . . oi . . . I'm dying! . . . Soon I will die! I will die! . . . . a!" Foam was rushing out of her mouth as if she were a crazed horse; it fell in blobs on the floor and smeared her face. Her hands flew about wildly and were drenched in blood because she had bitten them in her frenzy. She was surrounded by three women; two were somewhat older, the other was middle-aged—all were pregnant. With every contortion of the screaming woman, they jumped back in fear; with every burst of frenzy, they cried out in one voice, "Oi!" I should also mention that from behind one of the screens (to the left of the door), I could hear a thin little voice singing, with complete unconcern, a ditty our Petersburg Germans dearly love:

Mein lieber Augustin,
Alles ist weg!

Suddenly, the hysterical woman shrieked with a deafening cry. She moaned, "Oh, I feel so sick! Oh, dear sir, I'm so sick! Lord God, let my soul go in peace. . . . A knife! . . . Get me a knife! . . ." She then got on her feet.

The knife lay on the floor. The woman rolled over it several times, but no one had the courage to pick it up. The house serf now stepped forward and, having seen the knife, knitted his brows and yelled severely, "And what do you need a knife for, you damn witch! For what? I'll give you a knife! . . . Kir'yanych! Hey there, Kir'yanych! . . . Good God! You're just as bad as she is! Get the hell over here! . . . We got to take this woman and—"

But, at that moment, Kir'yanych was jumping up and down, banging his shoes terribly and trying to catch a spider that was crawling up the wall. He heard nothing.

The house serf spit, slowly untied his belt, and, throwing the woman a savage look, yelled with all his might, "Tie her up!"

The body of the hysterical woman suddenly began to tremble. The frenzied expression on her face was now replaced by a timid and imploring look. Like a leaf falling from a tree, she fell upon the feet of the house serf and plaintively asked for mercy.

"Back to your place!" her tamer cried solemnly, with a tragic gesture of his hand. "Back now, you old piece of gingerbread!" (The poor woman was pockmarked—the Russian has a knack for words.) "Back to work!" he added, stamping his foot. "Just make a sound, one more sound, and I'll tie you up and throw you into the cesspit to boot."

The landlady sat the woman down and set her to work. The now timid soul began to sew without stopping, fearing to raise her eyes to the house serf who, by contrast, was staring at her like an owl (so the proverb goes). He repeated in various tones, "No more nonsense now, no more."

I feel that I must tell now what I myself learned subsequently. In reality, Terentievna was not a "hysterical type" (so we call a Russian woman who has fallen victim to some stupidity or other). Rather, she was prone to delirium tremens which seized her regularly, particularly after a weeklong bout of heavy drinking. The house serf had been summoned repeatedly to save the day by the same (and most inexpensive) means. He invariably returned the frenzied woman to a more docile state and, at times, even knocked the tipsiness out of her. Whether the house serf did such a thing by means of an unusually sharp voice, a fierce glance (so the landlady thought), a special blessing of the fates, or simply by whatever the situation required—no matter how he did it, he enjoyed the endless admiration of the landlady and the women tenants for what they saw as his "magnetic powers." The house serf even thought to put his influence over Terentievna to his personal advantage. After he had calmed her down, he gave her some of his own underwear to mend. While she sewed, he repaired his shoes, standing there naked, holding his left leg quietly in its pant leg and not daring to move from the spot until she had finished.

On the way back to my quarters, I again noticed the screens from which the thin little voice had sounded. I now caught sight of a nice-looking young woman, who, like her colleagues in the cellar, was distinguished by the amplitude of her pregnancy.

"Why are they all pregnant?" I asked when we had entered the room.

"We all know why," the house serf answered. "Say you have this cook living with you . . . maid . . . some kind of a mam'selle, married or otherwise. Suddenly . . . You know how it is. . . . They can't hold off any longer. . . . So where do they go? . . . You can't march off into the street. You just don't do that. Fedotovna is a good soul too . . . an ordinary type. . . 'Come stay with me a little, my sweet! I will not hurt you!' someone says. And off to her place for a while. They would go to her place. And there—the deed was done. . . . Fedotovna liked it like that, pure and simple. . . . Now there was a woman! She'd put her heart and soul into everything she did. . . . You could search the whole wide world, but you'd never find one like her. They say there are two just like her in Moscow, but they can't be as good. . . . They'd probably bust up anybody they'd meet . . .

"One of the women died in childbirth the other day. . . . She was all in tears. She just moaned and groaned. . . . Fedotovna cleaned up everything neat as a pin. . . . She stuffed all the trash and stuff into her trunk. . . . 'What am I to do with my things,' she said, 'a deceased woman without kith or kin? They should be given to the poor. . . . Let them all pray for a dead woman. . . . I'll take nothing from them now, nothing, it will be of no use to me." Then she summoned the beggars, all of them young boys and girls . . . each one smaller than the other. . . . She asked, 'Is there any wine around?' . . . Now, there were only these two men. . . . They had already eaten . . . but they gave her something to drink, and would you believe it, off she went and stole one of their handkerchiefs. . . . Now, don't you leave your place. . . . Hey there, Kir'yanych, what do you say to another glass?!"

The house serf went up to the table and gasped in horror—the bottle was empty. Cursing, he kicked the green man repeatedly, hoping to wake him. The latter, however, was sleeping heavily, unconcerned as a babe in the middle of the floor. He did not move. Rather, in his stupor, he responded to the house serf's kicks with verses, taken from his pamphlet commemorating someone's name day, replete with well-wishes and blessings. I think he was raving; after all, no one in his right mind could possess such magnanimity.

"Ain't much can be done for a dog who keeps licking his tail," the house serf said with touching sympathy. He had his hat in one hand and in the other the bottle. "And just when I'm ready to lend him money, the taverns are closed!"

"And where are you off to, hedgehog face? Better tomorrow you eat with that money!"

"What will be, will be! And is that a good enough reason not to drink now? . . . Well, perhaps it is."

"One should remember," Kir'yanych said with an inner joy, "that 'the naked shed their tears, but God will calm their fears.' "

After the first glass, the house serf and Kir'yanych confessed how they had felt toward each other the first time they had met. After the second, they cried, hugged, and kissed repeatedly. After the third, they quarreled, and after the fourth, this modest drama followed the natural (and inevitable) outcome, which I here relate so artlessly: Our heroes got into a fight . . .

When I woke up the next morning, I became interested in snatches of a conversation:

"You got any dogs here?"

"Yes sir, I do. A pair of them, both reddish with spots . . ."

"Are the spots gray, perhaps? . . . Are their ears torn? . . . And does one have a small black spot on its tail?"

"It just might have. Why don't you take a look?"

When a person first awakes, he is often very lazy. I surely wanted to take a look at our early visitor, but I also was not up to turning over and opening my eyes. By the way, I later met this individual face-to-face. He is a most interesting gentleman! I'll introduce him to you when the opportunity arises.

We now bid farewell to Trostnikov's notes. (To explain precisely who this Trostnikov is would cause us to stray far from our subject; thus we do not include it here.) We have been proud, however, to have taken an excerpt from his writings and to have presented it for the gracious attention of our readers.[9]

—N. Nekrasov

9. It is of interest to note that "The Petersburg Corners," together with the novel *The Thin Man* (*Tonkii chelovek;* 1853–55), were the only two prose works that Nekrasov did not reject in later life.

The Alexander Theater

Vissarion Belinsky

O theater! O theater! What a magical place you always have been for me![1] How you have struck all the strings of my soul with your ineffable charm! What wonderful chords have you played on them! . . . In you, O theater, I have seen an entire universe in all its alluring diversity, splendor, and mystery! After seeing you, O theater, what did I care for the eternally blue cupola of the sky, its shining sun, its pale-faced moon, and its myriad languidly bright stars? After you, what did I care for the silent, gloomy forests, the green groves, and the lush fields? Indeed, what did I care for the sea itself, its heavily breathing chest, the incessant murmuring of its banks, and the sad whispering of its waves, breaking against the inaccessible shore! O great theater! Your painted sun, moon, and stars; your canvas trees; your clouds sewn from rags; your wooden seas and rivers have surpassed anything in nature to satisfy my thirst, to still the tormenting anticipation of the miracles in my soul! Your influence on me has been so powerful that even now when you disappoint and deceive me so cruelly, my heart is forced to quiver whenever I see a crowd gather slowly in your still half-empty but brightly lit amphitheater, when I hear the discordant tuning of your instruments, and when I am seized by the presentiment of some great mystery, of some great miracle that is about to unfold before my very eyes!

1. Belinsky was as good as his word, having written roughly 180 articles on the Russian theater during his critical career. See V. Berezina, "Problema chitatelia i zritelia v kritike Belinskogo," *Vestnik Leningradskgo universiteta,* issue 1 (January 1977), 69.

But then, O theater, you have given me even more than that! I remember how, with the final strike of the violin's bow, the mysterious curtain quickly rose, and how my impatient gaze rushed off to peer through it and to see more quickly the magical world that lay hidden behind. The actors who appeared onstage were not ordinary people. They were either so inexpressibly good or so horribly villainous. The women were so charming, so ineffably virtuous that one could give a thousand lives for just a mere glance at them! The enchanted stage was so wondrous, so completely enchanting that my heart beat in a slow and muffled way, and my breath died on my lips. The young, innocent feeling of the stage so gratified everyone there; and—Good God!—what fullness of soul, what emotions and impressions pervaded the people as they left there! Even if on some afternoon when I came across an old, dilapidated theater in some provincial city, [2] I looked at this "splendid" temple of art with such a reverential feeling that even though I find it awkward to remove my hat before people, I saw it as an unpardonable boldness to remain with a covered head in front of such a building.

Whenever I visited the theater, I imagined that each actor was a noble and happy being, a priest of high art who served with happiness, disinterest, and passion. Yes, I thought, fame had smiled upon such an individual, and stormy applause had surrounded him. Like a wizard or magician, the actor could at will force his listeners to laugh and cry by the way he cast a glance, pitched his voice, or moved his hands. He could rouse them to great thoughts and virtuous sentiments; he could stir in them a love for good and a hatred for evil. His calling was great, and his accomplishments were noble. With what worthy respect did he regard and serve art! With what force was he ennobled by it! As I saw it, anyone who wanted to become an actor was a great individual. I almost became one myself—an actor, that is, not a great man.

O, the dreams of youth! At that time, I did not suspect that some actors were not servants of art but its slaves and that they had every right to regard the stage as their corvée. I did not surmise that other actors were shackled to the theater like a bureaucrat to an office, like a shopkeeper to

2. Belinsky is referring to the Gladkov Theater in Penza (about 350 miles southwest of Moscow), where he had been a student. See *V. G. Belinskii v vospominaniiakh sovremennikov* (Moscow: Khudozhestvennaia literatura, 1977), 51–52.

a store. I also was unaware that the best of these "great" people were calculating and proud and that they had an exalted idea of their talent, be it genuine or fleeting. Indeed, it never occurred to me that such individuals did not understand art or that they looked upon it only as a job that, more for some, less for others, was burdensome and boring. Such things I found out later, after I had parted with provincial puppet shows and became acquainted with the "theaters" in our capitals—if I may beg your indulgence to use such a word to describe the dramatic institutions there.

But when I first saw the stage, I became enchanted with this thing called theater, this enduring idol of my soul.[3] My spirit soared; it grew and matured. Fantasy overtook reality. My mind came into its own and proudly turned its back on experience, possibility, and common sense. Vague ideals rose up in my soul, and the spirits of a better world, entities that could be heard but not seen, flew around me and beckoned me to a better place and sphere. Rather than to look at the stage and theater before me, I began to dream of another stage, another theater. And from behind the personages who came under my gaze, there began to appear other individuals—people with such marvelous expressions, unlike anyone in this earthly world. Before my very eyes, the stage for an absolutely innocent, commonsense vaudeville, for example, the living room of a landowner or a bureaucrat, turned into a long gallery. At one end, a terrible woman appeared in the half darkness, a haggard figure with a pale face, disheveled hair, and an open chest. Rolling the distended pupils of her horror-filled eyes and wiping one bare hand with the other, she whispered in an icy voice, "Out, damned spot! Out, I tell you! One, two! Who would have thought that the old man had so much blood!" The woman was Lady Macbeth. In the distance behind her, there towered the image of a man. His hand held a bloody dagger, his eyes wandered in a savage way, and his pale, bluish lips murmured indistinctly, "Macbeth has had a terrible dream and now he can no longer sleep!"

In the high-pitched voice of some vaudeville prima donna, singing a couplet with flat witticisms and coarse double entendres, I heard the pleading voice of Desdemona, her muffled sobbing, her predeath wails. In the crude avowals of some melodramatic lover for the "lady" who had

3. Belinsky is referring to the Russian actor Pavel Mochalov. See V. Belinskii, " 'Gamlet.' Drama Shekspira. Mochalov v roli Gamleta," in Belinskii, *Polnoe sobranie sochinenii,* vol. 2 (1953), 253–345.

captured his heart, I imagined Romeo and Juliet in the garden at night. I heard their harmonious words of love, so full of young, noble, and rapturous bliss that I myself was afraid that my whole being would waft away in their sigh of sacred love. Suddenly before me, there also appeared an old king who, together with the roar of a storm and the clap of thunder, heaped the terrible words of a father's curse upon his ungrateful and cruel-hearted daughters.[4]

What a wonderful world this was! In it I felt so good, so free. My heart lived a second existence; my inner gaze saw rows of bright spirits representing love and bliss. I came to possess not only another body but also another soul, loving and tender, like that of a splendid woman to whom I could pass on all my wondrous visions. I also felt, in a more forceful and tormented way, the angst of loneliness, a thirst for empathy and love. Whenever I visited the theater, the people onstage talked, walked, sang, and waved their arms. The public yawned and clapped, laughed and hissed, alternately excited and bored. But I did not see what was occurring on stage; rather, I saw a place in the distance, filled with my riveting visions. And I would leave the theater, not remembering what had gone on there but nonetheless content and filled with the feeling that I had been blessed passionately by my dreams and by my melancholy foray into the bright world of genuine and elevated art. My soul had waited for a miracle to happen, for a dream that was fulfilled *at least in part.* But my soul, happily and good-naturedly, took this "part" for the whole and was satisfied, solemnly and completely. Truth be told, no matter what bitter things life might send me, I will never forget that diminutive pale individual, his splendid and noble face, and his long black curls. I will never forget how he recalled his father in a voice that poured forth like the limpid waves of a sweet melody. I will never forget how he dissolved into leonine sobbing when he indicted himself for his shamefully weak will; or how he roared like thunder in the sky; or how his eyes, heretofore so melancholic and gentle, now blazed forth like lightning. I will never forget how this individual, having discovered the terrible murder of patricide, shook the amphitheater with inhuman laughter. And I will never forget

4. William Shakespeare wrote *Romeo and Juliet* in 1595, *Othello* in 1604, *King Lear* in 1605, and *Macbeth* in 1606.

how the audience, with frightened looks and bated breath, merged as one as it gazed upon the suffering artist, and how, with the unanimous cheers of a thousand thrilled voices and the equally united thunder of a thousand hands, it took its turn in bringing down the rafters![5] I also saw him—that black Moor, that great child who, having loved, could rein in the force of his love but who, having surrendered to suspicion, would not rest content until he had sacrificed his beloved, destroying with his own hand one of the best and most fragrant blossoms that had ever flowered under the sky. Oh, how even now is my sleep disturbed by those barely audible words: "What have you done, O shameless woman? What have you done?"[6] I also saw how this proud oak tree was brought down by a storm when this Moor, with wavering steps and wandering glance, first approached his innocent sacrifice and then rushed to the door where the terrifying witness to the innocence of his sacrifice was knocking. It seemed to my fevered imagination that the crowd about me was as great as the artist whom it applauded, that it understood art, and that, like the forest and the sea, it was filled with mystery and thought. And I was convinced that I had seen in the theater everything that it could show, everything that one could demand from it.

But as all good things come to an end, so did my enchantment with the theater. At first, I began to notice that in a Shakespearean play, I always saw only a single personage, not any other characters or the drama itself. I also saw that when this personage left the stage, everything grew dull and dark. It languished and died, became vulgar and boring, and lost all sense whatsoever. I quickly became convinced that although the talents of this actor equaled those of ancient Atlantis, he could not shoulder the huge edifice of a Shakespearean drama alone. I also realized that onstage, this actor was not always good but even sometimes poor and that he was noteworthy only when he vented his volcanic nature and gave way to fiery inspiration. Finally, I understood that when the audience applauded an artist onstage, it did so in a completely impulsive and unconscious way and that it did not distinguish between sudden flashes of genuine inspiration and buffoonish shenanigans, which, though bold in effect, were mundane and catered to the vulgar demands of the mob. I became annoyed and sick at heart.

5. Belinsky is again talking about Mochalov.

6. Belinsky is quoting from *Othello,* act 4, scene 2.

But the time has passed, my respected reader, when I no longer get annoyed at the theater except in those instances when I see a long poster listing several new plays and underneath them the fatal word "debut." Ever the inveterate reviewer, I enter the dramatic temple, though it has long since been a temple for me. Good God! How I have changed! But such a metamorphosis is something that everyone goes through, and you, my respected reader, will also change, if you have not done so already. But before you finish my elegy in prose, I wish to ask you one thing. You yourself can choose to read or not to read what I have written—that is up to you. But in any case, I ask that you not succumb to a harmful prejudice, that is, to see as evil and unkind anyone who, with years of severe experience, does not always look at everything in a happy way; who does not always judge things with tolerance and tenderness but with anger; and who exposes reality before your eyes, making you rub them from the bitter smoke of fantasies that he has exploded like rockets. If this person seems dour, it is perhaps because his soul harbored noble ideals and searched and yearned for way too much. No, this person seeks nothing and wants nothing. All his ideals have vanished in the cold light of experience, and with tiresome grumbling he seeks revenge anywhere and anytime on that reality which has deceived him so cruelly.

But I assure you, respected reader, that I am no longer a malcontent, for I gave up the foolish habit of grumbling a long time ago. Now I am an individual who is pleased with everything in the world. I do not abuse or scold but address everything with light praise. You will find it easy to get along with me, and I hope that you will be completely satisfied with me—if not my ability to delight you with witty and pleasing words, then from my patience for everything that you like and I do not.

After this somewhat long and poetic introduction, allow me, respected reader, to turn your attention to the more prosaic characteristics of the Alexander Theater.[7]

There is a Russian proverb that says a city has mores, but a village has customs. In reality, though, every city has something special about it, something personal that belongs to it alone. Simply put, every city has its

7. It is of interest to note that Belinsky's comments on the Alexander Theater were rebuked sharply by a reviewer for the *Northern Bee*. See Oksman, *Letopis' zhizni i tvorchestva V. G. Belinskogo*, 409.

own "mores." After all, could there be a Petersburg without its "mores"? The physiological life of Petersburg has many innate features, but the Alexander Theater is one of its most characteristic. In fact, it is one of the most prominent "mores" of our great and splendid capital. To describe the physiology of Petersburg and not to say a word or draw special attention to the Alexander Theater would be like drawing a portrait and forgetting to include the nose or making only a sketch of one. Anyone who wishes to see the external side of Petersburg as a great and splendid city, as the capital of Russia, and as one of the most important trading ports in the world has only to glance at the Alexander Theater. With its charming square in front, the arsenal of the Anichkov Palace[8] on one side, and the Imperial Public Library[9] on the other, the Alexander Theater is one of the most marvelous jewels of Nevsky Prospekt. But anyone who wants to see the private Petersburg—not only its homes but also the people who live in them—must first attend the Alexander Theater before he visits all other theaters in St. Petersburg. He must go to the Alexander long, often, and without fail; for only then will he gain the experience and understanding to see the mysteries of the characteristics of the Petersburg way of life unfolding before him. An old sage used to say to anyone he met, "Show me your friends, and I will tell you who you are." Although we do not have the honor of being counted among old sages or even our very newest ones, we nonetheless have the right to say to some people, "If you want to know Petersburg, go to the Alexander Theater as often as possible"; and to others, "Tell us how often you go the Alexander Theater, and we will tell you what kind of person you are." Everyone has his views—and so do we!

Every theater has two sides which, so to speak, make up its existence. They are the actors and the public; the theater cannot have one without the other. These two sides are bound together closely because it is always through the actors that one can accurately judge the public and vice versa. Another important aspect of theatrical life is its repertoire and, with it, contemporary dramatic writers. In all three aspects, the Alexander Theater is remarkably independent. It has its own public, actors, and repertoire.

8. The Anichkov Palace was built between 1741 and 1750 by Empress Elizaveta Petrovna for her lover, Alexei Razumovsky. It later became the winter residence for the heir to the throne.

9. The Imperial Public Library, now the Russian National Library, opened in 1814.

And, in all of these three aspects, the Alexander Theater fully justifies itself with the well-known Russian proverb, "One gets what one deserves."

As Petersburg is, at present, the representative of formal Europeanism in Russia, so is the Russian theater in this city the representative of the same European formalism on stage. For instance, it was a gracious host to the techniques of classical drama, for example, its actors sang declamations and did the two-step minuet. Theatrical classicism accompanied one generation after another. It began with Dmitrevsky and passed through Yakolev, Semyonova, and the Kolosovas; it ended with Mr. and Mrs. [Vasily] Karatygin, especially the former, who surrendered unwillingly to the spirit of the times and became the first actor to depart from the classical orthodoxy that had fostered him.

The classical era was a brilliant period for the Russian Theater in St. Petersburg. It engaged the upper echelons of the capital and the best-known writers of the age in an active way. Working on its behalf were first Sumarokov, Knyazhnin, and Fonvizin, and then Ozerov, Zhandr, Gnedich, and others. Pushkin came along in the twilight of the Russian classical theater in Petersburg. What he saw was still sumptuous and splendid; indeed, he resorted to classical antiquity when he wrote:

> Stern critic of the theater
> Honored citizen of the wings
> Fickler worshipper of actresses
> Lover of all dramatic things.
> Onegin flew to the theater
> Where everyone is a judge
> Ready to praise *entrechat* and *Moina,*
> But give *Phèdre* and *Cleopatra*[10] the nudge.
> The theater is a magic kingdom
> For in hoary times of old
> *Fonvizin,* the friend of freedom
> With his satires made quite bold,
> There *Knyazhnin* postured as a "master,"

10. Moina is the heroine of Vladislav Ozerov's 1805 tragedy *Fingal.* Phèdre is the title character of Racine's 1677 tragedy, and Cleopatra is the heroine of Étienne Jodelle's 1553 tragedy *Cleopatre captive.*

And *Ozerov* and young *Semyonova*[11] shared
The people's tears and laughter.
There that great genius, our *Katenin,*
Restored Corneille to the stage.
There *Shakovskoi* amused us all,
And lovely *Didelot* was the rage.[12]

The ballet, that genuine marvel of both classicism and the eighteenth century, joined with comedy and tragedy to capture the attention of the public. Didelot was considered a great artist. And who does not recall those poetic lines in *Onegin* about the dancer Istomina? Indeed, it was only in the verse of that work that one could talk about Taglioni and Fanny Elssler. The ballet is popular even now, but it has lost its importance. Crowds flock to the ballet only when they hear the name of Taglioni, but without her, only inveterate lovers of dance are fond of the form. In Pushkin's time, though, the ballet had conquered both classical tragedy and comedy:

There Melpomene[13] was greeted
With a prolonged and stormy howl,
There she stood before the callous crowd
And beckoned beneath her tawdry cowl,
There Thalia[14] dreamed in quiet
And did not heed the friendly waters' part
There Terpsichore[15] was the only one
Who could move the young man's heart,
(What was common in an ancient time
Still continues in yours and mine.)[16]

11. Ekaterina Semyonova was considered the greatest performer of the role of Racine's *Phèdre* on the Russian stage.

12. Belinsky is quoting, with some license, from the first chapter of Pushkin's *Eugene Onegin.*

13. In ancient Greek mythology, Melpomene is one of nine Muses, sister goddesses of the arts and sciences. She is the patroness of tragedy in both a figurative and a theatrical sense.

14. The ancient Greeks saw the Muse Thalia as the representative of comedy.

15. Terpsichore, another of the Muses, was seen by the ancient Greeks as the patroness of dancing and ballet.

16. Belinsky is now quoting from chapter 7 of *Eugene Onegin.*

The theater in Moscow developed much more freely than the one in Petersburg. The classicism in Moscow could not put down deep roots; it ruled the stage only when nothing could take its place. Thus, as soon as the word "romanticism" began to appear in Russian letters, classicism disappeared immediately from the Muscovite stage. One should also note that even during the heyday of classicism in Russia, the theater in Moscow did not observe the musical declamations and the two-step minuet in any strict manner. Mochalov, who debuted onstage in 1818, played the role of Polinik[17] in a natural way, not at all in the classical style.

In this regard, Moscow was way ahead of Petersburg. But such a development is not surprising given the fact that Moscow was not greatly influenced by the austere forms and standard decorum of Europe. Moscow does not chase after form, and even when it does, it does not observe it strictly. But as everyone also knows, Petersburg goes wild over such a thing. V. A. Karatygin was the first actor to take up theatrical reform, but he did so in an extremely restrained way. For a long time, he remained true to the traditions of classicism that had formed him as an artist. But little by little, his appearances on the Muscovite stage forced him to abandon the classical manner altogether. Indeed, classical drama was dropped completely even from the Petersburg stage because its writers and actors had just as completely given themselves over to the so-called romantic school. Because Karatygin's acting had become much more natural, he now played a variety of roles. But his classical formation was still of value to him because in any part he played, he preserved a picturesque pose and a graceful form, the lack of which neither talent nor inspiration can replace (just as pose and form cannot make up for a lack of talent and inspiration).

Naturalness is a key feature of drama, just like it is in any other art. But one must also not forget that naturalness in art is not at all the naturalness of reality. Only a few can possess the former, while almost everyone is privy to the latter. The fact that a person can be natural in his everyday speech in life does not mean that he can be natural in his speech onstage. A gifted actor must possess the ability to be natural onstage; but to do so, he must study and practice so that this ability becomes second nature to him. We have also come across performers whose acting is more repulsive than

17. Polinik is the hero in Vladislav Ozerov's 1804 play *Oedipus in Athens* (*Edip v Afinakh*).

natural and who testify to the fact that artistic naturalness must be graceful and artistic. In this regard, Karatygin is a genuine artist: he possesses fully the means and the ability to express gracefulness and art in his acting. That is also why he is all the more tied to his formation in the classical school, which paid almost no attention to nature but which focused exclusively on art. For many actors, such a situation has meant their ruin. That is, caught unawares by new conceptions of art, these actors immediately lost their talent, for what was considered their greatest asset had suddenly become their greatest liability. It was too late for them to relearn their craft because the classical manner of acting had become second nature to them. By contrast, Karatygin understood in time that he had to change his style of acting completely; and though he did such a thing, step by step, and not without considerable struggle, he emerged victorious, poised between tradition and the very newest demands. What was new did not depart from him, and what was old he used to his own advantage. The ability to act onstage not only with dignity and decorum but also with grace, the duty to respect any means to influence the public, and the commitment to constant study and to meticulous preparation for both major and minor roles became second nature to him. Because Karatygin turned his back on the musical declamation and the two-step minuet (a goose step with a solemnly raised hand), he gradually surpassed his earthly rival, Mr. Bryansky, a very gifted artist who attempted, unsuccessfully, to make musical declamations sound genuine but who thus, at the height of his powers, saw himself as losing his talent. In vain do young artists, by copying Karatygin, attempt to acquire the talent for high drama. Indeed, they succeed only in espousing the artist's shortcomings and not a single one of his strengths. Without any malice aforethought, they turn their performance into a somewhat vicious caricature of Karatygin's acting. All they have to do, they think, is mimic a gifted artist so that they can escape the hard work of studying art and of developing their own talent. These young actors do not understand that Karatygin had no role models for his art and that he had to labor a great deal and to develop whatever means he had at hand to work out a personal manner of acting.

Mrs. Karatygina is also an artist whose remarkable talent is similar to that of her husband. She too was raised in the old classical school but sought to rid herself of any forced manner in her acting. Mrs. Karatygina, though, has been only partially successful in her guise. When she performs in tragedies, she still retains extremely stylized poses, cries, and screams; when she acts in comedies, she is pretentious; and in both tragedies and comedies, her acting is more forced than natural. Generally speaking, Mrs. Karatygina is incomparably better in comedies than in tragedies. Even her husband does not have as many desperate imitators as she does, that is, young artists who, one can justifiably say, succeed completely in imitating and caricaturing her shortcomings. Thus, whenever Mrs. Karatygina and her imitators appear on stage, one has no choice but to see her as a grande dame surrounded by her local retinue. Her disciples especially struggle to copy her comme il faut acting, but they succeed only in mirroring her affectations. Apparently, they do not think that the ability to act comme il faut onstage depends upon the constant practice of acting comme il faut even at home, without guests, but alone with oneself. Regarding Mrs. Karatygina's traits as an actress, we must also note that she, over the course of her career, has prepared and performed each of her various roles—big and small, important and trivial—with the same exacting conscientiousness as her husband. Her performance on stage is sometimes good, sometimes poor, but never foolish or bad.

Returning to Mr. Karatygin, we cannot think of an actor who is more in love with his glory and craft or more ready to sacrifice everything for both. The passion and commitment with which Karatygin began his career on stage, he continues to this day and will continue into the future. Simply put, he is a slave to his art. He has done everything to develop his talents; he is committed to his acting in heart and soul. He is almost always excellent in roles that demand both intelligence and art from the actor. That is why his role as Ludwig XI in *The Enchanted House*[18] is his solemn triumph. Here he is inimitable, and only the most inveterate lack of taste can see his Hamlet and Othello as better.

Here we must also mention the public of the Alexander Theater, and how wonderfully it receives its favorite artist when he appears on stage as an old *Bürgermeister* who, having stopped on the steps of a tower, reproaches his repulsive grandson with bitter but quiet dignity.[19] It is difficult to

18. *The Enchanted House* (*Das böse Haus*) was written by Joseph Auffenberg in 1834.

19. Belinsky is referring to the knight Job in Victor Hugo's 1842 melodrama *The Burgraves* (*Les Burgraves*).

imagine a person more splendid and gracious than the thin figure of this hundred-year-old man who so resembles someone from another world. His body may seem decrepit, but his spirit is as if forged in iron: hale, hearty, and young. We do not need to mention that nature has endowed Karatygin with a good set of vocal cords and that his voice can move to a cry whenever he must express something with passion. Incidentally, we are far from the view that Karatygin is an artist who is devoid of emotion. No one can say that he is without feeling. Anyone who has seen him in the role of Jarvis (in the play of the same name)[20] must remember how Karatygin prepared himself for execution by arranging for the future of his daughter. No one who remembers him in this part can say that Karatygin lacks emotion.

Emotion and passion, though, are not always the same thing. The voice of passion is often great, but it never devolves into mere screaming. It affects a spectator's soul, not his ears. Generally speaking, whenever we call attention to Karatygin's emotion and warmth, we have in mind his roles in new dramas or those instances when he plays particular individuals. In tragic pieces, however, Karatygin tends to give way to declamations, which he tries to make as natural as possible but which, for their lack of emotion, are declamations just the same. But in instances which require artistic poses, deliberation, deftness, art, and effects, Karatygin is almost always magnificent. In this regard, he is a Petersburg actor par excellence, the alpha and omega as regards talent and other remarkable abilities. Karatygin is the alpha because he currently has no rivals on the Petersburg stage, and he is the omega because he has no heirs to his legacy.

To show the full difference between the theaters in Petersburg and Moscow, one need only establish a parallel between their two key tragic actors. Mochalov was not formed in any school. He emerged on the stage because he believed that he was a great talent. Without any deliberation on his part and without ever giving an accounting of himself in his art, he immediately became a reformer. In the role of Polinik, Mochalov purposely set himself apart from the classical mode by means of his fresh emotions and natural manner of acting. He remained committed to the truth that he had observed throughout the course of his life. But he did so

20. The play in question is *Jarvis the Honest Man* (*Javis l'honnête homme*) written by Alexander Dumas-père and Charles Lafont in 1840.

unconsciously, yielding only to his instinctual talent. At his disposal were a handsome face, fiery inspiration, burning passion, profound feeling, and a voice that was first solemn, then soft, but always harmonious and melodic. Mochalov is a small man. His figure is not prepossessing, his mannerisms are roughly hewn and seemingly without any finesse at all. He depends completely on the whim of inspiration; but once it awakens in him, the stunned spectator observes the great mystery of art, one that defies descriptions, words, and aesthetic theories and books. In these inspired moments, Mochalov's mannerisms are noble and elegant; he even seems to grow in height. But when this inspiration leaves him, he immediately becomes a completely different person. The audience sees nothing other than how he hunches his shoulders and slaps his hands on his hips. In a word, they see the most strange mannerisms and the most bizarre (for lack of a better word) poses and figures. They hear nothing but one cry after another. Sometimes this metamorphosis happens several times in the course of one role. Rarely does Mochalov give an even performance from beginning to end; but when he does, one sees the triumph of a great talent, but not of art. On the infrequent occasions when Mochalov is playing a role poorly, there are one or two flashes of wondrous inspiration that move the audience as if it has received an electric shock. It sometimes happens also that Mochalov plays a role that is indescribably poor from beginning to end. Thus, the people who see Mochalov as a great artist are as correct as those who see him as a poor, ungifted one. Mochalov has had considerable success on the Petersburg stage; but he could not enjoy constant acclaim there. The public of the Alexander Theater could not overlook his weaknesses for the sake of his strengths. By contrast, Moscow has always loved Mochalov and has willingly forgiven his shortcomings for his moments of inspiration. Only a very few Muscovites could not pardon Mochalov for his artistic foibles, but the more heatedly they rose up against his shortcomings, the more passionately they expressed their love and respect for his talent.

Karatygin enjoyed great success on the Muscovite stage, but each new visit of his there increased the number of people who sought to minimize his talent. Just as Mochalov could not claim continual success on the Petersburg stage, Karatygin could not enjoy constant acclaim on the Muscovite one. From these differences, one can see that Moscow wants inspiration from the artist, while Petersburg demands art and form. Strictly speaking, Mochalov is neither an actor nor an artist; rather, he is like an oracle who, when filled with the tormenting ecstasy of art, reveals its mysteries. By contrast, Karatygin is a consummate actor and artist who is always ready for his craft and is always good at what he does. That is why Mochalov is exhausted for several days after he plays well onstage, whereas Karatygin can appear twice a day for an entire week during Carnival in either dramatic or tragic roles. If someone would appear onstage who could combine the passionate and tempestuous inspiration of Mochalov and the rigorous, exacting study of Karatygin, we would have a truly great actor.

Generally speaking, in the sphere of dramatic art, Petersburg is different from Moscow in that it shows considerable ability in being—or at least seeming to be—satisfied with externals and forms. Simply put, the stage in Petersburg has more art, but its counterpart in Moscow has more talent. There is in Moscow, though, an artist who unites both conditions: talent and art. We are talking about Shchepkin. Shchepkin is so unique that, unlike Karatygin and Mochalov, he is beyond imitation (at least successfully). True, both the Petersburg and Muscovite stages have remarkable comic talents (e.g., Messrs. Martynov, Zhivokoni, Sadovsky, and Karatygin the Second), but Shchepkin's talent goes beyond comedy.

There is no argument that Shchepkin is excellent when he plays Famusov and the town governor in *The Inspector General,* but there are other roles that show his genuine forte. Whoever has seen Shchepkin play the minor part of the sailor in the play of the same name[21]—and who has not seen him in it?—can easily imagine the genuine range of his giftedness. Shchepkin is superb in those prosaic roles that depict common, everyday people and which demand from the artist not only comic but also deeply fervid emotions. Shchepkin was formed in the classical school and grew up on Molière (whom he saw as the highest ideal of comic drama). But the old repertoire did not offer him a single good role that could suit his talent. And, even if the plays of Molière and Kotzebue gave him models for reflection and study, he had to keep his talent within a sphere that was strictly comic and one-sided. Such a state of affairs taught Shchepkin little; so he had to learn how to be both a person and an artist from the few people

21. The play in question is Thomas Sauvage and Jules de Lurieu's 1833 comedy *A Sailor* (*Un Matelot*).

in our country who could teach him a thing or two. Shchepkin could not but note the revolution that occurred in our literature under the name of so-called romanticism. He took in Shakespeare greedily—at least those plays that were translated into Russian—and he joyfully sidestepped the biases of people already formed in their tastes to follow the progress of Russian literature. Shchepkin, though, has started to appear on our stage only very recently, and in only three or four plays to boot. He has appeared in the role of Shylock only once or twice, but he should play such a part at least ten times so that he can master it fully and show what a gifted artist as himself can do with such a part. Perhaps if Shchepkin had become acquainted with Shakespeare earlier, he would have been able to play the role of Lear, a role that lies in the realm of his talent as much as does the clown in this piece or, for that matter, Falstaff.[22] (Incidentally, only a few people in our country understand the deep significance of the clown in *King Lear;* that is why when Shchepkin does not play this individual, the role is always performed in such a remarkably pitiful and thoughtless way.) Perhaps many people will be surprised when we assert that an artist such as Shchepkin speaks with particular passion about the minor role of the gardener in *Richard II*[23] and that if he would appear in such a part, people would immediately understand that there are no minor roles in Shakespeare. Shchepkin is also excellent as the musician, Miller, in Schiller's play *Cabal and Love.*[24]

Unfortunately, Russian literature does not afford Shchepkin roles that would correspond to the fullness of his talent (for the roles of Famusov and the town governor are strictly comic). Translated and revamped vaudevilles offer him nothing, regardless of the characters in them. The persona of the sailor, though, is seemingly tailor-made for him and insures the triumph of his talent onstage. Shchepkin thus suffers from a small and limited repertoire. Generally speaking, Shchepkin's artistic lot has not been a happy one. For a long time, he was unaware of his genuine calling, and once he found it, he could not find a sufficient number of roles in our national drama. Such an unhappy circumstance, though, did not cause him to neglect the parts he espoused. He prepared for each part attentively and acted it in

22. Falstaff is a character in Shakespeare's *Henry IV* (1596–98), *Henry V* (1599), and *The Merry Wives of Windsor* (1597).

23. Shakespeare's *Richard II* appeared in 1595.

24. Schiller wrote *Cabel and Love* (*Kabale und Liebe*) in 1784.

a conscientious way onstage. Even if Shchepkin came across a part that had nothing going for it, he performed it in such a matter as to give it the things that it lacked, that is, sense and even entertainment. Shchepkin's techniques do not allow him to appear in many roles, for example, characters who are young as well as thin people of all ages. His main shortcoming as an artist is that because of his physical being, his acting can be somewhat monotonous. He also suffers from an excess of passion and emotion, which sometimes prevents him from fully rendering his role—a flaw that is purely Muscovite! Passion is the predominant element in Shchepkin's acting not only in dramatic but also in purely comic roles. Just as another actor would find it horrifying to play a comic role that demanded he speak from the soul or become serious or angry, so does Shchepkin find it difficult to keep comic inspiration within prescribed bounds. The triumph of Shchepkin's talent arises not only from the fact that he can simultaneously rouse the public to both laughter and tears but also that he can interest his spectators in the fate of the common man and force them to cry and tremble over the sufferings of some sailor in much the same way that Mochalov would have them cry and tremble over the torments of Prince Hamlet or General Othello. Shchepkin is on good terms with all kinds of audiences, and in this regard he is at home on the Petersburg stage as much as he is on the Muscovite one. But Shchepkin would enjoy even greater success if his aesthetic conscientiousness did not render him decidedly incapable of exploiting dramatic effects and of catering to the tastes of the mob. Shchepkin is primarily an actor for the chosen few, for people who can respect the shades and nuances of his genuinely artistic acting.

After Shchepkin, the most important artists of the Muscovite stage are Messrs. Zhivokini, Orlov, Sadovsky, Potanchikov, Stepanov, and Samarin. In Mrs. Orlova, the Muscovite stage has a remarkable actress for both drama and comedy. But it is Mrs. Repina, an unusually gifted individual, who has long been the true jewel of the Muscovite stage and whose roles and talent are analogous to those of Shchepkin. The most important artists in the troupe of the Alexander Theater (primarily comedies and vaudevilles) are Mr. Martynov, an artist with a great and far-reaching talent who, unfortunately, has so far figured only in roles that are comic, not dramatic; Mr. P. Karatygin, an individual who cannot play many parts but is extremely gifted just the same; and Mr. Sosnitsky, a very deft artist who is well-versed in theatrical matters and who, even when he does not prepare, can play any part in light comedy or vaudeville. One should also mention Messrs. Samoilov, Maximov, and Grigoriev the First, as well as Mesdames Dyur and Samoilova the Second, both of whom (especially Samoilova) enjoy favor with the public of the Alexander Theater in dramatic roles and who, sometimes not without success, play parts that lie outside serious drama but which could develop their theatrical gifts. We also include in this group Mrs. Sosnitskaya, an artist with an absolutely remarkable talent for comic roles; and Mrs. Valberkhova, an actress from the old classical school but who shows an exceptional ability for both drama and comedy, and who is (especially rare in our country) well educated to boot. (Valberkhova, though, now appears onstage rarely, and her time has already passed.) We also should mention Mrs. Samoilova the First, an actress who does very well in comic and vaudeville roles, especially when she plays simple naive girls, such as peasants, loose women, and the like. The public of the Alexander Theater, though, sees the now deceased Asenkova as the pinnacle of dramatic perfection; they were especially thrilled whenever she played male parts. Truly, Asenkova always acted with purpose, bravely, boldly, and with that assuredness which quickly makes a success of her talent, marks her as a fixture onstage, and earns the constant goodwill of the public.[25]

It would be difficult to summarize in a few words the key difference between the Russian theaters in Petersburg and Moscow; but the contrast between them is great nonetheless, for it is rooted in the publics of each capital. Speaking personally, Moscow has no single theater public. For instance, the Petrovsky Theater[26] in Moscow is host to people of varying education, ranks and stations, tastes and needs. Here one will see merchants with beards and merchants without beards, as well as students and people who live in Moscow only because they find it merry to do so and who are accustomed to living only in those places which make them happy. Here one will see fashionable jackets with yellow gloves as well as bold dolmans and other forms of outer apparel. Here there will also be fur coats,

25. See, for instance, Nekrasov's 1853 encomium to the actress, "To the Memory of Asenkova" ("Pamiati Asenkovoi").

26. The Petrovsky Theater was actually two theaters: the Bol'shoi, built in 1780, staged operas and ballets, and the Malyi, constructed in 1824, featured dramatic productions. Both theaters exist to this day.

full-length coats, and old-fashioned overcoats with collars. Completing the picture will be hats both large and small, peaked at the top, adorned with feathers, or covered with rabbit fur. There will also be kerchiefs that are brocaded and made of silk or cotton. At the Petrovsky, also, one will encounter people who think that *Filatka and Miroshka*[27] is an interesting and amusing play; or who claim that the European repertoire does not have all that many treasures; or who do not want to hear about anything other than Shakespeare. There one will likewise come across others who assert that Gogol's comedies are the height of perfection or that they are coarse farces but not lacking in talent. Finally, at the Petrovsky, one will meet still others who regard Kukol'nik's dramas[28] as model pieces or who see nothing but boredom in them. In a nutshell, the Moscow theater exhibits almost as many opinions and tastes as the number of people who make up its ranks. As a result, in the Moscow theater, it is not rare to come across the most precise, educated, and refined tastes alongside ones that are extremely vulgar and coarse. It is also not uncommon to hear the most intelligent opinion from the person sitting on the right and the most absurd view from the one sitting on the left.

But even people with the same degree of education do not speak in the same voice or use the same words because at the Petrovsky, everyone wants to have his or her own convictions and judgments about things. Muscovites love and value tragedies and dramas of pathos more than they do comedies and vaudevilles. Such a preference is understandable: comedies need a more educated public than tragedies do. Tragedies relate directly to the individual's emotions and passions, even if these feelings are unconscious; tragedies also stir up powerful feelings even in souls that have long been sound asleep. Comedies, though, need to be appreciated by people who have developed on the soil of a mature civilization. Comedies demand the most precise intelligence, observation, and taste, as well as the ability

27. *The Rivals, Filatka and Miroshka; or, Four Bridegrooms and One Bride* (*Filatka i Miroshka—soperniki, ili chetyre zhenikha i odna nevestka*) was an 1831 vaudeville written by Pyotr Grigoriev (Grigoriev the Second) in 1831. Interestingly, in his reviews, Belinsky often approved of the work in a highly favorable way.

28. Nestor Kukol'nik, a dramatist of middling talent, was primarily an author of patriotic plays on historical themes, his most famous being his 1832 work *The Hand of the Almighty Has Saved the Fatherland* (*Ruka vsevyshnego otechestvo spasla*). His fans called him the Russian Goethe; his detractors, in a play on his name, labeled his dramas *kukol'nye komedii,* or "puppet comedies."

immediately to seize upon every nuance, every barely noticeable characteristic. In Moscow, tragedies are loved even by merchants both with and without beards. Such a state of affairs is not surprising if only because most of the people in this group are difficult to arouse. Indeed, they succumb to only the most powerful emotions. Give them a fistfight that goes from one side of the room to another or a struggle between mastiffs and the famous bear Akhan. Should these merchants decide to go to the theater, give them Mochalov, whom they call Mocha*lov.* For one of his benefit performances, they will pay a hundred, two hundred, or even more for a box for which they could pay less than fifty. Our merchants absolutely love Mochalov; long before and after a performance, they love to stroke their beards and tell their acquaintances, "*You would not believe how much I had to pay for tickets to see him!*" Such boasting is a purely Muscovite feature, something that would never happen in Petersburg![29]

The public of the Alexander Theater in Petersburg is not at all like its counterpart in Moscow; this is a "public" in the current and genuine sense of this word. The public of the Alexander Theater does not have varying social strata; rather, it is made up entirely of working people of a well-known type. It does not have varying biases, opinions, and tastes. It demands only one thing; it seeks to be satisfied with only one thing. The public of the Alexander Theater never contradicts itself; it always remains true to who and what it is. It is a single individual, a single face. It is not a plurality of people but one person, solid, properly dressed, neither excessively demanding nor pliant. The public of the Alexander Theater fears any kind of an extreme and constantly holds to the judicious middle; it is an extremely honorable person with a well-intentioned exterior. Its members are akin to the most respected circles in Germany and France, that is, bourgeoisie and philistines. The public of the Alexander Theater are completely at home in its confines. Here they are so easy and free.

29. Consider this 1843 ditty entitled "The Petersburg Theatergoer" ("Peterburgskii teatral") written by Vladimir Zotov about merchant-"beards": "He lives only for the stage / He raves about it alone / And hardly does he see and hear it /Then passion grips him to the bone. / He begins his life at one / When the theater opens its door / But until that time, he suffers, waits, and grieves / More dead than alive, and wanting more." (*On odnim teatrom dyshit / Bredit tol'ko im odnim/ I ego lish' visit, slyshit / Strast'iu k zrelishham tomim. / Zhizn' svoiu on nachinaet / V chas, kogda v teatr idet / A do toi gory stradaet / Zhdet, tomitisa, ne zhivet.*) Quoted in I. Ignatov, *Teatr i zriteli: Chast' I. Pervaia polovina XIX st.* (Moscow: Zadruga, 1916), 212.

They do not like to be seen among "foreigners" who, incidentally, never go there. Individuals from elevated spheres and circles sometimes drop in at the Alexander Theater but only to see Gogol's plays. The regular public there soundly disapproves of such pieces and looks upon them with well-deserved contempt. (Such individuals dislike bawdiness and trivialities and see Gogol's dramas as an affront to their refined and high societal tastes.) People who do not belong to high society, who do not sympathize with the public of the Alexander Theater, and who feel that they are "foreigners" there go to the Mikhailovsky Theater.[30] And if they do not go there because they do not know French, they go nowhere at all.

Such a circumstance is most fortunate for the public of the Alexander Theater because it does not allow itself to be colorful or diverse but exudes only one hue, one strictly determined character. So if there is to be any applause in the Alexander Theater, everyone must clap their hands, and if there is silence there, it is because everyone is dissatisfied with what they have seen. Neither dramatic writers nor actors, if they are quick-witted people, dare risk putting their foot where it does not belong. One writes, the other acts—always without taking any chances, for they know how to please their public. Gratitude for services rendered—this quality of noble souls is one of the most praiseworthy features of the public of the Alexander Theater. Its members love their actors and do not stint on curtain calls or applause. With rapturous clapping, they greet their favorites, from Karatygin to Grigoriev the First inclusive.[31] But they do not

30. The Mikhailovsky Theater was built by the architect Alexander Bryullov in 1831–33 to honor Nicholas I's young brother, Mikhail Romanov. At this time, it hosted companies for Italian, German, and French opera and drama. The audience members for the Mikhailovsky Theater were far more restrained than their colleagues at the Alexander. "The Mikhailovsky Theater," a critic wrote in 1839, "is host to a public that is intelligent, educated, and impassive. . . . They applaud little and [after a performance] call for the actors onstage rarely, but their approval is valued highly." *Syn otechestva,* vol. 9 (1839); quoted in Ignatov, *Teatr i zriteli,* 201–2.

31. The same critic who wrote about the Mikhailovsky Theater noted also about its rival: "The Alexander Theater attracts an audience that is exclusively Russian. Provincials, on the following evening after their arrival to town, consider it their duty to visit there. How kind and undemanding is the public at the Alexander Theater! . . . In all of Europe, perhaps, there is not a single audience who enjoys the theater with such fanaticism as they. They love to make a fuss with their money; their palms hurt from applauding; the theater shakes at its foundation from the noise and cheers with which they greet a female actor." Ibid.

Also consider one of the many physiologies of the audience of the Alexander Theater in which spectators are considered both physically and socially: rows and occupations. "Iumoristika: Zametki peterburskgo zevaki; Teatral-liubitel," *Repertuar i Panteon,* bk. 3 (1845), 883–84.

act rashly and without calculation because they, like any educated and well-mannered audience, accord their rewards in proportion to an artist's services. Karatygin will do more than fifteen curtain calls in the course of one evening, but other artists will be called out more than once. The average number of curtain calls usually falls somewhere between five and fifteen, even though the audience has been known to summon Karatygin onstage no less than thirty times. The public of the Alexander Theater applauds without stopping, but they do so not from extravagance but because of the extremely apparent quality of all the plays that are given them, as well as of all the actors who play for their enjoyment. But if on that rare occasion an actor does not manage immediately to win over the public's favor, he does not hear any applause from it.

For the most part, the repertoire in Moscow features plays that have been written in Petersburg. Moscow can boast of only one great vaudeville actor: Mr. Sokolov. Moscow's other great vaudevillian, Mr. Korovkin, has left that city for Petersburg, exercising his full right to do so and venting his equally untrammeled willingness to make magnanimous sacrifices (on behalf of dramatic art). After all, everyone knows that the entire great foment in the Russian dramatic enterprise is occurring in Petersburg and that it is doing so right alongside all other types of literary production! But as regards theatrical writing in Petersburg or, more accurately speaking, about the dramatic repertoire of the Alexander Theater, it behooves us either to pass over it in silence or to comment upon it in a detailed way. We opt for the latter. Attention, readers! For our topic is both important and profound!

First of all, we must say that the repertoire of the Alexander Theater gives it every right to be seen as a playhouse that is both universal and all-inclusive. Classicism and romanticism, Racine and Shakespeare, Ozerov and Schiller, Molière and Scribe, tragedy and comedy, dramatic plays and vaudevilles, six-stopped iambic lyrics and vaudeville verse, genuine prose and hack writing—all is welcome on the stage of the Alexander Theater, without any partiality and with all possible graciousness. Indeed, when one sees one of these things alongside another onstage, one does not feel even the slightest surprise!

And Russian plays—what diversity do we have here! Historical plays, patriotic plays, plays taken from novels and stories, original plays, translated plays, and plays that render French mores into Russian ones! And the heroes of these plays: Alexander of Macedonia with royal pages and Turkish drums![32] We also have Lomonosov and Derzhavin, Sumarokov and Tredyakovsky, Charles XII and Queen Elizabeth, and Feodosiya Sidorovna and Susanin.[33] Why, one can't even begin to count them at all!

We must also say that, judging by what we have recently seen, the repertoire of the Alexander Theater, like the Alexander Theater itself, has acquired a definite character. Until 1834, it was the site of a futile battle between classicism and romanticism—a battle in which the former had the upper hand and in which even Karatygin had to perform the most ultra-romantic plays in a style that was classical, not romantic. But since 1834, with the appearance of Mr. Kukol'nik as a dramatic writer, the Alexander Theater has quickly begun to tilt toward romanticism; and since 1838, with the entry of Mr. [Nikolai] Polevoi on the dramatic scene, it has become decidedly ultraromantic if only because it was from this time on that the character of our newest dramatic plays—what we actually see today in our theater—finally took shape.

Before Kukol'nik and Polevoi, we regarded dramatic art with a respect that was somewhat mystical: Schiller and especially Shakespeare seemed to everyone to be unattainably great models of theatrical art. But after Polevoi and Kukol'nik, dramatic art became an industry unto itself; along-side machine tools and steam engines, it attended to our spiritual needs. Schiller and Shakespeare were cast aside,[34] and writing a play that was no

32. Belinsky is referring to Mikhail Markov's 1841 play *Alexander of Macedon* (*Aleksandr Masedonskii*).

33. Belinsky's reference here is to various popular plays at this time: Nikolai Polevoi's 1839 piece *Ode to the Very Wise Daughter of the Tsar, Felitsa* (*Oda premudroi tsarevne Felitse*); his 1842 drama *The Woods of Kostroma* (*Kostromskie lesa*); his 1842 work *A Comedy About the War of Fedosiya Sidorovna with the Chinese* (*Komediia o voine Fedos'i Sidorovny s kitaitsami*); and his 1843 drama *Lomonosov; or, A Life in Poetry* (*Lomonosov, ili zhizn' v poezii*).

Also in Belinsky's listings are such plays as Karl Topfer's 1839 work *Karl XII on the Return Home to Sweden* (*Karl XII auf dem Heimkehr*) and Pyotr Karatygin's *Elizabeth and the Earl of Essex* (*Elizaveta i graf Essekc*), a reworking of John Banks's 1682 play *The Unhappy Favorite; or, The Earl of Essex.*

34. Sadly, Belinsky's statement is true. For instance, Nikitenko reported, "The people at the Bol'shoi Theater gave a performance of *Richard* [*III*] presented in such a way that is seemed to come straight from Shakespeare's creative head. . . . But O Shakespeare! Shakespeare! What barbarians do you now encounter! Although the theater was full, one could count only eight or nine people who expressed their delight. Everyone else was mute, deaf, and sitting on their hands: there was neither rapture nor applause." Quoted in Ignatov, *Teatr i zriteli,* 207.

The story gets even better. In early 1841, a reporter from *Repertoire of the Russian Theater* noted that a performance of Shakespeare's *Coriolanus* was sold out for the first two performances but for the

worse than anything these two had written became easier than to write a historical novel "on order" or even to write history itself. The reason for such ease is that a play demands less time and perhaps can be cooked up for any benefit performance, especially when the artist for whom the benefit is given takes the time to order a work from an author a month or so in advance. That Mr. Kukol'nik is a gifted individual, this no one will argue, but he so genuinely opts for quantity over quality and for speed over thoughtful deliberation over plot, characters, and style. Hope in his talent, together with the absence of a discriminating public, negates all doubt that Mr. Kukol'nik will attain success. Mr. Polevoi has arrived much later than Mr. Kukol'nik, but he has decided that he needs neither a calling nor a talent for dramatic writing to be crowned with success on the stage of the Alexander Theater. Unfortunately, Mr. Kukol'nik bears out this truth because he is now appearing more and more rarely on stage. At the same time, also, Mr. Polevoi is garnering so many dramatic laurels that he is now considered the premier dramatist of the Alexander Theater. But Mr. Polevoi is not the only one who claims honor and glory there, for he shares the delight and ecstasy of the public with Mr. Obodovsky.

Mr. Obodovsky has sometimes been cited for his infrequent translations, such as the verse of Schiller's *Don Carlos.*[35] At that time, such pieces accorded him fame and sometimes even glory. But in recent times, Mr. Obodovsky has surpassed only Mr. Polevoi in the quantity and the hastiness of his dramatic reworkings. But how can one not envy the laurels garnered by both these dramatists? And how can one also not envy the happiness of the public of the Alexander Theater? After all, it is happier than the English public, who have only Shakespeare, and the German public, who have only Schiller. Indeed, in the personages of Messrs. Polevoi and Obodovsky, the public of the Alexander Theater suddenly has both Shakespeare and Schiller! Mr. Polevoi is the Shakespeare for the public of

third was curiously lacking an audience: "Wishing, no matter what, to see *Coriolanus,* I again set out for the Alexander Theater. Thank God, the sign that said sold out was no longer there. But when I entered the hall . . . I was greatly surprised to see that it was more than half empty. 'What is going on?' I thought. . . . Had all of St. Petersburg seen the play in the first two performances? Or had we made a mistake? Was this the day for *Coriolanus*? We looked at the poster. Yes, it said that *Coriolanus* was playing . . . only this time without *A Young Man at Sixty* and *Tarantella* . . . the plays *or nonplays* that had accompanied *Coriolanus* previously." Quoted in Ignatov, *Teatr i zriteli,* 224–25, italics in the original.

35. Johann Schiller published his poetic drama *Don Carlos* in 1787.

the Alexander Theater, and Mr. Obodovsky is its Schiller. The former is known for the diversity of his genius and for his profound knowledge of the human heart, the latter for the wealth of his lyrical sentiments, which pour forth like a stream of fiery lava. In those moments when Polevoi lacks genius or reveals shortcomings in matters of the heart, he usually comes running in with ballet scenes in which, to the tune of drawn-out and plaintive music, the most dear parents bid farewell to their tender children, or a faithful spouse takes leave of an adoring lover.[36] Similarly, in those instances when Obodovsky momentarily exhausts the native springs of his stormy, fiery passions, he quickly turns to dance, forcing the hero (and sometimes the heroine) of some pathetically patriotic drama to perform some kind of national two-step.[37]

People accuse Mr. Obodovsky of imitating Mr. Polevoi; but after all, Schiller also imitated Shakespeare! People likewise accuse Mr. Polevoi of stealing from Shakespeare, Goethe, Molière, Hugo, Dumas, and others, but what he has done is neither stealing nor borrowing. Everyone knows that Shakespeare took whatever he wanted, no matter where he found it, and Mr. Polevoi, in his capacity of Shakespeare of the Alexander Theater, does likewise. Mr. Polevoi writes dramas, comedies, and vaudevilles; but Shakespeare wrote only dramas and comedies. So it must be that the genius of Polevoi is more sweeping than the genius of Shakespeare. Schiller wrote only dramas, never comedies; Mr. Obodovsky also writes only dramas, not comedies. Mr. Polevoi began his dramatic career by imitating Shakespeare's *Hamlet;*[38] Mr. Obodovsky began his dramatic career with a

36. Belinsky is mocking Polevoi's 1838 drama *Grandfather of the Russian Navy* (*Dedushka russkogo flota*) and the previously cited play, *Lomonosov; or, A Life in Poetry.*

Belinsky was on dangerous footing, though, because Nicholas I was one of Polevoi's greatest fans. "The emperor is grateful to you," Benkendorf once wrote to Polevoi. "He has ordered me to tell you that although he has never doubted your extraordinary talents, he has never surmised that you were capable of such dramatic art. He asks you, he orders you to write for the theater. Give me everything that you will write. The emperor himself will read it all." Quoted in Ignatov, *Teatr i zriteli,* 208.

37. Here Belinsky is referring to Obodovsky's 1842 drama *A Russian Boyar's Wife of the Seventeenth Century: A Dramatic Piece in One Act with Wedding Festivities and Dances* (*Russkaia boiarynia XVII stoletiia: Dramaticheskoe predstavlenie v odnom deistvii s svadebnymi deistviiami i pliaskami*).

38. Belinsky has in mind here Polevoi's 1838 drama *Ugolino.* It should also be noted that Polevoi also translated *Hamlet* for the Russian stage in 1837, his goal being to reflect in the sufferings of the Danish prince the tragic fate of his own generation: the fear that had seized Russian progressives in the wake of the unsuccessful Decembrist Revolt of 1825. Polevoi's translation also gave birth to "Russian Hamletism," the tendency by national philosophers and writers to interpret the social and

translation of Schiller's *Don Carlos.* Like Shakespeare, Mr. Polevoi began his dramatic writing only as a mature man, and until he attained success, he, also like Shakespeare, received his training in the various forms of art that are innate to immature youth. Also as did the great English writer, Mr. Polevoi began his dramatic career by writing several lyrical pieces of which, at that time, the Russian public was made aware, courtesy of Mr. Svin'in. Mr. Obodovosky, like Schiller, began to write plays during the years of his fiery youth. Perhaps people will object to what we are saying, noting that Shakespeare never resorted to ballet scenes and that Schiller never forced his heroes to dance, so one should not posit any absolute similarities between these writers and Messrs. Polevoi and Obodovsky. Moreover, these same people will see dances and ballet scenes not as shortcomings of the Alexander Theater but rather as the apex of its new dramatic art. After Shakespeare and Schiller, dramatic art had to move forward—and so it did. Mr. Polevoi's drama gave special importance to the minuet and Mr. Obodovsky's pieces to the staccato quickness of the Ukrainian trepak. If anything, such effects show the middle age of the first writer and the youth of the second.[39]

As regards the differences between the careers of Shakespeare and Schiller and those of Messrs. Polevoi and Obodovsky, one can name a few: Shakespeare began his career in an unhappy way, Mr. Polevoi in a happy one. Shakespeare was not seduced by fame but looked at it with the smile of biting British humor. By contrast, Mr. Polevoi is fully capable of delighting in all the accumulated laurels that people have heaped on him on the stage of the Alexander Theater. Schiller was reviled in his youth and commanded respect only when he reached maturity. Mr. Obodovsky has been applauded and respected from the very day he began his dramatic career.

Indeed, were it not for the hard work and diligence of these worthy dramatists, Russian theater would have collapsed altogether because there

psychological plight of the Russian intelligentsia in the light of Shakespeare's character. For more on Belinsky's assessment of the Hamlet motif in Polevoi's work, see his article "Ugolino. Dramaticheskoe predstavlenie: Sochinenie Nikolai Polevogo 1838 goda," in Belinskii, *Polnoe sobranie sochinenii,* vol. 2 (1953), 437–48.

39. At this time, Polevoi was forty-nine; Obodovsky was thirty-eight. Obodovsky's play *Velizarius* was a reworking of the German playwright Eduard von Schenk's 1829 work of the same name.

would be no dramatic literature at all. In fact, it is only now, when the Russian theater is holding its own, that Messrs. Polevoi and Obodovsky can be called our Russian dramatic Atlantises. Usually, these two men operate in this way: When the theater has nothing left to stage, they write a new play, which is performed about fifty times in a row and then never again. Sometimes Mr. Obodovsky comforts the public of the Alexander Theater with his incomparable drama *Velizarius;*[40] other times he thrills the audience with his even more incomparable *A Russian Lady of the Seventeenth Century.* Mr. Polevoi particularly charms the public of the Alexander Theater with wondrous works of his creative genius, for example, *Elena Glinskaya*[41] and *Lomonosov.* The last one was performed nineteen times in a row in a very short period; the last stagings of the play were during Shrovetide in 1843. Was it, or will it be, performed a twentieth time? This we do not know; but as one newspaper wrote regarding the many stagings of *Lomonosov:* "After ten times in a row, the thing is already old! Everyone has seen it, everyone has enjoyed it, and whatever value it had is gone! If *Lomonosov* had been performed twice a week, it would have retained its freshness for a year. But now it is Shrovetide, and with the coming of Lent, the thing will be like a fish soup, which one likes the first time around but which gets boring when it is served up over and over again!"[42] We are totally at odds with such an assessment. Whatever is splendid will remain so, no matter how many times one enjoys it. *Woe from Wit* and *The Inspector General* will never be like warmed-up fish soup, nor will they ever be Shrovetide plays. It is very important for plays like *A Russian Lady of the Seventeenth Century* and *Lomonosov* to be performed nineteen times in the course of twenty days.

Mr. Polevoi's *Elena Glinskaya* is a parody of Shakespeare's *Macbeth* with borrowings from Walter Scott's novel *The Kenilworth.*[43] His *Lomonosov* is a reworking of a novel entitled *A Biography of Lomonosov,* written by Mr.

40. Platon Obodovsky's play *Velizarius* appeared in 1836.

41. Polevoi wrote *Elena Glinskaya* in 1839.

42. Surprisingly, the citation is from Faddei Bulgarin. See F. Bulgarin, "Smes'. Zhurnal'naia vsiakaia vsiachina," *Severnaia pchela,* February 15, 1843, 2.

43. In truth, *The Kenilworth Castle* (*Zamok Kenil'vort*) was a dramatization of Scott's 1821 novel *Kenilworth.*

Ksenofont Polevoi.[44] His *Parasha the Siberian Woman*[45] is taken from an old novel of Madame Cottin's, entitled *Elizabeth L. (Lupalova); or, The Trials and Travails of a Family, Which Is First Exiled to Siberia and Then Returns from There: A Remarkable Happening.*[46] His *Death and Honor!*[47] comes from Michel Masson's story "A Grain of Sand."[48] Indeed, there is no end to our list of sources through which Mr. Polevoi has rummaged to concoct his dramatic pieces. In this regard, he has far outstripped our well-known borrower of dramas, Knyazhnin.[49] In his rivalry with well-known dramatists from other countries, Mr. Polevoi wishes in no way to cede first place, if not in productivity, then also in talent to our native greats. He himself combines the talents of Il'in, Ivanov, and Prince Shakovskoi. In a word, this Sumarokov of our times, this many-sided, fruitful, active, and so very gifted individual is indeed just like the Sumarokov of the seventies of the preceding century; he is the diligent father of the Russian theater.

We would be acting unjustly if, in this survey of contemporary dramatic geniuses, we forgot to mention Messrs. R.Z. and V.Z.,[50] who, with great success, have followed Messrs. Polevoi and Obodovsky in pursuing an occupation in the dramatic field. Both these individuals are highly gifted and extremely productive. The first, though, is more of a classical writer, while the second is more of a romantic one. Generally speaking, though, such qualities as freshness, facility of style, and dramatic content rest primarily with the latter, not the former.

As regards vaudevillists and, generally speaking, translator-reworkers and writers of trifling plays—we will not list all of them here.[51] But, without

44. Ksenofont Polevoi wrote *Mikhail Vasilievich Lomonosov* in 1836.

45. Nikolai Polevoi's play *Parasha the Siberian Woman* (*Parasha-Sibiriachka*) appeared in 1840.

46. Most likely, the reference is to a Russian translation of Madame Cottin's 1806 novel *Elisabeth, ou les Exiles de Siberie.*

47. More accurately, Polevoi wrote his play *Death or Honor!* (*Smert' ili chest'!*) in 1839.

48. Michel Masson's story "Grain of Sand" ("Le Grain de Sable") was published in Paris in 1833.

49. From the late eighteenth century on, Yakov Knyazhnin enjoyed an unenviable reputation as an improviser upon subjects by Voltaire, Metastasio, Molière, and Goldoni. In fact, Knyazhnin's "borrowings" from dramatists were so well known in Russian society that even Pushkin, in the first chapter of *Eugene Onegin,* called Knyazhnin "imitative" ("*pereimchivyi*").

50. Belinsky is referring to the father-and-son dramatists Rafail and Vladimir Zotov.

51. Vaudevilles at the Alexander Theater grew steadily in this period. In the 1832–33 season, 41 vaudevilles were staged; in the 1836–37 season, 71; in the 1840–41 season, 99; and in the 1846–47 season, 99. Further, during this period, vaudevilles often made up roughly two-thirds of the annual repertoire of Russian theaters. K. Derzhavin, *Epokhi Alexansandrinskoi stseny* (Leningrad: Lengikhl,

a doubt, first place belongs to the gifted actor of the Alexander Theater, Mr. P. Karatygin. In Karatygin's vaudevilles there is sometimes a certain something that aligns them with the best qualities of this genre and that, more than other vaudevilles around, makes them most like Russian ones. We will not say that among the many vaudevillists of the Alexander Theater there cannot be found two or three people who are not with some degree of talent. But the indisputable truth is that the vaudeville has killed both the stage and the theater and that it is particularly in this genre that French content has been revamped along the lines of Russian mores.[52] The vaudeville is the child of French life, French humor, and French wit, one that is light and graceful like the bubbly foam of champagne. We are extremely alien to those pedants who focus their attention only on things that are weighty and serious and who dismiss everything that is light and merry as trifles. We will not compare the very best French vaudevilles with the dramas of Shakespeare or the tragedies of Schiller. Indeed, we would rather focus our efforts on a decent vaudeville or even a simple merry farce than on a middling tragedy. Simply put, we would rather laugh than yawn. But we would go to see a vaudeville or a farce only at the Mikhailovsky Theater, and only because we would want to see the French actors in it. We would want to enjoy the way they act *ensemble,* so replete with taste, decorum, and grace even when these actors perform a play that is not rich in sense and thought. The Russian vaudeville is as fraudulent as its English or German counterparts because the genre is the property of French humor. Like a Russian folk song or a story by Krylov, it defies translation. Our translators of French vaudevilles translate words, but they leave behind the life, wit, and grace of the original. Their witticisms are heavy, their puns grate on the ear, their jokes and remarks appeal to the minds and hearts of bureaucrats of the fifteenth class. Furthermore, these translations for the stage are hardly a godsend because our actors may play Frenchmen but, out of spite, they remain Russians—just as French actors, when performing *The Inspector*

1932), 36; A. Vasil'ev, "Lekgaia komediia i vodevil' i 'Bal'zaminovskaia trilogiia' A. N. Ostrovskogo," *Uchenye zapiski: Fakul'tet iazyka i literatury; Kafedra russkoi i vseobshchei literatury; Rostovskii na Donu gosudarstvennyi pedagogichekii institut,* vol. 3 (1940), 84.

52. Belinsky's misgivings aside, it is worth noting that of the more than 1,606 plays of various genres staged at the Alexander Theater between the years 1826 and 1855, 850 of them were vaudevilles. Of these, 520 were reworkings from the French, and 330 were originals. M. Paushkin, *Staryi russkii vodevil'* (Moscow: Khudozhestvennaia literatura, 1937), 17

General, act like Frenchmen. We repeat: the vaudeville is a wonderful thing in French, when acted out on the French stage, and when performed by French actors. It cannot be imitated by or translated into other languages. The Russian, German, and English vaudeville will always be a parody of the French vaudeville.[53] Not long ago a Russian newspaper published an article saying that as long as our vaudevilles imitate French ones, they are good for nothing. The same newspaper, though, also said that Russian vaudevilles were beginning to stand on their own and becoming very good—and even purer than their French counterparts.[54] Perhaps such an allegation is so, but only, we confess, if we should happen to see a Russian vaudeville that could actually stand on its own. But such a thing always hobbles along, and looking at it, we unwillingly recall the poetry of a Russian folk song:

> Ah, what looks like scissors is really a pitchfork.
> And what looks like a stream is really a rake!
> And what looks like a head is really a barrel for beer!
> And what looks like an eye is really a dimple!
> And what looks like a lip is really a finger![55]

53. Belinsky was not the only one among the literary progressives who disliked the vaudeville. For instance, Gogol, notwithstanding his own penchant for literary buffoonery and slapstick, wrote in an article "The Petersburg Stage for 1835–1836" ("Peterburskaia stsena v 1835–1836 godakh"), "What is now playing on our stage? The melodrama and the vaudeville, those illegitimate children of literature. . . . These light playthings could be born only in France whose [national] character lacks a profound physiognomy.

"But what happens . . . when one of our corpulent but witty and intelligent merchants who, having known nothing on his foot but a heavy boot, now tries on a narrow slipper, and a second remains in his boots but is the first to dance a French quadrille? That is our national vaudeville."

Among Russian dramatists, though, the vaudeville had its supporters. For instance, Pyotr Karatygin wrote, "The poor vaudeville! How much slander does it endure! How it is despised, almost trampled in the mud, and called an illegitimate child of art. . . . Why cannot we Russians see its tie to small light comedy . . . and that [from it] comes *balagan*-like farce, buffoonery, and clowning-about?" Quoted in Paushkin, *Staryi russkii vodevil',* 17.

Similarly, the actor Dmitri Lensky wrote in a theatrical couplet, "Will the vaudeville last for long? / Will it attain a ripe old age if it did? / But it would lose all its charm / If it did not babble on like a kid." (*Vodevil' kogda byl dolgovechnym? / Glubokoi starosti kogda on dostigal? / Dal esli b on ne lepetal rebenkom rezvym i bespechnym / On vsiu by prelest' poterial!*) Quoted in Paushkin, *Staryi russkii vodevil',* 17.

54. Belinsky is referring to Polevoi's review of Karatygin's vaudeville *The Bakery; or, The Petersburg German* (*Bulochnaia, ili Peterburgskii nemets*). See N. Polevoi, "Smes'. Zhurnal'naia vsiakaia vsiachina," *Severnaia pchela,* October 8, 1843, 4.

55. The citation is from a *bylina,* or folk heroic poem, "Dmitri Vasilievich and Domna Faleevna," published in M. Sukhanov's 1840 anthology *Ancient Russian Poems* (*Drevnie russkie stikhotvoreniia*).

Russian reworkings of French dramas are in especially great demand. Indeed, they make up a large part of our contemporary repertoire. The reason for their popularity is obvious: the public wants original plays and demands that the stage show Russian life and mores. Our homegrown dramatists, though, are poor in ideas and plots, so there is only one thing left to do. They must take a French play and translate it word for word. The action (which essentially can take place only in France) is moved to the Saratov[56] region or to Petersburg; the French names of the characters assume Russian ones. A prefect becomes the head of a section; an abbot becomes a seminarian; a brilliant society lady becomes a *barinya;* a lady-in-waiting becomes a maid, and so on. About these original plays, there is nothing more to say. At the very least, such reworkings have content, a beginning, a high point, and a denouement; original plays can do well without any other of the extra niceties of dramatic content. The public, no matter who they are, does not want to know that drama, no matter what kind it is, even if it is taken from contemporary society, must first and foremost be an accurate mirror of the life of contemporary society. The society, depicted by our dramas, might as well be Arab, not Russian. No matter what kind of play it is, no matter what its content, no matter what social group it depicts—high society, noble, bureaucrat, merchant, peasant—and no matter where it takes place—a salon, eating house, square, a boat—the content is always the same. Idiot parents have a sweet, educated daughter in love with a young man who is charming but poor. Usually, this young man is an officer, but from time to time, for the sake of diversity, he is a bureaucrat. The girl's parents, though, want to marry her off to some fool, psychotic, scoundrel, or all of them put together. Sometimes, the content is just the reverse. An ambitious mother and father have a son—the ideal of young manhood (i.e., an individual without color or character). He is in love with the *daughter of poor but noble parents.* Such individuals are the ideal of all that is sound and good; they are types that can find a place for themselves only in vaudevilles: models who espouse all kinds of perfection and who appear everywhere but in life. The young man's parents want to hitch him, that is, to marry him off to someone he does not love. By the end of the play, though, virtue is rewarded and vice is published. The lovebirds marry, their

56. Saratov is some four hundred miles southeast of Moscow.

very dear parents bless them, and the duped villain who has come between them is mocked by the audience. The action of such a play always follows this pattern: the maiden, alone and with a book in her hands, complains to her parents and reads sentiments about "the heart which loves without asking the permission of others." Suddenly the maiden says, "Oh! It is you, Dmitri Ivanovich or Nikolai Alexandrovich!" He responds, "Oh! It is I, Lyubov Petrovna or Ivanovna, or something else. . . . How glad I am that we are *alone!*" Having uttered such words, the tender lover kisses the little hand of his beloved. Notice that he has to kiss it without fail, otherwise the public would have no other way of knowing that this brave officer or virtuous office worker is precisely a lover or a fiancé! We have always been surprised by the matchless art of our dramatists, the way they hint so deftly and precisely at the relationships among the characters in their dramatic works. Later in such a play, the heroine asks her lover to leave so that her mommy and daddy do not see him. But he continues to kiss her little hand and to say how unhappy he is, that he is dying from torment, and that he will choose any means to pursue his love. Finally, he, for the last time, kisses her little hand and leaves.

There now enters the "villain" who immediately kisses the same little hand once, twice, three times, even more, depending on the circumstances. The young maiden pouts her lips and pours forth her feelings; mommy or daddy scold and threaten her; finally, a rich uncle helps her beloved, or the "villain" is shown to be a scoundrel. The dear ones bring their hands together as a couple in love. The hero grins tenderly, and so that he not stand on stage without anything to do, he takes up kissing the little hands of his intended, even smacking his lips. The young maiden smiles sweetly, if affectedly, as if reluctantly allowing her lover to kiss her hand. Looking at such things, one unwillingly exclaims:

> From whom have their portraits been drawn?
> From where have their conversations been heard?
> And should such things truly belong to them,
> We still think the whole thing absurd.[57]

57. Belinsky is quoting from Lermontov's 1840 poem "The Journalist, Reader, and Writer" ("Zhurnalist, chitatel' i pisatel' ").

If one would take our dramas seriously, one would think that the only thing that people do in holy Russia is fall in love, marry people whom they cherish, and until they do, keep kissing the petite hands of their beloved. This is a mirror of life, of reality, of society! The time has come to understand why we shoot blanks into the air; why we join battle with windmills and boars, not with knights and *bogatyrs;* why we depict rag dolls, not living people; and why we portray the world of edifying fairy tales that can amuse seven-year-olds, not contemporary society! The time has also come to understand that lovebirds, when they meet each other (even if they are the least bit like genuine people) talk less and less about their love and more and more about completely superfluous and insignificant things. Lovers understand each other in a silent way. Herein lies the author's art: to make his characters acknowledge their love before the public but without saying a word about it. Of course, lovers can speak about love, not in vulgar, worn-out phrases but in words that are new, spontaneous, and filled with significance and soul.

In our dramas, "lovers"—men as well as women—are the most colorless and consequently the most boring figures. They are simply puppets set in motion by an author who pulls their strings. Such a development is understandable: These "lovers" exist not for themselves but only to facilitate the external action of the play. That is why we always feel sorry for those actors whom evil fate has doomed to play the roles of male and female lovers. To them goes all the greater honor if they manage not to embellish their parts but only to play their roles with as much vulgarity as possible. Why do our dramatists always put forth such ill-starred lovers? Because with such characters, they do not have to put any content in their plays, that is, a knowledge of life, people, society, and the whys and wherefores of existence. Furthermore, our dramatists seek only to amuse the public with eccentrics and original types. They concoct characters who cannot be found anywhere; they attack vices that have nothing wicked about them; they laugh at mores they do not know and cling to a society to which they lack access. They usually poke fun at the merchant who has shaved off his beard, the young man who has returned from abroad with a beard, and the young lass who rides horseback and loves cavalcades. Simply put, our dramatists scoff at the cut of a dress, a hairstyle, the French language, a lorgnette, and yellow gloves. And God help us! What models of virtue do our dramatists draw from and put forth! Indeed, our comedy is exactly the same as it was in Fonvizin's time: stupid characters who are sometimes amusing, though caricatured, and smart ones who are always boring and naive.

Our tragedies are as mournful as our comedies. They depict Russian life with the same truthfulness but with even less success because they portray historical Russian life only from its elevated aspects. Leaving aside whatever worth these dramas may have, the main reason for their lack of success is their erroneous view of Russian history. They chase after nationality but continue to regard Russian history from a Western point of view. Otherwise, our Russian dramatists would not have begun looking for drama before the time of Peter the Great. Historical drama is possible only when there exists a struggle among various elements in governmental life. Not by chance did the apex of historical drama develop in England. Not by chance also did Shakespeare appear in England and not in some other country because nowhere else were the elements of governmental life so contradictory, so at war with themselves as in England. The key reason for this phenomenon was a triple conquest: the defeat of the local inhabitants first by the Romans, then by the Anglo-Saxons, and finally by the Normans. There was also England's struggle with Denmark, the centuries-old wars with France, and the era of religious reform or the struggle of the Protestants with the Catholics. Russian history has no such inner struggle of elements; that is why its character is more epic than dramatic. A welter of passions, a clash of inner elements, and a diverse society are the necessary conditions for drama. All three things are lacking in Russian history. For instance, Pushkin's *Boris Godunov*[58] is not a success, even though it is a deeply national work. Indeed, *Boris Godunov* is not so much a drama as it is a poem with a dramatic form. From this point of view, Pushkin's *Boris Godunov* is a great work, one that draws deeply from the treasures of the national spirit. Others of our dramatic poets have thought to see the national spirit in old Russian caftans and fur caps, not to mention folk speech. With this purely external national character, our dramatists have begun to dress Germans in folk costumes and put Russian proverbs in their mouths.[59] Thus, our tragedies are just the opposite of their

58. Pushkin wrote *Boris Godunov* in 1825.

59. Belinsky is again attacking the Slavophiles.

French pseudoclassical counterparts. French poets, in their tragedies, dress Frenchmen in Roman togas and force them to utter parodies of ancient idioms. But our poet-dramatists dress Frenchmen and Germans in Russian costumes and force upon them the specter and likeness of Russian speech. The words and clothes are Russian, but the feelings, sensations, images, and ideas are German and French.

Our commentary on our contemporary Russian drama also applies to our comedy and vaudeville. They too whirl about on effects that are extremely innocent and simple but also empty and trifling.

In their dramas, our authors rely on the emotional meeting of a father and son, of a mother and daughter, of lovers, and of husbands and wives. This sudden encounter—the unexpected acknowledgment that initial strangers are now close or loved ones—is always accompanied by cries, kisses, embraces, tears, "oohs," "ahs," and sometimes even by fainting. Similar effects always attain their goal: People applaud and go into ecstasies or frenzies. The comedy or the vaudeville (for some reason they are the same thing in our country) flaunts other effects that are just as insipid. In one such work, a smitten young man pretends to be insane and imagines himself as Eruslan Lazarevich[60] in order to be close to his love. He rides about stage on a stick and regards it as a horse, chasing after it with a whip, and speaking in the language of knightly Russian stories. The other characters in the play are so stupid that they actually see him as insane and allow him to deceive them. In the same play, one of the protagonists falls into a pool, puts an iron bucket on his head, and, to the applause and laughter of the audience, sings the aria of the knightly ruler from the opera *Ruslan and Lyudmila.*[61] About the value of these couplets, there is nothing to say. Let us just note that the public's wishes that these things be sung two or three times.

We should now expound upon the content of the most splendid works in our dramatic literature. Indeed, such an undertaking would take us very far because the subject is so interesting and vast that it would never be too late for it to serve as the topic of a special article. That is why we will limit ourselves only to those plays that the Petersburg public knows from the

60. Eruslan Lazarevich is the hero of a Russian folktale.

61. Belinsky is referring to the 1843 vaudeville by N. Aksel', *Liudmilla; or, A New Home of Madmen* (*Lyudmilla, ili novyi dom sumasshedshikh*).

Alexander Theater and that provincial spectators know from Mr. Pesotsky's *Repertoire and Pantheon.*[62] In other words, we are talking about dramatic works that could satisfy the best traits of the Alexander Theater since they have been graciously accepted by its public and acted out by its artists with great success. Of course, we will not list all of them, but the most remarkable are these: *Donna Luisa, the Portuguese Infant,* a historical drama in five acts, written in verse and with dancing and singing (the subject taken from a story by Mrs. Reybaud);[63] the first scene in the comedy *The New Minor* (the splendid work of Mr. Navrotsky);[64] *Alexander the Great,* a historical piece in five acts, written in verse with singing and military marches. The first act is entitled "Two Tsars"; the second, "The Conqueror"; the third, "The Amazon Queen"; the fourth, "Mother and Son"; and the fifth, "The Fall of Ancient Persia." The action here takes place in Persia about 350 years before the time of Christ (when royal pages and Turkish drums were the norm). Acts 1 and 2 take place in the ravines of Kilikia; act 3 in Babylon. The first scene of act 4 also takes place in Babylon, the second in a cave near Ecbatana. The first two scenes of act 5 occur in Persepolis, and the third on the border of Bactriana.[65]

Other pieces that have enjoyed success in the Alexander Theater include: *Neither Civilian nor Soldier, Neither Russian nor Frenchman; or, The Visitor from Abroad,* a romantic (!) vaudeville in one act;[66] *The Ship Master from Saardam; or, The Man Without a Name,* a *Russian* comedy in two acts;[67] *The Merchant Without a Beard, with Apologies to the Proverb:*

62. The citation is to the journal the *Repertoire of Russian and the Pantheon of All European Theaters* (*Repertuar russkogo i Panteon vsekh evropeiskikh teatrov*), published by Ivan Petrovich Pesotsky in St. Petersburg from 1842 to 1856.

63. The drama was written by Rafail Zotov, based on the 1838 story "Dona Luisa" by Madame Charles Reybaud.

64. In a review written in 1840, Belinsky castigated Sergei Navrotsky's 1840 comedy "The New Minor" ("Novyi nedorosl' ") for what he saw as its "Herculean lack of talent." Belinskii, *Polnoe sobranie sochinenii,* vol. 4 (1954), 336.

65. Ecbatana was the capital of Media, Persepolis the capital of Persia. Bactriana was a country located on land that is now part of Afghanistan, Uzbekistan, and Tajikistan; it was a crossroad for economic, religious, and artistic exchange between East and West.

66. Pyotr Grigoriev (the First)'s vaudeville *Neither Civilian nor Soldier, Neither Russian nor Frenchman; or, The Visitor from Abroad* (*Ni statskii, ni voennyi, ne russkii, i ne frantsuz, ili priezzhii iz-za granitsy*) was staged in St. Petersburg in 1841.

67. Rafail Zotov's *The Ship Master from Saardam; or, The Man Without a Name* (*Saardamskii korabel'nyi master, ili net imeni emu*) appeared in St. Petersburg in 1841.

Don't Trust a Horse in the Field or a Wife Who Is Free, an *original* comedy in three acts;[68] *A Boyar's Word; or, The Lacemaker from Yaroslavl*, a drama in two parts, the content of the first act borrowed from a segment of a French play;[69] *Ivan the Godfather,* an *original Russian tale* in two parts;[70] *The Schooner from New Carleby,* a *historical yarn* in two parts taken from the time of Peter the Great;[71] *The Forests of Kostroma,* a Russian tale in two acts with *singing;*[72] *Modern Beard Loving,* an original comedy in three parts;[73] *Prince Silver; or, Love and the Fatherland,* an original drama in four acts, written in verse;[74] *Father and Daughter,* a drama in five acts, written in verse and translated from the Italian;[75] *Elena Glinskaya,* a dramatic work;[76] *Christina, Queen of the Swedes,* a drama in three acts, translated from the German;[77] *Tsar Vasily Ivanovich Shuisky; or, Family Hatred,*[78] a dramatic work in five acts with a prologue, written in verse; and *Svyatoslav,* a dramatic work in four scenes, written in verse.[79]

We must also mention *A Great Actor; or, A Debutante's Love,*[80] a drama in *three* acts and *five* parts. Act 1 of part 1 is entitled "The Lamplighter of the Theater and the Flower Girl"; act 2 of part 2, "The Gamut of Passions"; and act 3 of part 3, "Riot in the Theater." Part 4 is entitled "The

68. *The Merchant Without a Beard, with Apologies to the Proverb: Don't Trust a Horse in the Field or a Wife Who Is Free* (*Sbritaia boroda vopreki poslovitse: ne ver' koniu v pole, a zhene v pole*) was an 1841 comedy by P. A. Smirnov.

69. Obodovsky's drama *A Boyar's Word; or, The Lacemaker from Yaroslavl'* (*Boiarskoe slovo, ili iaroslavskaia kruzhevnitsa*) appeared in 1841.

70. *Ivan the Godfather* (*Kum Ivan*) was written by Egor Alad'in in 1841.

71. Bulgarin penned *The Schooner from New Carleby* (*Shkuna Niukalebi*) in 1841.

72. Polevoi's *The Forests of Kostroma* (*Kostromskie lesa*) appeared in 1841.

73. *Modern Beard Loving* (*Sovremennoe borodoliubie*) was an 1841 comedy written by Dmitri Zubarev.

74. Nikolai Filimonov wrote *Prince Silver; or, Love and the Fatherland* (*Kniaz' serebriannyi, ili otchizna i liubov'*) in 1842.

75. Obodovsky's *Father and Daughter* (*Otets i doch'*) was staged in 1842.

76. Polevoi's *Elena Glinskaya* came to be in 1838.

77. *Christina, Queen of the Swedes* (*Kristina, koroleva shvedskaia*) was Obodovsky's 1842 translation of Wilhelm Vogel's 1841 play *Christine von Schweden.*

78. Obodovsky wrote *Tsar Vasily Ivanovich Shuisky; or, Family Hatred* (*Tsar' Ivanovich Shuisky, ili semeinaia nenavist'*) in 1842.

79. *Svyatoslav* was penned by Vladimir Zotov in 1842.

80. Pavel Kamensky's *A Great Actor; or, A Debutante's Love* (*Velikii akter, ili liubov' debiutanki*) appeared in 1842.

Reproachful Actress," and part 5, "Playing the Lyre at the Theater in Drury Lane Theater."[81]

We should also note *Our Wives Are Missing; or, The Bon Vivant Mayor,*[82] and *A Comedy About the Warrior Woman, Feodosiya Sidorovna, with the Chinese.*[83] The latter is a Siberian tale in two acts with singing and dancing. Act 1 bears the title "Russian Daring," *complete with dancing.* Mr. Pisheau and Mrs. Levkeeva will dance *in the Cossack style.* Act 2 is entitled "Chinese Bravery," *also with dancing.* Here Messrs. Sambursky, Svishchev, Timofeev, Volkov, and Nikolaev will dance *in the Chinese style.* Acts 1 and 2 also feature a choir singing national hymns.

The repertoire of the Alexander Theater also takes in *Lyudmila,* a drama in three parts, an imitation of the German ballade, "Lenore,"[84] and consisting of ballads and verses by V. A. Zhukovsky; *A Russian Lady of the Seventeenth Century,* a dramatic work in one act *with wedding dances and songs; Ruslan and Lyudmila Revisited; or, The New Insane Asylum,* a trifle-vaudeville in one act;[85] *Taking Petersburg Hostage,* a Russian dramatic tale in two acts; *The Magic Barrel; or, Dreaming for Real,* an ancient German fairy tale in two acts; *The Russian Sailor,* a historical tale;[86] *Once Upon a Time There Lived This Dog,* a vaudeville translated from the French;[87] *People of Novgorod,* a dramatic work in five acts, written in verse;[88] and *Cigarette,* a comedy in one act.[89]

81. The Drury Lane Theater, opened in 1663, is the oldest theater in England; it continues to stage performances to this day.

82. Pyotr Grigoriev the First, along with several others, wrote *Our Wives Are Missing; or, The Bon Vivant Mayor* (*Zheny nashi propali, ili maior bon-vivant*) in 1842.

83. Polevoi's *A Comedy About the Warrior, Feodosiya Sidorovna, with the Chinese* (*Komediia o voine Fedos'i Sidorovny s kitaitsami*) appeared in 1842.

84. "Lenore" was written by Gottfried Bürger in 1773. Bürger's bizarre piece is typical of the material from which Russian dramatists of the time drew their inspiration. In "Lenore," a ghostly rider, posing as Lenore's dead lover, carries the woman away on a macabre ride through an eerie night landscape illuminated by flashes of lightning. At its end, the rider is revealed as Death himself, a skeleton replete with a scythe and hourglass. Bürger's "Lenore," though, had a profound impact on the development of romanticism throughout Europe.

85. Aksel''s *Ruslan and Lyudmila Revisited; or, The New Insane Asylum* (*Eshche Ruslan i Liudmilla, ili novyi dom sumasshedshikh*) was staged in 1843.

86. Polevoi wrote *The Russian Sailor* (*Russkii moriak*) in 1844.

87. *Once Upon a Time There Lived This Dog* (*Zhila-byla odna sobaka*) appeared in 1844; the author is unknown.

88. Rafail Zotov wrote *People of Novgorod* (*Novgorodtsy*) in 1844.

89. Spectators enjoyed Polevoi's comedy *Cigarette* (*Sigarka*) in 1844.

Enough! We simply cannot list them all! But we do ask the reader to pay attention to the names of all these plays. The thoughts implicit in them open up an entire new world! Indeed, the titles of some of these plays can be the subject of an entire article. Even with translated works, the honor for coming up with witty, ingenious, and alluring names belongs to our Russian writers alone. For example, the name of one French play is a simple one: *Le Maître d'École;*[90] but translated into Russian, it bears the title: *The Schoolmaster; or, Teaching Idiots Is Like Treating the Dead.*[91] Another French play invested with Russian mores has the witty title *What We Have, We Don't Keep; And What We Have Lost, We Burst Out Crying.*[92] The well-known French play *The Husband in the Country*[93] has been translated with the title *Angel with the Wife at Home; Devil with People Outside.*[94] Many titles of plays show such homegrown wit, but in our view, there are also enough of them to show what our dramatic factory is like; after all, factories are known by their trademarks.

But the most harmful aspects of these dramatic-factory works are that they kill theatrical art. Dramatic works that feature reality and genuine characters unwittingly train even mediocre actors to learn not only the roles they must play but also life and reality itself. But our tragedies, dramas, *dramatic productions,* comedies, and vaudevilles focus not on reality and characters but on scenic effects that are melodramatic, amusing, or comic. In these works, there are neither personages nor characters, and artists, even the most talented, have unwittingly grown accustomed to playing them without any preparation or study, reflection or thought, and always in one and the same way. No matter what, they want to arouse only horror or laughter in their audiences. But who can blame them for that? This is what our dramatists demand from them; this is why the public rewards them with applause. About the truthful depiction of life, of characters—these

90. *Le Maître d' École* was penned by Joseph-Philippe Lockroy and Auguste Anicet-Bourgeois in 1841.

91. Karatygin the Second wrote *The Schoolmaster; or, Teaching Idiots Is Like Treating the Dead* (*Shkol'nyi uchitel', ili durakov uchit', chto mertvykh lechit'*) in 1842.

92. Sergei Soloviev's vaudeville *What We Have, We Don't Keep; And What We Have Lost, We Burst Out Crying* (*Chto imeem ne kranim, poteriavshi plachem*) appeared in 1843.

93. *The Husband in the Country* (*Le Mari à la Campagne*) was written by M. Bayard in 1844.

94. *Angel with the Wife at Home, Devil with People Outside* (*Doma angel s zhenoi, v liudiakh smotrit satanoi*) was written by Pavel Fyodorov in 1844.

are things that escape everyone's attention. Karatygin appears onstage and the public of the Alexander Theater already knows that it should go into ecstasy. Martynov appears onstage and spectators know that they must laugh. In light of such things, is it at all surprising that artists have, willingly or unwillingly, come to see their profession as a job and that for many of them, studying a role means merely to learn it by heart? As a result, art declines, talents fade, and the dramatic theater becomes a purely mechanical operation. But what keeps the public from being dissatisfied with their dramatists and actors is the same thing that keeps dramatists and artists from being dissatisfied with their public. And if everyone is satisfied, what else is needed?

In my article "Petersburg and Moscow," I noted that the middle strata of the Petersburg population has gone wild over high society and maintaining a "good tone." They have taken their passion for such things into the theater, and we have purposely listed the titles of many plays that have been staged at the Alexander Theater so as to acquaint our readers with the tone that is reigning in its sphere. To say literally everything that one should say about this subject, we must add that both the artists and the public of the Alexander Theater do not have a very sophisticated understanding of Gogol's dramatic talent. Such a shortcoming arises primarily because of the sharp expressions that fill Gogol's comedies and which can wear away at the bon ton of the partisans of the Alexander Theater. In light of such sharpness, it is not surprising to note that Gogol's comedies, whenever they are staged at the Alexander Theater, truly seem more like farces than comedies. That is why his play *The Marriage* failed decisively when it was first performed there.[95] It was only with the recent arrival of Shchepkin to the play that the Petersburg public took *The Marriage* for something new and unfamiliar, that it greeted each word of this comedy with hearty laughter and lively applause. But for such a thing to happen, it was necessary that Shchepkin play the role of Kochkaryov because his name brought to the stage not only the inveterate spectators of the Alexander Theater but

95. Gogol wrote *The Marriage (Zhenit'ba)* in 1842. Belinsky's remark is true. At its debut, the play was greeted by audiences with both boredom and hissing. See S. Danilov, *Gogol' i teatr* (Moscow: Gosudarstevennoe izdatel'stvo "Khudozhestvennaia literatura," 1936), 165–68.

others as well.[96] Is it any surprise that Petersburg actors (with the exception of Mr. Martynov) do not know how to play the roles created by Gogol? After all, they have grown accustomed to vaudevilles, which lack originality, life, and truthfulness, as well as to characters that are like puppets and dolls. But in Moscow, where the public is so extremely varied that it really is not a public at all—where people discuss and are concerned about art more than high society and good tone—there, in Moscow, Gogol's plays do extremely well. Along with Shchepkin, who is beyond words as the town governor, there are also Mr. Potanchikov, who plays the postmaster; Mr. Stepanov, who acts as the judge; and Mr. Orlov, who steps forth as Osip. But in Moscow, many things are played differently than in Petersburg. For instance, in Petersburg, the splendid play *Eight Years Older*[97] passed without comment, without any noise at all. In Moscow, though, it did splendidly, not only because it is a good drama but also because of the way Shchepkin played the role of the doctor and Mr. Samarin acted as the hero of the play.

Concluding this article, we repeat that Petersburg has a theatrical public, but Moscow has yet to have such a thing. As far as Petersburg is concerned, such an audience is an important advantage because the taste of the public there can and even must change with time. When this welcome turning point comes, the Petersburg theater will have a public that is not only educated but genuine, one that will function as one face, one individual. The authors of this article are still waiting for this turning point. In the meantime, we prefer to go to the Moscow Theater, which has more artists if not geniuses. At the Moscow Theater, the artists are richer in talent if not art; that is why the performances there are often quite successful. At the Moscow Theater also, actors stage Gogol's plays with special love and for a simple reason. The public there demands more creativity and thought from these plays, and from its actors, more inspiration and art rather than

96. Here Belinsky chooses to ignore two facts: *The Marriage* succeeded at the Alexander Theater only after the third performance in late 1842; and for the next five years, the play was staged rarely or disappeared altogether in the theatrical seasons from 1843 to 1848. B. Sokolov, *Gogol': Entsiklopediia* (Moscow: Algoritm, 2008), 177.

97. More accurately, *The Crime; or, Eight Years Older* (*Prestuplenie, ili vosem' let starshe*) was a play written by Auguste Arnould and Narcisse Fournier in 1837 and translated by Soloviev for the Russian stage in 1842.

just a "high tone." Finally, at the Moscow Theater, everyone judges things in his or her own way. They never agree with one another on anything, despite the fact that they are all very often equally close to the truth.

—A Theatergoer Ex Officio

The Bureaucrat

Nikolai Nekrasov

An individual of the judicious middle,
Who never wished for much in life,
He drank rowanberry liqueur before dinner
And foamy wine with his wife.

He ordered clothes at Kincherf's[1]
And for a long time (a forgivable fervor)
Nurtured a deep hope in his soul
To become a collegiate assessor.[2]

Since he had not the blood of nobles
But was of priestly strains,
He did not want his children
To be called nasty names.

Simple in looks and resigned to fate,
He held himself with a stoop.
But, unaccountably shy, he jumped from his chair
Whenever his elders came to snoop.

1. Kincherf's was a well-known clothing store that catered to actors and bureaucrats.
2. The position of "collegiate assessor" (*kollezhskii assessor*) occupied the eighth rank of the "Table of Ranks."

No matter what the reason or where he was,
From quarrels with the boss he shrank,
And took care that his walk, talk, laugh, and look
Were all in keeping with his rank.

Attentive and yieldingly meek
With relatives, his aunt, and his wife,
But with subordinates, he could,
Like any official, proudly vaunt his life.

At any time, he could scream and scold
Like all of us are wont to do.
He even made his eyebrows bend
When hell broke loose anew.

At a time when we appeal to reason,
When our age seeks to restrain the gut,
However anxious our existence,
We Russians do everything but.

Stocky hulks are rarely seen
We love to eat and drink—our fate.
And even though we twiddle our thumbs,
We rarely put on weight.

In these days, dear reader mine,
The proper place for the soul
Can be found, by the grace of God,
Even in a stagnant hole.

But my hero, though up with times,
Avoided the harmful influences of the age
And was simply a man, neither thick nor thin,
Fish nor fowl, dimwit nor sage.

On this collar there solemnly lay
An immensely fat, double chin,
But the space between his head and chest
Was so short that it seemed a sin.

Paralyzing stroke was a constant threat;
His spine was hunchbacked, so people claimed,
And his legs (I must whisper in your ear)
Were somewhat crooked—his nurse they blamed!!

Orphans and widows he did not assist,
But his solid belly waved to and fro.
He sometimes threw pennies to beggars:
A holy do-gooder from head to toe.

A wondrous, noble soul—with pride
So he proclaimed himself with élan,
And like all of us, for what faults he had
He blamed his wife and kids and clan.

At work, he was a model:
He never took a bribe or stole,
But for his wife, he said,
Bought a mansion atop a knoll.

A guarantee of carefree life,
This house was his greatest prize.
There were also Foma, Vanyusha, and Feklusha
Who all brought sweet tears to his eyes.

Anything extremely rich or poor
Disturbed him greatly. Order was his love.
All words that were harsh and daring
Made him shutter and seek solace from above.

He railed against writers—not without cause.
In fact, his face turned white, his body shook
Whenever a hated author garnered
Some official's kindly look.

He regarded books as a burden.
All stories were "tales"—things not nice.
He saw reading as a "waste of time"
And idleness as the mother of vice.

This is what he told his underlings.
Such thoughts are deep but extremely old,
And of all contemporary discoveries
He "paid fines" in cards when told.

It is time for me to tell you
How our model Russian, bureaucrat, and sage
Was mortally infected with a passion,
One that was common for our age.

A passion that sank its roots
Deep into our wide Russian land
Since we let the folk play whist
And watched the servant play this hand.

Preference is now the game to play:
How quickly, pleasantly the hours fly.
"Whoever invented this game was a genius!"
Said our hero, his face so sweet and sly.

He never enjoyed himself like this
How did he play?—That could make one cry!
A genius, perhaps, could give us a clue,
But since I'm here, I'll give it a try.

When dinner ended as it should,
Our hero, having crossed himself, went the extra mile.
Having ordered a table into the dining room,
He said with a kindhearted look and smile:

"What say, gentlemen, up for some fun?
Life is short, we don't have all day!"
So inspired, his breathing became quicker.
He forgot all about life; nothing else did he say.

His wife, his children fell by the wayside.
Like a druid, entranced, our hero starts.
For him, heaven and earth no longer existed
But merged in clubs and diamonds, spades and hearts.

Beyond cards, nothing did he know, hear, or see,
But he remembered every prize he won.
He hated players who were tightfisted and shy
But saw bets with bold ones as a lot of fun.

He was filled with deep admiration
For all winning hands or a trumped card.
He played whist without the least little fear,
But like many others, took losing hard.

When he lost, he was down at the mouth,
Angry, growling, like a ruffled cat.
But when luck was with him, he loved at every hand
To tap his fingers and say, "Take that!"

Like everyone, he uttered jokes,
He once said when others asked for more,
"Why, Pyotr Kuz'mich, you've served so long in court,
You really must know the law!"

Also like everyone, he poked fun
At jacks and queens, pretty but cold.
But about aces and other respected cards
He never made so bold.

Ladies and gentleman, perhaps you are yawning
At my well-intentioned story from spite.
You reproach me for excessive detail,
But I sing of triflings beyond your sight!

I sing of that which charms our Rus',
Of our days, wondrous to behold,
Of our life so full and rich and deep
Like that of the Crusades of old!

I'm not joking—Look with both your eyes!
From "native Moscow" to the sea in the West,
From the "stern Caucasus" to "Finnish cliffs"[3]
How our Slavic soul loves all that is best!

I confess my own passion for cards:
I really do like them a lot.
I lose my shirt, but I have to have them,
Otherwise I'll fall asleep on the spot.

What else can we do?—I ask you
Our saintly fathers were always at a feast or ball.
In spring they planted beets and cucumbers.
They hunted rabbits and wolves in the fall.

A pedigree dog, a stately horse
Amused them and aroused them so,
And eccentrics joined them at dinner
And sought to carry on the show.

3. Nekrasov is here paraphrasing several lines from Pushkin's 1831 poem "To the Slanderers of Russia" ("Klevetnikam Rossii").

Our saintly fathers loved to sit and talk,
Everyone at their beck and call.
They drank each other under the table
And fought like Russians with one and all.

We find our forefathers amusing,
But we outgrew them long ago.
Lucky us, we found our calling.
A sin to be idle, we play cards high and low.

Once a week, our most honored hero,
Tired of cards, takes to the street,
Attending benefits at the Alexander Theater
And paying twice the cost for a seat.

As was custom, he supported national genius
But thought a knowledge of drama a bore.
He loved when evil was punished in the end,
Along with wild shooting, blood, and gore.

Listening to a jester's couplets,
He lightly poked his wife.
Between acts, he loved to whisper to stately ladies.
Of such things, sly Petersburg is rife!

That drama needs passion and art,
That Shakespeare was one-of-a-kind
Was something he was so unsure of
That he daily kept changing his mind.

At work he was always well-intentioned.
He followed each and every rule,
So when satire reared its ugly head,
He thought its author a scoundrel and fool.

A pillar of society, a star of his world,
He cursed officials for taking bribes
But raged on, his heart exploding,
When writers published gibes.

Like all well-intentioned people,
He so was ashamed to see and read
Such "malicious" articles and stories
That he felt compelled to take the lead.

He drank twice as much as normal,
That's how annoyed he got,
And said that writers for their boldness
Should get Siberia for their lot.

—*N. Nekrasov*

The Omnibus: Scenes from Petersburg Country Life

Mikhail Kul'chitsky

Cast of Characters

Hero, a Petersburg German whose vocation seems to be unknown initially but who later seems to be something like a shoemaker
Mr. X, the hero's confidant
Mr. Z, another of the hero's confidants
Elephantine Gentleman
Average Lady
Boy, about ten years old, son of the *Average Lady*
Girl, about seven years old, daughter of the *Average Lady*
Bureaucrat, who wishes to pass for a fine diplomat
Sleepy Gentleman
Officer with a Huge Mustache
Gentleman with a Lorgnette
Gentleman in Glasses
Gentleman with a Stick
Gentleman in a Turban
Modest Young Maiden
Sensitive Lady
Merchant with a Beard
Conductor
Coachman

Passing Lad
Strange Officer
Attorney and several *Policemen*
Silent *Strollers* and *Passersby*

The action takes place at a dacha and also on the way to Petersburg.

Note: This play was written a long time ago, immediately after the first omnibus appeared in Petersburg, an event which, as often happens with the arrival of something new, was not without certain mishaps. As a result, all references to problems with omnibuses in this play should not be applied to contemporary conveyances of this sort because they function beautifully, are managed well, and are among the most useful contraptions in Petersburg.[1]

Act 1
A summer cottage outside of Petersburg. The month of July, but wet and cold. There is a tavern; from its windows one can hear the sounds of billiard balls knocking about. Surrounding the tavern are a park and other sights that recall the summer and the country. It is late afternoon. STROLLERS *take extreme pleasure in wandering paths made of crushed bricks.*

Scene 1
A GENTLEMAN IN GLASSES *and a* GENTLEMAN WITH A STICK.

GENTLEMAN IN GLASSES: Come on! Let's get on the omnibus.

1. The appearance of the "omnibus" was already a topic in literature. For instance, Nekrasov, in the already noted "Petersburg Dachas and Environs," sang an exaggerated paean to the vehicle which, the hope was, would transport passengers between the center of St. Petersburg and the dachas in the northern regions of the city. Beginning operation on May 15, 1844, the omnibus entered quickly in urban life and controversy. Cabbies, reeling from the competition posed by the vehicle, called it the "devil's puppet" (*chertovaia kukla*). See Oksman, *N. A. Nekrasov,* 56.

GENTLEMAN WITH A STICK: We have to ask the conductor when it leaves. Hey. Mr. Conductor!

[*The* CONDUCTOR *appears, an individual with an ordinary servant's mug and wearing a gold braid and a round hat.*]

GENTLEMAN WITH A STICK: When does the omnibus leave?

CONDUCTOR: At half-past nine.

GENTLEMAN WITH A STICK [*looking at his watch*]: That means in half an hour. It's exactly nine o'clock now.

CONDUCTOR: Yes. Only today we will seat earlier, at nine-fifteen.

GENTLEMAN IN GLASSES: What do you mean, "you will seat"?

CONDUCTOR: You know, to seat! Should you choose to get on, we will seat you, too.

GENTLEMAN IN GLASSES: Very well. But how come you are leaving earlier?

CONDUCTOR: All because there are a lot of people today, and it will take longer to seat them.

GENTLEMAN WITH A STICK: Can it be that all the seats are taken?

CONDUCTOR: No, nobody has taken any seats yet.

GENTLEMAN WITH A STICK: Give us two tickets, then.

CONDUCTOR: You don't need tickets. Just give me the money.

BOTH GENTLEMEN: Ha, ha, ha! Here's the money. Leave two seats for us.

CONDUCTOR: No, don't give me the money just yet. Better you give it to me when we start seating.

GENTLEMAN IN GLASSES: But how can that be, pal? You don't have any tickets, you don't sell any seats. So what are we supposed to do? Just sit in the carriage and wait?

CONDUCTOR: So you'll wait. You are waiting now already.

GENTLEMAN IN GLASSES: But isn't that a stupid thing to do?

CONDUCTOR: Well, if you don't want to wait, then go and take a walk; or here, sit down on the bench [*pointing to the bench*]; or do as the other gentlemen do: go to the pub [*pointing to the pub*]. . . . Perhaps you can get a bite to eat there . . .

GENTLEMAN IN GLASSES [*with an annoyed air*]: *C'est une bête!* Let's go.

[*They leave.*]

Scene 2

The GENTLEMAN IN A TURBAN, *with a grave and severe Asian face, and a* PASSING LADY *with special features.*

PASSING LADY: Si vous voulez partir avec cet omnibus, ne vous éloignez pas.

GENTLEMAN IN A TURBAN: Je crois qu'il vaut mieux prendre un billet.

[*They pass by.*]

Scene 3

MR. X *and* MR. Z (*very young people who could, in time, perhaps, become very fine shoemakers*).

MR. X: Hey, conductor! Mr. Conductor!

[*The* CONDUCTOR *appears.*]

MR. Z [*looking at the clock on the outside of the omnibus*]: Are you leaving soon?

CONDUCTOR [*also first looking at the clock and then scratching the back of his head*]: You can take your seats in five minutes; we'll be leaving in about twenty.

MR. X: But I thought we would take our seats in twenty minutes and leave in five. [*He laughs, pleased with himself.*]

[MR. Z *laughs, pleased with* MR. X.]

MR. X: OK, fine. All three of us will go. Here's fifty kopecks, give me five in change. I'm going—that's one. He's going [*pointing at* MR. Z.]—that's two. And there's also a third. That's three. He's over there [*pointing to the pub*]. Friedrich, komm hier!

VOICE FROM THE PUB: Nehmen Sie fur mich einen Platz! I'm starting another game. . . . I'm gonna win this one!

[*Exclamations from the pool hall can be heard.*]

MR. X: How about now? Can we take our seats?

CONDUCTOR [*again looking at his watch*]: Now you can take your seats!

MR. Z: God damn it! Where are the horses?

MR. X: You mean to tell me that there are no horses yet? Then why should we take our seats?

CONDUCTOR: It doesn't take long to harness the horses.

[*Puzzled,* MR. X *and* MR. Z *step aside.*]

Scene 4

An AVERAGE LADY, *a* BOY, *and a* GIRL.

AVERAGE LADY: Mr. Conductor! Here's for three tickets [*she gives him some money*]. Get in, children.

BOY: Oh, Mommy, how scary it is inside!

GIRL: Oh, it's so dark, so very dark.

[*They get in the omnibus; their mother follows them.*]

MR. X: God damn it, everyone's getting in. We should, too.

MR. Z: Friedrich! Hey, Friedrich! . . . Everyone's here.

[*They get into the omnibus.*]

Scene 5

A BUREAUCRAT, *who wishes to pass for a diplomat, with a great deal on his mind.*

BUREAUCRAT [*to* CONDUCTOR]: My dear! . . . Don't you think it's getting a bit crowded! [*He looks at the omnibus.*] Here's a four-spot; you owe me ten kopecks: that's right, isn't it? [*He takes the change.*] Much obliged!

[*He carefully boards the omnibus.*]

Scene 6

A MODEST YOUNG MAIDEN, *with an absolutely innocent look.*

MODEST YOUNG MAIDEN: Mr. Conductor! Let me in.

[*She takes fifteen kopecks from her bundle.*]

CONDUCTOR: Let me help you, miss.

[*He helps her with special care.*]

Scene 7

GENTLEMAN IN GLASSES *and the* GENTLEMAN WITH A STICK.

GENTLEMAN WITH A STICK: Hey, how about us? Let's get in, too.

GENTLEMAN IN GLASSES: We'll get in, we'll get in, but we have a problem. [*He motions his friend and half whispers*]: Do you have any money?

GENTLEMAN WITH A STICK: Not a kopeck.

GENTLEMAN IN GLASSES: Hm! . . . But I only have three ten-kopeck bits.

GENTLEMAN WITH A STICK: That's more than enough for where we want to go.

GENTLEMAN IN GLASSES: Nevertheless, I'm afraid.

GENTLEMAN WITH A STICK: Of what?

GENTLEMAN IN GLASSES: The devil knows what. . . . What if because so many people want to get on, the conductor decides to raise the fare and charge a quarter-spot instead of fifteen kopecks?

GENTLEMAN WITH A STICK: We can ask.

GENTLEMAN IN GLASSES: Please, you ask.

GENTLEMAN WITH A STICK: Why don't you want to ask?

GENTLEMAN IN GLASSES: Well, you see . . . er . . . To tell you the truth, pal, I'm afraid. . . . What if he says it will cost a quarter! That would be shame.

GENTLEMAN WITH A STICK: Why would that be shame? You'll simply go alone.

GENTLEMAN IN GLASSES: That's nonsense! In that case, we'd better get a cabbie.

[*They approach the omnibus.*]

GENTLEMAN WITH A STICK: Give me some money. [*To* CONDUCTOR] Hey, Mr. Conductor! How much does a ride cost?

CONDUCTOR: Fifteen kopecks silver.

GENTLEMAN WITH A STICK: Here's money for two.

[*Both get in.*]

Scene 8

A MERCHANT WITH A BEARD *and the* CONDUCTOR.

MERCHANT WITH A BEARD [*to* CONDUCTOR]: Most deeply respected one! The fare is still fifteen kopecks, isn't it? Yes? All right! Well, God bless you!

[*Breathing heavily, the* MERCHANT WITH A BEARD *boards the omnibus.*]

Act 2

In the omnibus.

On the right side of the omnibus sit the BOY, *the* AVERAGE LADY, *the* GIRL, *the* BUREAUCRAT, *the* MODEST YOUNG MAIDEN, *and the* MERCHANT WITH A BEARD. *On the left sit* MR. X, MR. Z, *the* GENTLEMAN IN GLASSES, *and the* GENTLEMAN WITH A STICK. *There also now enter a* SLEEPY GENTLEMAN *(an elderly man who looks like a mop and who sits down to the left of the* GENTLEMAN WITH A STICK*); a* GENTLEMAN IN A TURBAN, *who takes a seat to the right of the* MERCHANT WITH A BEARD; *and an* OFFICER WITH A HUGE MUSTACHE, *who sits next to the* GENTLEMAN IN A TURBAN. *All are pressed together and complaining about the stuffiness and heat.*

Scene 1

SLEEPY GENTLEMAN [*to* GENTLEMAN IN A TURBAN]: Permettez, monsieur, que je vous demande: êtes-vous Turc?

GENTLEMAN IN A TURBAN: Non, monsieur.

[*The* SLEEPY GENTLEMAN *closes his eyes. Silence ensues.*]

MR. X [*leaning out the window*]: Hey, Freidrich! Geschwinder!
MR. Z: Geschwinder! Geschwinder!

[*More silence.*]

Scene 2
A SENSITIVE LADY *appears, escorted by a* STRANGE OFFICER.

SENSITIVE LADY: Oh, dear Lord!! All the seats are already taken! [*Pausing at the footsteps, she says to the* CONDUCTOR] Mr. Conductor!

[*The* STRANGE OFFICER *stands outside the doors of the omnibus.*]

STRANGE OFFICER: Hey, Conductor! Just where do you think you're going, pal? The lady is asking you a question.
CONDUCTOR: What can I do for you?
SENSITIVE LADY: Where is my seat?
CONDUCTOR: You can take any seat you like.
SENSITIVE LADY: Any seat I like? And what if there are no seats to take?
CONDUCTOR: I beg your pardon! What do you mean there are no seats? There are eighteen seats and only thirteen people. There will be a place to sit. The gentlemen can squeeze in a bit. Please come on in.
SENSITIVE LADY: Thirteen people . . . But this is terrible! . . .

[*Everyone presses closely together. The* SENSITIVE LADY *gets on the omnibus and, with an unpleasant look on her face, sits to the right of the* GENTLEMAN IN A TURBAN.]

SENSITIVE LADY [*speaking to the* STRANGE OFFICER *through the doors*]: Imagine that! There are fourteen of us . . . And we're pressed in here like sardines in a can! . . . How stuffy it is . . . C'est affreux.

STRANGE OFFICER [*shrugging his shoulders*]: Que faire, madame? This is, so to speak, our common destiny. [*He smiles.*] Au plaisir de vous revoir. . . .

[*He scrapes his feet and walks away.*]

SENSITIVE LADY: *Bonjour!* [*To* CONDUCTOR] How come you're not taking off? It's time to go.

CONDUCTOR: We're leaving right away. [*To* COACHMAN] Go water the horses.

EVERYONE [*with horror in their voices*]: What? You mean the horses haven't been watered yet? So when are we going to leave? Mr. Conductor! This is absolutely unheard of! The devil knows what's going on. [*They all look out the window; four ragged-looking horses pass by.*] This is simply awful!

MERCHANT WITH A BEARD [*in his turn*]: My little bag! There's something in my little bag!

CONDUCTOR: Just a moment! Just a moment! We really can't go without drinking water.

MR. X AND MR. Z [*through the window*]: Friedrich! Friedrich!

Scene 3
In the doorway of the omnibus, there appears the full-moon-like figure of the ELEPHANTINE GENTLEMAN. *Everyone looks at him with a mixture of curiosity and horror.*

They ALL *exclaim:* Can such a person like this exist? No, it cannot be!

[*The* ELEPHANTINE GENTLEMAN puts *his foot on the steps and boards the omnibus.*]

The SENSITIVE LADY *goes pale, says:* Good Lord! *and hides in the corner.*

[*The* CONDUCTOR *assists the* ELEPHANTINE GENTLEMAN *in getting on, moving him over to the left side. The passengers there huddle together, wheezing and grunting. As the* ELEPHANTINE GENTLEMAN *takes a seat, the omnibus sways heavily to the left side. The* SENSITIVE LADY *lets out a scream; the* SLEEPY GENTLEMAN *opens his eyes. Everyone continues to press together and to gaze at the* ELEPHANTINE MAN *with horror.*]

SENSITIVE LADY: Good God! Where are they going to squeeze in three more passengers? [*She feels like crying.*]

ELEPHANTINE MAN [*looking at everyone with a questioning air and after some thought, raising himself over to the door*]: Conductor!

CONDUCTOR: What can I do for you?

ELEPHANTINE MAN: Are there any more seats?

CONDUCTOR: There are.

ELEPHANTINE MAN: Are there many?

CONDUCTOR [*counting the passengers to himself*]: Three, four, seven, ten, thirteen. [*Aloud*]: Three.

SEVERAL VOICES: How can you say three? Have mercy! What are you talking about? How can you say there are three more seats?

MR. X: Don't you remember that one seat has already been sold? That gentleman over there in the pub; he'll be coming soon.

CONDUCTOR: Yes, yes, you're quite right. So! There are still two seats. Precisely two seats. Two seats exactly.

ELEPHANTINE MAN [*taking out some money*]: Give me one more seat.

CONDUCTOR: You want another seat? Excuse me . . . but for whom? Is somebody else coming? . . . Your brother, perhaps? . . .

ELEPHANTINE MAN: No, for me.

CONDUCTOR: That means . . .

ELEPHANTINE MAN: For me alone. Here, take the money.

[*He throws the money at him.*]

CONDUCTOR [*to himself*]: This must be some big fish! He wants more than one seat.

Scene 4

EVERYONE *and the* HERO.

The HERO's *hair is dirty, his coat is covered with chalk. His eyes are a bit cross-eyed. He boards the omnibus, stepping on the others' feet, trying to get to his friends but offering no apologies for the ruckus he is causing.*

SENSITIVE LADY [*almost whispering*]: Well, now there's one more!

[*The* HERO *hears what the* SENSITIVE LADY *has said. He stops in the middle of the omnibus and addresses her coldly.*]

HERO: One seat, not two.

[*He then pushes himself forward and takes a seat between* MR. X *and* MR. Z.]

GENTLEMAN IN GLASSES [*speaking quietly to the* GENTLEMAN WITH A STICK]: Do you smell something . . . ?

GENTLEMAN WITH A STICK [*sniffing the air*]: Yes, very much so. . . . It seems like something from the pub.

[*Several passengers, looking at the* GENTLEMAN WITH A STICK, *also begin to sniff the air. The* HERO, *having leaned forward and not noticing anybody or anything, speaks loudly to the* CONDUCTOR.]

HERO: So tell me, Mr. Conductor! Is this your omnibus? Turn the thing on. . . . When are we going to get going?

[*His friends,* MR. X *and* MR. Z, *laugh. The* BOY *and the* GIRL *look at the* HERO *with curiosity. The clock strikes half past nine. The* CONDUCTOR *blows his whistle in a most mournful way. The omnibus moves from its place and slowly makes its way down the alley.*]

One hears the PASSENGERS *exclaim:* Thank God! Finally! We're off! We're moving!

[PASSERSBY *stop and stare.*]

HERO: Here we go, here we go! . . . We're off! . . . We're off! But I didn't get to finish my game. Balls thirty-five and twenty-eight. Yellow one in the middle—bam! And it was my turn to play! . . .

[*The* CONDUCTOR *continues to blow his whistle as he walks alongside the omnibus. The horses barely creep forward.*]

HERO: Keep blowing your whistle! Keep blowing the thing! I told you that the next time we play, it's my turn! The next time the latter half of the game is mine! The idiot probably didn't understand what "next time" means! Ah, the hell with it!

[*He makes a grimace. The* BOY *and the* GIRL *laugh. Several of the passengers move away. The* SLEEPY GENTLEMAN *closes his eyes. The* CONDUCTOR *continues to blow his whistle.*]

HERO [*sticking his head out the window*]: I don't care if you blow your whistle or not! . . . Aha! . . . You're not Rubini,[2] pal, you just blow a whistle! . . . Ah, the hell with it!

[*The* HERO *makes another grimace. The* BOY *and the* GIRL *laugh loudly.*]

GENTLEMAN IN GLASSES: Who is this character?

GENTLEMAN WITH A STICK: He's German. With him around, it's startin' to smell bad around here.

GENTLEMAN IN GLASSES: Just you wait until he gets carsick! . . . Then he'll really be pleasing to the ladies.

[*The* CONDUCTOR *continues to blow his whistle.*]

HERO [*waving his hand*]: Don't blow your whistle! Don't blow it at all! . . . All them cows is here . . .

2. It should be noted that in 1843 Giovanni Rubini performed in St. Petersburg and was also named Director of Singing and Colonel of Imperial Music by Nicholas I.

[*The* BOY *and the* GIRL *are laughing loudly; the friends,* MR. X *and* MR. Z, *are also chuckling happily. The* SENSITIVE LADY *is biting her lip, and the* BUREAUCRAT, *having looked at her, shrugs his shoulders. The* SENSITIVE LADY *is frowning. The* GENTLEMAN IN THE TURBAN *maintains his fixed grandeur.*]

SENSITIVE LADY [*addressing the passengers in a careless way*]: Who is that young man?

[*Silence.*]

GENTLEMAN IN THE GLASSES [*talking to the* GENTLEMAN WITH A STICK]: Whoever he is, he's not a bad chap. . . . Apparently, he is going to be our main character.

[*For the last time, the* CONDUCTOR *blows his whistle in a mournful way. He then takes a seat by the door. The omnibus leaves the park, makes for the open highway, and trots along with a great deal of noise. The hat belonging to the* SLEEPY GENTLEMAN *falls off his head and rolls to the feet of the* MODEST YOUNG MAIDEN. *The* GENTLEMAN WITH A STICK *looks at the hat and also at the* MODEST YOUNG MAIDEN. *The* MODEST YOUNG MAIDEN *looks at the hat and also at the* GENTLEMAN WITH A STICK. *They both smile.*]

HERO [*waving his hands*]: Aha! We're moving! We're off! This is some car we have here: Fu! fu! fu! fu. . . . V'room! . . . V'room! . . . V'room! v'room! . . .

SLEEPY GENTLEMAN [*waking up with a fright*]: Hey! What's going on?

[*The* HERO *turns to the* SLEEPY GENTLEMAN, *who in the meantime has picked up the hat and has put it on his knee.*]

HERO: I can see you're frightened. Huh? . . . But there's nothing to be afraid of! . . . The car is solid, made in England. . . . Fu! fu! fu! . . . We'll be at the station in five hours. Ah, what the hell!

[*The* HERO *grimaces for the third time. The* BOY *and the* GIRL *laugh loudly; their mother tries to restrain them. The neighbors turn their backs. The* SLEEPY GENTLEMAN *closes his eyes.*]

OFFICER WITH A HUGE MUSTACHE [*looking at the* HERO]: He's drunk, ain't he?

SENSITIVE LADY: Is that so? I'm afraid you're right. . . .

Scene 5

Outside the omnibus, one hears a scream: Do you have a seat on board?

The CONDUCTOR *replies:* Yes, we do.

The omnibus stops, and the passengers become excited. The doors open, and in steps a GENTLEMAN WITH A LORGNETTE, *a small and thin figure. He first bows politely to the* SENSITIVE LADY; *then, with ease, he takes a seat alongside her.*

HERO: Aha! . . . Now we've got still one more. . . . We've got an entire herd on now. . . . Mr. Conductor! You had better put away your whistle! . . . Well, we're off!

[*The omnibus takes off again. The* GENTLEMAN WITH A LORGNETTE *first looks around at everyone; he then points his lorgnette at the* HERO.]

HERO [*looking at him*]: Just what do you think you're doing? What's this? Some kind of inspection?

[MR. X *and* MR. Z *whisper something in his ear.*]

HERO: What? We're off! [*He frowns and brushes away a forelock.*] . . . Nobody can get this thing movin'! . . . But I've got my seat. . . . What kind of inspection is going on?! [*He sways and sings.*] Tra-la-la la-la!

[*The* GENTLEMAN WITH A LORGNETTE *continues to look at the* HERO. *The hat belonging to the* SLEEPY GENTLEMAN *falls off his knee; but he continues to sleep, knocking his head against the window frame. The* GENTLEMAN WITH A STICK *and the* MODEST YOUNG MAIDEN *again snicker about the hat.*]

GENTLEMAN IN GLASSES [*to the* GENTLEMAN WITH A STICK]: But this man is starting to get on my nerves! Look at how upset he's getting.

GENTLEMAN WITH A STICK: It's because the German's self-esteem has been insulted.

[*The* HERO, *forgetting all manners, waves his hands, stomps his feet, and the like.*]

HERO: Tra-la-la! La-la-la! . . . Must be some important person here. . . . He's gonna do some inspection . . . and he even has a lorgnette! I have lots of smashed glass. Twenty-five windows. . . . Oh, what the hell!

[*The* HERO *grimaces and spits. The strong smell of wine wafts through the omnibus. The passengers become indignant.*]

SENSITIVE LADY [*to the* OFFICER WITH A HUGE MUSTACHE]: Well, perhaps, he'll really try to start something. . . . I am afraid he will. . . . Tell him to stop before he starts . . .

OFFICER WITH A HUGE MUSTACHE [*calmly*]: There's nothing to worry about, madam.

GENTLEMAN IN GLASSES [*almost whispering*]: It's time to show him out the door.

SEVERAL PASSENGERS: Show him out! Throw him out! Look at the way he's behaving, Mr. Conductor. Stop the omnibus.

[*A mild uproar ensues. The omnibus stops; the* CONDUCTOR *opens the doors. The* GENTLEMAN WITH A LORGNETTE *sees that the decisive moment has come and that everyone's eyes are fixed on the* HERO. *He gets out of the omnibus. Everyone is silent.*]

HERO: What's going on? What stop is this?

SEVERAL PASSENGERS [*addressing the* HERO *in a rather shy way*]: Get out.

HERO [*his eyes popping out of his head*]: What do you mean, "Get out"?

OTHER PASSENGERS [*speaking to him more boldly*]: Yes, yes! Get out, get out!

HERO [*in a loud and very threatening way*]: But why?

[*Everyone is silent.*]

SLEEPY GENTLEMAN [*in his sleep*]: But I am not a Turk.

[*Everyone laughs. The* SLEEPY GENTLEMAN *wakes up and gives everyone a strange look.*]

SLEEPY GENTLEMAN: What's going on? Why have we stopped?

HERO: Would you be so kind and find out for me, too?! I've already asked.

GENTLEMAN WITH A STICK: You wanted to get off. So get off!

ALL THE PASSENGERS: Yes, yes! You wanted to get off.

HERO [*solemnly*]: Really. . . . I wanted to get off? Well, now if you must know—I don't want to now! Let's get going!

[*The* HERO *waves his hand in a commanding way and begins to whistle. The omnibus starts to move but hits a bump. The* GENTLEMAN WITH A STICK *and the* MODEST YOUNG MAIDEN *sway most of all; the latter, smiling, drops her eyes. The* SLEEPY GENTLEMAN *puts the hat under his feet and closes his eyes.*]

HERO [*triumphantly*]: I want to stay. . . . Aha! I want to stay on! . . . Perhaps I'll even want to stay on farther. . . . La, la, la! Phew, phew, phew! . . .

[*The* HERO *winks at the* MODEST YOUNG MAIDEN *and makes all kinds of signs to her.*]

SEVERAL PASSENGERS: So now what, people! He has to be shown out. [*To the* HERO] Dear Sir! You really are behaving in an indecent way. You are insulting the ladies. And we do have ladies here.

BUREAUCRAT [*amid all the noise*]: You are acting shamefully.

[*The* MERCHANT WITH A BEARD *wants to say something but instead of words gives out a terrible roaring sound.*]

MERCHANT WITH A BEARD: Rr-r-r-r-r! . . . I beg your pardon.

[*The* MERCHANT WITH A BEARD *closes his mouth and then strokes his beard.*]

GIRL [*whispering*]: Mommy! Why do I suddenly smell onions?
GENTLEMAN WITH A STICK [*to the* HERO]: You are not behaving politely.
SEVERAL PASSENGERS: You are offending all of us.

[*The* HERO, *having listened to the general talk, latches onto the word "offend."*]

HERO: I am insulting you! Ha! . . . Mr. Conductor. Stop the omnibus!

[*The* HERO *gets up on his feet. The omnibus stops.*]

SENSITIVE LADY [*crying out*]: *Ah, quelle histoire!*

[*She jumps up on the footstep.*]

HERO [*addressing everyone in a triumphant way*]: You, my dear sirs, say that I'm offendin' you. . . . Which one of you believes that? Be the first to say so! Who says that I am insulting him or her?

[*Everyone is silent; no one answers. The* HERO *turns to the* AVERAGE LADY. *The children cling to her in fear.*]

HERO: And you, my dear lady, have I offended you?

[*The* AVERAGE LADY *turns her back on him in silence.*]

HERO: No? [*Turning to the* BUREAUCRAT] Now it's your turn to answer me, my dear sir. Have I offended you?

[*The* BUREAUCRAT *lowers his eyes and gazes at the top of the stick of the* GENTLEMAN WITH A STICK.]

HERO [*to the* GENTLEMAN WITH A STICK]: Have I offended you?

GENTLEMAN WITH A STICK: You cannot offend me, but there are ladies here.

HERO [*waving his hands*]: But how can you say such a thing! Have mercy! After all, you are not a lady! . . . Get lost! [*Silence.*] Get lost! Hey, Mr. Conductor! I am an important man, you know. You will be held responsible for this! . . .

[*The* SENSITIVE LADY *boards the omnibus. The* CONDUCTOR *closes the doors. The omnibus begins to move.*]

HERO [*yelling with all his might*]: Aha! . . . Which one of you is so important? . . . Me insult you, indeed! . . . Tra-la-la-la. . . . [*He sings.*]

Saufen Bier und Brantewein
Schmeissen alle Fenstern ein . . .

[MR. X *and* MR. Z *whisper something in his ear.*]

HERO [*annoyed*]: You all go to hell! After all, is my money any worse than yours? Have I given you leather buttons, while these gentlemen have given you golden ones? I have the same seat as everyone else. Aha!

[*The* HERO *gives everyone a bold look; he then turns his head to the window.*]

HERO: Hey, coachman! T'fu! . . . .

[*The* HERO spits *at him. Then grabbing the handles about him, he swings the omnibus to and fro.*]

HERO [*singing*]:

Ich bin liederlich,
Du bist liederlich,
Sind wir nicht liederlich, Leute, a?!

SENSITIVE LADY: Dear God, he'll turn us upside down!
MODEST YOUNG MAIDEN: Hey, what's he doing now?

[*The* MODEST YOUNG MAIDEN *looks at the* GENTLEMAN WITH A STICK *and laughs.*]

GENTLEMAN WITH A STICK: Ah, it's nothing.

[*The* GENTLEMAN WITH A STICK looks *at the* MODEST YOUNG MAIDEN *and laughs. The omnibus rocks.*]

SLEEPING GENTLEMAN [*in his sleep*]: Good Lord! . . . . He can't be controlled . . .

[*The* SLEEPING GENTLEMAN *wakes up. His hat rolls under the feet of the passengers. He grabs hold of it and puts it securely on his head.*]

HERO: I can't be controlled! . . . Ai, ai, ai. . . . That's a good thing!

[*The friends* MR. X *and* MR. Z *laugh. The* SLEEPY GENTLEMAN *first looks at the* HERO *in a puzzled way and then closes his eyes.*]

GENTLEMAN IN GLASSES: That German may celebrate, but he'll end up in a police station yet. No wonder one of those police officers was looking at him in a strange way before.
GENTLEMAN WITH A STICK: I would be extremely happy if something like that would happen. Look, look at what he's doing now!
HERO [*to a* PASSING LADY]: Hey, toots! . . . You ain't bad lookin' at all. . . . Hey, you, get over here. . . . Psst, you!

[*The* HERO *waves his hand at her.*]

SEVERAL PASSENGERS [*indignantly*]: This is outrageous! This is awful.

[*The* HERO *looks at them with unsteady eyes. He is completely drunk.*]

HERO: Hello? . . . We there yet?
MORE PASSENGERS [*decisively*]: Yes, yes, it's a shame! Stop the omnibus! Mr. Conductor! Stop the omnibus!
HERO [*turning pale*]: Now whaaat?

[*The omnibus stops. Little by little* PASSERSBY *gather around it.*]

ELEPHANTINE GENTLEMAN [*solemnly*]: Mr. Conductor! Escort this gentleman off the omnibus.

[*The* ELEPHANTINE GENTLEMAN *points to the* HERO *with his finger; the* HERO*'s friends,* MR. X *and* MR. Z, *press up against the wall.*]

SENSITIVE LADY: Good Lord! . . . I will just die today.

[*The* SENSITIVE LADY *jumps up from the seat.*]

CONDUCTOR [*timidly to the* HERO]: This way, please.

[*The* HERO *pretends not to hear.*]

CONDUCTOR: Sir, you have been asked to leave.
HERO: Me? What for?
CONDUCTOR: Because. . . .
SEVERAL PASSENGERS: Because you have been acting badly!
CONDUCTOR: That's right. Your behavior is unacceptable.
EVERYONE: Yes, yes, unacceptable! Now get out!

[*The* HERO *brushes away a forelock with one hand and puts the other on his hip.*]

HERO: Now this is really something! . . . Ha, ha, ha, ha! . . . Like I don't know how to behave! . . . Ha, ha, ha! . . . So I'm behaving badly. . . . They want to shove me off! . . . Ha, ha, ha! Well, now what should we do? Who's gonna try?

[*The* HERO *gives a threatening look to the* CONDUCTOR.]

HERO [*to* CONDUCTOR]: Now you just an'sher me this! Didn't I pay the same money as the others? Did all these gentlemen pay more than I did? An'sher me!

GENTLEMAN IN GLASSES: Get out of the omnibus, sir, get out. You have been behaving badly.

HERO: How dare you say such a thing? Just what is proper anyway? . . . Perhaps we know how to behave better in society than you! Maybe it is you who don't know how to behave in society! We are welcome everywhere, and better places, too. Why, there are princes and counts where we visit. . . . Yes, oh me, oh my! . . .

[*The* HERO *taunts first everyone, then the* GENTLEMAN IN GLASSES.]

HERO [*to the* GENTLEMAN IN GLASSES]: And you, dear sir, just who are you?

GENTLEMAN IN GLASSES: Get lost!

HERO: Get lost yourself! A-ah! . . . You're wearing glasses, so you must be some big fish! No?! Then phooey! . . . You can't order us around!

GENTLEMAN WITH A STICK: Get out, or we'll call a policeman and he will haul you out of here.

HERO: A policeman! . . . Go ahead! Just you try! . . . It is I who will carry you all off to the police. I'm not afraid of anyone!

MANY PASSENGERS: Get out! Get out! You're holding up the coach! You're raising a ruckus! You're behaving improperly!

BUREAUCRAT [*amid the general noise*]: You're causing a revolt, a revolt!

MERCHANT WITH A BEARD: This won't do, my dear sir!

HERO [*addressing everyone*]: My dear sirs! One and all! Get lost, all of you!

[*The* HERO *takes out his wallet and turns to the* CONDUCTOR.]

HERO: Here is a hundred rubles. I will pay for everybody here! Now you all get off!

ELEPHANTINE GENTLEMAN [*solemnly*]: My dear sir! If you don't get off this minute, I will throw you out the window.

[*Everyone quiets down. The* HERO, *taken aback, keeps quiet for a while; he then speaks, but in a quieter tone.*]

HERO: Throw me out the window? . . . [*Moving forward*] I am not just some object. . . . I won't go. [*Moving even farther*] Here's a hundred rubles silver. I'll buy seats for an entire week! . . . Nobody will be able to get on. . . . Out the window, indeed!

[*The* HERO *again moves forward. Everyone falls back and presses closer to the side.*]

HERO: Just go ahead and try! . . . I don't want to go. [*Moving farther forward*] Is anyone else any better than me? . . . Through the window, no less! [*Approaching the door*] Now here's this very important person. Why, he's taller than the spire at the Admiralty.[3]

[*The* HERO *gets off.*]

SENSITIVE LADY [*outside the omnibus*]: Oh!

[*The* SENSITIVE LADY *jumps into the omnibus. The* CONDUCTOR *bangs the doors shut.*]

3. The original Admiralty was one of the first structures in St. Petersburg. It was designed both as a dockyard for the building of some of the first ships of Russia's new Baltic fleet, as well as additional defense for the newly acquired territory of the Neva delta.

The current Admiralty was built between 1806 and 1823. Its gilded spire, 73 meters tall and topped with a weather vane of a "little ship" (*korablik*), is one of the city's most famous landmarks.

The Admiralty served as the Naval Headquarters for Russia until 1917; it is now a naval college.

CONDUCTOR [*crying out*]: Get going!

HERO [*running after the omnibus*] Stop! . . . How dare you do such a thing? I will buy out all the seats for a year! . . . Here's a hundred rubles in silver! For an entire year, I tell you! I'll see you all in the police station! . . .

[*The crowd parts to let the* HERO *pass. He takes a cab and follows the omnibus, threatening the* CONDUCTOR *with his fist.*]

Act 3

Scene 1

Everyone is in the omnibus except the HERO. *All are silent. Little by little, people begin to talk.*

GENTLEMAN WITH A STICK [*to the* GENTLEMAN IN GLASSES]: Look at how the boy and the girl have quieted down. They'll remember this for a long time.

GENTLEMAN IN GLASSES: Yes, they certainly will.

AVERAGE LADY [*to the* BUREAUCRAT]: But the gentleman is following us. I'm afraid that he will do something unpleasant when we get off.

BUREAUCRAT [*with a gallant air*]: Oh, please don't worry, madam. A drunk, no matter what else he is, is still a drunk. A sober person still has an advantage over him.

AVERAGE LADY: But . . .

BUREAUCRAT: No, no, please believe me. One word explains it all—he's *drunk*. . . . [*In a more serious way*] I suppose, though, that this gentleman wasn't so drunk, so to speak, that . . .

AVERAGE LADY: What are you suggesting?

BUREAUCRAT: Yes, yes. It's only that . . . There was something else about him. . . . [*Even more seriously*] I'm suggesting . . . Hm! Hm! . . .

AVERAGE LADY [*surprised*]: Tell me.

[*The* BUREAUCRAT *shakes his head. In the meantime, the* HERO *is alongside the omnibus, holding the reins in his hands and threatening the passengers with his fist.*]

HERO: So you think the show is over! . . . No way! Stop! . . . I'll show you! . . .

SENSITIVE LADY: Tell me, is he going to embarrass us in this town? He's pointing at us with his finger. . . .

OFFICER WITH A HUGE MUSTACHE: I'm surprised that the police haven't caught up with him yet.

MERCHANT WITH A BEARD: It must be that they haven't noticed him.

OFFICER WITH A HUGE MUSTACHE: What did you say?

MERCHANT WITH A BEARD: I said. . . . [*Making a strange sound*] Grrrrr! . . . Excuse me! I said—it must be that they haven't noticed him.

SENSITIVE LADY: How can they allow all this trash—God knows where they come from—to act the way they do? . . .

[*The* SENSITIVE LADY *is suddenly overwhelmed by the smell of radishes and onions.*]

SENSITIVE LADY: Fu! Where is that coming from?

[*The* SENSITIVE LADY *looks at the* MERCHANT WITH A BEARD *and indignantly holds her nose.*]

BUREAUCRAT [*pointing to the back of the bus*]: I think they should put a sign with some rules telling people how they should behave. Then something like this would never have happened. If someone starts raising a ruckus, he should be shown the rules. He should be told, "Here, take a look." . . .

GENTLEMAN IN GLASSES: When one can't pound rules into someone's head, it's useless to post them on the walls.

BUREAUCRAT: He, he, he . . . That's quite right. But here you see . . .

HERO [*outside the omnibus*]: I'll see you all in the police station! . . .

GIRL: Mommy, will we be there soon?

AVERAGE LADY: Right away.

GIRL: And this gentleman. . . . The angry one. . . . Is he going to yell at us again?

AVERAGE LADY: No, dear.

GIRL [*pointing to the* SLEEPY GENTLEMAN]: And that man over there? Will he be staying here?

AVERAGE LADY: Be quiet.

GIRL: And who is going to wake him up?

HERO [*approaching the window and yelling with all his might*]: Aha! . . . No! Tbrru! . . .

SLEEPY GENTLEMAN [*waking up with a start*]: What? What's going on here? [*Looking around*] God damn it! When will we finally get there?

[*The omnibus stops on Nevsky Prospekt. The* CONDUCTOR *opens the doors.*]

CONDUCTOR [*to* SENSITIVE LADY]: If you please.

[*The* HERO *jumps up from his seat in the cab.*]

HERO [*to* CONDUCTOR]: No, stop! . . . Ah! . . . You dared! . . . Police, hey, police!

SENSITIVE LADY: This is a disgrace!

[*The* SENSITIVE LADY *hides in the omnibus.*]

CONDUCTOR [*to* HERO]: Let go of me, sir. I'm in a hurry!

HERO: So you're in a hurry! Well, we will just see about that! . . . Hey, you, Mr. Attorney!

[*A crowd gathers around the omnibus. An* ATTORNEY *and two* POLICEMEN *approach.*]

SENSITIVE LADY: Good God, what will happen to us next?

ELEPHANTINE GENTLEMAN: Don't worry, madam. Would you please let me off.

[*The* ELEPHANTINE GENTLEMAN *gets off with difficulty.*]

ELEPHANTINE GENTLEMAN [*to* POLICEMEN]: Take away this shoemaker. He kept bothering us the whole way.

[*The* POLICEMEN *seize the* HERO.]

HERO: A shoemaker? . . . What a stupid thing to say! . . . Let me go. . . . I'm not a shoemaker. Perhaps he's a shoemaker, or he has a father who's a shoemaker. . . . But I'm not a shoemaker. I've never even held a waxed thread in my hands. . . . I won't let you do this. . . . A hundred rubles in silver. . . . Let me go. . . . You are going to answer for this.

[*The* HERO *goes off in the distance, led by the two* POLICEMEN. *The passengers and the crowd disperse. It is getting dark out.*]

GENTLEMAN WITH A STICK [*to the* MODEST YOUNG MAIDEN, *who is walking away*]: Where are you off to?
MODEST YOUNG MAIDEN: Why do you want to know?
GENTLEMAN WITH A STICK: Maybe it's on the way to where I'm going.
MODEST YOUNG MAIDEN: Maybe so.

[*They disappear.*]

Scene 2
The CONDUCTOR *approaches the* COACHMAN, *who meanwhile has unharnessed the horses and put away the reins.*

CONDUCTOR: Would you like some, Eryoma?

[*The* CONDUCTOR *offers the* COACHMAN *an open tobacco box.*]

COACHMAN: Thank you very much. [*He takes some snuff.*] What's the problem, brother Pantelei? It seems that we are late. What's the story?
CONDUCTOR [*also taking some snuff*]: Yeah, there's a story, all right. For some reason, one gentleman didn't quite get along with another passenger. One said, "You get off." The other replied, "No, you get off."
COACHMAN: So?
CONDUCTOR: Well, one of them was shown out, but then he got angry, and then . . . started playing all kinds of games.

COACHMAN: Was he drunk?

CONDUCTOR: He didn't seem so to me. Perhaps, he was. . . . Who can tell with these people? . . .

COACHMAN: How could it have been anything else? He had to be drunk since he had to be led out by the hand as sometimes is the case for all of us. [*Shaking his head*] It's not for nothing that we have the proverb "Drink, but don't drown your brain."

CONDUCTOR: That's true enough. . . . Or how about the saying "You are free to use your tongue, but not your hands!" Well, I'm off. Are you also leaving soon?

[*The* CONDUCTOR *and the* COACHMAN *leave for the nearest "establishment."*]

COACHMAN: I'm coming.

[*The* COACHMAN *leads the horses away.*]

—*Govorilin*

The Literature of Petersburg

Vissarion Belinsky

The expressions—*Petersburg Literature, Muscovite Literature*—are not at all as arbitrary and inappropriate as those people who acknowledge only Russian literature are inclined to think. No one, of course, will argue that all of Russia—not just Moscow and Petersburg—lays claim to such writers as Lomonosov, Derzhavin, Fonvizin, Karamzin, Dmitriev, Krylov, Batyushkov, Zhukovsky, Pushkin, Griboyedov, Lermontov, and Gogol. Everyone will also agree that such individuals should be called Russian writers, not just Petersburg or Muscovite ones. Indeed, the time has passed when both our capitals were seen as the sole center of Russian literature and when each city tried to appropriate a famous writer for itself. Also long gone are those eras when Moscow tried to prove in print that some poet had grown up in its environs, only to provoke a response from Petersburg that this same individual was born and spent the greater part of his life in its surroundings. What nonsense! For instance, I. A. Krylov is primarily a citizen of Petersburg, a Russian city that was founded on German land, and that is half filled by Germans and rife with foreign ways. But show me another writer who was born, was raised, lived, and died in Moscow and who was closer to the people and more Russian than Krylov was.

Generally speaking, all of our writers belong to both Petersburg and Moscow. One was born in Petersburg but grew up in Moscow. Another lived and wrote in both cities. Still other writers were born and spent their childhood in the provinces but in the end were raised, lived, and wrote first in Petersburg, then in Moscow. For example, Lermontov was born and spent his childhood in the province of Penza.[1] He then studied at Moscow University but never completed the course of science there. Next Lermontov moved to Petersburg and entered the Military Academy in that city. Pushkin was born in the province of Pskov,[2] was raised in Petersburg, and spent the greater part of his life in our northern capital. Such circumstances, though, did not prevent him from knowing or loving his "native Moscow," as he himself used to call it.

The above said, one must acknowledge that exclusive citizenship in either one of our capitals has influenced many of our great writers. For instance, Pushkin, a poet who was more a citizen of Moscow than Petersburg, could not write *Onegin* in any other way than he did. Many of Gogol's most splendid plays show that he spent one of the freshest and most impressive periods of his life in Petersburg. Indeed, the imprint of Petersburg can be seen on many of his works, not because, of course, he owed his manner of writing to that city, but because he drew his characters from so many types there. Such works as "Nevsky Prospekt," *Notes of a Madman,* "The Nose," "The Overcoat," *The Marriage,* "The Morning of a Busy Person," and "The Departure" could have been written not only by a great talent with the outlook of a genius on life but also by a person who knew Petersburg firsthand, not from hearsay alone. Generally speaking, life in Petersburg aptly facilitates the development of humor and satire among our great talents. *Woe from Wit* portrays life in Moscow, but it could have been written by someone in Petersburg. Even in the taut, cold, unhappy, and passionate irony of Lermontov's verse, we see indications that he spent the best years of his life in Petersburg. If Griboyedov and Lermontov had spent the greater part of their existence in Moscow, one could reasonably assume that their works would be more peaceful and mild. They would also contain more positive elements than negative ones and consequently have less power and depth. Once again our two capitals show sharp and contradictory differences.

1. Penza is both a city and a province, roughly 350 miles southeast of Moscow. Belinsky is mistaken here, though. Lermontov was born in the inland capital.

2. Belinsky errs again. Pushkin was also born in Moscow but raised in Tsarskoe Selo (now called Pushkin), approximately 20 miles south of St. Petersburg. The writer did spend time in Pskov, roughly 400 miles north of the capital, the reason being his exile at the family estate of Mikhailovskoe there between 1824 and 1826.

If being a long-standing citizen of Moscow or Petersburg can influence the works of our great writers, individuals who represent the national spirit, then the fiction of ordinary writers shows more vividly to which of these two cities their talents belong. In this regard, though, the existence of a "Petersburg" or "Moscow" literature is even less doubtful than that of Russian literature. In the national written expression of any country, one should seek out not only the works of its great talents but also the products of its general, day-to-day activity. Such writing is the grand total of a nation's literature; it is its income minus its expenditures, the latter being the result of inner processes. Regarding these *totals,* the world of journalism usually gives us nothing because the works of unusual talents that appear in periodicals are later published independently, whereas everything else in them has a contemporary and thus relative interest. In no way, though, does such a situation deny the influence (and importance) of journals on the development of public education and enlightenment. Indeed, journalism makes up an important part of any literature. Ordinary talents may be insignificant in the eyes of posterity, but they are extremely valuable for their contemporaries. For one thing, they serve as mediators between the mob and writers of genius. For another thing, they bring the new ideas of great writers within the comprehension of the masses.

From this point of view, the difference between the artistic writing of Moscow and Petersburg is significant.

In our article "The Alexander Theater," we tried to show how the theatrical audience in Petersburg differs from its counterpart in Moscow. Indeed, what we said about the theatergoers in both cities can also be said about the reading publics there. People in Petersburg read more than people in Moscow do because they [those in Petersburg] attend the theater more frequently. Also, when it comes to social progress, one has to declare for Petersburg, but at present the art and literature that should arise from such an advantage is small. Everyone reads in Petersburg. But we need not explain what we mean by *everyone.* After all, there is hardly a person alive who does not know that *all* of Petersburg consists of working, "educated" people. In fact, in Petersburg, it would be hard to find an individual who, wearing a tailcoat and knowing how to speak Russian, does not read, for example, the *Northern Bee* and *Repertoire.* Such a situation is hardly the case in Moscow. There some people read everything, but others read absolutely nothing with the exception of the *Supplements to the Moscow News,*[3] the reason being that they do not want to waste money on the editorials and feature articles in the main edition. The number of people in the latter group is much larger and more encompassing than those in the former. People who read in Moscow see such an activity as a serious business; they know what and why they are reading. In Petersburg, however, reading is the habit of educated people, the fruit of civilization.

Who does not know that newspapers are a necessity for every literate person and that this necessity draws from that public awareness which is the foundation of European life? But by the same token, who also does not know that reading newspapers is not the same thing as reading in general? In Europe, people read newspapers to find out, on a daily basis, what is going on in the big wide world. There a newspaper is not a book but an informer, a postman who makes everyone read. In Russia, though, people turn to newspapers to find out about manufacturing and contracts. As do readers in Europe, most of the public in Petersburg reads newspapers and journals, poems and novels. They have to read everything that causes a stir, however external; otherwise they will not rest easily. As everyone knows, Eugene Sue's *Mysteries of Paris* caused a sensation throughout the world, and people in Petersburg read the work in both French and Russian[4] because they were convinced that this tale is a matchless and great work of art. If, at the very same time, though, the citizens of Petersburg would have read a genuinely splendid aesthetic piece—French or Russian, but which did not cause a stir at the time of its appearance—it would not have occurred to them that they had read a wonderful piece. Petersburg loves to read everything that is new, contemporary, and exciting, things that *everyone* is talking about. That is why it reads almost everything that appears in French bookstalls or in Russian journals. Petersburg also has a great respect for old writers, if they have been unanimously proclaimed as such, but because it does not read books, it does not read such people in depth. Petersburg does not have time to do so, for it is too busy with

3. Beginning in 1838, the *Supplements to the Moscow News* (*Pribavleniia k "Moskovskim vedomostiiam"*) complemented one of the most important newspapers in Russia with both official and personal advertisements.

4. Eugene Sue's *Mysteries of Paris* (*Les Mystères de Paris*) was published in 1842–43 and translated into Russian in 1844. It was the subject of a special article by Belinsky in 1844.

new things, starting with morning posters and feuilletons in the *Northern Bee* and ending with a newly appeared novel, short story, or drama. The citizens of Petersburg are busy working in offices, paying visits, taking walks along Nevsky Prospekt, and attending parties, clubs, theaters, and concerts. They thus have no time to think and distinguish between works that are truly good and those that are mediocre or poor. That is why the citizens of Petersburg love to be guided by the judgments of acknowledged authorities, be they their bosses at work or well-known critics and reviewers.

It is not easy to be recognized as an authority or critic in Petersburg. To do so, one has either to become the boss or to publish one's name in various editions for at least twenty years so that it becomes as familiar to people as a sign that is fortunate enough to hang on the last house of a many-cornered street and which cannot help being noticed no matter where a person goes. Any feuilletonist, any reviewer can become a passable authority, but only in his own circle, among his own friends. Also, if this individual should wish, he can have a small public that is devoted to him, never questions his judgments, and often eats and drinks with him! Regarding more major authorities, though, such individuals must hold a major rank or, failing such a position, have the honor of being the editor of a journal or a newspaper with a large circulation or, at the very least, of being a major collaborator in literary criticism in this journal or magazine. Superficial success in this area is always proof of intelligence, knowledge, talent, and impartiality. But that is not all; such an individual needs to satisfy still one more extremely important condition to become recognized as a critic, an authority. So long as a journalist or a critic has fresh and new ideas, people will regard him with caution, as an upstart who wants to be smarter than *everyone else,* and who argues against everything that *everyone else* is convinced of. Such a trend is usually rooted neither in conviction nor in an independent view of things, nor in a passionate love for the truth. Rather, it draws from bias, maliciousness, and other less-laudable sentiments. But when the literary ideas put forth by a journalist or a critic are accepted by society or when they become commonly accepted truths, the wounds arising from affronted pride become healed gradually. Once the journalist-critic is taken with his glory and success, though, he begins to consider works that at one time were the object of his merciless criticism,

intelligence, and taste.[5] The deed is done! He becomes an authority, incapable of being shattered or destroyed. His every word is law! People in Petersburg are immediately ready to believe the article of a critic who is not only unknown in their city but also attached to an authority in their city. The only thing necessary is that his article raises a considerable stir among the countless official and literary major and minor authorities. If a new book is published in Petersburg but has escaped the attention of a critical authority, people will believe the first review about it, no matter who has written it. The book then goes into circulation; everybody praises it, everyone approves of it. No sooner does an authority write about the work, though, than the book perishes, for everyone is saying bad things about it. In these polemical cross fires, Petersburg always believes the one who has fired the last shot, even though he has done so with an unloaded pistol.

Just as Petersburg journalists and critics have their own authorities, so do the writers in that city have their own experts and judges. Among these writer-authorities, one can point to Marlinsky in prose and to Mr. Benediktov in poetry. For some time now, though, these two authorities have not been on everyone's lips, but such a situation is not the fault of the critics so much as it is from the fact that the former belongs to a group of old writers, while the latter has not written for quite some time. On the other hand, Gogol has never had the honor of being an authority in Petersburg. Even worse, his works are not liked there, and as an author, he is considered an equal of Paul de Koch if only because he *copies* only *low nature in a faithful way*.[6] Most of all, the average reader prefers that a writer portray strong Marlinsky-like passions. He also wishes for that bon ton that shines forth in the matchless works of creators who have appropriated the social finesse at the "Club of the United Society."[7] Such preference, though, does not mean that Gogol is not being read in Petersburg or throughout Russia. In Petersburg, Gogol enjoys an exclusively and, in our opinion, most envious and splendid glory. The more he is abused, the more he is read. Of course, in Petersburg as well as in all of Russia, one can find

5. Belinsky is again mocking both Faddei Bulgarin and Nikolai Polevoi, specifically their pandering to the government.

6. Both Polevoi and Osip Senkovsky made such a comparison.

7. The "Club of the United Society" (*Klub soedinennogo obshchestva*) was founded in St. Petersburg in 1794 and consisted of important artists, merchants, and governmental employees.

several people who have a profound understanding and respect for Gogol's talent. *In this regard,* therefore, Petersburg is hardly an exception. But the majority judge Gogol in much the same way as do "respectable" people in Petersburg, that is, individuals of a certain age and rank. Thus there is the hope that when the younger generation in Petersburg becomes elderly and "respectable," they will acquire the right *to be bold enough to have their own view about things.*[8] The majority of people in Petersburg will then be firmly in Gogol's camp, even though such a development will not advance the aesthetic education of society in any significant way.

Everyone in Petersburg knows not only the name of Byron but also that he is a gloomy and satanic poet. Citizens of the city are also ready and willing to utter loud phrases to show their great respect for the colossal genius of Shakespeare, whom they have come to know at the Alexander Theater. The citizens of Petersburg fail to be surprised at the name of any famous author or at the title of any famous work. Simply put, they fail to be surprised at any famous phenomenon. They know everything there is to know, although not very deeply, so they will never argue about anything. Indeed, if the citizens of Petersburg ever should begin to argue with you about something, they will justify their opinion by telling you that everyone thinks like they do. But then, out of politeness, they will add that, perhaps, you are also right in your view. But to tell the truth, what is there to argue about? Why should anyone get upset? After all, as regards all these Byrons and Shakespeares, the Petersburg citizen has absorbed all the ready-made ideas of his boss, or of some other honorable individual, or of a famous critical authority, or, finally, of a friend who writes feuilletons. In his view, such people are more than sufficient to assert that he knows everything, that he understands everything, and consequently that he is an "educated" person and the key reason why he can stand tall in a crowd.

In Moscow, though, the situation is quite different. There, under the guise of good fashion, one can come across the most amazing and innocent ignorance of everything regarding education and literature. I very much love and respect the bearers of such ignorance. I am ready to talk to them only about those things that they themselves want to talk about, for example, the recently discovered and truly viable ways of growing hair on a

8. Belinsky is paraphrasing a line from the character Famusov in Griboyedov's play *Woe from Wit.*

bald head or how to have a splendid career in a very short time. Indeed, if any of these gentlemen would begin to discuss literature with me, I would be bored to death. On the other hand, in Moscow one often encounters people who talk about *Byron and other important matters*[9] and who do not just repeat what other people say. They know and understand what they are talking about because they are individuals who do not get confused or sidetracked by an authority or someone's opinion. In Moscow also, one can often run across people who have some rather strange ideas about things. One could even say they are often mistaken in their views, but at least they think in their own way, as they themselves see things, and not like what one or another gentleman thinks. But I much prefer these individuals over those who can talk about everything and who agree with everybody without knowing or being interested in anything. What about those various types of liars and lunatics that exist everywhere? If Griboyedov found Repetilov in Moscow, Gogol also found Ivan Aleksandrovich Khlestakov there. People in Moscow respect authorities much less than their counterparts in Petersburg not only as regards the truth but also the personal opinions of everyone around. Old names arouse a lot less trust in readers than newly arrived and younger talents. Expressions like "he has written himself out" or "he has fallen behind" are completely unknown in Petersburg, though to the indignation of aging geniuses, they are used quite frequently in Moscow. Moscow has authorities who have established themselves over the course of many years—one has written five short novels in twenty years; another has penned about two dozen picturesque poems,[10] and so forth. But these authorities are a *separate group unto themselves.* They attract their own public by praising each other via a third party who, expecting the same kind of praises from them, forwards such adulation to the intended party. In Moscow, though, the contemporary audience judges these "celebrities" in its own way, without paying much attention to what these famous people think about themselves. We already have noted that Moscow University gives its own special color to the reading public in that city because its members—those who teach and those who study—are the genuine cornerstone of the Moscow public. That is why Moscow has more

9. Belinsky is again citing *Woe from Wit.*

10. Belinsky is again mocking Polevoi and Alexei Khomyakov.

young people who belong to science and literature than anywhere in Russia. A significant number of the teachers, translators, and employees of journals in Petersburg, together with the civil servants there, are people who have moved from Moscow. Such a situation is hardly surprising because to those involved in literature or public service, Moscow does not offer a wide enough arena for those who wish to do something in these areas. That is why those who would rather "do nothing" than "not do anything" hurry to move from Moscow to Petersburg: they fear being transformed from people who can do things to those who only talk about doing things.

In Petersburg, people become writers by accident. They enter the literary profession not from calling or passion or capability but from poverty and circumstances. Petersburg has many periodicals and even the smatterings of a book trade. So writing hands are needed and are being sought everywhere. A young office worker has never thought of becoming an author because he has never read anything. By accident, though, he meets a writer, a feuilletonist, or a reviewer, and in a very short time, one of them convinces him that he too can be a writer who is no worse than anyone else. This young worker first writes feuilletons about tailors, as well as about cigarette and lipstick shops. He then begins to pass judgments on Russian literature. Finally, he himself begins to write stories, vaudevilles, even dramas and novels. After all, it is so easy to do such things! In Petersburg, literary fame is dirt cheap. One has only to work *a bit more cheaply* for some newspaper, which, like a basket, contains anything that people throw into it. One can also work for nothing at all for some magazine that loses a hundred subscribers yearly. In the former instance, the owner of the newspaper will immediately declare that you are a young man of literature with great hopes for the future. In the latter, the owner of a repulsive and asinine journal will proclaim that you are a genius, even though you are someone who has never been able to do the simplest thing. You will be required only to know how to use the commonplace expressions of contemporary journalism—a type of knowledge that is easier to acquire than to learn the three Rs. That is why there are scads of writers in Petersburg. Later, you as a writer will be asked to praise and extol your own people and to criticize foreigners. Such a thing is also easy to learn. In Moscow, if you are a reviewer or a critic and attack the works of some writer, not only the public but even the writer himself can understand that you are acting not from personal bias or from base calculation but from a conviction that is perhaps incorrect but sincere and honest. In Petersburg, though, such a situation is something that no one understands. "What have I ever done to him? Why is he taking out after me?" a writer will ask when you write an unfavorable review of his article or book. "I have always praised him. Besides, what is there for us to fight about? I just happen to write in a completely different style than he does, so I cannot be in his way or make him nervous." Love for the truth, the sacredness of conviction, the ability to take offense at a book or article because it itself offends aesthetic or common sense, these are things almost no one really wants to know. Nonetheless, Petersburg does not have a single scribbler who would not talk most of all about conscientiousness, good intentions, love for science, and striving for the success of Russian literature. Indeed, it is very often some literary associate who cries louder than others about such things, even though he has changed several bosses and has betrayed each and every one of them several times along the way. In Moscow, the people who write are scrupulous as regards their reputation and convictions. If you insult him in print, the Muscovite man of letters will not become your friend over a bottle of champagne. The custom of bearing no grudges and, generally speaking, the ability to forgive enemies at the first sign of something advantageous and profitable is one of the most remarkable virtues of Petersburg writers. In Moscow people with opposing convictions do not like to get together even in the simplest of everyday situations. And as we see it, the source of such conduct is also worthy of praise, though if carried to extremes, it can be subject to criticism. Several Muscovite writers have preserved this mode of behavior also in Petersburg, and they are regarded as moral monsters and depraved individuals. After all, in this city, the only thing of importance is social intercourse, not convictions.

In Petersburg, people publish books that are more beautiful than those of their counterparts in Moscow. A Petersburg novelist of the fifteenth rank writes all of the "certain characteristics" of the lives of great people, and in his works, the honor of being a hero goes only to Napoleon, Frederick the Second, and the like.[11] Muscovite scribblers in their novels

11. Belinsky has in mind Rafail Zotov and such novels as his 1834 work *The Mysterious Monk; or, Several Features of the Life of Peter I* (*Tainstvennyi monakh, ili nekotorye cherty iz zhizni Petra I*); his 1837 tome *Nicholas, the Bear's Paw, Ataman of the Contrabandists; or, Several Features from the Life of*

portray family life: a *he* and a *she,* "cursed places," and similar things.[12] They also depict the shattering of the Tatar yoke in Sokol'niki and the heroic deeds of Tan'ka, the villain in Marina's Grove.[13] The Petersburg scribbler has never even seen the entrance hall of a decent home, but in his stories and novels, he portrays high society, bon ton, aristocrats, and life as it exists with these people and things.[14] The Moscow scribbler describes a jackass rebel and discloses the dissolute life of merchants' sons in Marina's Grove.[15] So now do you see the difference between the scribblers of both our capitals! Moscow has few feuilletonists and reviewers, if only because there are absolutely no newspapers there. Journals in that city also do not exist. But in Petersburg, feuilletonists and reviewers make up a special and numerous guild. Generally speaking, anyone who wants to have a closer look at everyday scribblers in Petersburg would be advised to read Mr. Panaev's "The Louse"[16] and "The Feuilletonist" in an attentive way. In time we will also present an article entitled "Men of Literary Effects and Masters of Book Matters,"[17] in which we will disclose the secrets and other curious phenomena of the petty literary and book world of Petersburg.

Just as new ideas and movements have already belonged to Moscow, so now do new journals belong exclusively to Petersburg. But until 1834 Petersburg had been poor in such things because at that time, Moscow was the center of journalistic activity. The reasons for the decline of journalism in Moscow are quite obvious. Moscow can reflect and understand, but it is

---

Frederick (*Nikolas, medvezh'ia lapa, ataman kontrabandistov, ili nekotorye cherty iz zhizni Fridricha II*); and his 1840 piece *Leonid; or, Several Features of the Life of Napoleon* (*Leonid, ili nekotorye cherty iz zhizni Napoleona*). It should also be noted that Belinsky's scorn of Zotov could hardly be greater, when one considers the fact that Peter the Great's Table of Ranks consisted of only fourteen ranks!

12. The citation is to Mikhail Voskresensky's 1836 novel *He and She* (*On i ona*) and his 1838 work *The Cursed Place* (*Prokliatoe mesto*).

13. Belinsky is referring to an 1834 pulp work, *Tan'ka, the Rostokinsky Pirate; or, The Harems of the Tsar: A Historical Story of the Eighteenth Century* (*Tan'ka, razboinitsa rostokinskaia, ili tsarskie terema: Istoricheskaia povest' vosemnadtsatogo veka*).

14. The individual in question is Leopold Brant, a colleague of Bulgarin, whose works—for example, *The Woman Aristocrat: A Tale of Recent Times* (*Aristokratka: Byl' nedavnikh vremen*), published in 1842, and *Life as It Is* (*Zhizn', kak ona est'*), printed a year later—displayed a pretentious and lackeylike view of aristocratic life.

15. Belinsky brings to minds two works: the 1836 anonymous pulp work *The Merrymaking of Merchant Sons in Marina's Grove* (*Razgul'e kupechekikh synkov v Mar'inoi roshche*) and N. Bazilevich's 1841 work *The Jackass Rebel; or, Masha's Wedding* (*Kozel-buntovshchik, ili Mashina svad'ba*).

16. Panaev published "The Louse" ("Tlia") in 1843.

17. Such an article never came to be.

not good at making things happen—at least in the literary sphere. Many people ridicule the punctuality with which issues of Petersburg journals come out over an appropriate period of time, but no matter how people laugh at such a phenomenon, it is a virtue, not a vice. In the course of every six months, Moscow will suddenly be host to the first books of this year, the last books of the previous one, and sometimes, as often happens, books of the year before that. Also nothing resembles anything else. Furthermore, Moscow does not have a single journal that comes out on a regular basis. The reason for such a shortcoming is that Muscovites are still faithful to the old pre-Petrine ways, that is, they love to do everything without too much knowledge and effort. They still have not grown accustomed to thinking that literary affairs have everyday, tiring, and practical aspects that demand a special type of talent, and that if one does not know such things, he cannot take his ideas very far. In Moscow, journals are published—how best to put this?—in a patriarchal way. Payment for writing articles or collaborating on issues is considered strange, exceptional, and even beneath the dignity of literary culture, even though such a "noble" attitude does not at all prevent publishers from spending the profits from their publications. Moscow was the home of *Herald of Europe,* the oldest and, until 1825, best journal in the Russian language. It was published first by Karmazin in 1802 and then by Zhukovsky, who sometimes worked together with Kachenovsky, who eventually took over the publication completely.[18] The greatest flowering of Muscovite journalism was from 1820 to 1830, inclusively. In that year [1830] also, there closed suddenly several other publications: *Herald of Europe,* the *Moscow Herald, Atheneus,* and *Galateus,* which since 1831 has been revived under the name of the *Telescope.*[19] But even though this publication brought together the efforts of almost all the people who had worked for the four aforementioned journals, it still was not a success because it did not command the attention of the public. The number of subscribers never crossed the wished-for line of a thousand people, and so

18. *Herald of Europe* (*Vestnik Evropy*) was a journal published in Moscow between 1802 and 1830 and devoted to literature, art, and political affairs.

19. The *Moscow Herald* (*Moskovskii Vestnik*) was a biweekly literary magazine that was edited by Mikhail Pogodin and published in Moscow between 1827 and 1830. *Atheneus* (*Atenei*) was a journal devoted to philosophy; it existed between 1828 and 1830. *Galateus* (*Galatei*) was published in Moscow between 1829 and 1830 before it was resurrected in 1831 by Nikolai Nadezhdin as the *Telescope* (*Teleskop*) for an additional five years.

it died a slow death.[20] By the same token, though, the best periodical of the time, the *Moscow Telegraph,* which was famous for just about everything including its *huge* number of subscribers, never had more than fifteen hundred readers and most of the time held at twelve hundred. All these journals came out in rather thin issues with small formats.[21]

Finally, Petersburg felt that its time had come. It understood that besides talent, the great driving force in journalism was material largesse. It also grasped that even if money does not give birth to talent, it can still force whatever talent there is to become more industrious so as to insure its position in society and to liberate it from the need to look for means of support other than literary activity. Such an idea could be born only in Petersburg and least of all in Moscow. For instance, the *Library for Reading*[22] understood that journals could not maintain their existence exclusively by espousing a particular direction that would attract masses of similarly minded people. So the *Library for Reading* decided first (as much as was possible), to bring together the work of all more or less famous writers, and second, to satisfy the demands and tastes of its extremely diverse audience. To do such a thing, it decided to publish a thick issue once a month and to make the encyclopedic variety of its content the basis for its existence. It turned out that such calculations were correct, the proof being that the *Library for Reading* had *five thousand* subscribers in the first years of publishing. Although time would show that the *Library for Reading* could not provide a united exterior from a disunited interior and that during more recent years its subscribers were fewer than those in the first year of its publication, the journal had nonetheless started out on a firm footing. From that time on, a journal that had fewer than a thousand subscribers and thus had been considered prosperous previously, hardly had any chance of surviving. But now people have discovered that the secrets for success are based in material largesse. Indeed, much to the dismay of journals in

20. This is not true. The *Telescope* was closed by Nicholas I for publishing the first of Pyotr Chaadaev's *Philosophical Letters* (*Filosofskie pis'ma*), written in 1829.

21. The *Moscow Telegraph* (*Moskovskii telegraf*) was a biweekly literary journal published in Moscow between 1825 and 1834. As was the case with the *Telescope,* the *Moscow Telegraph* was closed by Nicholas I, in this case for an unfavorable review by Polevoi on Kukol'nik's play *The Hand of the Almighty Has Saved the Fatherland.*

22. The *Library for Reading* (*Biblioteka dlia chteniia*) was a monthly journal published in St. Petersburg from 1834 to 1865. In the 1830s, it carried more than seven thousand subscribers.

Moscow, the idea and motive for publishing have moved to their counterparts in Petersburg.

The *Library for Reading* is a journal that is permeated with the Petersburg genius and thus completely unlike any Muscovite publication. As journals in Moscow espouse enthusiasm and love for the ideal, the *Library for Reading* vaunts a positive spirit of irony and ridicule about things about which one is not forbidden to joke but that nonetheless deserve attention and respect. Incidentally, this tendency to poke fun at things has had a positive effect because it serves to counter the childish and unfounded idealism and enthusiasm that, even when they are quite moderate, are laughable and, when they are extreme, are simply unbearable. One extreme always cures another. Nevertheless, the appearance of the *Library for Reading* has had a great influence not only on Russian journalism but also on Russian literature in general. We recall that when the journal first came into existence, many writers were scandalized by the fact that it paid their writers for each and every line, and very well to boot. As a result, the fact that the owner of a publication was making a profit meant that the people who worked for him also had the means to exist. We are now so far from the childish outlook on so-called commercialism in literature that we even find it difficult to understand how it ever existed at all.[23] A writer-tradesman is ready to write both *for and against* something that he has been hired to write, whereas a man of literature will never betray his convictions for the sake of money. Pushkin said:

> A work of art is not for sale
> But manuscripts can be sold.[24]

Suppose that from honor, a market could give away beef and bread, and stores could hand over cloth and goods. If such things were so, one could write for journals not only for money but also for honor. Byron was

23. Belinsky is here taking issue with Stepan Shevyryov, who in an 1836 article "Literature and Commerce" ("*Literatura i torgovlia*") argued for unmercenary considerations in art. Also see Belinsky's 1836 article "About Criticism and the Literary Opinions of the 'Moscow Observer'" ("*O kritike i literaturnykh mneniiakh 'Moskovskogo nabliudatelia'*"), in Belinskii, *Polnoe sobranie sochinenii,* vol. 2 (1953), 123–77.

24. The citation here, with some license, is from Pushkin's 1824 poem "A Conversation of a Bookseller with a Poet" ("Razgovor knigoprodavtsa s poetom").

never a tradesman—he never sold his inspiration and never wrote for journals—but nonetheless, he received enormous sums for his manuscripts.

Generally speaking, all of what we have said comes down to one and the same thing, that is, both Petersburg and Moscow have their own importance and significance for Russia, and their collective assets will become more obvious once railroads connect the two cities. This railway will be a great thing. It will be a wide path for civilization, enlightenment, and education. Most of all, it will be a commercial affair, the offspring of calculation and money.

—V.B.

The Lottery Ball

Dmitri Grigorovich

On September seventeenth[1] in Petersburg (not to mention other cities in Russia), there occurs an event that is unlike any other day of the year.

Carriages regularly collide with each other at the entrances to stores. People of all ranks and stations, even individuals who have nothing interesting about them, come out of confectioners' shops with packages and baskets under their arms. Clothing and toy stores run out of wares. There is no way that one can even enter the English store. Crowds stampede and swarm through the department stores. On September seventeenth, it is not only in the streets but also in each and every home that the hustle and bustle grows with incredible speed. In one place, people counter the everyday atmosphere by polishing parquet floors and hanging curtains in the windows. In a second, people seek to break the established routine by replacing tallow candles with stearin ones. In a third, homeowners add two or three card tables to the two or three already there, something they do every evening with German punctuality. In short, every roof harbors plenty of commotion, rearranging, and running about.

Perhaps you find it extremely strange that all these goings-on are happening on September seventeenth. But have mercy! How can it be otherwise? Judge for yourselves! One has a wife, Sofia; another has two daughters, Vera and Lyubov'; a third has a sister, Nadezhda; a fourth has

1. According to the Russian calendar (old style), September seventeenth was the name day for individuals with the names of Vera, Nadezhda, Lyubov', Agafokleya, and Sofia.

a sister-in-law, Agafokleya (fortunately, such names are becoming rarer now), and, finally, a fifth has the fate of having family members with all these names—Vera, Lyubov', Nadezhda, Agafokleya, and Sofia. After all, how can it be otherwise? But relatively speaking, all this hustle and bustle means absolutely nothing when compared to what happened on September seventeenth last year in the Petersburg district, in the house of the collegiate secretary, Foma Fomich Krutobryushkov.

Just imagine: fate, this very fate which pays positively no attention to rank and consequently to the wages associated with it, this fate frowned on Krutobryushkov's wife and his three daughters. Foma Fomich, having foreseen the tragic situation and expenses that he incurred by celebrating his daughters' name days on three separate occasions (for even in our time, such celebrations are considered a sacred obligation), decided that his children would celebrate their name days at one time, on one day alone.

Incidentally, people who are not in the same situation as Krutobryushkov also do such things. But I am certain there that their purpose has an even more economical basis than the pleasure of portraying the family in an allegorical style, as a cross, an anchor, and a burning heart.

A name day would not have produced any special revolution in the home of Foma Fomich, nor would it have been celebrated with the usual quiet and modesty, had it not occurred to the respected official about two months before the events that we are describing here: Foma Fomich wished to organize a lottery. It seems that this idea was exactly like all the others Foma Fomich had in that it had entered his head not as the result of thinking but by accident. Indeed, this one was no exception.

Foma Fomich had an older brother who kept a little shop located between the third and fourth lines on Vasilievsky Island, one that sold all kinds of ancient things such as furniture, tin plates, pictures, and books. This brother died suddenly and, in his will, left all his property to Foma Fomich. Foma Fomich was so firm in character, though, that despite the sorrow burdening his soul, he began selling off some of his inheritance the day after the sorrowful event. But some things he saved. Furthermore, Foma Fomich, having heard from good and kind people about the incredible profits one could make by having a lottery, decided to take a chance and to arrange one himself. As a matter of fact, hardly a month had passed to show that the advice of his friends had been well founded and that Foma

Fomich's dreams had come true beyond anyone's expectations. Tickets for the lottery were sold with incredible speed.

Despite the fact that most of the tickets had already been taken, Krutobryushkov would have done what so many extremely respected people usually did: He would have no doubt postponed the drawing until some other day, continuing the lottery forever. But he was kept from doing so by an extremely important event.

It so happened that one day Foma Fomich was sitting in the department next to the councillor, Alexander Petrovich Tsvirkuliaev, an individual who, in all of life's events, maintained an air of incredible importance but who, at this particular moment and for some unknown reason, could not conceal his high spirits and was in an extremely good mood.

Krutobryushkov, impelled by an unusual feeling of tender emotion (a feeling which arises in every subordinate who has the good fortune of sitting down next to his superior just at the right moment) could not help but tell him of his intentions to have a lottery. Alexander Petrovich, wishing to show that he was a very tolerant boss, not only approved of his subordinate's undertaking but also took two tickets and promised to be present for the drawing.

So you see, there was no possibility of postponing the lottery, and Foma Fomich, wishing to avoid extra expenses, decided to have the drawing on the same say as the name day of both his wife and daughters.

But before we begin describing the preparations for the celebration, we should acquaint the readers with the individuals who will play the major roles in the event.

Foma Fomich Krutobryushkov is not a tall man but a rather fat individual, with an unusually red face and a polished bald spot on the top of his head. There is nothing particularly extraordinary about Foma Fomich's appearance except for the fact that he has no eyebrows whatsoever. Such a lack gives his face a honey-sweet and, at times, affected expression. Foma Fomich is extremely religious and works extremely hard at a job he has held for fifteen years. He is also a good head of the household. His grammar is quite poor, but he has an unusual interest in speculative transactions. Foma Fomich's wife, Sofia Ivanovna, is a woman of medium build who looks just like her husband except for her eyebrows, which are extremely thick and black. Her women neighbors assert that she loves to gossip, but such an opinion I attribute more to spite than truth because Sofia Ivanovna is the godmother of a garrison mayor. Mrs. Krutobryushkova is also an extremely hot-tempered woman who, by virtue of the physical force granted to her by nature, uses her talents for the wrong purposes. (Even Foma Fomich has admitted to such.) She rules her daughters with an iron hand. She reigns over her household with similar determination and takes command of the kitchen when, for dinner, people wanted *kulebyaka,*[2] a dish for which she is famous throughout the neighborhood. One of Sofia Ivanovna's most remarkable traits is her memory. Indeed, she is so fortunate in this regard that she can remember every date on the calendar. Ask Sofia Ivanovna the dates for Saint Mamel'fa's or Evpsikhii's or Evtikhii's feast day and she can tell you, accurately and right away, on which day the church celebrates the feast days of Mamel'fa, Evtikhii, and Evpsikhii. Sofia Ivanovna also loves to have people in her home. She invites one for tea, another for *vatrushka,*[3] and still another for an omelet. After her guests leave, though, she usually curses them soundly and assures everyone that she and all her habits of Muscovite generosity have been taken advantage of. But such anger does not prevent Mrs. Krutobryushkova from being a good hostess and kind spouse.

As regards Foma Fomich's daughters, a certain poem from Kazan'[4] will free us from the need to describe them:

> One of them, Vera, is a brunette,
> The second, Lyubinka, is a coquette,
> The third, Nadin'ka, is a blonde
> And the best of all, I'll bet.

As a matter of fact, Nadin'ka, the youngest daughter of our respected official, differs from her sisters in that she has a rather pretty face, which arouses jealousy in Vera and Lyubov'. Lyubochka, the oldest of the three girls, has already passed the deadline for being a bride. She is only twenty-seven, but such a circumstance arouses in her an even greater desire to flirt and be liked. Lyubochka has already had a number of romantic adventures,

2. *Kulebyaka* is a type of pie with meat, cabbage, and/or salmon filling.
3. A *vatrushka* is a savory open tart, topped with *tvorog,* or Russian farmer cheese.
4. The reference for this poem is unknown.

one of which is worth mentioning. She was once in love with a collegiate registrar who used to visit the Krutobryushkov's home quite often. The registrar had raised great hopes that Lyubochka would be his spouse. But it turned out that he did so only to while away the time. (He later married a merchant woman.) Initially, Lyubov' Fominishna, in a fit of jealousy and rage, had wanted to jump into the Malaya Neva. But fortunately she limited herself to writing to her traitor a letter that went like this:

> You oughta be 'shamed of yerself for decievin' me, not only before you, but in front of God, too. My honer is dear to me. God will punesh you; how could you do such a thing! . . . Oh, its' unbarable to get sich bad news after all the good i did, i read your note and fainted it would have been better if you shot me with a pistel so I wouldn't suffer so much. . . . Oh, oh how i am suff'ring 'cause of you with all the goodness of my heart. God will punesh you but good. But God be with you I am dyin' from 'tacks of sadness, oh, oh, you villein, you. . . .

Having expressed her despair is such a way, Lyubov' Fominishna seemingly took revenge on her treacherous lover by flirting with every one of his friends, without caring who the person was. But since none of these individuals seemed to notice her advances, she remains even now in the status of a maiden.

Verochka is the exact opposite of her sister because she is extremely sentimental and shy. She also has a highly developed sensitivity to things. If a rooster attacks a hen in a yard, she cries; if she fails to thread a needle, she cries anew; and if she happens to drop a plate or rip her apron, she is in tears once more. In a nutshell, she is ready to cry anytime, anyplace. Verochka always keeps some gloomy novel under her pillow, for example, *The Love of a Negro; or, A Black Man Unlike Many Whites,*[5] and other books in that vein. Also, Lyubochka gets inexplicable pleasure from teasing Verochka and calling her a *sissy.*

5. *The Love of a Negro; or, A Black Man Unlike Many Whites* (*Negr, ili chernyi, kakikh malo byvaet belykh*) was a Russian reworking of a piece by the French writer Joseph Lavallée; it was first published in Russia in 1797–98.

Nadin'ka is a complete child and sings nonstop: "Suddenly the piano sounded a chord—u-u-u-u—fly away, sadness of mine" and other similar things.

Without exception, all three girls adore dressing up and strolling through the department stores.

To complete the picture of the family life of our college registrar, one should also acquaint the reader with Savishna, who holds the position (a purely formal designation) as the cook in the household. Savishna, like all Russian common womenfolk who are engaged in the domestic arts, cannot boast of any special cleanliness as regards her person. She is also not particularly bright because she has just recently been brought in from Kaluga, her birthplace. Savishna absolutely hates to dust. In fact, she cannot even understand why anyone does such a thing. Indeed, when Sofia Ivanovna orders her to do so, she says: "Damn you! . . . Really, one can dust as much as one pleases, but there'll be twice as much of the stuff the next day." Savishna calls Lyubov', Vera, and Nadin'ka "young ladies," and whenever she has spare time, she takes out a pack of cards and tells their future for them in a rather successful way.

On September seventeenth, the family of the collegiate secretary rose much earlier than usual. After everyone had expressed his or her best wishes to everyone else, and after Savishna had presented Sofia Ivanovna with a pretzel shaped in a knot, the family settled around the steaming samovar and drank tea.

"Well, Mother, today is your name day," Foma Fomich said, sipping his tea. "And you, Nadya" (she was his favorite) "will probably be glad that guests are coming today. Yes, I believe that you've been looking forward to and dreaming about such a day for an entire two weeks now, am I right?. . ."

"Better we talk about business," Sofia Ivanovna answered in a serious tone. "It's no fun to think about all the people who are going to be showing up here. . . . Where are we going to put them all? We have to think carefully. After all, we have only two rooms. . . ."

"What else can we do?! . . . Besides our own family and friends, we are also going to have all those people who took tickets for the lottery. . . . I myself also thought that our apartment might be too small, but perhaps not all of them will come. . . ."

"How can they not come! You are such a ninny, such a simple-soul ninny! Don't you know that this is all that people have been looking forward to—to eat and drink at someone else's expense?"

"That is very true, Sofia Ivanovna, but God knows, perhaps we will manage somehow. . . . Wait a minute! We need to see how many tickets are still unspoken for."

Having said this, Foma Fomich ran to the wardrobe, opened and pulled from the bottom of the second drawer a piece of paper on which he had written the winning prizes and their numbers. For a long time, he had known the list by heart, as if it had been a member of his family. But he looked at the list again because he took great pleasure in admiring it. The list, after all, had been his *idea* and it guaranteed him quite a bit of money. (Several of the officials had bought their tickets on credit.)

Here is what the collegiate secretary read for the hundredth time:

> This will be an amiable lottery with a ball, music, dances, dinner, and other entertainment.
>
> The prizes will be:
> 1. A diamond ring.
> 2. An English silver watch.
> 3. A gold chain with a key.
> 4. A piano.
> 5. A large clay pipe in a silver setting and a large long-stem smoking pipe.
> 6. A box from Italy with such lady's things as scissors, a thimble, a pincushion, a threading needle, two mother-of-pearl spools, and a mirror.
>
> The price of a ticket is one silver ruble.

At the bottom of the page were the lottery numbers together with the names of Foma Fomich's friends and acquaintances who had written their signatures alongside them. Small crosses made by the conscientious host on the left side of some of the tickets indicated that they had been bought for cash. In short, everything was the way it was supposed to be. Only one thing could seem strange to someone who was not an official like Foma

Fomich. The majority of officials did not write their last names; rather, the page was covered with various allegorical inscriptions. For instance, across from the number eight was written: "*a lucky man*"; next to another, most likely some amusing person or so-called *soul of departmental society* had penned in rather carefully: "*adoo, moan cher ami*"; still alongside a third, someone had written, for some reason and in place of a name, the following words: *my respects,* and so on.

It seemed that Foma Fomich was extremely pleased with such sweet inscriptions and continued reading: "The end of these tickets, collegiate secretary, Foma Krutobryushkov, August 17, 1844."

"Only Mikhailo Mikhailovich Zhelchnyi has not bought a ticket," Foma Fomich said, after he had finished reading the list. "No," Zhelchnyi had told him. "We all know these lotteries. Moreover, whenever I buy a ticket, I never win. So I vowed that I would not do so again."

"A miser of a man," Foma Fomich said to himself. "The only thing Zhelchnyi knows is how to spread rumors and impose himself on his hosts. Well, someday I will teach him a lesson. . . . I should read again who is going to come, I have to prepare something to eat. . . .

"First of all, there will be Alexander Petrovich Tsvirkuliaev, our councillor. . . . He bought two tickets. . . . Please, Lyuba, don't forget to serve him first when you come in with the apples, appetizers, and whatever else you will be serving. . . . And all of you, try to please him as much as you possibly can. Vakh Onufrievich will also be coming. . . ."

"Oh, Foma, and he will get as drunk here as he did at the baptismal party at Ivan Ivanovich Maslyanikov's?"

"Well, to keep such a thing from happening, we will give instructions that no one gets more than one class of *pernch*. . . . Also coming are Methody Karpych, the collegiate assessor; Akula Gerasimovich Ershov, the executor; the children's godmother, Arina Petrovna—but then again, she's practically family; Sila Mamontovich with a spouse. . . . Ivan Ivanovich Maslyannikov. . . ."

"Now just tell me, Foma Fomich, how can we possibly feed all these people? This is no joke. You are going to have almost the entire department here. . . . What are we going to do?"

"There is no other way, my dear. Besides we are going to have a lottery, so we are not wasting all this food for nothing. . . . There will also be Voloskov, the assistant to the head of the department; Vladimir Makaronich Semyanichkin with his spouse . . . Natalia Kuzminishna. . . . It seems that I almost forgot Ivan Ivanovich Yelkin. . . . a splendid young man who is very well respected by his superiors and makes a good salary, to boot. . . . He'd make a good fiancé for Lyubochka. . . ."

"Oh, he's a good one, your Yelkin," the Krutobryushkovs' elder daughter replied in a rude and abrupt way. "I'd sooner hang myself than marry such a pipsqueak. . . ."

"No one is good enough for you! What's wrong with Yelkin for a fiancé? I simply don't understand you! I hope that Apollon Ignat'evich doesn't let us down. He promised that he would come without fail and even play the piano once he gets here. But God knows if it will be our misfortune that he drinks too much 'cause then we will never get to see him. . . ."

"Well, children, be on your best behavior," Foma Fomich continued, "and for Christ's sake, be as pleasant with the guests as possible, especially our councillor. He's an older man and someday may be in a position to help us."

"But what would anyone want to do with us?" Lyubochka said, pushing away her cup. "You should have had some new dresses sewn up for us. Why, we look like beggars in what we are wearing now. . . ."

"What's this? What are you talking about?" Sofia Ivanovna exclaimed suddenly, approaching her daughter. "Is your mother any worse than you, I'd like to know! Your mother has been going about in the same old house-coat that she has to wear inside out every two years to make it last. . . . Are you worse off than your sister, perhaps? Tell me! . . ."

"That's enough, Sonyushka. . . . Leave her alone . . . if only for the sake of this day," Foma Fomich said, holding his spouse's hand, which was ready to fall on his daughter's shoulders. (We have already noted that Sofia Ivanovna loved to take strong measures.)

"No, no, perhaps, your mother is worse off than you?"

"Oh, really, why do you always have to yell so much?" Lyubocha screamed. "Let these other fools obey you, I don't even want to know you!"

"Oh, oh, oh," Verochka began squeaking in a pitiful way. "How dare she call us fools."

Lyubov' Fomininshna ran out into the other room, having slammed the door loudly behind her. Soon everyone heard a terrible moaning, which immediately calmed them down. Sofia Ivanovna, who was used to such scenes, poured herself a second cup of tea. Verochka stopped whining, and Foma Fomich spread himself out on the sofa.

"Well, Mother," he said. "You give orders as you please about the things that have to be bought, and I and the children will tidy up the place. We can't leave it like this."

"Here's two red rubles for you," he continued, taking some money out of his greasy leather wallet. "I really can't afford any more than that. . . ."

"I think that it will be enough," Sofia said, "But perhaps it might be better to write down everything that I need to buy or else I will forget. . . . Get up! How can you just lie down all sprawled like that? This is hardly the time to relax. . . ."

Foma Fomich got up, pulled a bottle of ink closer to him, and began to write down what his wife dictated to him.

"Half a pound of tea, a bottle of rum, two pounds of wine cherries, fruit pastilles, shoes for Nadya, five lemons, about eight stearin candles. . . ."

"Mommy, please buy me some lipstick, but only pink-colored," Nadin'ka interrupted.

"Yes . . . All right, get this down: pink lipstick, black shoelaces, two yellow ribbons, eight pounds of veal. . . ."

"If you keep going on like this, you might as well decide to buy the whole city of Petersburg. . . . Have mercy, Sofia Ivanovna, you simply don't have enough money. . . . For example, what do you need the veal for? Why the hell do you need veal? . . ."

"Would you please be so kind and not butt into business that is not yours? Just keep on writing. . . ."

"Good God, Sofia Ivanovna, veal is totally unnecessary. . . . As I see it, you would do better to buy caviar, fresh, good caviar. . . . Such a thing would be better and cheaper, too. . . ."

"Well, all right, all right, write it down. . . ."

"Caviar. . . . Well, it seems that's it. . . . Go with God, and we will also get busy with things here. Get a move on. Soon it will be ten o'clock and nothing is ready yet."

Sofia Ivanovna put on her coat, put her shopping list together with the money into a handkerchief, and, accompanied by Savishna, quickly left in a coach for the city.

The task that the esteemed father of the family had undertaken was made all the more difficult because the rooms in the apartment were arranged in quite an awkward way. First of all, all apartments in Petersburg are arranged badly, beginning with the kitchen. From there stretched a narrow hallway that was totally impassable because there had been no other place to put the king-size bed of the spouses. So to get to the next room down the corridor, one cannot do anything else but walk sideways, with his back to the wall. Indeed, if some portly figure gets in the way, he has to jump over the bed altogether. Incidentally, portly figures are totally incapable of making such a move. At the end of the corridor are two rooms: The first one serves as a living room and a hall, the second as a bedroom for Verochka, Nadin'ka, and Lyubochka.

Despite all these difficulties, Foma Fomich did not get discouraged (such was his nature). In the middle of the first room, he put the piano as the key object and prize of the lottery. On it he arranged the other prizes in an extremely artful way, particularly showing off the box from Italy and the large clay pipe, which had been mounted on a colorful plate. All around were placed chairs and two sofas that were covered with a somewhat old but also quite pretty oilcloth. The milky gray walls shone forth with a great many pictures, the most noteworthy of these being a portrait of the head of the department where Krutobryushkov worked (a necessary possession that any *striving* official has to have) and some landscape that was painted in oil colors but that had become so blackened that one could scarcely make out the sky from the earth. Across from one of the sofas, Foma Fomich put a little round table which he bought for an occasion a long time ago. A wall clock hung in its old place by the window.

Arranging the second room of the apartment demanded still more work. Lyubochka absolutely refused to move despite her father's requests and Verochka's tears. Finally she gave in, and the bedroom of the three girls took on a more appropriate look, being designated for those people who would be playing cards.

Foma Fomich and his daughters had not yet managed to tidy up the apartment completely when the godmother, Arina Petrovna, came through the door with a rather huge knot-shaped pretzel (a common gift of cooks, godmothers, housekeepers, and old women who had rendered some kind of service).

"Hello, Foma Fomich, hello, girls," she said, putting her gift on the circular table. "Congratulations from the bottom of my heart." Making the sign of the cross, she continued: "May God grant you all every happiness, well-being, and good fiancés." (Arina Petrovna kissed one girl after another.)

"And just where is your wife?" she said, suddenly changing the intonation of her voice. "She must have gone to buy things and other fuss and bother. God grant that she do it all cheaply. Nowadays fish is so expensive; those damn merchants rob you without any conscience at all." She uttered the last words extremely quickly.

"Well, yes, it goes without saying, dear one, that all this business is costing me quite a lot," Foma Fomich said, somewhat unhappy about the ill-timed visit of the godmother and, more important, about the news of the high cost of food. "I am most grateful that you have not forgotten us and have paid us a visit."

"How could I forget you? Why, I even brought you a knot-shaped pretzel. I thought, 'Well, they can probably find a use for it,' and so I went out and got it. . . . Are you expecting a lot of guests tonight?"

"Yes, dear Arina Petrovna, quite a few . . . quite a few. . . . Do sit down, why are you standing? . . ."

"No, thank you. I've only come for a minute to congratulate you on your holiday. . . . I know that you have enough things to worry about without me adding to your troubles. . . . But I will be coming tonight. . . ."

"Come without fail. . . . We will be expecting you." After several new hugs and kisses, Arina Petrovna left, accompanied by her goddaughter, Nadin'ka. Krutobryushkov's family resumed working. Everything was ready when Sofia Ivanovna entered, bearing all kinds of packages and parcels. Having glanced at the rooms, she was quite pleased with the way they looked. Only one thing bothered her: the huge king-size bed that stuck out so inappropriately in the hallway. Having had a quick lunch, the family of the collegiate secretary began working on their own appearances.

At half past seven, the staircase at the Krutobryushkovs' home was illuminated with lighted tallow candle ends, which had been painstakingly saved by the mistress of the house. These candle ends were arranged quite artistically inside huge turnips, the middle of which Foma Fomich had drilled with holes. At the entrance of the apartment burned two dishes with lighted candles. Also, almost every table was host to *stearin* candles in tall candleholders. Judging by the illumination, the ball promised to be magnificent. Foma Fomich, wearing a white tie and a new dress coat, was running from one room to another, rearranging first some piece of furniture, then a candle, which poorly obeyed his shaking fingers. (He was in a state of great excitement.) Finally, he turned to his daughters, imploring them to finish with their toilet as soon as possible.

Sofia Ivanovna had already been in the kitchen for a long time. Thanks to the efforts of the thoughtful hostess, the plates bore hefty amounts of wineberries, pastilles, and Crimean apples that were cut in halves (a necessity for all kinds of balls, parties, and picnics). Sandwiches also played a significant role. Rows of glasses, at this point empty, extended along the service table in the kitchen, ready to exchange their emptiness for that salutary nectar which the official had baptized with the name of *punchik*. Despite being busy with all these things, Sofia Ivanovna found time to look after Savishna, who was preparing a *kulebyaka* on a trunk. (All the tables were occupied.)

"Now remember, Savishna," Sofia Ivanovna said. "Make sure you do everything like I told you. Serve punch to the male guests and tea to the ladies. And don't forget: do not pour a second glass of anything until I tell you to do so. . . . Oh! And do not burn the *kulebyaka*. . . ."

"Yes, ma'am, Sofia Ivanovna, I won't. . . ."

"Well, you might as well start slicing it. . . . No, no, I will do it myself. . . . But only serve it when I tell you to do so."

"Yes, ma'am, Sofia Ivanovna. . . . Are there gonna be a lot of g'ists?"

"Yes, yes, God forgive me, the devil should take them all. There's going to be quite a few. . . ."

"But why is it that they're not here yet, Sofia Ivanovna?" Foma Fomich uttered, entering the kitchen. "It will soon be half-past eight. . . ."

"They still have plenty of time. . . . Well, how about Lyuba and Nadya? Are they ready? Surely they have had plenty of time to make tea. . . ."

"They still haven't done it, though I told them many times to do so. The guests will be coming soon, but all those two care about is a scarf or a pin. . . . They give me nothing but trouble."

"Just watch. I'll move them along!"

And with that, Sofia Ivanovna headed for the living room where the celebrants were getting ready for the ball.

"Well, are you going to be ready soon?! How long are you going to sit there and make faces in front of the mirror?"

"Good Lord! They don't even give us enough time to get dressed around here! Do you want us to show up looking like beggars? . . . We look pretty bad as it is. . . ."

"Look you two. I have had more than enough out of you. . . ."

At that very minute, though, there was a noise in the kitchen, and Sofia Ivanovna, without finishing what she was about to say, immediately rushed into the hallway. Vera, Lyuba, and Nadya instantly hid the lipstick, mirror, and combs under the sofa and took their places at the doors. When the mistress of the house entered the kitchen, Foma Fomich was helping Natalya Vasilievna Semyanichkina with her fox-fur coat. She had arrived with her husband and two daughters, Anfisa and Ashin'ka.

"Hello, my dearest Sofia Ivanovna," Semyanichkina said. (She was passionately fond of playing the role of a society woman.) "Here we are. Congratulations on your name day and that of your daughters. . . . I have brought my own children with me. . . ."

"Yes, we have brought our children with us," Semyanichkin repeated in a mutter.

"Oh, when I think of all the trouble that you have gone to, darling Sofia Ivanovna. I was just telling my husband today that one has to be as good a hostess as Sofia Ivanovna to have the time to prepare everything for so many guests. . . ."

"Yes, that's just what my wife said," Semyanichkin muttered again.

"Do please come into the room. . . . Natalya Vasilievna. . . . Vladimir Markovich. . . Anfisa Vladimirovna. . . . I humbly implore you. . . ."

"Vladimir Markovich, I humbly implore you," Foma Fomich said, inviting his guest with his hand.

The Semyanichkins began moving, Natalya Vasilievna taking the lead. She was dressed, as they say, in her very best, with yellow ribbons that made her very much like some Indian god. Following her were two young ladies who were not at all bad-looking. The parade was ended by the timid

Semyanichkin, a small and quite thin and yellowish individual, dressed in a baggy and ill-fitting dress coat and with a left eye that was constantly tearing. Having made their way through the pass at Thermopylae[6] (the narrow space between the wall and the bed), the Semyanichkins successfully reached the living room, where Krutobryushkov's daughters awaited them.

But hardly had Sofia Ivanovna managed to seat her guests on the sofa and to begin an interesting conversation—about how expensive the apartment was, about its warmth, conveniences and inconveniences—when there again arose a noise in the kitchen and one heard Foma Fomich's voice announcing the arrival of new guests. Sofia Ivanovna found it necessary to rush off and meet them.

This time, she saw the accountant, Sila Mamontovich Buslov. Groaning and puffing, he was taking off his summer coat. (Sila Mamontovich was never cold; that is why he did not consider it necessary to wear heavier clothes in the wintertime.) His thick fingers, looking very much like carrots, did not obey their master and seemed to spread out more and more. Having finally gotten rid of his coat, the corpulent accountant first shook Foma Fomich's hand and then addressed Sofia Ivanovna.

"I am so very happy, madam, to have the occasion personally to congratulate you on your name day as well as our esteemed Foma Fomich. . . . I also brought my wife and daughter with me. . . . And I ask that you please make them feel at home. . . ."

With these words, he stepped aside and introduced to Sofia Ivanovna a woman who was as thin as a rail, with hair pushed way up, and wearing a dress that was so starched that if necessary, it could have served as a shelter to Sila Mamontovich himself. For her part, Mrs. Buslova introduced her daughter, a young girl about nineteen years old.

After the usual hugs and kisses, the ladies headed for the living room where the scent of *carnation eau de cologne* became more noticeable.

"Sofia Ivanovna," Semyanichkina said, getting up from the sofa, "I still have yet to see the prizes. Are they really all here?"

6. The Battle of Thermopylae took place in 480 B.C. and is one of history's most famous last stands, pitting a vastly outnumbered Greek force against invading Persians at the pass of Thermopylae in central Greece.

"All of them are here, Natalya Vasilievna. Take a look at this box, such fine work. Why, it's simply adorable. Genuine French craftsmanship."

"Yes, the box is very nice. . . . What would you like to win, Anfisa?" Semyanichkina continued, turning to her daughter after the hostess had left. "Perhaps a sewing box or a piano? I'd expect that you would be eager to get the piano?"

"No, mommy, I would rather have the diamond ring."

"And I would prefer to win the gold chain with the little key," Ashin'ka said.

"Well, I simply believe that we will not get anything at all," Natalya Vasilievna added in a whisper. "Most likely, the host and hostess hid the best tickets for themselves. . . . You will see. . . . Vladimir Markovich, where are you hiding? There he is sitting in the corner. Why, he doesn't wish even to take a look at the prizes!"

At this point one should note that Mr. Semyanichkin has this trifling weakness: he falls asleep immediately after he takes a seat. Furthermore, Semyanichkin could move to sleep from wakefulness so quickly that even before one turned his back on him, he could already have closed his eyes and let loose with a small nasal whistle. Indeed, he slept so constantly that real life appeared to him as a dream.

His spouse's voice (the only thing that could arouse Vladimir Markovich from his lethargy) woke him right away.

"What is it . . . Natalya Vasilievna?" he said, approaching his wife.

"Well, what would you like to win?" she asked. "Surely the clock?"

"A clock, Natalya Vasil'evna. . . . ."

"Well, but you wouldn't turn down the piano either?"

"The large clay pipe is absolutely marvelous, Natalya Vasilievna. . . ."

"Well, how can you say such a thing! A large clay pipe! . . . I wouldn't take such a thing if someone gave it to me as a gift! . . . But then this sewing box. . . . Now that's another thing altogether. . . ."

"Yes, the sewing box . . . is better. . . ."

Sila Mamontovich's rail-thin wife and his daughter took no part in the lottery whatsoever and sat as if glued to their seats.

Soon one could hear heavy sighs emerging from the hallway and announcing that the fat accountant was trying to squeeze in between the bed and the wall. But to everyone's surprise, he appeared promptly in the living-room.

While this respectful gentleman—a passionate lover of music, theater, and, generally speaking, such elegant things as painted Muscovite snuff-boxes, guns, and statues that are sold in the streets—conversed with the ladies about the pleasure that these things gave him, the Krutobryushkov's apartment gradually filled with people.

One after another there appeared Vakh Onufrievich Peterka, who is already known to the reader; the godmother Arina Petrovna who worked as an accountant's assistant; and Aristarkh Vissarionovich, whose eyes were incredibly like those of a curly-haired lapdog being fed meat by its naughty mistress, that is, they looked like they were drowning in some kind of red bilberry jam.

Foma Fomich's living room was already crowded when there also entered Ivan Ivanovich Maslyannikov with his very young son, Vanyusha; Mikhailo Mikhailovich Zhelchnyi, a retired official; and Apollon Ignatievich, the very one who was supposed to play the piano. The appearance of the latter brought especially great peace and joy to Foma Fomich.

"Foma Fomich! Hey, Foma Fomich! Hey, pal, are we going to have the lottery soon?" Mikhailo Mikhailovich Zhelchnyi asked, when the group finally settled down.

"We're just waiting for Alexander Petrovich . . . our counselor. . . ."

"You don't say! And he will come, too. . . . Wow! Alexander Petrovich will be here! . . . Now this was something that I did not know," Sila Mamontovich said, wiping off the sweat that was dripping from his nose. "Well, Foma Fomich, I certainly can see that your ball is no joke. . . ."

"Why, Alexander Petrovich even bought two tickets. . . ."

"You don't say? And he bought two tickets, too! Good for you, pal, good for you!"

"He must have somehow really made a pest of himself," Zhelchnyi whispered into the ear of Akula Gerasimovich Ershov, who worked as an executor.

"Akula Gerasimovich, my most profound respects," Foma Fomich pronounced, coming up to him. "I thank you for coming. . . ."

"Don't mention it. . . . I'm very glad to be here. . . ."

"Hello, Ivan Ivanovich," Krutobryushkov continued, catching sight of Maslyanikov and Vanyusha. "Long time, no see. . . . Are you in good health?"

"Thank you for your prayers, dearest Foma Fomich. . . ."

"Hello, Vanya. . . . Oh, he's such a clever boy. . . ."

"Sweetheart, kiss the gentleman," Ivan Ivanovich said, patting his son on the head.

"And how old is he?"

"He turned five on the feast day of Saints Frol and Laurus."

"Five already! . . . People are calling me, Ivan Ivanovich. . . . You will excuse me. . . ."

Foma Fomich went into the hallway.

"Daddy. . . . Daddy . . . What's that thing over there?" Vanyusha asked, pointing to the piano.

"Why, it's music, little one. . . . That's what they are playing."

"Music. . . . And what's this?" the child continued, climbing up onto the piano and touching the clock, the clay pipe, and the box from Italy.

"Don't touch anything, don't touch anything, little one . . . or else you will break it. . . . It's a pipe."

"A pipe!"

"Tell me, please, Ivan Petrovich, how's your wife feeling these days?" Sofia Ivanovna asked.

"I humbly thank you for your prayers. . . . I hope that the end will soon be in sight."

"You mean she hasn't given birth yet?"

"No, but any time now. . . ."

"Foma Fomich! Sofia Ivanovna! What about the lottery?" several voices said.

"This minute, ladies and gentlemen, this very minute. But wait just a little more. . . . I think that Alexander Petrovich will be arriving shortly, and you understand that we really can't start without him, can we? . . ."

"As I see it, you still haven't done anything with the tickets," the godmother, Arina Petrovna, said.

"Everything is ready except for Alexander Petrovich, who's not here yet. . . ."

"Who is going to draw the tickets?"

"Anyone can do it. It's no big deal."

"No, Foma Fomich, the child should be the one to do it. . . . That's the way it's done everywhere," Mikhailo Mikhailovich said, taking great pleasure in putting everyone in a difficult situation.

"Yes, indeed," Sila Mamontovich continued. "Yes, a child should be the one to draw the tickets. . . . He is, so to speak, the emblem of innocence, God's little angel. . . ."

"In that case, Ivan Ivanovich will let us borrow his Vanichka."

"I would be very happy to do so. . . . It would be very pleasant to do so. . . . Vanya, Vanya, do you want to do the drawings for the lottery?"

"Yeah, I want to . . . the lottery. . . ."

"What a dear little boy," Natalya Vasilievna said, approaching Maslyanikov with Krutobryushkov's daughters. "How old is he?"

"He turned five on the feast day of Saints Frol and Laurus."

"Give me a kiss, sweetheart," Mrs. Semyanichkina said.

"Go kiss auntie. . . ."

Ivan Ivanovich was extremely pleased that Foma Fomich's guests were taking such an interest in his son. He sat the boy down on his lap.

"So, my mischievous imp, whom do you love more: Mommy or Daddy?"

"Ma . . . Ma . . . Daddy."

"Oh, what a smart little boy! Give me a kiss, sweetheart! What a clever little boy! One sees right now that he will be a very intelligent person," said someone from the crowd that surrounded Ivan Ivanovich.

Maslyanikov was beside himself with joy, and so as to brag even more to the guests about Vanyusha's wit, he asked the boy, "Well, my little one, what would you wish your mother to give birth to—a little brother or a sister?"

"A ho . . . ho . . . horsie," Vanyusha answered boldly. The crowd burst out laughing. Ivan Ivanovich, not expecting such an answer, became so embarrassed that he put the child down on the floor and, for no reason at all, began feeling through his pockets.

At that very moment, the councillor, Alexander Petrovich Tsvirkuliaev, appeared at the door with the host in tow. Having greeted everyone with a rather important bow, Alexander Petrovich said to Foma Fomich in a somewhat forced tone, "Introduce me to your wife. . . . I wish to meet her."

"Sofia Ivanovna. . . . Sofie. . . . As you wish. . . . Alexander Petrovich. . . ." Krutobryushkov said, pushing his wife and daughters forward.

"Well, my friend, I see that they are still quite young," the councillor said with a certain importance, not standing on any ceremony and taking Nadin'ka by the chin. . . . "Well, what about the lottery?"

"This minute, Alexander Petrovich, this very minute. . . ."

All the guests gathered around the piano. Mikhailo Mikhailovich and the executor tried more than anyone else to be noticed by the councillor.

Vanyusha, to the extreme delight of his father, was seated on the piano between the sewing box and the clay pipe, which was still lying on the plate. He would be the one to draw blank papers for the prizes. Anfisa Vladimirovna, the daughter of Mrs. Semyanichkina, announced the numbers.

The lottery began.

Only two people did not take part in the lottery: the sensitive Vera Fominishna and Dmitri Alexeevich Voloskov, who had been irresistibly attracted to her for quite a long time. They had gone off to the side and had given themselves over to a silence that was broken only with periodic sighs. That was how they showed their love.

Meanwhile, in the other corner of the room, completely opposite sentiments were exciting the crowd. Every time Anfisa Vladimirovna drew a number, and especially when little Vanyusha unwrapped a piece of paper that was either a blank or a winning number, the crowd, tortured by anticipation, kept pressing toward the piano with all its might.

"Number nine!" said Anfisa Vladimirovna.

"Nothing!" Mikhailo Mikhailovich said with a happy smile.

"Number fifteen!"

"Nothing!"

"Oh, God damn it!" said Akula Gerasimovich Ershov. "I lost! But I knew it all along that I would lose. Why just today I told Mikhailo Alexandrovich Poplyovin that I would most likely lose. . . . That's my fate! That's the way it always is with me!"

"I've already told you," Zhelchnyi whispered in his ear, "that there must something crooked about the whole thing, completely crooked. . . . Just you watch, the councillor is going to win something."

"Number twenty-one!"

"Nothing!"

"Ninety-seven!"

"Nothing!"

"Three!"

"Nothing!"

"One!"

Natalya Vasilievna held her breath. It was her number.

Ivan Vasilievich, inseparable from his son, helped him unwrap the piece of paper and, seeing something written in there, read in a rather coherent way:

"The clay pipe, trimmed in silver with a big . . .

"I knew it! . . . Instead of winning the work box! . . . It's always something for Vladimir Markovich!"

But there was no reply. It must have been that Mr. Semyanichkin was off sleeping, leaning against something somewhere.

The lottery continued.

"Number thirteen!"

"Nothing!"

"A hundred!"

Ivan Ivanovich read:

"The box from Italy."

"Don't tell me that I won?" the councillor said with a self-contented smile. "To tell you the truth, I wasn't expecting to. . . ."

"Allow us the honor of congratulating you," Ershov and Zhelchnyi said at the same time.

"Alexander Petrovich, would you like us to deliver the box to your home, or would you like to take your prize with you?"

"No, why should I put you through all that trouble? Better that I take it home myself," the councillor answered.

"I told you there was something hokey going on," Mikhailo Mikhailovich whispered to the executor.

"I myself now see that very well," he replied.

Soon the lottery was over. The piano went to some official who was not even present at the party; and almost all of the remaining things passed into the hands of the master of the house.

Alexander Petrovich, despite all the requests of Sofia Ivanovna and Foma Fomich to have at least one cup of tea, immediately left after the drawing, taking his box with him and explaining his early departure by saying that he had other things to attend to. Vanyusha also parted with the guests and was put on the king-size bed by his caring father and Nadin'ka. The rest of the guests wandered through the rooms, talking about the tricks of fortune and the whims of fate.

After Alexander Petrovich had left, Krutobryushkov became somewhat unduly familiar with his guests, running from one to another with cards in his hands, trying to persuade them to set up a couple of games.

"Tell me, please, my dearest Akula Gerasimovich," Mikhailo Mikhailovich said in a whisper, "surely they must have invited us here with the intention of starving us to death. . . . Some party this is! . . . It even said on the invitation: 'with food and all kinds of fun and games.' . . . Some fun it is when they don't give you anything to eat. . . ."

"Yes, I myself am also feeling somewhat hungry. . . ."

"Well, thank God, it seems that they are at least bringing in some punch. . . ."

As a matter of fact, Savishna appeared from the corridor, carrying a huge tray stacked with cups and saucers. She was followed by Nadin'ka, who, with downcast eyes, was bringing in a basket with biscuits and slices of white bread.

The guests gathered around the tray.

"Well, this punch is only punch in name," Mikhailo Mikhailovich continued into the executor's ear. "Why, it's simply some weak tea. . . . Akh! Hee, hee, hee! . . ."

"Well, I believe that, you know, we could add a little chamomile into it."

"My dear, what is your name?"

"Savishna, sir."

"Do you know, Savishna, where we could get hold of a little rum to put in our glasses?"

"No, Sofia Ivanovna is angry enough as it is. She says I am pouring way too much as it is. . . . "

"Why, you're lying, you great big idiot!" Sofia Ivanovna screamed, her face purple with anger. "I beg your pardon, Mikhailo Mikhailovich, she's a stupid women who's straight from the country. . . . Kindly give me your glass."

"Countryside simplicity, madam," Mikhailo Mikhailovich noted with an evil grin. "Oh you, Savishna, Savishna! Yesterday's country girl!" he continued, looking at the embarrassed woman.

Natalya Vasilievna Semyanichkina, her daughter, the godmother Arina Petrovna, Krutobryushkov's daughters, and Ivan Ivanovich were all settled on the sofa and chairs about a little round table. They were listening attentively to Sila Mamontovich Buslov, who, not without particular eloquence, was praising some singers both at the post office as well as those who were under the direction of one Zhukov. He kept insisting that since the latter group sang *phononically,* he preferred them to the former.

While this conversation was going on, there entered into the Krutobryushkovs' living room the widow Pelageya Kuz'minishna Kurykova, with her two daughters and son, a young, extremely lively lad who was dressed in a carefully tied topknot. All of his movements sought to give the impression that he was a very successful young man. He was wearing a brown tailcoat with light buttons, a blue tie, a violet waistcoat, and elastic trousers, which he appeared to like very much since he kept stroking them with the palm of his hand as he stretched his leg forward.

Pelageya Kuz'minishna brought her daughters up to the mistress of the house. The young Kurykov made his way down the line of ladies, kissing each and every hand.

"Oh, what a pity, Pelageya Kuz'minishna, that you missed the lottery."

"Well, what could I do, darling Sofia Ivanovna? There was no chance for me to come earlier. . . . And just where is Foma Fomich? . . ."

"As usual, he has just sat down to play cards with friends. . . . Allow me to introduce you to a friend of mine, Natalya Vasilevna Semyanichkina."

"I am very pleased to meet you. . . . I hope that we can be friends. . . ."

The ladies kissed each other.

In the meantime Pyotr Petrovich (that was the young man's name) had already managed to utter a ton of pleasantries and had entered into everyone's favor. He now stood opposite Lyubov' Fominishna and begged her to dance the first French quadrille with him.

"Pelageya Kuz'minishna, please . . . have some tea," Sofia Ivanovna said, pointing to the tray that Savishna was carrying. "Young ladies, would you like some tea? . . . Pyotr Petrovich! . . . Some tea?"

"No, but I thank you humbly. After all, what you have here is much nicer than any tea . . . all the more so since I have the pleasure of talking to your daughter."

"My, my. . . . He is really something else, Pelageya Kuz'minishna. . . . He seems to be where the young ladies are. . . . "

"Oh, you don't have to tell me, he's such a *faire-le-coeur* that we really have a problem here. . . ."

"Well," Natalya Vasilievna interrupted, "It's quite all right for a young man to behave like that. Why, it's even necessary that he does so. Indeed, I find your son to be quite a sophisticated and educated young man."

Apollon Ignatievich, a thinnish but extremely tall official dressed in a formal light green uniform, sat down behind the piano. Sounds of "Well, Karlusha, don't be shy" signaled the beginning of the ball. The gentlemen engaged the ladies; the others leaned against the walls.

The dance started.

Meanwhile, in the other room, the game became more and more heated. Despite Sofia Ivanovna's orders to the cook not to serve more than one glass of punch to the guests, Vakh Onufrievich had somehow managed to down a couple of glasses and, unlike the others there, had become very agitated.

"No, pal, just do as you please," he cried out to Akula Gerasimovich, striking the wall with his fists. "But don't you dare toss away your queen of clubs; just don't dare do that, pal! . . ."

"In the first place, don't address me in such a familiar way," the executor answered him angrily. "And in the second, since I do not have the honor of knowing you personally, I would like to ask you—who gave you the right to be so bold and to start yelling here? . . ."

"What? What did you say? . . ."

"That's enough, gentlemen! Vakh Onufrievich, you ought to be ashamed of yourself!" Foma Fomich said. "Really, what's the harm if Akula Gerasimovich got rid of his club. You should have trumped him. Yes, that's what you should have done, and that would have been the end of it."

I do not know how this whole matter would have ended had not the sounds of the first French quadrille, together with the steps of the dancers and the especially passionate stumping of the young Kurykov, aroused in the players a desire to see what was going on in the living room. As a matter of fact, there was much to admire there. Pyotr Petrovich, who was dancing with Lyubov' Fomishina, seemingly wanted to outdo himself. First he let his eyes follow his lady with passionate anticipation; then he suddenly rushed off sideways and minced his steps in an extremely quick way. When his partner was supposed to curtsy, he knelt in front of her, waved his handkerchief in the air, and smiled in such a way that Lyubochka instinctively had to lower her eyes.

Other people were worthy of attention. For example, there was Voloskov and another young official in a black suit who was dancing with Sila Mamontovich's daughter and who was sparing no effort to attract attention. The couple, though, seemed to fade in the light of Pyotr Petrovich's boldness.

"Well, I must admit, madam, your son is such a good dancer that words simply fail me," the portly accountant said to Pelageya Kuzminishna. "Where did he learn to dance so well?"

"My Peten'ka is still taking lessons. . . . Every Saturday he attends dance class faithfully."

"So I assume that there are good teachers there?"

"He says that there is no other place where one can learn to dance so well. . . . Besides, at these classes, there is society, *good company,* and everything is so great, so concerned with good manners and style . . ."

"Of course," Natalya Vasilievna said, "such a thing means a great deal for a young man with education, and especially if, as you say, these classes feature people of society who can teach him luster and polish, you know, the necessary . . . *laizzez-aller.* . . ." But here the lady got quite confused, or as Gogol puts it, she let her tongue run away with her.

"And, if I may ask, madam, how much does one have to pay for these lessons, or does one simply need some kind of invitation?" the simple-souled accountant continued to ask.

"Oh, no, sir, the fees are the same as those at the Club of the United Society," answered Pelageya Kuzminishna, who was as simple-souled as the accountant. "Only I don't know how much they charge. . . . But here he comes; Petin'ka, Petin'ka! How much do you pay per lesson for your dance classes?"

"One ruble!" the young Kurykov called out in a sonorous voice as he was doing an entrechat.

"You don't say! Why, that is simply wonderful."

"Yes, it certainly is . . ."

Quadrilles followed one after another, being interrupted only when Sofia Ivanovna and Savishna seemed purposely to stop them to serve apples, pastilles, and wineberries.

The animation and excitement of the dancers increased with every hour. Even Dmitri Alexeevich Voloskov, who had been dancing throughout the entire ball with Verochka but who had not uttered a single word to her, finally struck up a conversation.

"Oh, how palish you are. . . ." he said in a trembling voice and with downcast eyes.

"What are you saying, sir! I am not palish at all! . . ."

"Oh yes, you are very pale . . ."

But their conversation did not last for long. The two became embarrassed at the same time and fell silent.

Even Ivan Ivanovich Maslyanikov could not keep from joining in the fun, having invited the younger daughter of Mrs. Semyanichkina to dance with him.

The leaps and jumps of the young Kurykov kept attracting more and more attention. But when the time came for a mazurka and he began dancing the first turn with Nadin'ka, there were not only exclamations but even applause coming from several ends of the room.

"Good Lord! What happiness to have such a son! What a wonderful young man! What a great dancer he is!" could be heard from all sides.

Pelageya Kuzminishna was beside herself with joy and maternal pride.

The crowd continued to crowd around the dancers. Kurykov became more and more excited, but suddenly, at that very moment when he moved to the middle of the living room to do some kind of caper, his trousers, which had been made to be elastic for the sake of still greater effect, betrayed him. A foot strap broke, and the young man found himself in the middle of the room showing a bare leg!!

Who can describe the effect this unfortunate circumstance made on Krutobryushkov's guests! What brush can paint the figure of Pyotr Petrovich, who was forced to show all of society the natural beauty of his leg?

The mazurka stopped, and roars of laughter could be heard everywhere. (Mikhailo Mikhailovich laughed louder than the others.) Pelageya

Kuzminishna could not endure such a sudden twist of fate; she fell ill. The commotion was, in a word, indescribable.

Kurykov, having somehow covered his leg with a handkerchief, ran as fast as he could into the kitchen. When he got there, he knocked Savishna off her feet, causing her to drop a tray with prepared sandwiches on the floor. But Kurykov, heedless of the consequences of his flight, headed for home.

Such an event, though, greatly affected everyone there. Pelageya Kuzminishna, despite all attempts to the contrary, could not agree to stay at the party after the scandal that had happened to her beloved son and left right away. Those who had been playing cards and had seen their game interrupted in the middle by the commotion did not express any great wish to continue playing, all the more so since Vakh Onufrievich was again boiling with anger, threatening the executor that he would destroy him if he again dared get rid of his queen of spades. Apollon Ignatievich also did not express a particular desire to continue playing the piano and kept making excuses that he was tired. In sum, everyone contributed to the end of the festivities.

All the people there, though, decided that it was time to have a bite. We will not go into details about the dinner. We will only say that the *kulebyaka* and especially the sandwiches were found to be extremely tasty and earned Sofia Ivanovna flattering praises from everyone except Mikhailo Mikhailovich Zhelchnyi, who again could not help whispering into the executor's ear that the *kulebyaka* was overcooked and that the sandwiches were topped with dust instead of Parmesan. The caviar was also greatly appreciated, but Foma Fomich was becoming increasingly desperate when he realized that he had been wrong in his calculations, that is, the caviar that had replaced the veal had made his guests quite thirsty and had caused them to keep helping themselves to the drinks until there was not a drop left. Vakh Onufrievich, while eating appetizers, had so helped himself to the various kinds of vodka that, ignoring his sense of duty, honor, and politeness, he took off his dress uniform and, despite the presence of the young ladies, said a great many outrageously inappropriate things, for which he was taken by the hand outside into the street.

Soon after the guests had eaten, they gradually prepared to take their leave. The Semyanichkins were the first ones to desert the group.

"Well, good-bye, dearest Sofia Ivanovna. Thank you for your hospitality and see that you don't forget us. . . . Ashin'ka, did you forget to take the pipe?"

"No, Mommy, I have it with me."

"Well, good, but where is Vladimir Markovich! Vladimir Markovich! . . ."

But there was no answer forthcoming, and he was nowhere in the rooms. Everyone looked for him. They searched all the rooms, but Semyanichkin was nowhere to be found. Foma Fomich was running back and forth from the living room to the kitchen and from the kitchen into the living room, looking even under the tables and sofas, but still he could not find Semyanichkin. Everyone there took an active part in searching for the lost official. Natalya Vasilievna was greatly excited, Anfisa and Ashin'ka were crying. Finally, Mikhailo Mikhailovich whispered something into Foma Fomich's ear, and the host said with a smile, "Don't worry. I will bring him out this very minute. . . ."

Soon he appeared, holding Vladimir Markovich by the hand, his eyes still sleepy and his clothes in a terrible mess.

"Oh, good God!" Natalya Vasilievna screamed, turning red. "Where has he been? Where? . . ."

"Vladimir Markovich . . . took off . . . well, then he fell asleep . . ."

"No . . . I . . . just for a little. . . . I didn't mean to. . . . I'm all right. . . . It's nothing . . ."

"What's the weather like outside?" Mikhailo Mikhailovich asked, smiling at Semyanichkin.

Everyone burst out laughing.

"I humbly thank you. . . . it's cold out . . . ," Vladimir Markovich muttered, looking all around shyly and not finding a place to hide.

"Good-bye, Sofia Ivanovna," Natalya Vasilievna said. "Foma Fomich, my respects. . . . Are you going to get it when we get home . . . you little fool! . . . So you took it into your head to embarrass me. . . . Just you wait! . . . " she continued whispering into her husband's ear as she kept pushing him along the corridor.

"My word of honor. . . . Natalya Vasilievna. . . . It's all right. . . . just. . . . only . . ."

"I'll show you 'just.' . . . Just wait till we get home. . . . Good-bye, dear Sofia Ivanovna. . . . Good-bye . . ."

Foma Fomich took a candle into the kitchen to see the other guests off because when he was looking for Semyanichkin in the passageway, he found only old ones that were burned out, and instead of candles, he found only turnips on the staircase.

"My respects, Natalya Vasilievna . . ."

"Good-bye, Foma Fomich. . . . Take care that you don't catch cold."

Vladimir Markovich said nothing because he was neither dead nor alive in anticipation of the thunderstorm that his precious other half had promised him.

Mikhailo Mikhailovich and Akula Gerasimovich promptly said good-bye to the Krutobryushkovs. During the course of the way home, the former never stopped cursing out to the latter each and every one of the people who had been at the gathering. In vain did Foma Fomich keep attempting to convince Sila Mamontovich to stay another hour and to play preference. Sila Mamontovich also followed the example of everyone else and declined the invitation. While all the guests were busy taking their leave, and the host and hostess were in the kitchen, Dmitri Alexeevich Voloskov stopped Verochka by the window in the living room, since he had firmly decided this time to make a formal declaration of love to her.

"No, you will now forget me," he said, rummaging through his hat with his fingers. "Vera Fominishna, you will not even want to remember. . . ."

"Oh, stop this. . . ."

"No, in no way can I stop. . . . I. . . . You. . . . You have built in the hearts of the people who love you . . . a temple of endless torment. . . ."

"Oh, no, on the contrary. . . . It is you who are tormenting me. . . ."

"No, Vera Fominishna. . . . I cannot torment you. I would not so much as dare torment you. . . . I wish that I could be with you all my life. . . . Now I am alone. . . . And without you, I am ready to die. . . ."

"I also will be alone. . . . And . . . when you leave. . . . the bright flowers will be very few. . . ."

God knows where the dialogue of these loved ones would have gone had not the godmother, Arina Petrovna, come into the living room to look for Vera, whom she absolutely needed to bid farewell. Young Voloskov, against his will, had to part without his beloved.

It took less than fifteen minutes for the Krutobryushkovs' apartment to empty. The only problem was Ivan Ivanovich Maslyanikov's difficulties with Vanyusha, who, having awakened from his nap, was not in a very good mood and, despite Sofia Ivanovna's gentleness and affection, kept hitting his father's right cheek in a merciless way.

Everyone left on foot or by vehicle with pockets and handbags full of gossip and extremely sharp remarks regarding the ball and the members of the Krutobryushkov household. But what could be done? It's like that everywhere; that is what makes the world go round.

As far as Sofia Ivanovna was concerned, she, having said the last sweet word to the last guest behind whom she closed the door, immediately changed the intonation of her voice and rushed at the simple-souled Savishna.

"You really outdid yourself tonight, my dear; you might as well have cut my head off! . . . Is there no end to your stupidity, you idiot, you village ninny!? . . ."

At this point, Sofia Ivanovna, who had taken up scolding her cook with a feeling of insulted dignity, suddenly began, as her husband would express it, to *treat* the latter to such select words that we do not dare convey them here on paper.

Savishna stood before her mistress but began to doze off. In fact, having listened to Sofia's preaching, she almost lost her balance from sleepiness.

Foma Fomich himself could hardly stand on his legs, but he nevertheless walked around the room for a rather long time. Not-so-ordinary thoughts were racing through his head. Foma Fomich was tortured by the demon of ambition and pride. He was quite certain that he had gained a great deal with his ball. That everyone had gotten drunk on his punch—this alone comforted him as a host to a great degree. When he returned to his department tomorrow, he would be able to tell about this evening's gathering in an animated but deft and modest way. In particular, he would tell how Vakh Onufrievich, while an honorable man, had lost all control of his rational faculties because of the splendid feast and hospitality of the master of the house. For only twenty rubles, Foma Fomich reasoned, he would acquire the reputation of being a generous host. He was also pleased that it had been the councillor who had won the box from Italy. "It is all very good," Krutobryushkov thought, "even though it is nothing really. Perhaps he doesn't even need the box from Italy; tomorrow perhaps, he might even give it away to benefit Avdot'ya Semyonovna or will do something else with it. But just the same, with this box, I managed to make this man happy, to please him. I succeeded in getting around him—something which is good and will come in handy someday. . . ." And Foma Fomich fell asleep with thoughts as to how it can be to one's benefit to get on someone's good side.

Meanwhile, Sofia Ivanovna first thought about the punch. Then her thoughts gradually moved on to the ribbons in Natalya Vasilievna's bonnet and the eight pounds of veal that had been replaced by the caviar. After that, she gradually turned to Vanyusha, who had hit his father in the right cheek and also scuffed Nadya's new shoes. Next she reflected upon how expensive the firewood had become, as well as upon the half-ruble coin that some rather good-looking merchant with a torn sleeve had given to her as change. Then for a long, considerable time, she thought about the pretzel that the godmother Arina Petrovna had brought her, and finally, with pleasure, about how she had dwelled on Sila Mamontovich's portliness. . . .

Verochka kept on dreaming about Voloskov for a long time. Her thoughts also jumped from one thing to another, but all of them revolved around the object of her affection. As far as Lyuba and Nadya are concerned, they simply fell asleep. Generally speaking, all three of them were very pleased with events.

But Savishna was not pleased—in the first place because Mikhailo Mikhailovich Zhelchnyi had told her that she was not a spring chicken, when everyone knew that she was only half through her golden age, and in the second place because the mistress had been way too harsh with her.

We really do not know where her thoughts wandered, but we do know for a fact that in this absolutely true story, Savishna for a long time kept stretching and yawning a great deal. Several times she rose on her elbow from the bed to shout at a hungry cat, which, with some frenzy, was munching on a bone:

"Get out of here, you wretched thing!! . . ."

—D. Grigorovich

The Petersburg Feuilletonist

Ivan Panaev

> I myself will follow your example, my very dear Tryapichkin. I too want to take up literature. It is boring, brother, to live in any other way; so if you really want to write, write to your heart's content. I see that I really need to be engaged in something spiritual.
>
> —*The Inspector General*

In Russia, *he,* the future Petersburg feuilletonist, is raised just like other noblemen's children. He lives at home until an appointed age, in villages, amid dirty and wretched serf boys and girls over whom he, as a child, rules like an autocrat. The story of his childhood is not unusual; so we need not go into detail here. His tender and caring parents do what all tender and caring parents do: they stuff him with rolls and cookies from morning to night. God be praised, the child's appetite is enormous; after all, he is in constant motion all day long. He spends his waking hours running around the courtyard, chasing after the serf boys with his whip, and talking back to peasant women and servants. In between, he somehow studies something; to use an expression from school, he even *crams down* lists of French words. At about age twelve, he is already quite tall. His tender and caring parents (whose original two hundred serfs have dwindled down to forty-five mortgaged and remortgaged souls) see it as inappropriate to keep him at home, so they send him off to a boarding school in Moscow. There he is taught a little bit of everything but never learns anything. By age fifteen, though, he is a rather capable translator of French to Russian; he also begins to have a small passion for poetry. On his school bench, and in secret from his teachers and tutors, he rereads all kinds of novels (in Russian translation) from Mmes. Cottin and Genlis to Walter Scott.

These works arouse in him a vague but disquieting wish to be a writer.

His teacher of literature—a pedant-seminarian—praises the lad, thereby sharpening his desire. My hero, in those hours when he is free from lectures, sits in a corner of his classroom and keeps writing on scraps of paper. He takes care, though, to hide everything that he has written from everybody.

One time as he was sitting over his scraps, munching on his pen, shaking his head, and muttering something under his breath, one of his friends stole up to him deftly and made off with a cherished poem. The future feuilletonist cried out from fright and threw himself cruelly on his friend. The latter, though, with one shove, rendered the poet helpless and took off with his trophy. Two minutes later the entire school surrounded the poet. "Oh! Oh! A writer! A writer!" the boys cried, laughing at him, teasing him, and sticking their tongues out at him. From that moment on, they did not give to the poet a minute's peace; but despite the torment of friends, he held fast to his wish to write. He kept marking up paper with scribbles or reading random volumes of Russian journals.

Little by little, the poet's friends gradually gave up tormenting him; and while they still laughed at him, they grew accustomed to the thought that he was a writer. The poor soul (he is now almost seventeen) is somewhat encouraged, and in imitation of the journals he has read, he wants to publish a similar publication for his class.

For this future journal, he buys a splendid little notebook. For two weeks, he works on a title page; for another two weeks, he draws a vignette. When both are finished, he begins to think about the content of his journal, and for it, he writes poems, stories, and critical articles. But poems and stories do not come easily to the boy. "To work on rhymes is not so easy, and to think up *little plots* for stories is also quite a burden," he thinks. "But criticism is easier; perhaps that is my 'true vocation.'" (The rascal—this phrase he has taken from a journal.)

"*Criticism?*" he asks. "But what if one day I become a *real* writer? Why, one could seemingly go mad from joy, seeing his work in print!" And, surrendering to these irresistible dreams, he—quiet and modest boy that he is—rewrites his works in his little notebook in a careful and beautiful way. Two months later, the entire notebook is filled with his writings. His journal is ready, and he begins to make the rounds of his friends. A terrible moment for a publisher! . . . He holds his breath.

How will his fate be decided? But no one is laughing at him anymore. He is being read, he is even being praised a bit. . . . It is fun to be a writer!

Soon his secluded life comes to an end. From a boy, he becomes a young man who takes his exams for the university.

He is finally a student! Instead of collars, he now wears a tie. He walks the streets and boulevards of Moscow without an escort; after school, he runs off to Pierre's to eat a meat pie. The future is opening to him: How many temptations there are! The theater, layered pies, pretty young girls, wine, and magazine articles.

Little by little, the young man takes advantage of all that life has to offer. Moving on to the second year, his physiognomy takes on a more serious expression. He wears glasses, yawns during lectures, looks timidly at hats, whistles melodies from vaudevilles, and dreams about his future literary glory. Meanwhile, for his own amusement, he translates various short stories and poems from French magazines.

His glasses give him a somewhat important air and invest him with a bit of arrogance. "Why don't I give it a try?" he says to himself, arranging his glasses. "Why don't I send at least one of my translations to a journal? It is quite possible that they will publish it. . . . As I see it, my style is not bad at all. . . . Yes, I'll give it a try!"

The letter and article are sent. From that moment on, the sickness of waiting takes hold of the young man. Even before the new issue of the journal comes out in print, he begins to feel feverish; his heart beats a bit too strongly. The new issue is out. He runs to the bookstore, pushing and knocking off their feet everyone who gets in his way. It is impossible to recognize him. He is without his glasses, his breathing is heavy, and streams of sweat run down his face. Stammering, he can barely say to the owner of the bookstore, "Please let me look at . . . the last issue of . . ."

Greedily he grabs the issue; his hands shake fearfully as they turn page after page. . . . Oh God! . . . He cannot believe his eyes. . . . Published! His translation is published! . . . He reads it through from beginning to end and then again from the end to the beginning. . . . The editing has not been bad at all! Without end, he admires the printed letters. With difficulty he tears himself from the issue and returns home, humming vaudeville verses in a state of indescribable delight.

His fate has been decided for good. Already believing himself to be a writer, he tells an officer, a relative of his who has come from Kharkov to Moscow on vacation, "My dear, I am swamped with translations. After all, I am a major contributor to the journal *NN.*"

"Bravo!" says the officer, curling his mustache and clicking his tongue. "God damn it, you are one fine fellow, Petya! Why, you little devil, you'll be the next Pushkin!"

The student cannot hide a pleasant smile. He firmly shakes the officer's hand and runs off to the journalist to enjoy his literary fame right away. The journalist receives him with an air of dry importance, but when the young man declares with trepidation that he is forever prepared to work for the journal *for free,* the severe and wise forehead of the journalists loses its frown.

"For free!" the journalist thinks. "Now that is something else! . . . No doubt about it, this young man is a very decent individual. I just love these hot-tempered novices! Besides, his translations are not bad, not bad at all. We can use him."

In his mind, the journalist is already letting go an employee who charges him twenty rubles for a page of translated text; and, turning to our hero, he says with a smile, "Would you like to smoke a pipe, my dearest? Ah? I will read the proofs and we will look for some work for you to do. So you just sit there and have a smoke. . . ."

What happiness! With humble delight the young man looks about the small room in which, as he sees it, only the cleverest of the cleverest, the chosen of the chosen, are allowed to congregate. Piles of manuscripts, books, newspapers, and French and German journals are scattered all over the tables, dusty and untidy. Proofs are falling to the floor. (At that time, journalists did not decorate their places with flowers and furniture from "Gambs."[1]) In this rather dirty room, my hero sees something mysterious and inviting. After all, the ruler of this room, he, this great man, for whom there are no literary mysteries; he, the ruler of these paper and dusty treasures; this powerful dispenser of immortality and glory; this stern and

1. Gambs was a well-known furniture store, founded in St. Petersburg in 1795.

merciless judge sitting before a poor and unknown student; he, with his all-powerful pen, is making magic signs on dirty proofs. What wondrous moments! For this great person, not only is my student ready to work for free, but he also willingly would give his own money—if he had any—for a flattering invitation to take part in this individual's journal. The poor feuilletonist! At this minute, he is the pitiful tool of the despicable will of his master, some newspaper publisher or journalist; he is nothing but a piece of dirt in his treacherous hand!

Perhaps, you too, reader, have forgotten the days of your innocence, the unselfish dreams of your bright youth! . . . But why do I need these digressions? Such things are vulgar and old.

Now, where was I? Oh yes, my hero soon moves from being a student to taking his candidacy exams. His old father passes away; his mother has been dead for a very long time. He is a complete orphan and a free bird, the heir of forty-five mortgaged and remortgaged souls. He sells them and, after paying his debts, comes away with five thousand rubles.

School notebooks are now under the table. In its place are a bottle of champagne and a receipt for several pawned things.

"Let's have a toast, *mon cher!*" he tells his relative, the officer, who, we cannot help pointing out, has already retired and gotten married in Moscow. "My rank is no lower than yours. I am a candidate for a degree. So don't joke around with me, my friend!"

"Let's have a toast, dear friend, let's raise our glasses!" the retired officer answers with a sigh. "What is rank after all, my boy? It doesn't mean a thing! What you need is freedom. That's what you need." (The officer waves his hand.) "Do not get married, Petya, do not get married, dear one. . . . Write, my boy, write some couplets against marriage. Good God, write them . . . and for that I will thank you very much. . . ."

How becoming it is to see the new candidate wearing his dress tailcoat with padded shoulders, a high collar, and long tails! A glittering button sparkles on his black shirtfront; his chin keeps diving in and out of a brightly colored, wavy tie; his face shines with self-contentment. His little room is arranged with great taste. On the wall hang small pictures and portraits of great people. On a shelf stands a silver sugar bowl, four books in a colorful binding, and a wallet, the gift of a *cousine,* on which, against a pink background, someone has sewn steel beads that spell out *souvenir.* He sits at his desk and writes an article, entitled "The Theory and Practice of Eloquence"—a most profound and thought-provoking piece!

People say that all candidates in Moscow begin their careers with teaching. So my young man also started out that way.

The administrators where he teaches are quite happy with his performance. He is praised and rewarded. Rumors about his talents and, most important, the care with which he does his job spread all over Moscow. Parents look for him and, in some families, pay him as much as ten rubles an hour!

Life opens up for him more and more. Sometimes he dines at the "Yar";[2] after dinner, he plays preference and whist at homes of friends. He dances at balls in the Zamoskvorechie. He does not miss a single tragedy with Mochalov in the lead role. But money keeps slipping through his fingers. Damned money! Good-bye to you, innocent dreams of youth! And farewell to you too, work done for free!

Having resolutely stamped his foot, he thinks, "I won't publish a single line without getting paid! . . . One should drink and make merry!"

In due time, he is privy to *ideal* love. After all, how can one live without *ideal* love? My hero falls in love with a young lady; he sighs, writes poems "to her," and publishes them. Beaming, he looks at the *dear little thief of his peace of mind.* The retired officer comes up to him, slaps him on the shoulder, and says, "Hey, you are one hell of a Marlinsky![3] Watch yourself, you dreamer! . . . Stay on the alert, my boy! Otherwise you won't notice that you have lost all your willpower!"

But my hero really does not need any warnings. He has fallen in love only to write poems "to her." At this point, he does not have love on his mind. He is dying to become the editor of some newspaper, some periodical. That's it precisely! Everywhere the idea pursues him mercilessly. But it is a good one! People say that it is most flattering for one's self-esteem to see his name printed in *capital letters* at the end of a newspaper or even the stock market section! But even as my young man writes manifestos for journals and newspapers, even as he talks about literary loyalty and conscientiousness, he has no hope of getting permission to publish a journal or newspaper.

2. The "Yar" or "The Ravine" is a famous restaurant that opened in St. Petersburg in 1826 and is still in operation today.

3. The reference is to the romantic writer Alexander Bestuzhev-Marlinsky.

Soon he becomes uncomfortable and bored in Moscow. There are no newspapers or feuilleton-type literature there; its citizens do not like light reading.

Moscow does not pay attention to the written articles of my young man. But why should it? Wisdom-loving Moscow constantly busies itself trying to resolve huge Slavic-Christian issues.

But Petersburg is quite a different thing! Petersburg is interested only in money. It is a haven for literary speculators, clowns, and baboons. There adroit people amass great capital with their diverse literary tricks; there gentlemen who never wrote a single line enjoy literary fame. There. . . . Well, so why not Petersburg?

Here is an excerpt from a letter which the author of "Theory and Practice," the future Petersburg feuilletonist, received from his friend, another Petersburg feuilletonist who actually writes the things.

"Yes, Petya, our Moscow is a village when compared to our Petersburg. . . . Why should you work, without glory or pay, for those Muscovite journals, the existence of which no one in our country even suspects? I know that you earn no more than 25 rubles per page, though you, you rascal, pretend to be charging no less than 150 rubles. Here any proofreader makes 4,000 rubles a year. Here, dear one, people gain fame by proofreading. About myself, I will tell you that besides my wages that you are well aware of, I take advantage of other innocent incomes. For example, all the confectioners know me; every day I drop into their places of business and eat as much as I please. I court them mercilessly, my friend. Merchants, actors, and officers treat me to liqueur with cream. In sum, here is a genuine heaven on earth. . . .

"In Petersburg, also, education extends to all social classes. Whenever I walk along Nevsky Prospekt, all the passersby say, 'Here comes the feuilletonist so-and-so. . . .' By the way, have you finished your little vaudeville which you read to me last year during my last stay in Moscow? I recall that some of your verses were simply marvelous! I myself have written a little vaudeville . . ." and so on and so forth.

"To Petersburg! To Petersburg!" my hero exclaims, having read these lines from his friend. "I know a well-known journalist in Petersburg. I will write to him and offer my services to him. He is a conscientious individual—that is important—and we will probably get along just fine. . . . In several years, I'll have some money to my name. Perhaps I'll acquire my own carriage, my own little horses. . . . But meanwhile I will also get a job. In Petersburg, one cannot but get a job. . . . Money is money and rank is rank. One thing should not interfere with the other. . . . Just the reverse. . . . I will belong to the conscientious literary party. . . ." and so on and so forth.

Everyone knows that Russian literature, the existence of which many intelligent people still doubt, is divided into *parties.* As a result, people say that the reading public is also divided into *parties.* To what party do you belong, my reader?

Here is what my hero writes to his friend, the Petersburg feuilletonist:

> The deed is done, my dear, I am coming to Petersburg. I have sold my furniture, and I am packing up my paintings so that the glass will not break on the way there. Find an apartment for me, *mon cher.* After all, as you know everybody and everything, such a thing should not be a problem for you. I have struck a very good deal with A. The feuilletons in his newspaper will be completely at my disposal.
>
> An acquaintance of mine also found me a job in some civil department. The money that I will be earning there will keep me going; I will even be able to make merry once a month. So, all I need to do is to get to Petersburg and make some money. In my repertoire, I now have three vaudevilles that I have reworked from the French. I will release them for the Petersburg stage. I have to tell you truthfully that these vaudevilles have some verses that are really naughty. . . .
>
> I hope, my dear friend, that even though we are feuilletonists who work for rival newspapers, we will not let such a thing interfere with our friendship. You have no reason to question my loyalty to you. I also want, my friend, to do a translation of Shakespeare in verse. It is time to introduce this great writer to our readers. You know that I have always been a fan of Shakespeare, *mon cher.* Besides, with a translation of Shakespeare in verse, I could easily

make a great name for myself in literature. To Petersburg! To Petersburg! . . .

To Petersburg—is not that where I should go?
To heaven on earth—for you I burn.
Do not fear. . . . Write bravely, my boy,
And have fun with the money you earn!

Adieu. I am yours "whilst this machine is to him," as Hamlet says. . . .

When our feuilletonist arrives in Petersburg, he gets his hair curled at *Fage*'s; he buys his ties at *Churkin*'s, his hats at *Falaleev*'s, his scented gloves at *Olen*'s. He puts on a frock coat with tassels and Brandenburg gold lace, the work of a tailor from *Au journal,* and goes for a walk along Nevsky Prospekt. How elegant he looks in this dandyish outfit! And, perhaps being aware of his newfound status, he appears for the first time as a feuilletonist under the name of a "society man." His frock coat with tassels and gold lace justify the courage of such behavior. The debut of my feuilletonist is brilliant. He imitates the playful and witty language of Janin. Here is an excerpt:

The most delightful, the most enjoyable, the most recent, and at the same time the most ancient piece of news in Petersburg is—*autumn!* . . . O yes . . . autumn, dirty, pale, cold, damp, with sunshine, but with the gray sky, the gray days, and the dark nights. . . ."

It is sad in the Summer Garden. Yellow leaves lie on the paths like shreds of torn paper on the floor of a writer's study or like curling papers in the dressing room of a lady aristocrat. There are almost no strollers there. The Summer Garden in spring and autumn—what a huge difference between the two! It is light and dark, day and night, smiles and tears. (Autumn in Petersburg is rainy.) . . . Many people complain about the Petersburg climate, but everyone knows that in April the Summer Garden is rife with roses that are charming, lush, luxurious, fluffy, and fragrant. There one also sees lilies—tender, transparent, and so illumined by the Russian sun that they seem whiter than Karasky marble, brighter than the Russian snow. . . .

My feuilletonist finds a job in the civil service.

He begins work with a passion. He is the first to arrive in the office and the last one to leave. . . . The boss is extremely pleased with him and even talks about him with the chief of the section. His remarks go like this: "This I must tell you, Ivan Kuz'mich, such a nice young man . . . that I simply must tell you! If he keeps going the way he does . . . Well, then, he will go far, he will be a reliable official, sir."

But alas! My hero does not meet the expectations of his boss. . . . Two months later, he is sick of his job. He stops going to the office, and, after several remarks from the head of the section concerning his lack of discipline, my hero quits his position altogether.

"I quit," he tells one of his pals from the pub, "because, *mon cher,* you know how it is, I need to get more serious about the freedom to pursue literature."

Our feuilletonist is not pleased with the Alexander Theater, but he does not miss a single performance there, making the excuse that he is obliged to go there because that is his *job.* (That last word he utters in a particularly strong way.) He does not like the actors, but he gets to know everyone and even becomes good friends with many of them. He not only devotes himself to learning all the petty behind-the-scenes gossip, but he also takes a personal and active part in it. All his articles on the theater reflect his activities. He chooses one actor (with whom he could not but strike up a friendship) and one actress (who is the object of rage of his actor-friend), and in each and every article and in the name of art, he takes them to task, often placing four exclamation points in parentheses behind their names. He pokes fun at the public of the Alexander Theater, even if half the stalls and boxes harbor bosom buddies whom he has known for less than half a year.

He makes his way amid the theater rows, throwing his coat to an usher, who bows to him and says in a pleasant way, "Hello, respected sir, Pyotr Semyonych." The feuilletonist wipes his glasses and eyes and asks the usher, "What? Have they started yet?" "No, sir, not yet," the usher replies.

Smiling a meaningful smile, and with a sense of his own self-importance, he comes up to a friend, a literary "factor," who, despite being completely illiterate, has gained some fame among literary circles by having published several literary plays, almanacs, and various types of other books that are selling quite well.

"Hello, my dear," the feuilletonist says to him, patting him on the shoulder.

The factor turns around.

"Ah, Petya! Why are your eyes so sleepy-looking?"

The feuilletonist adjusts his eyeglasses.

"I somehow overslept, my dear."

"Listen here, Petya, do you know that . . ."

The "factor" leans over to the feuilletonist's ear and whispers something. . . . One can hear only individual words: *carousing and boozing, drunk, I am publishing, praise it; Repertoire . . . sweetheart; I was promised . . . The* Bee . . . *The* Invalid . . . *So watch out*! . . .

The factor threatens the feuilletonist with his finger and laughs, adding, "You really are a rascal, pal!"

A minute of silence ensues.

The factor attentively looks over to the first row of chairs; then he purposely turns to the feuilletonist and says, "Petya, Petya! Just look at who wound up in the first row. . . ."

The feuilletonist wipes his glasses.

"Wow! Can it really be Maxim Petrovich?!"

Maxim Petrovich—or, more exactly, Maxim Petrov—is a bookseller, and a "conscientious" one at that. In any case, that is what the other "conscientious" journalists call him.

Of course, with this "conscientious" bookseller, my hero is quite close and on the most friendly terms.

"Maxim Petrovich! Maxim Petrovich! . . ." he mumbles in a friendly way, nodding to him and waving his hand.

The bookseller is burdened with a lot of accessories from the haberdasher's, but he comes up to the feuilletonist and the factor, who both shake his hand with feeling.

"Well, well, Maxim Petrovich! Aren't you quite the dandy!" the feuilletonist exclaims, examining the bookseller from head to toe. "What can I say? You are quite the fashion plate."

The bookseller smiles.

"It's really nothing," he says, straightening up with pleasure.

At that moment he is approached by an officer who, having some inclination toward literature, has just written a small vaudeville. Again there is the mutual shaking of hands.

The officer looks at the feuilletonist with feeling.

"With what delight," the officer tells him, "did I read your last article on the benefit performance for Tolchyonov. . . . How you kept managing to describe it in such a lively way. Why, you are always so good at your writing . . . that it seems like it comes naturally. . . ."

The officer stops talking because he no longer knows what else to say.

"Yes, my dear sir," the "conscientious" bookseller remarks. "*They* are experts in such things. . . . The way *they* write is simply *charming!* Good God, it's like they don't have to write at all."

The eyes of the feuilletonist take on a glistening expression. He is melting from such praise.

"Pyotr Semyonych," the bookseller continues, "after the *pirformince,* should we not drop into a restaurant? . . . It would not be a bad idea to drink a bottle or two of champagne."

"With pleasure."

The curtain rises. During the performance, the "factor" and the feuilletonist wink at each other in a significant way.

After the performance, all the gentlemen leave for dinner at the expense of the "conscientious" bookseller.

How nice and cheerful it is to live in Petersburg! My feuilletonist likes it there very much. He especially enjoys having lunch at the expense of the literary "factor" and dinner at the expense of the "conscientious" bookseller.

The wine is splendid, and the conversations are also not half bad. In the course of these encounters, he often succeeds in scrounging up several successful couplets with a certain actor—verses which, people say, are enthusiastically applauded on the stage of the Alexander Theater.

Besides vaudevilles, the feuilletonist also writes short stories. For the most part, the heroines in these works are Marlinsky-type maidens who are sensitive and ideal; who passionately love *poetry* that is *light, hazy,* and *vague,* and whose hair is

> . . . uncontrollably askew
> Steel-like in endless spirals!

Their heroes are stormy young men who strive for somewhere and something. Rife with boiling passions and despite everything earthly and common, they rise constantly into the *heavenly ethers;* and over pancakes at Izler's, they talk about things which are splendid and high. They sip what one of our poets energetically called *the nervous juice of grapes* and

> . . . the bloody stream
> Drink it to the dregs!

The ideal maidens *usually chain themselves to the fates of these passionate youths,* and their stories always have a tragic end.

During the first days of the feuilletonist's stay in Petersburg, he becomes very angry at several unscrupulous journalists and newspaper men who base their authority on twenty-five years of experience. He curses them soundly because they have insulted him. He has heard rumors that these authorities with their twenty-five years of experience have called him an *undereducated brat,* so he wants revenge by sharply criticizing them in an article.

He writes to his friend in Moscow:

"When I arrived here in Petersburg, I was attacked most cruelly by N.N. and F.F. These literary vampires also wanted to suck my blood; but I managed to strike back at them so very well that they have kept their tongues quiet about me for a very long time. Their lack of conscientiousness is outrageous. I thank God that I belong to that literary party which enjoys the respect of all worthy people. . . . Yesterday I was at a literary gathering given by prince. . . ." and so on and so forth.

But, as he writes, an inner voice tells him, "Listen here, my pet, what if you are making a mistake in calling Messrs. N.N. and F.F. vampires? What kind of vampires are they? They are very kind and merry people and good writers, to boot. The only reason they do not acknowledge your good qualities is that you work for their sworn enemy. All you have to do is leave him, and they will accept you with open arms. They will admire you, praise you, and discover a wonderful talent in you. . . . They could bring you the genuine fame for which you have long been striving, but without any success. . . ."

As he smokes his pipe, the feuilletonist becomes lost in thought.

"Would they really take me into their open arms?" he questions his inner voice in a doubtful way, but also with a pleasant grin. "In any case, even if such a thing would really happen, would I be able to go against my very self, to betray my thoughts, convictions, and feelings?"

His inner voice answers, "How many years have I been telling you that you have no thoughts, convictions, or feelings? You only pretend to have such things, not to mention a vapid and stupid idealism that brings you and everyone like you nowhere. You talk constantly about some literary conscientiousness. What do you mean by such a thing? Today you are hired by one journalist, and so from necessity, not conviction, you praise your boss. This present boss of yours is really no better than the others, his enemies whom you now attack so ruthlessly. Tomorrow, due to *circumstances,* you will cross over to these others (know that because of your own personal powerlessness, you will always be a pitiful slave to these *circumstances* and *accidents*). Tomorrow, I repeat, you will join those other bosses for an extra five hundred rubles a year, and those at whom you are now hurling polemical catapults will become your idols. Furthermore, on the order of these new idols, you will call 'black' what yesterday you called 'white,' and vice versa. Furthermore, it costs you nothing to do so. You do not have your own opinion, your own will. My friend, you sing other people's tunes; you are always at another's disposal. Take away someone else's will from you, and immediately you will become a robot, a doll, a nothing. . . ."

The feuilletonist jumps up from his chair. He indignantly throws away his pen, nervously rearranges his glasses, and paces the room in panicky agitation. Never has there been a moment when his inner voice has spoken to him so sharply.

"No, all this is outrageous!" he exclaims. "My inner voice is telling me the most intolerable impertinent ideas! Why on earth should I start listening to it now? I will strangle it. . . . How dare it slander me like that! As if I do not have my own opinion, my own will! No, I am no deserter. . . . I will show my inner voice. . . . My convictions are unassailable. . . . I am not . . ."

He does not finish his thought, but, in noble indignation, he only inhales and exhales a cloud of smoke from his mouth.

"Do not be angry, my dear," his inner voice continues calmly. "You most certainly have no opinion of your own. You either write your articles first by plagiarizing someone else and then, ingrate that you are, by cursing those benefactors who have furnished you with new thoughts and words; or you simply dash off pieces on the order of your bosses. . . . Your own witty creations are all too well known to me. One time, you inform the public of news that it is fall in Petersburg; another time, you tell them that lilies and roses are blooming in the Summer Garden . . . a third . . ."

The feuilletonist looks around timidly. He is afraid that someone may be eavesdropping on his conversation with his inner voice.

"Do not be afraid," his inner voice tells him. "No one can overhear us. . . . I speak in a very low voice. . . . Everything will remain between you and me; so don't be angry. . . . All I am doing is explaining yourself to you a bit, along with those vague, narrow-minded ideas that wander through your head. Your views about conscientiousness are the height of vulgarity. They only show how limited and immature you are. Conscientiousness is a trivial and beaten horse upon which literary clowns and speculators have long ridden as they, to the public's shame, pose and dissemble before each other in the literary arena. Just like you, none of these gentlemen have any convictions or ideas. . . . They only worry about how to make as much money as possible and to live like *barons* and *lords.*

"Few are the people in our literature with convictions and ideas. And who understands them? Who knows and values them? At this moment in history, nobody envies their fate. They sweat and slave to earn a crumb of bread, but they are at the mercy of literary speculators who take advantage of their mind, work, and talent and who, at their expense, grow rich, fat, and famous. Such things you know all too well. But there is nothing you can do with these few writers with convictions and ideas, for there is no place for you in their society. You would have long died from boredom if you had spent time with them and had not come across other people, for example, individuals who find themselves at home at the Alexander Theater or who, as *pillars of society,* dine at Palkin's[4] or some other café-

4. Palkin's is the oldest restaurant in St. Petersburg; it opened in 1795 and still continues today.

restaurant and who live a grand life with a bottle in one hand and cards in the other. . . .

"The former group despises you. In their company, you do not dare open your mouth. You just sit there smoking your pipe, your eyebrows frowning. With them, your self-esteem, that tireless little worm, eats away at you, and, hiding your distress, you rearrange your glasses constantly. Indeed, that habit of yours comes from your inner nervousness at being with such people. By contrast, the latter group always greets you with open arms because you are one of their 'chosen,' an oracle in their society. They applaud when you read them your vaudeville couplets and stories; they ask you for advice. . . .

"You have nothing in common with the first group; but with the second, you have ties of family and blood. You do not have the willpower to be a *man* and to live in human society. You have been branded a feuilletonist, and you will be one until the day you die. So go and live with people like yourself. . . . Literary factors, booksellers, actors, and the like await you at Izler's. . . ."

The feuilletonist feels a heaviness in his head and a dryness on his tongue. . . . He paces the room and rearranges his glasses. Again he inhales deeply and becomes lost in thought. The pipe drops from his hands.

At that moment, the feuilletonist's door opens with a bang, and he shudders from the noise. In front of him stands his friend—the literary factor.

"Petya, what's with you?" he exclaims. "You look like you are upset about something, or perhaps you're writing an article, you rascal?"

"No. . . . I don't know. . . . I have a bit of a headache."

"And I'm here because I have a piece of news. . . . B.B.B. has quit writing feuilletons for the newspaper. You, Petya, should get that job of his! Why, pal, you have gotten tied up with such a stupid crowd! After all, no one reads your newspaper, but ours has three thousand subscribers. Are you listening? Three thousand people will read your feuilletons! . . . So what do you say? I'm telling you the truth; anyway you look at it, *our* paper is better than yours. . . . *We,* pal, have substance, everything. In our newspaper, you will be praised for everything you do. After all, F.F. is a wonderful man! His life is a lot of fun. . . . We dine at his place on Sundays. . . . He sets a wonderful table, and his wine is simply something to behold! . . . He has already asked about you. I have to introduce him to you."

"How strange!" the feuilletonist replies, as if speaking to himself. "Just now my inner voice has been giving me the same advice."

"Who is this? What inner voice?"

"Oh, it's nothing really. I meant to say something else."

"Really, my friend, make up your mind right now. I am running off to F.F.'s right this very minute. I will tell him that you have agreed to come over to our side. We can conclude everything today. . . . So, Petya, do we have a deal? . . . You'll be earning plenty of money, and everything will go your way. Let's have some champagne to celebrate our happiness. . . . Well, make up your mind."

The feuilletonist rearranges his glasses.

"You see, my dear, I am a little ashamed to do such a thing because of my current boss at . . ."

"Good Lord, pal, don't even think about him, and don't tell him anything either. He won't even find out about coming over to us. Just leave him and be done with it. . . . And if he starts to question you . . . you just tell him that . . . Well, you will think of something to say that is much better than I can come up with. . . . So, Petya, do we have a deal?"

"Let me think about it a bit, my dear. . . . To tell you the truth, I could start writing articles for *your* newspaper even as we speak. . . . But as far as giving you my complete consent . . ."

But after several minutes, the feuilletonist solemnly offers his hand to the factor. The deal is done! Only the first step has been difficult; after that, there is nothing to fear. The feuilletonist strikes up a favorable deal with that very newspaper man whom only a week before he has called a *vampire.* Quietly, on tiptoes, he moves over to this individual's newspaper and, having received his blessing, begins to work at a new place.

The feuilletonist is very pleased with his new boss. They often go out together for a drink. Ever the hypocrite, he looks his boss straight in the eye. He mercilessly takes out after everyone who belongs to that literary party of which, just the day before, he had been a member. He begins to attack his former boss. To tell the truth, he does so first rather timidly, with some consideration, but then boldly, arrogantly, and rudely. Poor thing, he goes overboard in showing his loyalty to his new boss.

Gradually, the feuilletonist loses all sense of shame and decency—the last human feeling that distinguishes him from an animal. He has become capable of anything. In a most primitive way, he pokes fun at a noble scientist whom his boss dislikes. He accuses of ignorance and illiteracy a man of letters who works modestly and unselfishly in the quiet of his study, only because this individual does not wish to participate in the editions of his boss's friends. For a sweet pie, he writes a kind word about a confectioner; for ten cigars, he praises a tobacco factory; for a pound of caviar, he writes nice things about a vegetable stand. Inside the literary arena, he stands tirelessly at the doors of his boss's carnival booth and cries, "Come and join us! We offer the best goods, our objectivity is the best, the public loves us, we are more clever and educated than everyone else, all our workers have diplomas. But in that shop across from us, good God, all of them are ignoramuses who have never gone to the university. Believe me, the ideas that they preach over there are all empty and silly. . . . So come and join our side. You will be happy you did!"

Cynicism takes complete hold of my feuilletonist. He now appears unwashed in public, he lies in filth at home. . . . The glass in his framed pictures is broken, spiderwebs hang from his walls, layers of dust lie on his furniture, bottles of wine and overturned glasses grace his table, cards and tobacco ashes are spread out over his floor.

"You really are a rascal, Petya, don't you agree? You are really a rascal," an actor cries out to him as he spreads out without his jacket on the shabby sofa. . . . "Hey, you rascal, pour me another glass of wine. . . ."

But the feuilletonist's hands shake, and he spills the wine as he pours it.

The factor, the officer who had written the little vaudeville, and the "conscientious" bookseller laugh loudly.

The officer cries out, "Petya, I will put you in my new vaudeville without fail."

The bookseller adds, "And we will publish your vaudeville and with illustrations, to boot."

A proofreader enters with some proofs.

The feuilletonist unsteadily rushes toward the proofreader, a glass of wine in his hands. He grabs holds of the proofs and yells, "Just pitch this rubbish, pal. . . . Throw it all out. Let's just raise a friendly toast, simply, without ceremony. . . . The wine is splendid. . . . We are all brothers, friends, and I love you all from the bottom of my heart. . . ."

Such shenanigans occur more and more frequently. Less and less does my feuilletonist bear the name of "my hero." His eyes are puffy and always sleepy-looking. Because he reads the proofs for his works in a haphazard way, there are numerous misprints when they appear in the newspaper. In the end, the feuilletonist's innate apathy turns to repulsive stupidity and laziness. The vampire-journalist, his new boss, fires him. Indeed, the journalist has no mercy. He does not take into account the previous favors of his former supporter. He forgets that the poor feuilletonist has not spared himself in becoming a clown before his boss and friends and that he has not spared his vocal cords when he invited passersby into the boss's circus tent.

So where will my fired feuilletonist go now? What is he to do? His vaudevilles have been hissed off stage; his furniture has been sold to pay his debts, his clothes are shabby and worn. His situation is not unlike that of the pecked and plucked crow in Krylov's fairy tale. His heart raked raw, he goes to his former friend and drinking buddy—the "conscientious" bookseller—and humbly begs him for work. The bookseller, loaded with all kinds of clothing accessories, stands indignantly at the entrance to his place of work. Without looking at the feuilletonist, he mutters, "Come back later. . . . I have no time right now. . . . You see for yourself that I am busy. . . . I don't have any time for you. . . ." A week later, however, he orders the feuilletonist to translate a book for children by the arrival of Holy Week, paying him pennies to do so. He also orders the feuilletonist to translate two little booklets. The first concerns the *best way to get rid of bedbugs* and the like; the second is about *the most amazing elixir to grow thick and splendid hair on bald spots.* People say that such books are in great demand.

"So is this the literary fame that I have been striving for?" the feuilletonist asks, rearranging his broken glasses that he has tied together with a string. Instead of tears, drops of cold sweat run down his face. His inner voice arouses him for a final time; it points at his powerlessness and nothingness, telling him with malicious delight:

> So if you are born a dwarf
> Don't ever try to be a giant.

A year goes by. The former feuilletonist wanders aimlessly. He is dressed in an old overcoat that is covered with mud, pieces of cotton hanging like fringe at the bottom. He drops by a confectioner's shop, sits down on a chair, and dozes off. Shouting and noise, though, force him to wake up. Into the room walk all his former literary friends: the literary factor, the vaudeville actor, the officer who wrote the small vaudeville, B.B.B. who, again having taken the calling of a feuilletonist, has assumed my hero's place, and the "conscientious" bookseller, loaded with all kinds of clothing accessories. . . . They are all very merry. The former feuilletonist, having caught sight of them, covers his face with a huge sheet from a French newspaper; for a long time, he sits without moving behind the screen.

"Well, just take a look here," the factor says, screwing up his eyes and pushing B.B.B. with his elbow. "Why, there's Petya, *mon cher!* Poor thing, how low he has fallen! Why, it's awful even to look at him! . . . Garcon! A glass of liqueur! . . ."

"Didn't I tell you, gentlemen," B.B.B objects, addressing the factor, the officer, the actor, and the bookseller, "that your Petya would never amount to anything. He is absolutely unsuited to write feuilletons; after all, gentlemen, for such things, one needs wit, agility, and a special kind of talent. . . ."

"And I recall his little vaudevilles," the actor remarks . . .

> Vaudevilles like his
> Are worse than any stupidity. . . .

"Bravo! Bravo!" the officer exclaims. "Now there's the beginning of a couplet."

The former feuilletonist tries to crawl quietly to the exit. But, accidentally, he runs into the "conscientious" bookseller, loaded with clothing accessories. The "conscientious" bookseller looks at him with contempt; then he walks over to the mirror to tidy himself. By that time, my hero has disappeared without a trace. He is nowhere to be seen, neither on the streets, in the taverns, nor in the confectioner's shops. He has left the country. But in his place comes another feuilletonist, one no less worthy than he.

Gogol branded such Russian feuilletonists *Tryapichkins.* One could not think of a better name for them! After all, Tryapichkins' friends are *Khlestakovs* and *Nozdryovs.*

—Iv. Panaev

APPENDIX: SELECTED LIST OF INDIVIDUALS MENTIONED IN THE TEXT

Addison, Joseph (1672–1719), English politician and writer

Aksakov, Konstantin Sergeevich (1817–60), Slavophile ideologue and journalist

Aksel', Nikolai Fyodorovich (pseudonym of Lindfors, Nikolai Fyodorovich, 1818–42), poet, dramatist, and translator

Alad'in, Egor Vasilievich (1796–1860), writer, dramatist, translator, and publisher

Alexander I (1777–1825), emperor of Russia, 1801–25

Alexander the Great (356–323 B.C.), king of Macedonia, 336–323 B.C., and conqueror of Asia

Algarotti, Francesco (1712–64), Italian writer

Anicet-Bourgeois, Auguste (1806–71), French dramatist

Anna Ivanovna (1693–1740), empress of Russia, 1730–40

Annenkov, Pavel (1811?–87), literary critic and memoirist

Arnould, Auguste (1803–54), French dramatist

Asenkova, Varvara Nikolaevna (1817–41), actress

Auffenberg, Joseph von (1798–1857), German playwright

Babel, Isaac Emmanuilovich (1894–1941), short-story writer

Bakhtin, Mikhail Mikhailovich (1895–1975), philosopher and critic

Balzac, Honoré de (1799–1850), French writer and dramatist

Banks, John (?–1706), English dramatist

Bashchutsky, Alexander Petrovich (1803–76), writer

Batyushkov, Konstantin Nikolaevich (1787–1855), poet and essayist

Bayard, M. (Jean-Francois-Alfred, 1796–1853), French dramatist

Belinsky, Vissarion Grigorievich (1811–48), critic

Bellinsgauzen, Faddei Fadeevich (1778–1852), navigator

Bely, Andrei (pseudonym of Bugaev, Boris Nikolaevich, 1880–1934), novelist, poet, theorist, and critic

Benediktov, Vladimir Grigorievich (1807–73), poet

Benkendorf, Alexander Khristoforovich (1783–1844), statesman and head of the Third Section during the reign of Nicholas I

Benois, Alexander Nikolaevich (1870–1960), artist, critic, and theatrical director
Bestuzhev-Marlinsky, Alexander Alexandrovich (1797–1837), writer, poet, critic, and translator
Biron, Ernst Johann (1690–1772), German adventurer and adviser to Anna Ivanovna
Blok, Alexander Alexandrovich (1880–1921), poet and playwright
Blücher, Gebhard Leberecht von (1742–1819), Prussian field marshal in the Napoleonic Wars
Botkin, Vasily Petrovich (1811–69), critic and publicist
Brant, Leopold Vasilievich (1813–84), writer and critic
Brillat-Savarin, Jean Anthelme (1755–1826), French lawyer, politician, epicure, and gastronome
Brodsky, Iosif Aleksandrovich (1940–96), poet and essayist
Bryansky, Yakov Grigorievich (1790–1853), actor
Bryullov, Alexander Pavlovich (1798–1877), architect
Bulgakov, Mikhail Afanasievich (1891–1940), writer
Bulgarin, Faddei Venediktovich (1789–1859), writer and journalist
Bürger, Gottfried August (1747–94), German poet
Butkov, Yakov Petrovich (?–1856), writer
Byron, Lord (1788–1824), English poet
Cassander (358–297 B.C.), king of Macedonia, 305–297 B.C.
Catherine the Great (Catherine II, 1729–96), empress of Russia, 1762–96
Chaadaev, Pyotr Yakovlevich (1794–1856), philosopher
Charles XII (1682–1718), king of Sweden, 1697–1718
Chateaubriand, François-René de (1768–1848), French writer
Chekhov, Anton Pavlovich (1860–1904), writer and dramatist
Churchill, John (1650–1702), Duke of Marlborough and English general and political leader
Churchill, Winston (1874–1965), British statesman and prime minister
Clarke, Edward Daniel (1769–1822), British traveler
Cook, James (1728–79), British naval captain, navigator, and explorer
Cooper, James Fenimore (1789–1851), American writer
Corneille, Pierre (1606–84), French dramatist and poet
Cottin, Madame (Sophie, 1770–1807), French writer
Couailhac, Louis (1810–85), French writer

Dal', Vladimir Ivanovich (1801–72), writer and scholar
Dante (Alighieri, 1265–1321), Italian poet
Davydov, Denis Vasilievich (1784–1839), poet and memoirist
Derzhavin, Gavrila Romanovich (1743–1816), poet, statesman, and soldier
Diaghilev, Sergei Pavlovich (1872–1929), ballet impresario
Dickens, Charles (1812–70), English novelist
Didelot, Charles Louis (1767–1837), French choreographer
Dmitrevsky, Ivan Afanasievich (1734–1821), actor, poet, and playwright
Dmitriev, Ivan Ivanovich (1760–1837), poet
Dostoevsky, Fyodor Mikhailovich (1821–81), short-story writer and novelist
Dumas-père, Alexandre (1803–70), French novelist and dramatist
Dumont d'Urville, Jules-Sébastien-César (1790–1842), French navigator, naturalist, and oceanographer
Dyur, Maria Dmitrievna (1815–68), actress
Elizabeta Petrovna (1709–62), empress of Russia, 1741–62
Elizabeth I (1533–1603), English queen, 1558–1603
Elssler, Fanny (Franziska) (1810–84), Austrian ballerina
Evreinov, Nikolai Nikolaevich (1879–1953), director, dramatist, and critic
Falconet, Étienne-Maurice (1716–91), French sculptor
Filimonov, Nikolai Ivanovich (1805–70), dramatist
Fonvizin, Denis Ivanovich (1745–92), playwright
Fournier, Narcisse (1800–1880), French dramatist
Francis I (1768–1835), Austrian emperor
Frederick II (1712–86), also known as Frederick the Great, king of Prussia, 1740–86
Frol (second century A.D.), stonecutter and saint
Fyodorov, Pavel Stepanovich Fedorov (1803–79), dramatist
Garshin, Vsevelod Mikhailovich (1855–88), short-story writer
Genlis, Stéphanie Félicité de (1746–1830), French writer and educator
Glinka, Fyodor Nikolaevich (1786–1880), poet, publicist, and prose writer
Gnedich, Nikolai Ivanovich (1784–1833), poet and translator
Goethe, Johann Wolfgang von (1749–1832), German poet, dramatist, novelist, and statesman
Gogol, Nikolai Vasilievich (1809–52), novelist and short-story writer
Goldoni, Carlo (1707–93), Italian dramatist
Goncharov, Ivan Alexandrovich (1812–91), novelist

Gorky-Peshkov, Alexei Maksimovich (Maxim, 1868–1936), writer, activist, and critic

Granovsky, Timofei Nikolaevich (1813–55), historian

Grebenka, Evgeny Pavlovich (1812–48), Ukrainian writer

Grech, Nikolai Ivanovich (1787–1867), journalist, writer, and philologist

Griboyedov, Alexander Sergeevich (1795–1829), diplomat and dramatist

Grigoriev, Pyotr Grigorievich (1807–54), also known as Grigoriev the Second, actor

Grigoriev, Pyotr Ivanovich (1806–71), also known as Grigoriev the First, actor

Grigorovich, Dmitri Vasilievich (1822–1900), writer

Hegel, Georg Wilhelm Friedrich (1770–1833), German philosopher

Herzen, Alexander Ivanovich (1812–70), publicist, writer, and thinker

Homer (ninth century B.C.), Greek epic poet

Hugo, Victor (1802–85), French writer

Il'f, Ilya (pseudonym of Fainzilberg, Ilya Arnoldovich, 1897–1937), writer and journalist

Il'in, Nikolai Ivanovich (1777–1823), dramatist

Istomina, Avdot'ia Il'inichna (1799–1848), ballerina

Ivan VI (1740–64), emperor of Russia, 1740–41

Ivanov, Fyodor Fyodorovich Ivanov (1777–1816), dramatist

Izmailov, Alexander Efimovich (1779–1831), journalist, writer, fabulist

Janin, Jules Gabriel (1804–74), French writer

Jodelle, Étienne (1532–73), French dramatist

Josephine (Bonaparte, 1763–1814), French consort of Napoleon and empress

Jouy, Étienne de (1764–1846), French writer and dramatist

Kachenovsky, Mikhail Trofimovich (1775–1842), journalist, historian, professor, and literary critic

Kaidonov. Ivan Kuzmich (1780–1843), historian

Kamensky, Pavel Pavlovich (1812–71), dramatist

Karatygin, Pyotr Andreevich (1805–79), also known as Karatygin the Second, actor and brother of Vasily Karatygin

Karatygin, Vasily Andreevich (1802–53), actor

Karatygina. See Kolosova.

Karamzin, Nikolai Mikhailovich (1766–1826), prose writer

Karr, Alphonse (1808–90), French writer

Katenin, Pavel Alexandrovich (1792–1853), poet, playwright, translator, critic, and literary theorist
Khomyakov, Alexei Stepanovich (1804–60), poet, playwright, philosopher, and theologian
Kireevsky, Ivan Vasilievich (1806–56), Slavophile, editor, and critic
Kireevsky, Pyotr Vasilievich (1808–56), Slavophile and ethnographer, brother of Ivan Kireevsky
Knyazhnin, Yakov Borisovich (1742–91), playwright, poet, and translator
Kock, (Charles) Paul de (1793–1871), French writer
Kolosova, Evgenia Ivanovna (1780–1869), ballerina and mother of Alexandra Kolosova-Karatygina
Kolosova-Karatygina, Alexandra Mikhailovna (1802–53), actress and wife of Vasily Karatygin
Komarov, Matvei (1730? –1812), writer
Korovkin, Nikolai Arsenievich (1816–76), vaudevillist
Kotzebue, August Friedrich von (1761–1819), German dramatist
Kozlov, Ivan Ivanovich (1779–1840), poet
Kraevsky, Andrei Alexandrovich (1810–89), editor and journalist
Kruzenshtern, Ivan Fyodorovich (1770–1846), navigator
Krylov, Ivan Andreevich (1769–1844), journalist, playwright, and fabulist
Kukol'nik, Nestor Vasilievich (1809–68), novelist and dramatist
Kul'chitsky, Mikhail (1817–45), writer
Kustodiev, Boris Mikhailovich (1878–1927), painter and stage designer
Lafont, Charles (1808–64), French dramatist
Lafontaine, August (1758–1831), German writer
Lanner, Josef (1801–43), Austrian composer, director, and musician
Laurus (second century A.D.), stonecutter and saint
Lavallée, Joseph (1747–1816), French writer
Lavater, Johann Kaspar (1741–1801), Swiss poet and physiognomist
Lazhechnikov, Ivan Ivanovich (1792–1869), writer and dramatist
Lenin, Vladimir Ilyich (1870–1924), revolutionary and politician
Lensky, Dmitri Timofeevich (1805–60), actor
Lermontov, Mikhail Yurievich (1814–41), poet and novelist
Levkeeva, Elizaveta Ivanovna (1851–1919), actress
Lockroy, Joseph-Philippe (1803–91), French dramatist
Lomonosov, Mikhail Vasilievich (1711–65), writer and scientist

Lotman, Yuri Mikhailovich (1922–93), critic
Louis XVI (1754–93), king of France, 1774–92
Louis-Philippe (1773–1850), king of France, 1830–48
Lugansky. Pen name of Vladimir Dal'
Lurieu, Jules Joseph Gabriel de (1792–1869), French dramatist
Lurine, Louis (1816–60), French editor
Magellan, Ferdinand (1480–1521), Portugese navigator and explorer
Maikov, Apollon Nikolaevich (1821–97), poet
Makovsky, Konstantin Yegorovich (1839–1915), painter
Marie-Louise (1791–1847), Austrian archduchess and second wife of Napoleon
Markov, Mikhail Alexandrovich (1810–76), poet, dramatist, and writer
Marlinsky. See Bestuzhev-Marlinsky.
Marquis de Custine, Astolphe-Louis-Léonor (1790–1857), French aristocrat and writer
Martynov, Alexander Estafievich (1816–60), actor
Masson, Auguste-Michel-Benoit (1800–83), French novelist and dramatist
Maximov, Alexei Mikhailovich(1813–61), actor
Mazepa, Ivan Stepanovich (1639?–1709), hetman of eastern Ukraine, 1687–1709
Mercier, Louis-Sébastien (1740–1814), French dramatist and writer
Metastasio, Pietro (1698–1782), poet and librettist
Mil'keev, Evgeny Lukich (1815–45?), poet
Mira, Pietro (pseudonym of Petrillo, Adam, 1700?–82?), Italian violinist and clown
Mochalov, Pavel Stepanovich (1800–1848), actor
Molière (pseudonym of Poquelin, Jean Baptiste, 1622–73), French dramatist
Mussorgsky, Modest Petrovich (1839–81), composer
Nadezhdin, Nikolai Ivanovich (1804–56), publicist, critic, and ethnographer
Napoleon (Bonaparte, 1769–1821), French Emperor, military leader, and conqueror
Navrotsky, Sergei Nikanorovich (1808–65), dramatist, critic, prose writer, publicist, and translator
Nekrasov, Nikolai Alexeevich (1821–78), poet, writer, and publisher
Nevsky, Alexander Iaroslavich (1220?–63), prince of Novgorod and national hero

Nicholas I (1796–1855), emperor of Russia, 1825–55
Nijinsky, Vaslav Fomich (1890–1950), ballet dancer and choreographer
Nikitenko, Alexander Vasilievich (1804–77), literary historian, critic, and memoirist
Novikov, Nikolai Ivanovich (1744–1818), writer, journalist, critic, and publisher
Obodovsky, Platon Grigorievich (1803–64), dramatist, poet, and translator
Odoevsky, Vladimir Fyodorovich (1804–69), writer, critic, educator, and public servant
Ogaryov, Nikolai Platonovich (1813–77), poet, essayist, and editor
Olearius, Adam (1603–71), German scholar, mathematician, geographer, and librarian
Orlov, Pavel Nikolaevich (1869–1932), actor
Orlova, Praskovia Ivanovna (1815–1900), actress
Ostrovsky, Alexander Nikolaevich (1823–86), playwright
Ozerov, Vladislav Alexandrovich (1769–1816), dramatist
Panaev, Ivan Ivanovich (1812–62), writer and journalist
Panaeva-Golovacheva, Avdot'ya Yakovlevna (1819?–93), writer, memoirist, wife of Ivan Panaev and mistress of Nikolai Nekrasov
Pesotsky, Ivan Petrovich (?–1849), editor and publisher
Peter the Great (1672–1725), also known as Peter I, tsar and first emperor of Russia, 1682–1725
Peter II (1715–30), grandson of Peter the Great and tsar of Russia, 1727–30
Peterburgskaya, Ksenya (ca. 1731 – ca. 1803), wanderer and saint
Petrov (pseudonym of Kataev, Evgeny Petrovich, 1903–42), writer and journalist
Petrov, Vasily Petrovich (1736–99), poet
Pindar (522?–433 B.C.), Greek poet
Platov, Matvei Ivanovich (1751–1818), hetman of the Don Cossacks and hero of the Russian war against Napoleon
Pogodin, Mikhail Petrovich (1800–1875), historian and journalist
Polevoi, Ksenofont Alexeevich (1801–67), writer and brother of Nikolai Polevoi
Polevoi, Nikolai Alexeevich (1796–1846), journalist, critic, dramatist, and historian
Potanchikov, Fyodor Semyonovich (1800–1871), actor

Potemkin, Grigory Alexandrovich (1739–91), general, administrator, and imperial favorite of Catherine the Great

Pushkin, Alexander Sergeevich (1799–1837), prose writer, playwright, and poet

Racine, Jean (1639–99), French dramatist

Radishchev, Alexander Nikolaevich (1749–1802), writer and social critic

Razumovsky, Alexei Grigorievich (1709–71), lover of Empress Elizaveta Petrovna

Repina, Nadezhda Vasilievna (1809–67), actress

Reybaud, Madame Charles (Fanny-Henriette, 1802–71), French writer

Richardson, Samuel (1689–1761), English novelist

Romanov, Mikhail Pavlovich (1798–1849), prince and brother of Nicholas I

Rousseau, James (1797–1849), French writer

Rubini, Giovanni Battista (1794–1854), Italian tenor

Ryleev, Kondraty Fyodorovich (1795–1826), poet and revolutionary

Ryurik (ca. A.D. 860, semilegendary founder of the first Russian state

Sadovsky, Prov Mikhailovich (pseudonym of Ermilov, Prov Mikhailovich, 1818–72), actor

Saltykov-Shchedrin, Mikhail Yegrafovich (1826–89), writer

Samarin, Ivan Vasilievich (1817–85), actor

Samoilov, Vasily Vasilievich (1812–87), actor

Samoilova, Nadezhda Vasilievna (1818–99), also known as Samoilova the First, actress

Samoilova, Vera Vasilievna (1824–80), also known as Samoilova the Second, actress and sister of Nadezhda Samoilova

Sand, George (pseudonym of Dudevant, Amandine Aurore Lucie, 1803–76), French writer

Sauvage, Thomas Marie Francois (1794–1877), French dramatist

Schelling, Friedrich (1775–1854), German philosopher

Schenk, Eduard von (1788–1841), German dramatist

Schiller, Johann Christoph Friedrich von (1759–1805), German dramatist

Scott, Walter (1771–1832), Scottish novelist and poet

Scribe, Augustin Eugène (1791–1861), French dramatist

Semyonova, Ekaterina Semyonova (1786–1849), actress

Senkovsky, Osip Ivanovich (1800–1858), writer, critic, scholar, and publisher

Shakespeare, William (1564–1616), English poet and playwright

Shakovskoi, Alexander Alexandrovich (1777–1846), dramatist
Shalikov, Pyotr Ivanovich (1767?–1852), writer and journalist
Shcheglov, Ivan Pavlovich (1856–1911), actor and activist
Shchepkin, Mikhail Semyonovich (1788–1863), actor
Shevyryov, Stepan Petrovich (1806–64), literary historian, critic, and poet
Shklovsky, Victor Borisovich (1893–1984), critic and writer
Smirdin, Alexander Filippovich (1795–1857), publisher and bookseller
Sobolevsky, Sergei Alexandrovich (1803–70), poet, publisher, and bibliographer
Sokolov, Ilya Osipovich (1777–1848), dancer, musician, and choir director
Sollogub, Vladimir Alexandrovich (1813–82), writer
Solounsky, Dmitri (early fourth century A.D.), martyr and saint
Soloviev, Sergei Pavlovich (1820–79), writer
Somov, Orest Mikhailovich (1793–1833), writer, journalist, and literary critic
Sosnitskaya, Elena Yakovlevna (1799–1855), actress
Sosnitsky, Ivan Ivanovich (1794–1871), actor
Soulié, Frédéric (1800–1847), French writer
Stalin, Joseph Vissarionovich (1878–1953), leader and dictator
Steele, Richard (1672–1729), Irish politician and writer
Stepanov, Pyotr Gavrilovich (1800–1861), actor
Stravinsky, Igor Fyodorovich (1882–1971), composer and conductor
Stroev, Vladimir Mikhailovich (1812–62), writer
Sue, Eugène (1804–57), French novelist
Sumarokov, Alexander Petrovich (1718–77), poet, dramatist, journalist, and critic
Susanin, Ivan (?–1613), peasant and folk hero
Svin'in, Pavel Petrovich (1787–1839), editor
Swift, Jonathan (1667–1745), English satirist
Taglioni, Maria (1804–84), artist, teacher, and ballet mistress
Timm, Vasily Fyodorovich (1820–95), artist and illustrator
Tolchyonov, Ivan Ivanovich (1786–1840?), actor
Tolstoy, Leo (Lev, 1828–1910), short-story writer and novelist
Topfer, Karl (1792–1871), German dramatist
Toporov, Vladimir Nikolaevich (1928–2005), philologist and critic
Tredyakovsky, Vasily Kirillovich (1703–68), poet, philologist, and translator
Turgenev, Ivan Sergeevich (1818–83), novelist and playwright

Tvardovsky, Alexander Trifonovich (1910–71), poet and editor
Uvarov, Sergei Semyonovich (1786–1855), statesman
Valberkhova, Maria Ivanovna (1788–1867), actress
Veltman, Alexander Fomich (1800–1870), poet, writer, and scholar
Virgil (70–19 B.C.), Roman poet
Vistengof, Pyotr Fyodorovich (1811–55), essayist and fiction writer
Vogel, Wilhelm (1772–1843), German dramatist
Voltaire, Francois Marie Arouet (1694–1778), French author and philosopher
Volynsky, Artemy Petrovich (1689–1740), general and official
Voskresensky, Mikhail Il'ich (1803–67), dramatist
Vyazemsky, Pyotr Andreyevich (1792–1878), poet
Weber, Carl Maria von (1786–1826), composer, conductor, pianist and critic
Yakolev, Alexei Semyonovich (1773–1817), actor
Yazykov, Mikhail Nikolaevich (1803–46), poet
Zagoskin, Mikhail Nikolaevich (1789–1852), dramatist, novelist, and short-story writer
Zhandr, Andrei Andreevich (1789–1873), dramatist and translator
Zhivokoni, Vasily Ignatievich (1805–74), actor
Zhukovsky, Vasily Andreevich (1783–1852), poet and translator
Zoshchenko, Mikhail Mikhailovich (1895–1958), writer
Zotov, Rafail Mikhailovich (1796–1871), writer and dramatist
Zotov, Vladimir Rafailovich (1821–96), writer, dramatist, journalist, and son of Rafail Zotov
Zubarev, Dmitri Eliseevich (1801–50), writer and dramatist

INDEX